T0318283

Digitalisation and Organisation Design

Digitalisation and Organisation Design aims to address key topics related to organisation design and knowledge management in the digital economy with organisational context, particularly in Asia. Asian nations are moving fast toward the digital economy. Doing business in the digital economy is different from the old way, and the role of organisation design and knowledge management is crucial to support innovative and creative ideas for tapping the huge market opportunities in which people are ready for digitalisation.

Chapters in the book cover important topics related to organisation design and knowledge management for organisations, especially business organisations in Asia, to prepare and cultivate necessary means for advancing in the digital economy. This book offers readers a unique value, bringing new perspectives to understanding emerging business opportunities and challenges in Asia. It will present a valuable collection of chapters with empirical studies from leading researchers on the related topic within the main theme (Asian economies, digitalisation, knowledge management, organisational design). The collection of chapters will be conceptually and practically beneficial for academics, students and policy makers interested in the latest developments in organisation design and knowledge management in the digital economy in Asia.

This book can be used as a main or supplementary resource for undergraduate and postgraduate students in business and related areas.

Mohammad Nabil Almunawar is currently an Associate Professor at the School of Business and Economics, Universiti of Brunei Darussalam (UBDSBE), Brunei Darussalam. His overall research interests include applications of IT in management, e-business/commerce, digital marketplace/platform, digital business ecosystem, health informatics, information security and cloud computing. Currently, he focuses his research on digital platforms and the digital business ecosystem. He has published more than 100 papers in refereed journals, books and book chapters. He is an associate editor of *Asian Business and Information Management* (*IJABIM*) and is a member of many editorial boards of international journals.

Md Zahidul Islam is an Associate Professor at the School of Business and Economics at University Brunei Darussalam (UBD). His teaching and research interests focus on strategic management, human resource management and knowledge management. His research work has appeared in journals such as *International Journal of Information Management, Management Decision, Journal of Database Management, Corporate Social Responsibility and Environmental Management* and *VINE: The Journal of Information and Knowledge Management Systems.*

Patricia Ordóñez de Pablos is a Professor in the Department of Business Administration in the Faculty of Economics and Business of the University of Oviedo, Spain. Her teaching and research interests focus on the areas of strategic management, knowledge management, intellectual capital, human resources management and IT. She is Editor-in-Chief of the *International Journal of Asian Business and Information Management* and serves as Executive Editor of the *International Journal of Learning and Intellectual* too. She is also the Editor-in-Chief of the book series titled *Routledge Advances in Organizational Learning and Knowledge Management.*

Routledge Advances in Organizational Learning and Knowledge Management
Edited by **Patricia Ordóñez de Pablos**

Key topics such as Organisational Learning (OL), Knowledge Management (KM) and Intellectual Capital (IC) are of increasing interest to both the academic community and organisations operating globally, in this post-crisis situation. They have a bearing on innovation and learning and can influence the achievement of competitive advantage for institutions, universities, organisations and regions. The existing literature on knowledge management and intellectual capital suggests that competitive advantage flows from the creation, ownership, protection, storage and use of certain knowledge-based organisational resources. Superior organisational performance depends on firms/universities/regions' ability to be good at innovation, learning, protecting, deploying, amplifying and measuring these strategic yet intangible resources.

This series brings together a selection of new perspectives from leading researchers from around the world, on topics such as knowledge management and learning in cities and regions; knowledge management and intellectual capital reporting in universities, research centres and cities, to name but a few. Not only are the volumes of the series supported by quantitative and qualitative analysis but reinforced by the experiences of practitioners as well.

The series gives readers the chance to explore cutting-edge research in the fields of knowledge management, intellectual capital and organisational learning not only from Europe and the USA but from Asia as well, an area which has been largely overlooked.

Digital Transformation Management
Challenges and Futures in the Asian Digital Economy
Edited by Mohammad Nabil Almunawar, Md Zahidul Islam and Patricia Ordóñez de Pablos

For more information about this series, please visit: www.routledge.com/Routledge-Advances-in-Organizational-Learning-and-Knowledge-Management/book-series/RAOLKM

Digitalisation and Organisation Design

Knowledge Management in the Asian Digital Economy

Edited by
Mohammad Nabil Almunawar,
Md Zahidul Islam and
Patricia Ordóñez de Pablos

Routledge
Taylor & Francis Group

LONDON AND NEW YORK

First published 2022
by Routledge
2 Park Square, Milton Park, Abingdon, Oxon OX14 4RN

and by Routledge
605 Third Avenue, New York, NY 10158

Routledge is an imprint of the Taylor & Francis Group, an informa business

British Library Cataloguing-in-Publication Data
A catalogue record for this book is available from the British Library

Library of Congress Cataloging-in-Publication Data
A catalog record has been requested for this book

ISBN: 978-0-367-75746-5 (hbk)
ISBN: 978-0-367-75747-2 (pbk)
ISBN: 978-1-003-16382-4 (ebk)

DOI: 10.4324/9781003163824

Typeset in Times New Roman
by codeMantra

Contents

Contributors

Mohammad Alif Azizi Abdullah is currently a PhD student under the School of Business and Economics – UBDSBE, Universiti Brunei Darussalam. He received his bachelor's degree (BSc Computer Science) in 2017 from the University of Chester, UK, and master's degree (Master of Management by research) in 2020 from the School of Business and Economics, Universiti Brunei Darussalam. His overall research interests include digital marketplace, electronic business/commerce, big data and digital ecosystem.

Jama AlGaizi AlFalasi is a manager of the Intellectual Property Disputes Unit in the Department of Economic Development in Dubai, United Arab Emirates. He received his MPA from the Mohammed Bin Rashid School of Government in the UAE. His research interest includes digitisation of public services and intellectual property rights reforms.

Diyana Najwa Ali is a PhD candidate of Universiti Teknologi Brunei (UTB) School Business. She gained an MSc in Management & Technology and a bachelor degree (Hons) in Business Information Systems. Her research interests are in knowledge management and business information systems where she has co-authored in Scopus indexed journal and book chapter.

Mohammad Anshari joined Continuing Education Centre (CEC) UBD in 2014. Currently, he is Senior Assistant Professor of Business Information Systems at Universiti Brunei Darussalam School of Business & Economics (UBDSBE) and also since 2018 he has been serving as Deputy Director at the Institute of Policy Studies, UBD. His professional experience started when he was IT Business Analyst at Astra International. After completion of his PhD, he worked as a research fellow at National Taiwan University sponsored by the Government Republic of China (Taiwan). Before that, he pursued research fellowship at King Saud University – the Kingdom of Saudi Arabia in 2009. He has also been Adjunct Senior Researcher at UIN Yogyakarta, Indonesia, since 2006. Details of his research interests are Business Information Systems, E-Health & Mobile

Health, Digital Business & Social Computing, Big data in business, ICT & Area Studies, ICT in Education and FinTech.

Omkar Dastane is a Senior Lecturer and Head of Postgraduate Centre at FTMS Global Malaysia (offering UK universities' PG programs in Kuala Lumpur, Malaysia). Omkar is a founder member of ASCENT international conference series and associate editor of the *International Journal of Accounting, Business and Management*. He also serves on a reviewer board of international journals. His research interests include consumer perception, choice modelling, electronic commerce and mobile commerce. He published widely in different refereed journals including *Journal of Consumer Studies and Retailing*. His book chapters are published in several research handbooks including *Handbook of Research on Disruptive Innovation and Digital Transformation in Asia* and *Handbook of Research on Innovation and Development of E-Commerce and E-Business in ASEAN*.

Simin Ghavifekr is an Associate Professor in the Department of Educational Management, Planning and Policy, Faculty of Education, University of Malaya. She is teaching and supervising many postgraduate students including Master's and PhD. She has many publications including books, chapters in books, journal articles and proceedings that are published in local and international journals such as Scopus and ISI indexed. She is also Editor-in-Chief for the journal *Malaysian Online Journal of Educational Management (MOJEM)*, which is a Scopus indexed journal by Elsevier. Moreover, Dr Simin is cooperating with many well-known journals from Taylor & Francis, Springer, SAGE and Emerald publications as reviewer and consultant. Her research interests include K-12, higher education, educational policy, leadership, management, administration, as well as e-learning and integration of ICT in educational setting.

Shankar A Govindasamy is currently the Head of Marine Assurance with a well-known ship manager, Eaglestar (a group of MISC subsidiaries) based in Singapore. Prior to that, he was seconded briefly to INTER-TANKO, an international organisation, and served as secretariat in a similar discipline, but to a wider maritime members of international independent tanker owners, ship managers and associates. He himself by profession is an ex-Merchant Navy officer (Master Mariner) with over two decades of sea-going experience. He sailed on gas carriers where high standard of safe operation and knowledgeable mariners are essential. Over the years, his quest for knowledge sharing and how it perceives among merchant navy officers, especially in current technology-driven and digitalisation of maritime assets that face shortage of merchant navy officer, contribute significantly to his work on this article.

Hartrisari Hardjomidjojo holds a PhD degree in Industrial Systems Engineering. Currently, she is working as an Associate Professor in the

Department of Agro-Industrial Technology, Faculty of Agricultural Engineering and Technology, IPB University (Bogor Agricultural University), Bogor, Indonesia. Her current research interests include Spatial, Expert Systems and Decision Support Systems.

Md. Harun Ur Rashid has been serving as a full-time faculty of Accounting at the Department of Economics and Banking in International Islamic University Chittagong. He has completed his BBA and MBA from the Department of Accounting and Information Systems, University of Rajshahi. Now, he is pursuing his MPhil at the Bangladesh University of Professionals. He has various publications in referred journals. His research interests include CSR, green/climate financing, taxation, corporate governance, technological adaptation and Shari'ah regulations. He is proficient in research tools such as SPSS, AMOS, Smart-PLS, Eviews, DEAP and STATA.

Fahmi Ibrahim, PhD, is Assistant Professor of School of Business, Universiti Teknologi Brunei (UTB), Brunei Darussalam. He gained his PhD from Glasgow Caledonian University, Glasgow, UK and MSc in Business Information Technology Systems (BITS) from the University of Strathclyde, Glasgow, UK. He has a wide range of academic experience gained in higher education establishments in the Brunei Darussalam and UK. His current teaching and research areas are in the field of Strategic Management, Knowledge Management, Management Information Systems (MIS), Human Resource Management, Operations Management and Tourism Management-Development within public, private and SMEs organisations. His consultancy experience is in the area of Business Transformation, particularly in SMEs. The consultancy expertise is supported by and complemented by his research interests. His research output includes book chapters, journal articles and conference papers. In recent years, his research interest has evolved to be contextualised around the strategic development of organisations in complex and transitional environments.

Nurul Indarti is a Professor from the Department of Management, Faculty of Economics and Business, Universitas Gadjah Mada. She holds master's degrees from the University of Agder, Kristiansand and Norwegian School of Economics and Business, Bergen, Norway and PhD degree from the Faculty of Economics and Business, University of Groningen, the Netherlands. Her research interests include knowledge and innovation management, entrepreneurship and small- and medium-sized businesses.

Nurul Amirah Ishak is a second year PhD candidate in Management at UBD School of Business and Economics (UBDSBE). Her research interests broadly centre around Strategic Knowledge Management and Organisational Behaviour. Recently, she has presented in an international conference and published in peer-reviewed journals including *VINE: The Journal of Information and Knowledge Management Systems.*

Shahidul Islam is a PhD candidate at UBD School of Business and Economics, Universiti Brunei Darussalam. He is also affiliated with Comilla University, Bangladesh, as Assistant Professor of Marketing. He publishes paper on healthcare, service quality and consumer behaviour.

Ajeya Jha is currently an Associate Director at the Sikkim Manipal Institute of Technology, Sikkim Manipal University, Sikkim. He was HoD of Department of Management Studies, Sikkim Manipal Institute of Technologies. He received his bachelor's degree and master's degree (MBA) in 1980 and 1982, respectively, from the Central University of Sagar, Madhya Pradesh, India". Dr. Jha has published more than 170 papers in refereed journals, books, book chapters and international conference proceedings. He has more than 23 years of teaching experience in the area of Marketing. His overall research interests include Social Media promotion on prescription drugs, DTCA.

Mohammad Khanafi Jumat received his BSc and MSc degrees from School of Business, University of Technology Brunei. Currently, He is a professional of IT Implementation for education sector.

Karman is a researcher at The Center of Research and Development of Informatics Application and Public Communication, The Agency of Human Resources Research and Development, Ministry of Communication and Information Technology, Republic of Indonesia. He has a great interest in research on communication and media, especially in religio-political context of Islam.

Vai Shiem Leong is a Senior Lecturer at UBD School of Business and Economics, Universiti Brunei Darussalam. She publishes on service marketing and consumer behaviour.

Andy Susilo Lukito-Budi is an academician from the Atma Jaya Catholic University of Indonesia. He holds Master of Commerce degree from the Business School, the University of Queensland, Brisbane, Australia and Doctorate degree from the Faculty of Economics and Business, Universitas Gadjah Mada. His research interests are Innovation, Knowledge Management, Organisational Learning and Information System. Andy Susilo is the corresponding author.

Hardo Firmana Given Grace Manik is an academician from the Faculty of Business, Duta Wacana Christian University. He holds a master's degree in Science in Management Programme from the Department of Management, Faculty of Economics and Business, Universitas Gadjah Mada. His research interests focus on Knowledge Management, Organisational Wisdom, Entrepreneurship and Strategic Management.

Marimin Marimin is a Professor of Industrial System Engineering at IPB University (Bogor Agricultural University), Bogor, Indonesia. His current research interests include Intelligent System, Decision Analysis and Decision Support System, Supply Chain Management, Green and Sustainable Industrial Development.

Fadzliwati Mohiddin is a Deputy Dean at the School of Business, Universiti Teknologi Brunei (UTB). Prior to joining UTB, she was the Chief Information Officer, the Director of ICTC and the Dean of the Faculty of Business and Management Sciences, Sultan Sharif Ali Islamic University (UNISSA). She also held the post of Deputy Dean at the Faculty of Business, Economics and Policy Studies, Universiti Brunei Darussalam from 2009 to 2010. She lectures in business information systems and general management. She was involved with several ICT projects that include knowledge management systems and e-learning systems for the Ministry of Education. And, she has been appointed as a judge for several business and ICT competitions such as the Asia Pacific ICT Award (APICTA) and the Brunei ICT Award (BICTA) since 2010. She holds a BA, Management Studies (Universiti Brunei Darussalam); an MBA (Lancaster University, UK); and a PhD, Information Systems (Curtin University of Technology, Western Australia). Her current research interest includes information systems success, knowledge management, e-government and general management.

Bambang Mudjiyanto is a principal researcher (professor) at The Center of Research and Development of Informatics Application and Public Communication, The Agency of Human Resources Research and Development, Ministry of Communication and Information Technology, Republic of Indonesia. Professor Bambang is currently actively teaching at various universities in Jakarta in the field of communication and media studies. Professor Bambang has a great interest in research on communication and media studies, especially in journalistic, new media and broadcasting.

Nazlida Muhamad is a Senior Assistant Professor at UBD School of Business and Economics, Universiti Brunei Darussalam. She publishes on religion influence on consumer behaviour.

Samrat Kumar Mukherjee is currently an assistant professor at the Sikkim Manipal Institute of Technology, Sikkim Manipal University, Sikkim. He received his bachelor's degree in 2000 from West Bengal University of Technology, Kolkata, and master's degree (MBA) from the Narula Institute of Technology, West Bengal University of Technology, Kolkata, India in 2010. Mr. Mukherjee has published more than 18 papers in refereed journals, book chapters and international conference proceedings. He has more than 11 years of teaching experience in the area of Marketing.

His overall research interests include Social Media promotion on prescription drugs, DTCA.

Ari Cahyo Nugroho is a senior researcher at The Office of Human Resources Development and ICT Research of Jakarta Region, The Agency of Human Resources Research and Development, Ministry of Communication and Information Technology, Republic of Indonesia. Ari currently serves as Deputy Head of The Office of Human Resources Development and ICT Research of Jakarta Region. Ari is an expert in the field of media framing and media politics, as his field of expertise as a researcher is in the field of communication media.

Vivek Pandey is currently a research scholar at the Sikkim Manipal Institute of Technology, Sikkim Manipal University, Sikkim. He received his bachelor's degree in 2015 from Lovely Professional University, Punjab, and master's degree (MBA) from the Lovely Professional University, Punjab, India in 2017. Mr. Pandey has published more than three papers in refereed journals and international conference proceedings. His overall research interest is in online patient support group.

Mohammad Habibur Rahman received his PhD in Public Administration from the University of Wales in the UK. He is currently a Professor at the Mohammed Bin Rashid School of Government in Dubai. Professor Habib was a Senior Fulbright Scholar at the Maxwell School of Syracuse University in the USA and Visiting Fellow at the York Centre for Asian Research of York University in Canada. He has more than 30 years of experience in teaching and research in the fields of public administration, political science and development studies in universities in Bangladesh, Canada, Fiji, Brunei and the UAE. His current research interests include public sector reform, e-governance/smart governance, strategic management and public–private partnerships. Professor Habib contributed several consulting and advisory support to government, international organisations and industry.

Didi Rosiyadi received a PhD degree in Computer Science and Information Engineering from National Taiwan University of Science and Technology (NTUST), Taiwan, in 2013. Currently, he is a researcher in Research Center for Informatics, Indonesian Institute of Sciences (LIPI) and also a lecturer in many universities in Indonesia. His research interests include digital image watermarking, steganography and cyber security. He has published more than 50 research papers.

Noor Maya Salleh, PhD, is newly appointed Director of Institut Perkhidmatan Awam (IPA) of Brunei. She was former Assistant Vice Chancellor (Academic) and Dean of School of Business, Universiti Teknologi Brunei. She gained a bachelor's degree in Public Policy and Administration from University Brunei Darussalam, MA in Training and HRD from the University of Warwick and a PhD in Management from the University of Southampton. She has 26 years of teaching experience and was awarded

Excellent Teacher Award in 2015. She also had experience in providing professional training on Human Resource Management for Brunei senior government officers. Her research and teaching interest is on emotional intelligence, human resource management and development, change management, organisational behaviour and knowledge management.

Desi Setiana received a BSc and an MSc in Psychology Behavior of Information Technology, respectively, from the University of Indonesia and the University of Brunei. She is a researcher at the Ministry of Law and Human Right, Republic of Indonesia. Her research interests are in the areas of psychology of information security, user behaviour towards cyberbullying and IT emerging technology for psychology education. She is now in-pipeline to pursuing PhD in IT Psychology for Cyberbullying and Security Protection for Prisoners.

Ahmad Budi Setiawan is a senior researcher at the Center of Research and Development of Informatics Application and Public Communication, The Agency of Human Resources Research and Development, Ministry of Communication and Information Technology, Republic of Indonesia. Currently, Ahmad is also serving as the Head of the Information Division of the Indonesian Researcher Union. He has a great interest in research on information system and socio-informatics, especially in IT governance, cybersecurity, big data, e-business, e-government and digital economy.

Ankit Singh is currently an Assistant Professor at the Symbiosis Institute of Health, Symbiosis International (Deemed University). He received his bachelor's degree in 2010 from the Institute of Management Studies, Devi Ahilya Vishwavidyalaya, Indore, and master's degree (MBA) from the Institute of Management Studies, Devi Ahilya Vishwavidyalaya, Indore, India in 2012. Mr. Mukherjee has published more than 19 papers in refereed journals, book chapters and international conference proceedings. He has more than 7 years of teaching experience in the area of Marketing. His overall research interest is IoT on healthcare industry.

Wardah Azimah Haji Sumardi is a faculty member at Universiti Brunei Darussalam specialising in Human Resource Management (HRM). She earned a doctoral degree in Business Management from Alliance Manchester Business School under the People, Management and Organisation (PMO) Division, University of Manchester, UK. Her thesis looked at employee involvement and participation in Brunei public sector undergoing change. She graduated from the University of Manchester in 2008 with an MSc Human Resource Management and Industrial Relations. She submitted a dissertation that examines the effectiveness of human resource management in the banking sector in Brunei. She earned a bachelor degree in 2006 from Universiti Brunei Darussalam (UBD) in Business Administration. Her primary research interest is in employee involvement and participation (EIP) particularly in the critical and comparative works of EIP. In a larger field of study, research interests are in the areas of human resource management, organisational behaviour and human resource development.

Alifya Kayla Shafa Susanto is a student from Information Security Department, School of Computing and Informatics, University of Technology Brunei, Brunei Darussalam, after graduated her senior high school at SMAN 4 Depok, Indonesia. She is now on the early stages of her research tracks. Her research areas include Information Security Management, Business Process Reengineering, and Blockchain for Financial Technology. Alifya is awarded by the best presenter on IC3INA conferences (International Conferences on Computer, Control, Informatics and Its Application), Bandung-Jakarta, Indonesia, 2021. Alifya has published around 5–10 articles in the International journals, conferences, and books.

Wardah Hakimah Sumardi is a Lecturer specialising in Marketing at School of Business and Economics, Universiti Brunei Darussalam, where she has been a faculty member since 2007. She received her PhD in Business and Management and MSc Marketing from Alliance Manchester Business School, University of Manchester, UK. Her current research interest is in transformative service research and consumer wellbeing. In a larger field of study, her research interests are in the areas of service marketing and social marketing.

Suprihatin Suprihatin is a Professor of Environmental Engineering and Management at IPB University (Bogor Agricultural University), Bogor, Indonesia. His current research interests are green process engineering, environmental management system, cleaner production, water and wastewater treatment technology and hazardous wastes management.

Heru Susanto is currently a Researcher at Research Center for Informatics, the Indonesian Institute of Sciences, and Assistant Professor at School of Business, University Technology of Brunei. He is also an Honorary Professor in the Department of Information Management at College of Management, Tunghai University, Taichung, Taiwan. Dr. Susanto has worked as an IT professional in several roles, including Web Division Head of IT Strategic at Indomobil Group and Prince Muqrin Chair for Information Security Technologies. His research interests are in the areas of information security, 5G technologies, grid application, big data, business process re-engineering and e-marketing. Dr. Susanto received a BSc in Computer Science, an MBA in Marketing Management, an MSc in Information Systems and a PhD in Information Security. Dr. Heru successfully authored more than 35 books published by Taylor & Francis, including eight full authored books and 30 book chapters, and more than 80 international publication in peer-reviewed and high impact journals.

Rindra Yusianto holds a master's degree in Industrial Engineering. He works as an Associate Professor in Industrial Engineering, Dian Nuswantoro University, Semarang, Indonesia. Currently, he is a PhD candidate at Agro-Industrial Engineering, Department of Agro-industrial Technology, Faculty of Agricultural Engineering and Technology, IPB University (Bogor Agricultural University), Bogor, Indonesia. His current research interests include Green Logistics, Spatial Information Systems and Intelligent Decision Support Systems.

Preface

Introduction

We are living in the age of digitalisation. The digitalisation of businesses is happening very rapidly. Digitalisation helps us to perform activities such as managing our works, making efficient decisions and sharing information and knowledge with others in the organisation. Digital transformation is changing the old ways of doing business in a new way. In other words, our organisation is moving from the old economy to a digital economy.

To make sure the transformation process advances in the right direction to support the new way of doing business, organisations need an innovative and creative way of anticipating the future. The abundance of information and knowledge that can be accessed through the Internet and plenty of tools that can enhance knowledge management such as Cloud Computing, Artificial Intelligence and Big Data, as well as affordable knowledge sharing tools, needs to be utilised effectively and efficiently by organisations. However, to do these, organisations need to have a proper organisation design to achieve the goal. In other words, an organisation needs to rethink its existing design, whether to adjust to the new way of doing business to make sure goals can be achieved and the organisation is competitive and agile.

The book aims to address key topics related to organisation design and knowledge management in the digital economy with organisational context, particularly in Asia. Asian nations are moving fast towards the digital economy. Doing business in the digital economy is different from the old way, and the role of organisation design and knowledge management is crucial to support innovative and creative ideas for tapping the huge market opportunities in which people are ready for digitalisation. Chapters in the book cover important topics related to organisation design and knowledge management for organisations, especially business organisations in Asia to prepare and cultivate necessary means for advancing in the digital economy in Asia.

This book offers readers a unique value, bringing new perspectives to understanding emerging business opportunities and challenges in Asia. It will present a valuable collection of chapters with empirical studies from leading researchers on the related topic within the main theme (Asian economies, digitalisation, knowledge management, organisational design).

The collection of chapters is conceptually and practically beneficial for academics, students, policy makers and the general public. Readers are likely to be academics, students, researchers, policymakers and practitioners for references on the latest development organisation design and knowledge management in the digital economy in Asia. This book can be used as a main or supplementary textbook for undergraduate and postgraduate students in the business or related areas.

Contents of the book

The book is organised into four main parts, addressing key issues in the digital economy: organisations and their environments in digital economy, people and knowledge management, information and knowledge management and finally, technology for information and knowledge management. Let's present a summary of the collection of 14 chapters of this book.

Part 1 "Organisations and their environments in digital economy" starts with Chapter 1, titled "Dynamic Capabilities, digital innovation and sustainable transformation of social enterprises" (by Md. Harun Ur Rashid). It states that:

> "...in the age of technological advancement, along with digital innovation and dynamic capabilities, the laws, regulations and policies implemented by government agencies and other public bodies require the social enterprise a legislative transformation which is a major challenge for the social enterprise. Firms that have remained competitive over time have received increasing interest from researchers. The study aims to explore whether dynamic capabilities play a role in the sustainable transformation of social enterprises encompassing the mediating role of digital innovation. The study interviews the social enterprises of Bangladesh and attempts to integrate dynamic capabilities and digital innovation for the sustainable transformation of social enterprise through an institutional entrepreneurship framework. The findings show that dynamic capabilities and digital innovation play a significant role in the sustainable transformation of social enterprises. Digital innovation also plays a crucial mediating role in the relationship between dynamic capabilities and sustainable transformation of social enterprises. The study provides valuable insights into the management of the social enterprises and regulatory bodies which help the enterprises formulate a sound policy to sustain in the competitive era."

Chapter 2, titled "Digital ecosystem: the case study of BruHealth" (by Mohammad Alif Azizi Abdullah, Mohammad Nabil Almunawar and Mohammad Anshari), affirms that:

> "...the current age of digitalization has made the majority of organisations and businesses shift towards digital mediums of conducting their operations, made possible through the rapid advancement of technology. The implementation of a two-sided or multi-sided platform

globally has accelerated digital transformation and ensures a smooth transition in facilitating interactions and transactions of interdependent user groups. A platform and its entities are observed as a digital ecosystem. Actors in the digital ecosystem exchange values between them and collectively create a network of exchange values. The objective of this chapter is to introduce a framework to design and review the digital ecosystem of BruHealth. This chapter discusses BruHealth, initially a contact-tracing application that has expanded into a growing multi-sided e-health platform in Brunei Darussalam, as a case to examine and test the framework in representing BruHealth's ecosystem, and determining development opportunities through analysing entities and the values they exchange within its ecosystem. The framework can also be used as a reference to develop a new ecosystem."

Chapter 3, titled "Examining the digital transformation of intellectual property (IP) infringement services in the Department of Economic Development (DED), Dubai" (by Jama AlGaizi AlFalasi, Mohammad Habibur Rahman), states that:

"...in the United Arab Emirates (UAE), intellectual property (IP) management falls within the remit of the Ministry of Economy (MoE), which is responsible for overall regulation of the implementation of the relevant federal laws in all seven Emirates. Nonetheless, each Emirate enacted decrees and laws concerning how such federal laws are implemented within its jurisdictions. The objective of this chapter is to assess the digital transformation of the procedures to protect trademark IP in Dubai. Practices and procedures for the protection of trademarks in the United States of America (USA) and Singapore are studied for comparisons and to examine their policy implications for Dubai's Department of Economic Development (DED). The findings indicate that trademark IP protection in the UAE is enabled by both customs registration and via relevant authorities, according to the local laws in force in each Emirate. It is also found that registrars in both countries (i.e. USA and Singapore) operate independently, and alternative dispute resolutions (ADRs) are used when trademark infringement occurs. Finally, the chapter recommends a digital operational model for trademark IP enforcement to strengthen the current structure in Dubai. The proposed gateway could streamline and ease the trademark infringement complaint process to facilitate investment."

Part 2 "People and knowledge management" starts with Chapter 4, titled "An analysis the influence of introversion personality on tacit knowledge sharing" (by Diyana Najwa Ali, Fahmi Ibrahim and Noor Maya Salleh). It studies:

"...how introversion may influence tacit knowledge sharing. The common perception of many is that through cultural cues, introversion is a problem because introverts are known for being reserved, quiet, and overwhelmed by an excess of social stimulus. Meanwhile, extroverts tend to be sociable and communicative, and they are seen as possessing the desirable set of personality traits for success in today's working environment. Based on this argument, tacit knowledge sharing is mostly associated with extroversion rather than introversion which provides the significance of this study. A qualitative approach was conducted through in-depth interviews with 11 knowledge workers from public and private sectors with diverse occupations in Brunei Darussalam. Therefore, the objective is to examine and analyse the knowledge-sharing behaviour within this group of categories. It was indicated that personality proved to have a stronger impact on knowledge sharing. However, the findings of this study demonstrated some contradictions that has been discussed in previous studies. The findings may promote understanding what influences introverts to share or not to share their knowledge."

Chapter 5, titled "Unveiling the potential mediating role of knowledge sharing in linking job satisfaction and organisational commitment" (by Md. Zahidul Islam, Wardah Azimah Haji Sumardi and Nurul Amirah Ishak), states that:

"...knowledge sharing (KS), organisational commitment (OC) and job satisfaction (JS) have become the essential drivers for attaining organisational success in the current knowledge era. This chapter aims to bring the three aforementioned key elements together and develop a theoretical framework. By taking a distinct approach from previous studies, the framework presented in this chapter proposes knowledge sharing as a potential mediator in linking job satisfaction and organisational commitment. This is an important contribution to the body of knowledge, as such a link has been largely unexplored in previous literature. The proposed framework is built upon well-established Blau's (1964) Social Exchange theory and Meyer and Allen's (1991) Three-Components Model of organisational commitment. Essentially, the framework postulates that job satisfaction may encourage knowledge sharing behaviour among employees, and subsequently fostering their organisational commitment."

Chapter 6, titled "Establishing mentoring and coaching mechanisms for preserving indigenous knowledge" (by Hardo Firmana Given Grace Manik, Andy Susilo Lukito-Budi, Nurul Indarti), states that:

"...indigenous peoples possess idiosyncratic traditional knowledge, and pass it down from generation to generation. This traditional knowledge is related to natural resources management, handicrafts, agriculture and maritime knowledge to maintain the livelihoods and survival of indigenous communities, including those in Southeast Asia. Thus, the preservation of indigenous knowledge is a must to do. Encouraged by this concern, we propose a framework mechanism that can be used, as one traditional culture preservation method, for mentoring and coaching in indigenous communities by utilising several well-established concepts in the knowledge management literature, such as the knowledge management cycle, knowledge management maturity, SECI model, learning theory and community of practice (CoP). This chapter contributes to the knowledge management body of knowledge by presenting a mechanism that describes the dynamics of knowledge accumulation (know-why and know-how) process through the mentoring and coaching experienced by an indigenous community member."

Chapter 7, titled "Determinants of knowledge sharing behaviours among merchant navy officers" (by Capt. Shankar A Govindasamy and Omkar Dastane), examines:

"...key elements that influence knowledge sharing behaviours among merchant navy officers sailing on-board Malaysian registered vessels. The study used a quantitative method, with data collected using on-line, self-administered questionnaire from 272 officers using snowball sampling. Normality and reliability of the data were assessed following which confirmatory factor analysis, the validity of the measurement model, and structural equation modelling was used to test the hypothesis. The findings revealed that interpersonal trust among co-workers plays a significant role in encouraging knowledge sharing behaviours among the employees. Additionally, intrinsic motivation driven by knowledge self-efficacy and enjoyment in helping others positively affects knowledge sharing behaviours. Organisation culture did not show significant relationship towards knowledge sharing while organisation rewards displayed negative significant relationship. Surprising and contrary to common findings, the usage of information and communication technology (ICT) reflected a negative and insignificant effect. This study suggests, to promote knowledge sharing activities in the shipping industry, it is vital to create a people-oriented environment rather than technology-oriented. Since there is a dearth of research in relation to knowledge management in the shipping industry, this chapter hopes to provide a theoretical basis for future research, as well as practical implications for ship managers."

In Part 3 "Information and knowledge management", Chapter 8, titled "Value co-creation in the social media platform: the perspectives of organizations and prosumers" (by Shahidul Islam, Nazlida Muhamad, Vai Shiem Leong and Wardah Hakimah Sumardi), states that:

"...value co-creation for organization, customer and society is an integral element of overall business strategy. As a collaborative and knowledge sharing tool, social media offers significant opportunities to organisations through effective resource integration and co-creating value facilitations, and prosumers through an unprecedented level of freedom and innovative mechanism in order for organisations and prosumers to engage in value co-creation. However, a holistic understanding of how organizations and prosumers are involved in the value co-creation process through social media is needed to manage significant challenges for organisations to develop social media strategies within a new reality of increased control and capability in the hands of prosumers. Hence, this paper aims to help understand value co-creation in the social media platform from the perspectives of organisations and prosumers. On the basis of past literature, this chapter provides insights into organizational push and pull strategies of value co-creation and extends the existing knowledge on value co-creation through social media in the Asian context. The study also offers a conceptual model on prosumer motivation to co-create value with firms and other customers, bringing together the integrative knowledge from several leading papers on customer and employee value co-creation. This chapter offers a rounded knowledge of the entire value co-creation process by bringing collective insights from knowledge management using social media, social media marketing and value co-creation through social media."

Chapter 9, titled "The use of big data technology to support the transformation of public content management towards knowledge management" (Ahmad Budi Setiawan, Ari Cahyo Nugroho, Karman and Bambang Mudjiyanto), states that:

"...big data technology is a phenomenon, and many organisations are trying to integrate it into their business processes to obtain added value as well as support business processes. Big Data can be used in various ways, one of which is public communication management. Along with the growing dissemination of public issues on social media and other internet contents, the Ministry of Communication and Information of Indonesia made it easier for various stakeholders to handle public issues and internet content by utilizing Big Data technology. In addition, after the process of handling the public issue, the knowledge management concept, which is integrated with big data, will help turn information into useful knowledge. The research was carried out with a qualitative method and described the use of huge amounts of information from big data technology on Big Data machines to monitor negative internet content. The results of this study show the use of Big Data and Knowledge Management technology in dealing with internet content and public issues circulating on the Internet, in particular, to support the public policymaking process."

Chapter 10, titled "Implication of Knowledge Management Systems Adoptions: Higher Education Institutions Context" (by Fadzliwati Mohiddin, Mohammad Khanafi Jumat, Heru Susanto, Fahmi Ibrahim, Desi Setiana and Didi Rosiyadi), addresses three main aspects. First one is:

"...identifying management tools used at the organisational level, second, the supportive and hindrance factors on the adoption of KMS, and last, the user perception and practices of KMS in the institution. A mix of methodologies is adapted to generate findings for this research. Both quantitative and qualitative methods will be used for this research through a questionnaire approach. The questionnaire is constructed in such a way that close-ended questions and open-ended questions are included. The research has led to several important outcomes for the implementation of KMS. This researcher has proposed a conceptual framework and the support from other research outcomes, i.e. identification of the management tools used, the support and barriers for implementation, and user perception and practices for the KMS implementations. It is recommended that by using the right conceptual framework, knowledge sharing in the organization is encouraged and the benefits of adoption will bring about further advantages to enhance the equality of information sharing and use. Efficient information captured, encapsulation, structuring, dissemination and employment of the organizational knowledge will support the achievement of organizational goals and objectives."

Finally, Part 4 "Technology for information and knowledge management" presents Chapter 11, titled "Strengthening artificial intelligence implementation of security business management in time of digital economy innovation" (by Heru Susanto). It states that:

"...the important aspect of the application of AI is how the organization uses AI to boost its business operations. This study will investigate the current state of artificial intelligence in business management in Brunei Darussalam. Most of all, this study is to reveal and manage any AI-related applications that can boost business management in Brunei. In addition to that, this study will also be analysing the impact of the recent COVID-19 on businesses and how can AI be able to help businesses to cope in such times. The challenges that the business faced that prevented them from implementing AI were lack of fund and the business does not believe that there is a significant benefit to be gained from adopting such technology. At the same time, AI is found to be able to increase the satisfactory level of businesses in terms of effectiveness and efficiency in business management. There are also several benefits that businesses can gain from AI that are revealed where even MSMEs can gain benefit from adopting AI."

Chapter 12, titled "Expanding and enhancing knowledge using artificial intelligence (AI) in the Asian agro-industrial sector" (by Rindra Yusianto, Marimin Marimin, Suprihatin Suprihatin and Hartrisari Hardjomidjojo), states that:

"...the support of Artificial Intelligence (AI) and the Internet of Things (IoT) into sustainability concept will improve the robustness of sustainable agro-industry. This research aims to increase the potato agro-industry competitiveness by predicting the harvest number using IoT, determining optimal logistics routes using AI and tracking and tracing potato commodities in Asia, especially Indonesia. The research contribution elaborates a sustainable agro-industry using remote sensing with a multi-thresholding and synergy spatial perspective based on AI. The results showed that the spatial perspective, namely altitude (>1,300 masl), soil texture (andosol), slope (8–13%), rainfall (300mm/month) and temperature (17–20°C), affected increase in the potato harvest number. This research has succeeded in predicting the harvest number with an accuracy rate of 89.35%. This research also shows that the proposed new method, namely spatial Dijkstra, can provide the most optimal alternative logistic route solution than the classical Dijkstra. This research also established accuracy with tracking and tracing based on an AI of 89.21%. This new approach has demonstrated the supply and demand balance in an adaptive, sustainable agro-industrial model simulation. This model needs to be implemented in the Asian sustainable agro-industry so that decision-makers can more quickly and accurately recommend a decision."

Chapter 13, titled "Social Media as collaborative and knowledge sharing tools in Malaysian schools" (by Simin Ghavifekr), affirms that:

"...the academic use of social media revolves around its functions in ensuring collaborative learning and knowledge sharing. Although challenges in terms of privacy and ethics continue to exist, certain measures are employed by academic institutions and educators to ensure that students make the most out of social media in the learning process. This conceptual chapter discusses the prevalent challenges and strategies in the use of social media in various academic institutions in different parts of the world, particularly in Malaysia. The discussion on the use of social media as a collaborative and knowledge sharing tool in Malaysia covers how this technological innovation has been used in teaching and learning, connecting stakeholders and improving learning management systems in primary and secondary schools, as well as in higher education institutions. Further research directions in this subject matter should cover behavioural and social factors that influence the effectiveness of social media in terms of collaboration and knowledge sharing. The implications of this conceptual paper on educators, academic institutions and government agencies focus more on infrastructure development and initiatives to improve the usage and usefulness of social media in schools and universities."

The last chapter of the book, Chapter 14, titled "Emergence of social media as a collaborative and knowledge sharing tool of health information during pandemic" (by Samrat Kumar Mukherjee, Vivek Pandey, Ankit Singh and Ajeya Jha), states that:

"...social media is a new and dominating means of communication that helps users to communicate with each other through email, images, pictures and music. With Covid-induced disruption, social media could play a key role as a medium for dialogue for health providers, physicians, consultants and health agencies to promote more informed decision-making between populations and individuals relevant to health or care. The purpose of the research presented in this chapter is to understand how social media is used for collaboration and knowledge sharing of health information and find challenges faced during the usage of social media for collaboration and knowledge sharing. The paper is conceptual and is based on a literature review. Findings of the study are: the collaboration challenges are its misuse, a large amount of potentially hazardous misinformation, increased pandemic concerns, tendency of doctors to maintain one-way relationships and confusion in terms of ethical online practices. It also concludes that social media can be effective in this context by instilling health information support, informational support, emotional support, esteem support and network support."

Acknowledgements

This book is composed of hard work and dedication made by authors, who are academics, researchers or practitioners in Asia. The editors would like to sincerely thank all authors for their contributions to this valuable book.

The editors would also like to extend heartfelt appreciation to all reviewers who had participated in the reviewing process. Their time and expertise in evaluating the suitability of submitted chapters for publication in this book had significantly contributed to the completion of this edited book.

Moreover, we are also profoundly thankful to our colleagues at the School of Business and Economics (UBDSBE), Universiti Brunei Darussalam, for their continuous support.

Finally, we also like to express our sincere gratitude to the editorial team from Routledge, CRC Press, Taylor & Francis Group for their wise feedback, advice and support to publish this book.

Mohammad Nabil Almunawar
UBD School of Business and Economics,
Universiti Brunei Darussalam, Brunei Darussalam

Md Zahidul Islam
UBD School of Business and Economics,
Universiti Brunei Darussalam, Brunei Darussalam

Patricia Ordóñez de Pablos
Faculty of Economics and Business of the
University of Oviedo, Spain

Part 1

Organisations and their environments in digital economy

1 Dynamic capabilities, digital innovation and sustainable transformation of social enterprises

Md. Harun Ur Rashid

Introduction

In recent years, businesses and entrepreneurs have increasingly prioritised sustainability to create sustainable value for stakeholders (Ince & Hahn, 2020). Social enterprise is defined as an organisation that "pursues a social mission while engaging in commercial activities to sustain their operations" (Battilana & Lee, 2014). These businesses offer solutions to such social challenges that neither the economy nor governments can adequately solve. With increasing the number of social enterprises, the research on their sustainability is increasing in the competitive and digital era (Ince & Hahn, 2020). Although prior researchers have focused on the social enterprise from the non-profit views, priorities have shifted to some extent not only for their business to achieve their social objectives but also to survive in the commercial environments (Eriksson, 2014). With the advent of novel and powerful digital technologies, it is essential to transform social enterprise by incorporating digital platforms, infrastructures and digital innovation for sustainability. Moreover, in the modern era, social enterprises (SEs) are facing an increasingly competitive business environment as they have to compete with the profit-making business (Hudon, Labie, & Reichert, 2020). Coping up with technological innovation and advancement is thus a major challenge for the social enterprise. Hence, it demands an ongoing sustainable transformation.

The social enterprise is a legally organised entity that seeks to combine social intent and economic benefit through business operations (Choi, Berry, & Ghadimi, 2019). On one hand, the social business needs to identify target market segments, changing customer needs and customer innovation with such a strategic business model which incorporates a customer solution (Rashid et al., 2020). To meet the customer changing needs, the social enterprises are to cope up with new technological knowledge into the process and product innovation to grab new opportunities for their sustainability. In this case, the social enterprises face challenges not only to cope up with new digital technologies but also digital innovation to extend their business compared to competitors. On the other hand, the government

DOI: 10.4324/9781003163824-2

imposes a wide range of regulations, incentives and procurement policies to shape social enterprise ownership, financing and control across the countries which may impact the social enterprise as per the publicness theory (Bozeman, 2007). In this case, Choi et al. (2019) documented three major barriers for social enterprise in terms of social outcomes: legal barriers regarding the distribution of ownership and top management; financial constraints due to the reduction of funding and control by the political and legal institutions. It is also a challenge for social enterprises complying with the legislations imposed by the governments and regulatory bodies for their sustainability. Therefore, along with digital innovation and building dynamic capabilities, the laws, regulations and policies implemented by government agencies and other public bodies require the social enterprise a legislative transformation. In this case, the concept of institutional entrepreneurship defines the deliberate act of transforming the existing institutional arrangements (e.g., policies, systems and operational processes) into new ones (Ko & Liu, 2020). For a sustainable transformation of social enterprise, sustainable designs are essential, which in turn involves interoperations that bring alignment of internal organisational components to the relationships with digital innovation and the coevolution of other entities such as society (Kompella, 2020).

To the best of my knowledge, no studies to date have explored dynamic capabilities, digital innovation and sustainable transformation of social enterprise from an institutional entrepreneurship perspective. Based on the literature gap, the study raises two research questions:

(RQ1) how can the social enterprise adopt dynamic capabilities and digital innovation for sustainable transformation?
(RQ2) whether digital innovation mediates the relationship between dynamic capabilities and sustainable transformation of social enterprise?

Therefore, the study poses a conceptual framework to integrate digital innovation and dynamic capabilities for the sustainable transformation of social enterprise through institutional entrepreneurship. Moreover, this chapter aims to examine whether social enterprises are adopting sustainable transformation considering dynamic capabilities and digital innovation. Further, the study contributes to the existing literature in the following ways. First, using the qualitative data (interviewing with open-ended questions), the study will examine the mediating effect of digital innovation on the relationship between dynamic capabilities and transformation of social enterprise. Second, it will provide social enterprise and its management a solution on how to cope up with the ongoing technology-based challenges to compete with a for-profit business. Third, through the theoretical lens of institutional entrepreneurship, the study identifies different domains of institutional work that support the incorporation of commercial practices within the technologically changing environment. Fourth, the study will provide academicians and researchers a novel methodological approach from an institutional entrepreneurship perspective that enables them to conduct more empirical research on the business models in the future. Finally, the study provides the different stakeholders, governments and regulators crucial insights to execute strategies to make the social enterprise sustainable.

Literature review

The recent expansion of the resource-based view into dynamic markets gives a new viewpoint on how companies build new capabilities to deal with evolving markets. According to this theoretical viewpoint, the ability of a company to "integrate, develop, and reconfigure internal and external competencies to meet rapidly evolving environments" is at the heart of its ability to innovate (Rothaermel & Hess, 2007). Dynamic capabilities facilitate a firm not only its ability to detect possible technological changes but also to respond to adapt through innovation. According to publicness theory, the government determines whether a social enterprise is market-oriented or serves a social objective based on three dimensions: ownership, funding and control. If there is a mismatch between supply and demand for social enterprises, particularly in terms of public value formation, policymakers may use policy instruments like legal definitions and conditions, government incentives, procurements and service provision contracts to improve a specific dimension, directing a social enterprise towards social outcomes rather than financial gain (Choi et al., 2019). In elaborating on social entrepreneurship research and practice, the study offers a comprehensive framework delineating the key practices integrating digital innovation and dynamic capabilities for the sustainable transformation of social enterprise presented in Figure 1.1.

Dynamic capabilities

Dynamic capabilities mean the organisational abilities to handle all resources that are needed for a business to achieve high organisational success in a continuously changing environment. Weritz, Braojos, and Matute (2020) defined and described dynamic capabilities "as an amalgamation of abilities and skills to generate, identify and analyze new knowledge within the organization." Both internal and external knowledge, competencies and organisational tools are among these abilities which help to acquire and apply expertise as well as develop new opportunities and resources (Bhatt & Grover, 2005). Dynamic capabilities provide the social enterprises competitive advantages due to its ability to integrate, build and reconfigure internal and external competencies to address rapidly changing environments (Heider et al., 2020; Ince & Hahn, 2020). Their mission is to better coordinate and communicate newly acquired knowledge, develop missing resources and integrate them into organisational routines and norms to remain innovative and competitive (Yeow, Soh, & Hansen, 2018). The qualitative research of Warner and Wäger (2019) explored how incumbent firms in conventional industries create a diversified and sustainable transformation capability. They proposed a model comprising nine micro-foundations to reveal the generic contingency factors under digital sensing, digital seizing and digital transforming that trigger, activate and impede the building of dynamic capabilities for digital transformation. In line with their research, analysing how dynamic capabilities facilitate the social enterprise for sustainability, Ince and Hahn (2020) documented three aggregate drivers: (1) outreach to heterogeneous stakeholders, (2) signalling business model and (3) collaborative management as the central mechanism for the sustainable transformation of social enterprise. To develop a digital business model, companies need a system of dynamic capabilities to utilise resources (Velu, 2017). Prior studies have identified three dimensions of dynamic capabilities: sensing, seizing and transforming (Kump et al., 2019; Schoemaker, Heaton, & Teece, 2018; Teece, 2007; Weritz et al., 2020). Building sensing, seizing and transforming capabilities helps a company to develop a long-term strategy that develops, refines and defends a viable business model, directs organisational change and offers a long-term source of competitive advantage (Teece, 2018).

Sensing

It identifies, creates, collaborates on and evaluates digitalisation patterns and technological opportunities in relation to consumer needs. Customer satisfaction can be generated by being able to understand, perceive and follow emerging technologies (infrastructure, content, platforms, services, e-business applications and so on). The collection of appropriate marketing intelligence information, which is a critical action of the sensing capacity, is made easier with digital technologies (Matarazzo et al., 2021). This capacity helps companies to gain deep insight into consumer motivations and create customised customer value by detecting and analysing the new background of the customer (Goerzig & Bauernhansl, 2018). Sensing is concerned with how to cope effectively with confusion and new opportunities. As a result, businesses must recognise and comprehend technological and customer-demand shifts in the environment (Teece, 2007). As a next step, organisations must determine the necessary resources to respond to the identified changes and opportunities. The aim is to recognise specific gaps and vital skills that are lacking. Organisations align these tools to the plan as a final step in the transformation process. As a result, companies create new competencies to fill in the gaps in their skills (Teece, 2007). To summarise, organisations must be able to sense their surroundings, promote and form learning processes and shape interaction processes.

Seizing

The term "seizing" refers to the process of identifying and pursuing business opportunities that are compatible with the organisation's environment, as well as its strengths and weaknesses (Teece, 2007). As a result of seizing, market opportunities are successfully exploited, and threats are avoided. Seizing information and expertise from both the outside and inside are closely linked to strategic decision-making, especially when it comes to investment decisions. Capacity-building begins with a plan that allows for the recognition of valuable knowledge. This assessment is based on prior experience and leads to a decision among several strategic options. An organisation's seizing capacity is high if it can determine whether some information has potential value and convert valuable information into concrete business opportunities that fit its strengths and weaknesses and make decisions based on that information (Kump et al., 2019). The firm must also seize opportunities in timely ways by successfully innovating and implementing new systems that take advantage of external changes (Schoemaker et al., 2018).

Transforming

Teece (2007) defines transformation as "enhancing, combining, protecting, and, when necessary, reconfiguring the business enterprise's intangible and tangible assets" in order to avoid path dependencies and inertia. To put it another way, transforming entails putting decisions for new business models, product or process developments into action by putting in place the necessary structures and routines, providing the necessary infrastructure, ensuring that the workforce has the necessary skills and so on (Kump et al., 2019). The actual realisation of strategic renewal within the organisation through the reconfiguration of resources, systems and processes is referred to as transforming. The ability to recombine and reconfigure assets and organisational structures as the enterprise expands, and as markets and technologies change, is described by Teece (2007) as transforming (reconfiguring). Transforming is thus comparable to implementation capacity, which is characterised as "the ability to execute and coordinate strategic decision and corporate change, which includes a variety of managerial and organizational processes, depending on the nature of the goal" (Li & Liu, 2014). Communicating, interpreting, implementing and enacting strategic plans are all examples of implementation. Renewal occurs only when new information and ideas are implemented; otherwise, they remain theoretical inputs and potential changes within an organisation. An organisation with a high transforming capacity constantly executes planned renewal activities by delegating tasks, allocating resources and ensuring that the workforce has the new skills needed. When dealing with a Volatility, Uncertainty, Complexity and Ambiguity (VUCA) environment, it is often insufficient for businesses to incrementally respond to changes. To fully benefit from new business models, they may need to reshape themselves and maybe their habitats (Schoemaker et al., 2018). On the other hand, a digital transformation must take into account how advances in digital technologies can affect a company's business model, organisational structures and processes (Hess et al., 2016).

Digital innovation

While transforming the social enterprise, it is crucial to consider digital innovation – a result of the digitisation of daily physical goods that provide new functions that significantly enhance the design of products, production, delivery and use (Warner & Wäger, 2019). Yoo, Henfridsson, and Lyytinen (2010) defined digital innovation as the digitisation of everyday physical goods which offer novel functions that greatly enhance product design, production, distribution and use. The three features of digital technologies such as re-programmability, data homogenisation and self-referential nature pave the way for a layered modular architecture that allow digital components to be embedded into physical products, making them a strategic option for companies looking to innovate digitally (Yoo et al., 2010).

Digitalisation has created an avenue of different ways for businesses to connect with their consumers, resulting in a slew of new and unforeseen business model developments (Khanagha, Volberda, & Oshri, 2014; Warner & Wäger, 2019). The "business model," especially in a digital context, has evolved into a new unit of analysis that explores how a company generates and provides value to its customers, as well as how it captures profits from managing a networked system of operations (Warner & Wäger, 2019). Digital innovation paves the way for social enterprise towards digital transformation. It varies from conventional modes of strategic transition in that it has increased the speed of change, resulting in much more environmental instability, complexity and ambiguity (Loonam et al., 2018). According to Hess et al. (2020), a digital transformation must take into account how progress in digital technology can affect a company's business model, organisational structures and processes. Summarising 11 papers on digitisation, the study of Nambisan, Wright, and Feldman (2019) identified three key themes, openness, affordances and generativity related to digital innovation.

Sustainable transformation

Many businesses still place too much emphasis on regulatory compliance when it comes to sustainability. This is a crucial aspect of maintaining a license to operate. However, it is critical to go further: incorporating sustainability into a company's strategy, operating model and day-to-day processes allow it to fully realise the value creation potential of sustainability. As a result, every company's boardroom should discuss sustainability. Goldstrom (2019) discusses four steps that organisations must take to achieve a successful sustainable transformation. The steps are as follows.

First and foremost, the company must change the way it operates. To produce products, an execution engine and a process is crucial, just like a manufacturing company. However, in this case, the process is being used to transform ideas into projects that improve the bottom line. Second, concentration should be given to skills, which entails not only reviewing the business processes but also the company's human resources. Transformations that incorporate and build on this type of formal capability analysis are twice as likely to succeed. Third, the plan should focus on growth. Most successful transformations necessitate organisations being as obsessed with growth as they are with cost reduction, if not more so. Finally, and most importantly, the business should consider altering its culture to reinforce these three points. The right culture will result in a healthy organisation that not only focuses on performance but also promotes long-term health.

Evaluating field interviews with 64 institutional entrepreneurs from UK-based social enterprises, Ko & Liu (2020) highlighted the institutional entrepreneurship perspectives of organisational transformation: (1) adopting new strategies to exploit fresh opportunities, (2) designing new organisational frameworks and operating processes (i.e., organisational form) to respond to the changing environment and (3) the establishment of legitimacy to address stakeholders' concerns about institutional change.

Methodology

The study uses primary data to develop a conceptual framework. To conduct the survey, the senior executives of two social enterprises of Bangladesh were interviewed using an open-ended questionnaire. The questionnaire has been developed based on prior studies (Ince & Hahn, 2020; Kompella, 2020; Kump et al., 2019) presented in Appendix A.

Face-to-face interviews were conducted in order to collect data and allow for personal contact (Alvesson, 2003). The senior advisors in the interviews were asked to share their perspectives on sustainable transformation and their vivid experiences with it. The study used a practitioner conceptualisation of the dynamic capabilities framework to guide the debate. This interactive exercise allowed participants to use the dynamic capabilities framework to freely discuss their understanding of and experiences with guiding client firms through digital transformation. This interactive exercise helped us fine-tune our conceptual model and determine which kinds of dynamic capabilities and digital innovation are necessary for the sustainable transformation of SE. The research has used tables and figures to achieve the objective of this study and develop a sustainable transformation model of SEs.

Results and discussion

Dynamic capabilities and sustainable transformation

In the rapidly changing market, dynamic capabilities offer the Bangladeshi SEs a competitive advantage towards sustainable transformation integrating, developing and identifying both internal and external capabilities. All three categories of dynamic capabilities build the business model of SEs for long-term sustainability to avail the competitive advantage (Teece, 2018).

Sensing and sustainable transformation

Following the study of Kump et al. (2019), the interviewees were asked regarding the sensing, seizing and transforming of their business. They responded to the queries whether their firm knows the changes in the current market and how to keep their firm up to date in the current situation as follows.

> Our firm is well informed about the current market situation and we always try to cope up with updated knowledge and technological progress. We use their marketing wings to search and collect new information from the national and international market and acquire new technological equipment.

The study also interviewed whether their firms are enough to identify target market segments, changing customer needs and customer innovation. The respondents' answers were optimistic that they always keep them up to date regarding the changing customer needs and thereby segment the target markets. Moreover, the SEs identify and realise the technological and customer-demand shifts in the changing market (Teece, 2007) which pave the way for sustainable transformation of the firms.

Seizing and sustainable transformation

The social enterprises are also in the process of recognising and following new business opportunities that are compatible with the firm's environment, as well as its strengths and weaknesses, within the regulatory bodies' laws for sustainable transformation (Teece, 2007). We have asked how their firms outline customer solution-based business models. They confirmed that

> We try to identify the proper problems faced by the customers in the changing environment. Moreover, we can determine whether some information is potentially valuable and convert valuable information into concrete business opportunities that fit the organization's strengths and weaknesses and make decisions based on that information. We are also well-informed about our competitors' activities and strategies to sustain in the competitive era.

Their discussion supports the prior studies (Kump et al., 2019). This research uses some clients, informers and published notices to know the competitor strategies of the recent changes in the current situation. Further, we asked how their firms cope up with new technological knowledge. The executives explained that they try to acquire new technological knowledge first, and to cope up with this knowledge, they convert it into the process and product innovation. Current information also leads to the development of new products or services of their firms, which in turn makes their SE towards sustainable transformation.

Transforming and sustainable transformation

In line with the study of Teece (2007), the executives of SEs believe that a firm that has a high renewal capacity would typically make these decisions by assigning roles, allocating resources and ensuring that their workforce has the necessary new knowledge. For sustainable transformation, they clearly define their duties and responsibilities and successfully implement plans. When the study inquired whether and how the plans for changes are flexible to adapt to the current situation in their company. They explained that

> We are always ready to accommodate the projects which change continuously even when unforeseen interruptions occur. We also practice the plans for changes in the daily business to grab new opportunities.

These findings are consistent with the study of prior studies (Heider et al., 2020; Kump et al., 2019). Sometimes, they emphasise their strength to flexibly adapt the plans for changes to the current situation.

Digital innovation and sustainable transformation

For a sustainable transformation, Bangladeshi SEs are involved in interoperations that bring alignment of internal organisational components to the relationships with digital innovation and the coevolution of other entities such as society (Kompella, 2020). For sustainable transformation, the firms need a rapid and widespread proliferation of novel and powerful digital technologies, platforms, digital infrastructures, which have changed how innovation and entrepreneurship are implemented (Nambisan et al., 2019). Further, the executives of the SEs were asked whether their firm is capable to cope up with new digital technologies and how does the adoption of new digital technologies influence to extend their business compared to competitors.

> We certify that our firm is capable enough to cope up with new digital technologies. But before adopting such new digital technologies, we would like to ensure that it is suitable for our business in generating

revenues with customer satisfaction. We also consider whether these technologies and processes make the firm efficient and attract more customers to extend our business.

In line with the study of Nambisan et al. (2019), the researchers wanted to know that how their firms cope up with three key themes, openness, affordances and generativity related to digital innovation. The study explored elaborately that the digitisation-based mechanisms aid their firm in resolving conflicts at different levels, while openness encourages and shapes the SEs' innovative and entrepreneurial pursuits. Though the SEs are taking potential actions offered by digital technology concerning specific uses of innovation, such as digital affordances, spatial affordances, institutional affordances and social affordances, it is weakening spatial and institutional affordances to promote firms' geographical and institutional distance interactions, such as foreign markets. Moreover, they mentioned their capacity by digital technologies to generate spontaneous change as follows.

> Our current knowledge of the origins and mechanisms of technology generativity offers insight into the possible interaction effects between technical systems, governance processes, and individual/firm activities, as well as the influence on a variety of outcomes at multiple levels.

Finally, when the respondents were asked how digital innovation helps their firms to transform their business with sustainability, they explained that their firms are in the continuous process of developing new organisational structures and operational procedures to respond to the changing environment

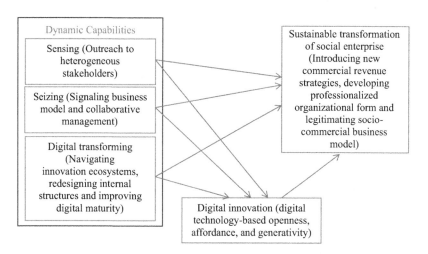

Figure 1.1 Integrating dynamic capabilities and digital innovation for the sustainable transformation of social enterprise through institutional entrepreneurship framework.

complying with existing institutional regulations. Thus, digital innovation paves the way for social enterprise towards digital transformation.

The mediating role of digital innovation between the relationship between dynamic capabilities and sustainable transformation

Social enterprises must build dynamic capabilities with sensing, seizing and transforming opportunities in timely ways by successfully innovating and implementing new systems that take advantage of external changes (Schoemaker et al., 2018). Tortora et al. (2021) found dynamic capabilities affecting firms' digital innovation in terms of the creation of new offerings, processes or solutions using a wide range of digital technologies, considering the snowballing importance of digitalisation to portray companies' competitive advantages and it, in turn leads firms towards sustainable transformation. To sustain in this digital world, social enterprises are to cope up with new technological advancements along with different types of institutional regulations. According to the publicness theory, the government implements a wide variety of laws, incentives and procurement policies to influence social enterprise ownership, funding and control across countries (Choi et al., 2019). In the explanation of establishing legitimacy to address stakeholders' concerns, they replied as follows.

> Along with adopting digital innovation and technological advancement, we try to comply with the legitimacy of regulatory bodies to address stakeholders' concerns about institutional and technological change.

The executives of social enterprises emphasised that not only technological progress but also digital innovation play a significant role in the sustainable transformation of their business. It provides the competitive advantages to operate their business towards sustainable transformation. Finally, when the executives were asked about the mediating role of digital innovation, they commented that in the presence of technological advancement, digital innovation accelerates the SEs towards sustainable transformation.

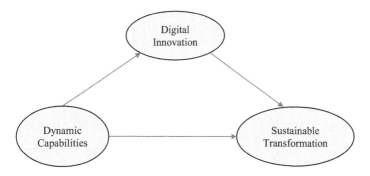

Figure 1.2 Conceptual framework.

Table 1.1 Items of dynamic capabilities and digital innovation for the sustainable transformation

Item code	
	Sensing
SE1	Our company knows the best practices in the market
SE2	Our company is up to date on the current market situation
SE3	Our company systematically searches for information on the current market situation
SE4	As a company, we know how to access new information
SE5	Our company always has an eye on our competitors' activities
SE6	Our company quickly notices changes in the market
	Seizing
SZ7	Our company can quickly relate to new knowledge from the outside
SZ8	We recognise what new information can be utilised in our company
SZ9	Our company is capable of turning new technological knowledge into the process and product innovation
SZ10	Current information leads to the development of new products or services
	Transforming
T11	By defining clear responsibilities, we successfully implement plans for changes in our company
T12	Even when unforeseen interruptions occur, the changing projects are seen through consistently in our company
T13	Decisions on planned changes are pursued consistently in our company
T14	In the past, we have demonstrated our strengths in implementing changes
T15	In our company, the changing projects can be put into practice alongside the daily business
T16	In our company, plans for change can be flexibly adapted to the current situation
	Innovation
O17	The digital technology and digitisation-based mechanisms help address problems and shape the innovation of our company
O18	The digitisation-enabled openness promotes innovative and entrepreneurial pursuits at our firm
A19	The affordances associated with organisational and digital infrastructures shape the ways by which innovation and entrepreneurial initiatives unfold in different contexts of our company
A20	The digitisation compensates for weakening spatial and institutional affordances to facilitate firms' geographically and institutionally distant interactions
G21	Digital technologies exhibit the capacity to produce unprompted change
	Sustainable transformation
ST22	We introduce new practices to exploit fresh opportunities
ST23	We develop new organisational structures and operate procedures to respond to the changing environment
ST24	We attempt to establish legitimacy to address stakeholders' concern about institutional and technological change

In the relationship between dynamic capabilities and sustainable transformation, the study explores whether digital innovation mediates. The study proposes the following conceptual model where the mediating effect can only be justified if a relationship between the independent variable (IV) and mediator (M) and between the dependent variable (DV) and mediator (M) is established (Hair et al., 2010). In our study, the mediating effect of digital innovation can only be supported if a significant relationship sustains between dynamic capabilities (IV) and digital innovation (M) (Kraay & Kaufmann, 2002) and association between digital innovation (M) and sustainable transformation (DV) as shown in Figure 1.2.

Based on the discussions related to dynamic capabilities, digital innovation and sustainable transformation, the study develops the conceptual framework presented in Figure 1.1. Moreover, the research develops a questionnaire based on the conceptual model and discussions shown in Table 1.1. The questionnaire is expected to help work with quantitative data and justify the conceptual model. Likert-scale-based study with structural equation modelling (SEM) can be used to testify the mediating effect on the relationship between dynamic capabilities and digital innovation.

Conclusion, implications and limitations

The findings emphasise the importance of sensing and learning capabilities as digital transformation triggers. This study offers some managerial implications for digital transformation in the SEs operations, in addition to providing a theoretical contribution to the current literature on digital innovation, organisational capacity and sustainable transformation. Moreover, the study provides academicians and researchers with a novel analytical approach from the perspective of institutional entrepreneurship, allowing them to perform more empirical business model research in the future. The findings also present key lessons to various stakeholders, government leaders and regulators in order to adopt policies that will ensure the long-term viability of the social enterprise.

First, the study provides an insight into how the SEs are adopting both digital innovation and dynamic capabilities to sustain their business in the changing environment. The firms are also adopting all the regulations and policies relating to ownership, control and funding imposed by the government and regulatory bodies. In the presence of technological progress, digital innovation accelerates the SEs towards sustainable transformation in the current market situation. Second, the study integrates digital innovation and dynamic capabilities for the sustainable transformation of social enterprise and develops a conceptual model through the theoretical lens of institutional entrepreneurship. Third, the study develops a questionnaire based on the conceptual model which may help conduct the Likert-scale-based statistical analysis in the relationship between dynamic capabilities and sustainable transformation encompassing the mediating role of digital innovation.

Finally, the study suggests the firms that establishing dynamic capabilities along with technological advancement, and digital innovation hastens the business towards sustainable transformation. It implies that digital innovation mediates the relationship of sensing change, seizing opportunities and transforming capabilities with sustainable transformation.

The study suggests the management of the SEs that they should be in the continuous process to establish a high renewal capacity in decision-making to assign roles, allocate resources and ensure that their employee has the necessary new knowledge to adopt digital innovation and technological advancement. The SEs should also be well informed about their competitors' activities and strategies in the recent changes to sustain in the competitive era. For sustainable transformation, they need to acquire and utilise new technological knowledge in the process and product innovation. Moreover, the firms should make their plans in such a way that the management can implement the plans for changes in the daily business to grab new opportunities. In addition to developing new organisational structures, the firms need to design the operating procedures in such a way that responds to the changing environment. Further, along with adopting digital innovation and dynamic capabilities, the firms should comply with the rules and regulations to address stakeholders' concerns about institutional and technological change. Finally, the SEs must be aware of generating revenues with customer satisfaction while coping up with new digital technologies as inefficiency in adopting innovation and new technologies may lose customers.

Furthermore, this study has significant managerial implications. Digital innovations aid SEs in traditional sectors, where a firm's reputation, brand recognition and customer relationships are critical strategic indicators for success. At the international level, sustainable transformation is a requirement for value creation, especially in SE where brand awareness is critical. Neglecting digital instruments is unsafe and could jeopardise the firm's existence. Furthermore, incorporating these innovations is not without obstacles, necessitating management and vision adjustments that stem from the acquisition of new organisational and marketing capabilities.

Despite the significance of the empirical findings and their practical consequences, this study has several flaws that could be addressed in future studies. First, the study was conducted based on developing countries; the results may not be applicable to developed countries. Second, the study surveyed only two SEs towards developing a new conceptual model; it may not represent all SEs. Future comparative research could take into account the limitations of this study. Geographical location, industry emphasis, brand positioning, governance structure and age, allowing for a more in-depth analysis of different digital transformation, applications and triggers can be considered. Future studies may also consider the Likert-scale-based quantitative method with statistical analysis. The conceptual model of this research provides a guideline for future research and can also be examined in other types of businesses.

Appendix A

1 How can your company know the changes in the current market and how to keep your firm up to date in the current situation?
2 Does your company know how to access new information? If yes, how does it search in the current market?
3 Are the processes of your firm enough to identify target market segments, changing customer needs and customer innovation?
4 How has your firm delineated a customer solution-based business model?
5 Are you well informed about your competitors' situation/activities/strategies? How?
6 How can your company cope up with new technological knowledge in process and product innovation?
7 Are the plans for changes flexible to adapt to the current situation in your company? If yes, how do you implement/practice the plans for changes in the daily business to grab new opportunities?
8 Is your firm capable of coping up with new digital technologies? How does the adoption of new digital technologies influence to extend your business compared to competitors?
9 Is your firm developing new organisational structures and operating procedures to respond to the changing environment? How?
10 How does your firm establish legitimacy to address stakeholders' concerns about institutional and technological change?
11 Do you think digital innovation plays any role in the sustainable transformation of your business? How?
12 How does digital innovation play a mediating role between technological advancement and sustainable transformation?

References

Alvesson, M. (2003). Beyond neopositivists, romantics, and localists: A reflexive approach to interviews in organizational research. *Academy of Management Review*, *28*(1), 13–33.

Battilana, J., & Lee, M. (2014). Advancing research on hybrid organizing: Insights from the study of social enterprises. *Academy of Management Annals*, *8*(1), 397–441.

Bhatt, G. D., & Grover, V. (2005). Types of information technology capabilities and their role in competitive advantage: An empirical study. *Journal of Management Information Systems*, *22*(2), 253–277.

Bozeman, B. (2007). *Public values and public interest: Counterbalancing economic individualism*. Washington, DC: Georgetown University Press: Jossey-Bass.

Choi, D., Berry, F. S., & Ghadimi, A. (2019). Policy design and achieving social outcomes: A comparative analysis of social enterprise policy. *Public Administration Review*, *80*(3), 498–505.

Eriksson, T. (2014). Processes, antecedents and outcomes of dynamic capabilities. *Scandinavian Journal of Management, 30*(1), 65–82.

Goerzig, D., & Bauernhansl, T. (2018). Enterprise architectures for the digital transformation in small and medium-sized enterprises. *Procedia Cirp, 67,* 540–545.

Goldstrom, S. (2019). Keys to a sustainable transformation: A conversation with Seth Goldstrom. *McKinsy & Company,* https://www.mckinsey.com/business-functions/transformation/our-insights/keys-to-a-sustainable-transformation-a-conversation-with-seth-goldstrom#.

Hair, J., Anderson, R., Babin, B., & Black, W. (2010). *Multivariate data analysis: A global perspective* (Vol. 7). Upper Saddle River, NJ: Pearson.

Heider, A., Gerken, M., van Dinther, N., & Hülsbeck, M. (2020). Business model innovation through dynamic capabilities in small and medium enterprises: Evidence from the German Mittelstand. *Journal of Business Research*, 130, 635–645.

Hess, T., Matt, C., Benlian, A., & Wiesböck, F. (2016). Options for formulating a digital transformation strategy. *MIS Quarterly Executive, 15*(2), 123–139.

Hudon, M., Labie, M., & Reichert, P. (2020). What is a fair level of profit for social enterprise? Insights from microfinance. *Journal of Business Ethics, 162*(3), 627–644.

Ince, I., & Hahn, R. (2020). How dynamic capabilities facilitate the survivability of social enterprises: A qualitative analysis of sensing and seizing capacities. *Journal of Small Business Management, 58*(6), 1265–1290.

Khanagha, S., Volberda, H., & Oshri, I. (2014). Business model renewal and ambidexterity: Structural alteration and strategy formation process during transition to a Cloud business model. *R&D Management, 44*(3), 322–340.

Ko, W. W., & Liu, G. (2020). The Transformation from traditional nonprofit organizations to social enterprises: An institutional entrepreneurship perspective. *Journal of Business Ethics, 171,* 15–32.

Kompella, L. (2020). Socio-Technical transitions and organizational responses: Insights from e-governance case studies. *Journal of Global Information Technology Management, 23*(2), 89–111.

Kraay, A., & Kaufmann, D. (2002). *Growth without governance* (Vol. Working Paper 2928, available at: www.google.com/url?siteresources.worldbank.org/ DEC/Resources/GG LAC11.pdf): The World Bank.

Kump, B., Engelmann, A., Kessler, A., & Schweiger, C. (2019). Toward a dynamic capabilities scale: Measuring organizational sensing, seizing, and transforming capacities. *Industrial and Corporate Change, 28*(5), 1149–1172.

Li, D.-y., & Liu, J. (2014). Dynamic capabilities, environmental dynamism, and competitive advantage: Evidence from China. *Journal of Business Research, 67*(1), 2793–2799.

Loonam, J., Eaves, S., Kumar, V., & Parry, G. (2018). Towards digital transformation: Lessons learned from traditional organizations. *Strategic Change, 27*(2), 101–109.

Matarazzo, M., Penco, L., Profumo, G., & Quaglia, R. (2021). Digital transformation and customer value creation in Made in Italy SMEs: A dynamic capabilities perspective. *Journal of Business Research, 123,* 642–656.

Nambisan, S., Wright, M., & Feldman, M. (2019). The digital transformation of innovation and entrepreneurship: Progress, challenges and key themes. *Research Policy, 48*(8), 103773.

Rashid, M. H. U., Nurunnabi, M., Rahman, M., Masud, M. A. K. (2020). Exploring the relationship between customer loyalty and financial performance of banks: Customer open innovation perspective. *Journal of Open Innovation: Technology, Market, and Complexity*, *6*(4), 108.

Rothaermel, F. T., & Hess, A. M. (2007). Building dynamic capabilities: Innovation driven by individual-, firm-, and network-level effects. *Organization Science*, *18*(6), 898–921.

Schoemaker, P. J., Heaton, S., & Teece, D. (2018). Innovation, dynamic capabilities, and leadership. *California Management Review*, *61*(1), 15–42.

Teece, D. J. (2007). Explicating dynamic capabilities: The nature and microfoundations of (sustainable) enterprise performance. *Strategic Management Journal*, *28*(13), 1319–1350.

Tortora, D., Chierici, R., Briamonte, M. F., & Tiscini, R. (2021). 'I digitize so I exist'. Searching for critical capabilities affecting firms' digital innovation. *Journal of Business Research*, *129*, 193–204.

Velu, C. (2017). A systems perspective on business model evolution: The case of an agricultural information service provider in India. *Long Range Planning*, *50*(5), 603–620.

Warner, K. S., & Wäger, M. (2019). Building dynamic capabilities for digital transformation: An ongoing process of strategic renewal. *Long Range Planning*, *52*(3), 326–349.

Weritz, P., Braojos, J., & Matute, J. (2020). Exploring the antecedents of digital transformation: Dynamic capabilities and digital culture aspects to achieve digital maturity. *AMCIS 2020 Proceedings*, *22* https://aisel.aisnet.org/amcis2020/org_transformation_is/org_transformation_is/22.

Yeow, A., Soh, C., & Hansen, R. (2018). Aligning with new digital strategy: A dynamic capabilities approach. *The Journal of Strategic Information Systems*, *27*(1), 43–58.

Yoo, Y., Henfridsson, O., & Lyytinen, K. (2010). Research commentary—the new organizing logic of digital innovation: An agenda for information systems research. *Information Systems Research*, *21*(4), 724–735.

2 Digital ecosystem

The case study of BruHealth

Mohammad Alif Azizi Abdullah, Mohammad Nabil Almunawar and Mohammad Anshari

Introduction

The analogy of 'ecosystem' has been a developing area of interest recently, continuously linked to the advancement of technology where ecosystem is considered to be resilient, extendable structures that can decode dynamic and sophisticated challenges. Digital ecosystem imitates that of a biological ecosystem which is related to the intricate and interrelated networks and their fundamental structures, where all of the components interact and present themselves as a complete self-organising, extendable and maintainable function (Li, Badr, & Biennier, 2012). Currently, information and communications technologies (ICTs) are inevitable in storing, retrieving and transmitting data and in supporting consistent interaction through digital mediums via the Internet and mobile devices. These large volumes of data generated daily and the growing difficulty of ICT-enabled systems have introduced the idea of "digital ecosystems." Digital ecosystems are made up of various and self-reliant entities such as organisations, individuals, services, applications and software that contribute to one or numerous tasks and concentrates on the connection between them.

The consistent progress towards digitalisation through the utilisation of digital technologies is key in achieving a digital economy. As the digital economy continues to grow through advances in technology and infrastructure, digital ecosystems are gaining increasing attention as a topic of research (Yamakami, 2010). Digital ecosystems observed in major companies such as Alibaba.com and Gojek have thrived within their current ecosystem that plays a significant role in its massive growth in their respective industries of e-commerce and MSP (multi-service platform). In today's most prominent companies are those that incline in bringing and binding distinct groups of entities in their business structure (Eisenmann, Parker, & Van Alstyne, 2006).

In Brunei Darussalam, the term digital ecosystem is still new and underutilised by organisations and government bodies. While it may exist without the knowledge of entities within existing ecosystems, BruHealth presents an intriguing matter in this research. BruHealth is an e-health

DOI: 10.4324/9781003163824-3

initiative that acts as a contact tracing tool implemented by the government of Brunei to combat the outbreak of COVID-19. Developed in the form of a mobile application, BruHealth is also perceived as a platform that provides e-health capabilities to its users. The primary objective of this research is to present a framework to examine the e-health ecosystem in Brunei and utilise it to recognise or establish a development strategy through the inclusion of additional values into its current ecosystem. This research uses BruHealth as a case study, a growing digital platform with a large userbase in Brunei, to assess the proposed framework in depicting BruHealth's ecosystem and investigating its growth potential. The main contribution of this research is the proposed framework to design and review Brunei's e-health ecosystem. Implementation of the framework to BruHealth enables additional questions to be examined: (1) What is BruHealth's core ecosystem? (2) What values are exchanged between the entities within the ecosystem?

The rest of the paper is organised as follows: Section "Literature review" is a literature review on some theories and associated issues; Section "Research methodology" is the methodology; Section "Value exchange network: an e-health ecosystem framework" is the discussion on the proposed framework; Section "Applying the framework: the BruHealth's ecosystem" is the application of the framework; Section "The foundation of BruHealth's core ecosystem" is the foundation of BruHealth's ecosystem; Section "BruHealth's ecosystem development" is the ecosystem development and final section is the conclusion.

Literature review

E-health

In the 1990s, when the Internet was recognised globally, several e-terms started to emerge and spread. E-mail introduced new prospects for individuals to communicate swiftly and share their experiences; e-commerce brought new approaches to do business and financial transactions via the Internet. The establishment of e-health presented an encouraging way to health and the healthcare system through information and communication technologies (Alvarez, 2002). Digital technologies are affecting the welfare and financial development globally (Stroetmann, 2018). In the last decade, the world has experienced expeditious progress and acceptance of technologies that have transformed the way individuals live and will have an equally changing impact on health care.

E-health is known as the Information and communication technology (ICT) measure that is established in the healthcare organisation. E-health provides many benefits such as cost-benefit, the ability of the operation and providing self-government for the patient. According to Eysenbach (2001), e-health is a rising area in the interchange of medical informatics, public health and business. The term e-health refers to the services and information that are provided in health care and improved through the Internet and associated technologies. Some interpretations of e-health are closely related to the Internet, emphasising its increasing significance in providing better health care. A health system incorporates the entire operations and constructions whose main objective is to affect health (Arah et al., 2006). Current developments of e-health services focus on empowering its users (patients) as a significant element of e-health. User empowerment can be in different types of interaction between users to the operator such as accessing services online, making online booking appointments and making payment online. A research by Anshari et al. (2013) argues that empowerment in any level of interaction with patients in a healthcare institution is difficult to provide. The research highlighted that empowerment for customers (patients or users) in an e-health system comes in many forms and standards in which digitising medical records is the bare minimum that gives users empowerment. A healthy connection between a healthcare provider and its patients is considered to boost customers' satisfaction, as a result making them dedicated customers.

Digital ecosystem

An ecosystem is more than just a metaphor, Briscoe et al. (2007) claimed that the development of a digital ecosystem intends to exploit dynamics of the complexity and distinct adjustments of living organisms that of a biological ecosystem. The theory of a digital ecosystem is suggested as a method to recognise the complicated and interrelated system being established (Fiorina, 2000). According to Li et al. (2012), digital components within a digital ecosystem is any valuable ideas, expressed by a natural or formal terminology that are digitalised and moved within the ecosystem, where it can be processed by computers and humans. Nachira et al. (2007) claimed that the emergence of digital ecosystems was made possible by the overlapping of the ICT, social and knowledge networks, where these networked connections are enabled by the Internet and the World Wide Web. Large corporations such as Alibaba.com and Gojek have applied the concept of digital ecosystem as a business ecosystem that has enabled them to significantly expand the functionalities and operability of their business.

Similar to that of an ecosystem in Ecology, a business ecosystem is formed by different interrelated actors or entities, where every one of the entities generates value within the ecosystem. The theory behind business ecosystem was established by Moore (1993, 1996) in explaining that a business is interrelated and collaborates with other business or company entities in generating value to meet customers' demands. From the perspective of business ecosystem, a business is present within the system itself where it affects and is affected by other entities or actors within the ecosystem. The business affects other entities by giving value to them and is affected by receiving value from other entities. According to Iansiti and Levien (2004b), within each business ecosystem, there exists the keystone that manages the interactions and transactions in the ecosystem. Within a business ecosystem, the keystone's value creation is created through the value generated by other entities. Therefore, the keystone is required to pay attention to the value, welfare and expansion of other entities in the ecosystem. Particularly, the keystone must ensure a mutually beneficial connection with other entities and between entities to co-create values and preserve a healthy business ecosystem (Anggraeni et al. 2007; Iansiti and Levien, 2004; Moore, 1997). The case of BruHealth presents an interesting matter to be investigated where the keystone is a government department (Ministry of Health) that provides directions and manages the values of other entities within its ecosystem.

Digital platform

In the current business world, most businesses have been transformed by digital platforms, and it is selected as the primary approach in arranging a wide variety of human proceedings that include political, economic and social interaction (Tan et al., 2015). Spagnoletti et al. (2015) refer to digital platforms as "a tall block that provides an essential function to a technological system and serves as a foundation upon which complementary products, technologies, or services can be developed." A digital platform is also identified as a two-sided market that includes a virtual space where the supplier and consumer groups participate in making transactions and trade (Amit & Zott, 2001). According to Spagnoletti et al. (2015), digital platforms are changing the progression of every IS landscape. The communication between consumers and businesses is evolving as digital platforms offer support to consumers that are made up of online communities. The growth of digital platforms has developed successful companies, for instance, in hospitality (WWOOF, Airbnb), in transportation (Uber, Gojek) and software development (Microsoft Windows, iOS and Android). The way people interact with each other has changed due to social media platforms such as Facebook and Instagram. Financial industries are being disrupted by the emergence of operating system platforms such as Apple Pay, PayPal and Square. A sharing economy is created with the development of peer-to-peer digital platforms such as Airbnb, Gojek and TaskRabbit. The rivalry between businesses no longer focuses on the management of the value chain but involves engaging in productive activities connected with a platform. Disruptive crossovers from digital technologies to finance (e.g., Kickstarter), mobility (e.g., Uber) and health care (e.g., PatientsLikeMe) are all motivated by the concept of a digital platform. Digital platforms are rivals on many levels of the technological structure, for example, the operating system and web browser in the mobile domain (Pon et al., 2014). As platforms are appearing in many diversified industries like banking (de Reuver et al., 2015), health care (de Reuver et al., 2013), energy

(Kiesling, 2016) and transportation (Svahn et al., 2015), the scope and diversity of scientific discourse are snowballing.

There are different characteristics of digital platforms that can benefit businesses. First, digital platforms assist businesses with considerable transaction costs that involve search, contracting, monitoring costs and distribution (Eisenmann et al., 2006; Pagani, 2013). For instance, digital platforms, such as TripAdvisor and Expedia, gather and integrate travel information from various sources into one digital platform. Doing so reduces the cost of searching (search cost) for information and getting assistance from intermediary agents. Second, with the encouragement of government authorities and digital scalability, the inclusion of technological progress of products is supported by the digital platform (Boudreau, 2010; Tiwana et al., 2010). For example, Google's Android and Apple's iOS offer regulatory and technical frameworks that aid in promoting and sustaining in creating applications. Apart from these areas, another area broadly discussed is the cross-side network effect (Evans et al., 2011; Hagiu, 2014). This network effect shows that the user's significance on one side of the platform grows as the number of users on the other side increases.

Two-sided and multi-sided network

Two-sided networks, or in another term also mentioned as two-sided markets, consist of platforms that facilitate the interactions between a specific but inter-dependent group of users. These groups usually involve the buyers and sellers that make platforms operating as two-sided markets a core aspect in the modern business environment. Presently, recent and future projects are established using the model of two-sided and multi-sided networks, and merchants are suggesting the employment of platform-type services that will enable buyers to connect with numerous sellers all at once (Koh & Fichman, 2010). In a two-sided network, the mediator manages the transactions between the inter-dependent group of users. Katz and Shapiro (1985) theory of network externality is particularly associated with two-sided and multi-sided networks. Network externality is the result of the addition of users and customers of a specific product or service on its usefulness between current users and customers for the same product or service (Torrent-Sellens, 2015). Positive externality refers to the rise of usage in certain products or services generated by the increased users and consumers, whereas negative externality is the other way. For example, the telephone is a product that can illustrate the network externalities. The usefulness or importance of a telephone grows if the quantity of the telephone rises.

Katz and Shapiro (1985) also emphasise the indirect network externalities, which were debated further by Clements and Ohashi (2004). Complementary products or services create indirect network externalities. For instance, the benefits of a smartphone will increase with the growth of social media applications, which can be used through the smartphone; subsequently, the number of these applications increases with the growth of smartphone users. These indirect network externalities can be found in the various network that is linked by intermediaries. For example, the usage of a credit card platform for customers will expand if there is an increase of businesses that approves the credit card released by the platform. Correspondingly, the number of customers on the platform will increase along with the benefits of the credit card platform to businesses increases. Intermediated indirect externalities are two-sided networks where the network externality of one side is dependent on the side of the other side (Rochet & Tirole, 2006; Roson, 2005). In two-sided networks, network externalities are categorised as either intra-network externalities or inter-network externalities. Inter-network externalities are features of one side of the platform that affect users on the other side of the platform. In most situations, the inter-network externalities on the two-sided networks are positive, where the expected increase of users on one side of the platform rises with growing activity levels on the opposite side of the system (Eisenmann et al., 2006).

Value exchange and value network

Value exchange is determined as the exchange of fixed or specific values between two entities. Allee (2008) distinguished the types of values that can be categorised as tangible and intangible values. Goods, services, revenue and fund are perceived as tangible values. Goods are any tangible or virtual object passed from one entity to another entity. Revenue is any financial or non-financial object acquired by an entity from another entity in exchange for goods or services. The fund is a budgetary or non-financial matter invested from an entity to another. The main belief of Allee's value network is the conversion of value where entities undertake intangible and tangible exchanges to reach a financial or social benefit. A business implements a value network if it acts as an intermediary for the customers or clients. The business provides a network that provides service to assist the exchange between customers, where the network is the representation of the interaction between customers, and the value network is the value formed through the service provided that assists in customer matching.

The theory of value exchange is heavily connected to the theory of social exchange (Blau, 1964). In the theory of social exchange, giving and taking are usually present in a social connection between individuals. This means that the value and benefit must be maintained in the social connection, which can be sustained through balancing the value and benefit of the connection. Blau (1964) confines social exchange as conditional and beneficial activities from others, which is a conditional and beneficial practice between two participants concerning transactions (Emerson, 1976). In businesses, the social exchange is limited to that of value exchange when one group presents a value and expects to gain a similar or better value from the other group. However, it is known that business proceedings include many actors; thus, a value exchange network is developed.

Research methodology

This research proposes a new framework that is constructed from selected literature that serves as a base to support the proposed framework (Almunawar & Anshari, 2020, 2021; Almunawar, Anshari, & Lim, 2020, 2021). The literature review of the research has determined the concept and beliefs that validate this research and in studying the growth aspect of an e-health ecosystem. The proposed framework of an e-health ecosystem is derived from relevant literature on two-sided networks and value exchange to support the design of the framework. The case of BruHealth is investigated to test the framework, in which BruHealth is a growing digital platform imposed by the government of Brunei. The framework is implemented to outline Bru-Health's ecosystem and examine its development opportunities.

The research focuses on secondary data sources consisting of timelines and official statements from government publications (press releases). Data collected from previous press releases, official government news) will then be analysed to provide clarification of relevant information on BruHealth. Data collection prioritises the features and regulations of BruHealth that have been introduced by the Ministry of Health (MOH). BruHealth features and regulations have been introduced in phases through press conferences since its launch to provide effortless transitions among users. An observational research method was used in this study to provide relevant information on features that are accessible for users and investigate entities' interactions within the ecosystem of BruHealth. The collection of data also includes other important factors of the research which includes determining the entities that are present within the ecosystem of BruHealth. Analysis of data collected will identify entities of the ecosystem before investigating their interactions in facilitating processes and operations inside the ecosystem with the support of other secondary data sources (online journals, e-books, official trusted web sources and articles). Determining entities within Bru-Health will assist in identifying the value exchanged between them.

Value exchange network: an e-health ecosystem framework

Value exchange network (VEN) is a network of value exchanges between entities within an ecosystem (Almunawar et al., 2020). While there is a constant presence of cash flow and transactions within a business ecosystem framework, an e-health ecosystem in the case of BruHealth focuses on the intangible values exchanged between entities within its ecosystem.

Value exchange

Information or knowledge, *benefits* and *option* are perceived as intangible values. *Information or knowledge* is the information or knowledge passed between entities. *Benefits* is the service or gains from an entity to another.

Option is an array of alternatives given by an entity to another entity. Several tangible and intangible values may not be present in the e-health ecosystem due to its current stage of extension where intangible values are primarily observed between the entities. Let *A* be an entity and B another entity, where value exchange occurs between them. Figure 2.1 shows a simple value exchange without the presence of *revenue*. Entity *A* collaborates with entity *B*. *A* transfer *benefits* and *information or knowledge* to *B* {b, ik} and *A* receives *benefits* and *information or knowledge* {b, ik} from *B*. It should be noted that the *ik* that passed from *A* to *B* is different to the *ik* that passed from *B* to *A*.

Figure 2.2 shows a simple two-sided market situation without the presence of *revenue*. *A* and *B* are a group of entities (collaborators and users) and *C* is a two-sided digital platform that facilitates the values exchange for *A* and *B*. Figure 2.2 portrays *C* as an intermediary between *A* and *B* that manages the value exchanges. Any user in *B* uses services from any collaborators in *A* through *C*. A user from *B* receives service {s} from a collaborator in *A*, and collaborator receives information or knowledge {ik} from the user in *B*. *C* receives information or knowledge {ik} from *B* and *B* receives {ik, b, s, o}, containing information or knowledge, benefits, services and options and intangible values including ease of use and contentment from *C*. *A* receives {ik, b, s}, containing information or knowledge, benefits and services from *C* and *C* acquires information or knowledge and benefits from *A*.

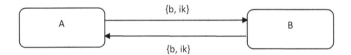

Figure 2.1 *A* exchanges values with *B*.

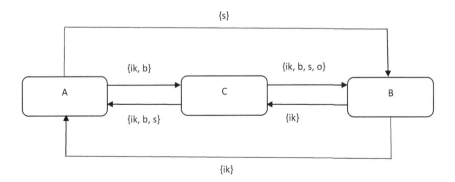

Figure 2.2 The VEN of a two-sided platform.

Table 2.1 The VEN table of Figure 2.2

Entities	A	C	B
A	–	{ik,b}	{s}
C	{ik, b, s}	–	{ik, b, s, o}
B	{ik}	{ik}	–

A value exchange network diagram portrayed in Figure 2.2 increases in size and complexity and is challenging to monitor when numerous entities are involved in the ecosystem. A value exchange network diagram can be depicted as a table that has the ability to show values carried by entities clearly. Table 2.1 depicts the value exchange network in Figure 2.2.

Applying the framework: the BruHealth's ecosystem

This research uses a case study to exhibit the capability of the proposed framework in illustrating the health ecosystem and to interpret the growth opportunities to grow the ecosystem. BruHealth is selected to prove the application of the proposed framework for the purposes:

1   BruHealth is a one-stop digital platform in Brunei Darussalam, initially used for contact tracing purposes during the spread of COVID-19 in Brunei which has developed into a more elaborate multi-sided platform with a developing ecosystem.
2   BruHealth unique state is interesting to investigate due to the daily obligatory of the population to use the platform, with the ecosystem being clearly observed through a VEN.

E-health in Brunei Darussalam and BruHealth

Before the widespread of the COVID-19 pandemic, e-health in Brunei is mainly dependent on Bru-HIMS. Bru-HIMS was introduced as a national e-health initiative by the Ministry of Health (MOH). Bru-HIMS system uses the idea of a 'One Patient One Record' where patients' medical details that were documented from all government health institutions, outpatient facilities, treatment premises and clinics can be viewed in a single electronic patient record (Ministry of Health Brunei Darussalam, 2012). Each patient will have one patient record that comprises a complete compilation of their medical record including details related to patients prescribed medicines and medical tests. Bru-HIMS enable patients to register through an online web portal, mobile applications and through a physical counter. While Bru-HIMS have provided a modern and efficient system that effectively manages patients' healthcare information, it still lacks functionality from the patients' perspective. Registering for Bru-HIMS enables health practitioners to better diagnose patients with all the information accessible to them, but this information is not accessible by the patients. It was expected that the introduction of Bru-HIMS would provide patients to possess a certain level of control over their medical records, even only just to view them. This actively demonstrates that the value of using Bru-HIMS is less advantageous to patients compared to the value health practitioners gain from it.

During the outbreak of the COVID-19 pandemic, an e-health application was introduced by the MOH as a response to the outbreak. The platform application was developed under the collaboration of the government of Brunei and EVYD Technology – a locally established medical artificial intelligence (AI) firm, a sub-company of YiduCloud, a major medical AI and big data firm located in China. The application was in a form of a contact tracing application called BruHealth. BruHealth is a 'one-stop' mobile application for anything COVID-19 related in Brunei Darussalam. The application initially included several features that include epidemic update, personal assessment code, self-assessment tool, Friday prayers code, COVID-19 knowledge, FAQs on COVID-19, nearby and QR code scan. The epidemic update enables users to see the latest trends and statistics of the global COVID-19 situation. Personal assessment code indicates the infectious possibility of the user and will decide the type of activities the user is allowed to perform. The self-assessment tool evaluates users' risk factors to COVID-19 to be used as an acknowledgement in which the tool does not offer medical examination, medication guidance and treatment advice. Friday prayers code is used to book a slot for an upcoming Friday prayer, to identify the user's health to attend the prayers. COVID-19 knowledge shows users the press releases published by the government related to the pandemic. Nearby feature pinpoints the activity trace of the confirmed cases in Brunei and the locations of medical facilities. QR code scan permits users to scan QR codes provided at the business premise depending on the event code of the user.

The outbreak of the pandemic has forced the closure of business premises such as gyms and fitness centres, driving schools, indoor and outdoor sports facilities, worshipping centres (mosques and churches), restaurants (cafes and food courts) and stalls (markets) for an indefinite period. Despite restaurants and cafes remaining open, these premises are only operating strictly for take-outs. These restrictions were enforced by the government on 17 and 18 March 2020, respectively, following the detection of the first confirmed COVID-19 case in Brunei on 9 March 2020. The imposed regulations have proved to be effective in containing the pandemic under strict social distancing measures in preventing huge crowds from gathering. The nation has been recording successive zero cases and has flattened the curve of cases since March. As arrangements for a 'de-escalation' plan to gradually open up business premises, BruHealth was introduced to the public in

May 2020. BruHealth was released to the public following the announcement of 'de-escalation' or the easing of COVID-19 restrictions from 16 May 2020.

BruHealth is a digital foundation for business establishments that permits business owners to validate customers using BruHealth that visits their premises within the quota determined by the MOH. At the initial stage of its release, the quota for business premises is 30% of its full capacity during standard operating time; for example, if the business normally serves 30 customers, only 30% of the total 30 customers, or a maximum of nine customers, are allowed to stay inside the business premise. The main function of BruHealth is for contact tracing purposes by generating a QR code to scan before entering business premises nationwide. The application originally operates as a two-sided network, particularly consisting of two main groups of businesses and users on each side of the network.

From the user's perspective, before BruHealth produces an event code (*Kod Acara*), users are required to do a 'self-assessment' through the application to determine the health status of the user before entering the premises. There are five event codes – green or yellow code implies that users are permitted to enter the establishment. While users with red, blue or purple event codes are not permitted to enter the premises. After an event code is generated, valid users with green or yellow codes are required to scan a unique QR code which varies differently between businesses. Users must first activate their 'Bluetooth' function before scanning the QR code and scanning it again before exiting the premise. BruHealth operates as a monitoring mechanism in containing the spread of COVID-19 through collecting data of individuals entering business premises and the number of individuals at a particular area in a given time. BruHealth allows the MOH to carry out contact tracing if there is a probable second-wave outbreak.

Since the emergence of BruHealth on 14 May 2020, a total of 436, 047 registration was recorded in the application, representing 94.8% of the population of Brunei. BruHealth was initially released as a contact tracing application in May 2020, where it has been showing encouraging potential to be further developed to improve the healthcare infrastructure of the nation. One of the main particular reasons for this circumstance is the majority of the population uses the application daily. As an initiative to transform healthcare delivery through the employment of artificial intelligence, new features were added to the BruHealth application in September 2020 (Han, 2020). New features such as online visit appointments, online personal health records and online consultation are to provide the population with tools to improve their health management. The new features will allow BruHealth users to book medical appointments, access their health records through the application, allowing users to book an online consultation with healthcare practitioners (doctors) via video call and make an online payment. The accessibility of health records for BruHealth users can provide better knowledge about their disease diagnosis, view tests that users have conducted and display prescribed medicines by public health institutions. The addition of these new features enables the government to collect relevant data in supporting the MOH to have a more comprehensive visualisation of the health conditions of Bruneians. Other Southeast Asian countries such as Malaysia and Singapore have also adopted digital technologies to facilitate contract-tracing capabilities to combat the outbreak of the virus in their respective countries.

The foundation of BruHealth's core ecosystem

The BruHealth's core ecosystem is a multi-sided network ecosystem, which comprises the keystone of the ecosystem or the Ministry of Health (MOH) of Brunei, healthcare institutions, BruHealth's platform and the users. Figure 2.3 is the foundation of BruHealth's core ecosystem including the keystone which is the MOH. Figure 2.3 portrays the value exchanges between four primary entities, MOH, *healthcare institutions, BruHealth's platform and users.* As the keystone of the ecosystem, MOH is in charge of the development and well-being of the ecosystem under its command. MOH is required to effectively control the value exchanges between the entities within the multi-sided ecosystem. MOH provides directions {di} to BruHealth in terms of functional capability, management, development and sustainability. Values exchanged from BruHealth platform to MOH are {i, s, sp} that includes information on data collected through the application, services the application provides to enable MOH to regulate and improve e-health infrastructure as a whole, and support the application provides with issues and complications. Figure 2.3 represents a case of value exchanges if a user (patient) wants to use the BruHealth application. A user, using their smartphones, to use the BruHealth application, obtaining a set of values {i, s, a, sp} that includes the information of global and local COVID-19 situation, services (book medical appointments online, access to user-health records, book online consultation via video call), authorisation of entering business premises through generated event codes after completing self-assessment, support provided by BruHealth allowing users to appeal their event codes in the situation of incorrect information provided during self-assessment. In the situation of booking medical appointments and online consultation, once the user decides the service to apply from BruHealth, their request will be sent to the healthcare institutions intended. The healthcare institutions receive the request through the BruHealth platform. The healthcare institutions then gain service and intangible benefits from the platform {i, s}. The intended healthcare institutions send the detail of available slots and practitioners to the platform, which will be passed to the user, which is i in {i, s, sp} where indirectly the healthcare institutions are providing service to the user {s}. Next, the platform will manage the connection and bookings depending on user decision and provide the service to the user {s} in {i, s, a, sp}.

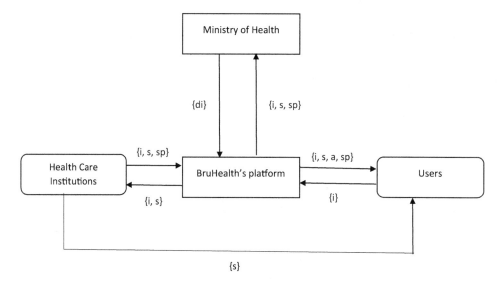

Figure 2.3 The foundation of BruHealth's core e-health ecosystem.

Figure 2.4 represents BruHealth's core ecosystem. BruHealth platform is vital in the ecosystem that facilitates the continuous connection between the entities. BruHealth provides value as a mediator between entities and provides them with a platform to obtain information and service or both at the same time. In Figure 2.4, Bru-HIMS plays a role in the ecosystem by providing {i, s} to the platform which are information that patients still use going to physical health institutions with unique Bru-HIMS code and providing support in validating and updating medical records of current BruHealth users. The e-health ecosystem of BruHealth is unique due to the absence of revenue between entities and still manages to grow. While the platform is central to interactions between entities, the information and services given to entities within the ecosystem is regulated by the keystone. BruHealth generates its value primarily through the platform and the users. Increasing values exchanged between the platform and the users have the potential to increase its sustainability in the future. Figure 2.4 displays the value exchange are similar from the platform to business premise, restaurants, government/educational institutions and indoor/outdoor facilities where the set value of {di, i, s} that includes direction from BruHealth to supervise the operations of these entities based on the guidelines set by MOH, information given to them through the BruHealth platform and the support they get from the platform in terms of issues with the application. Note that these entities use a different application called PremiseScan, which is under BruHealth. However, the value exchange in Figure 2.4 between the platform and business premise, restaurants, government/educational institutions and

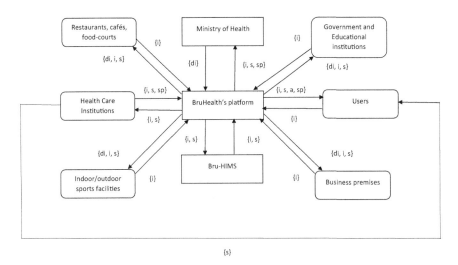

Figure 2.4 BruHealth's core e-health ecosystem.

indoor/outdoor facilities are inadequate due to the value {i} which is the information they get from the platform are less advantageous to them. The only benefit these entities gain from PremiseScan is the ability to see or view active BruHealth users within their premise.

BruHealth's ecosystem development

Developing the ecosystem of BruHealth is important in sustaining its usage even after the pandemic subsides in Brunei Darussalam. Additional values provided by BruHealth will enable the ecosystem to expand and give its users benefits other than being used as a tool to enter business premises. Creating more features that empower users, giving access to private clinics and granting businesses more value are a few development opportunities to expand the BruHealth ecosystem.

User empowerment

In the early stages of implementation, BruHealth is an important applica-tion for individuals to have on their smartphones during the outbreak of the virus. The closure of restaurants and eateries, sport facilities and gyms nationwide has affected the daily habits of individuals. The disruption to these daily habits developed a sense of concern among the community on when circumstances are going back to normal. When 'de-escalation' plan began to commence followed by the introduction of BruHealth, the appli-cation was extensively downloaded by the locals. The initial feature of the application was to facilitate contact tracing, allowing users to enter business premises through valid event codes generated by the application. While individuals can return back to their daily habits, they needed to adjust and adopt a 'new normal.' However, the usage of the application is mandatory rather than optional for the population. The population only considers the application as a tool to enter and exit premises without offering much value to the users. This means that users by no means feel empowered in using the BruHealth application.

A research by Anshari et al. (2013) argues that empowerment in any level of interaction with patients in a healthcare institution is difficult to provide. The research highlighted that empowerment for customers (patients or users) in an e-health system comes in many forms and standards in which digitising medical records is the bare minimum that gives users empowerment. User empowerment can be in different types of interactions between users to the operator such as accessing services online, making online booking appointment and making payment online. The new additional features added to the BruHealth application have shown to provide empowerment to its users by enabling them to book medical appointments, access their health records through the application, book an online consultation with healthcare practitioners (doctors) via video call and make online payment through the application. It is considered that better benefits that create value to the customer will generate confidence and dedication that assist customers and health institutions in maintaining the relationship for collaborative benefits (Anshari et al., 2013). This implies that when users feel empowered using the BruHealth application, the more likely users will continue to use it even when COVID-19 has subsided.

Accessibility to private clinics

The establishment of the BruHealth platform has clearly provided an improved e-health system to the population of Brunei. Users benefit from the service and information accessible to them through the platform. However, accessibility to the platform is only limited to public health institutions where private clinics are yet to gain access to the platform. It is an interesting situation where users (patients) visit public health institutions such as government hospitals where their diagnosis, prescribed medicines and tests are recorded into BruHealth, while users (patients) visiting private clinics will not get their diagnosis, prescribed medicines and tests recorded into BruHealth. Granting access to private clinics will include them as a part of the proposed BruHealth ecosystem. For example, consider a situation where user A visits a public hospital for a fever where health practitioners' diagnosis of user A is recorded into BruHealth; after a few days, user A is still not feeling well and decided to visit a private clinic, where medical records of user A are not present. Suppose the private clinic has access to BruHealth and can see user A's medical records, with relevant information accessible to them, they can potentially diagnose user *A* better. The value private clinics can give is the information (diagnosis) they have recorded from users (patients) of BruHealth giving a more comprehensive detail of an individual's medical status or condition.

Value to businesses

In the current state of BruHealth application, it has been observed that the value of the platform to businesses premises and facilities is only limited to the number of active users residing in their premises. The information provided to them through the extension of the platform called PremiseScan is less favourable to the business side in terms of value they gain. Once a registered user scanned the provided QR code of premises, the PremiseScan will then only show the number of active users on the application. However, other additional significant information such as time entered and duration of stay within the premise is not available from the application. One way to increase the value of businesses using the platform is to provide this information in the form of statistics available through PremiseScan. In doing so, it can generate strategies to increase the revenue of business premises and facilities by utilising the information. For example, restaurant *A* has been recording the most customers dining in at their restaurant during lunch hours (12–2 pm) on a Thursday; with this information, restaurant owners can create promotions and offerings to attract more customers to their premise and boost their revenue during these peak hours. Another advantage is that the restaurant can expect the number of customers dining in at a specific time, where they can develop a plan to improve their customer service in terms of the arrival of orders and staff management. Consider, for example, that restaurant *A* experiences a shortage of attendants to cater to their customers during the peak hours and food was arriving late to their customers. Utilising the information will enable the restaurant to resolve these issues.

Conclusion

BruHealth's growing multi-sided networks ecosystem began as a two-sided network comprising Bru-HIMS initiative with two inter-dependent groups of health institutions and users (patients). The immediate development was stimulated by the introduction of BruHealth application as a mechanism to combat the COVID-19 pandemic and an e-health initiative. Additional factor significant to its rapid progression is the massive user base that BruHealth has due to the mandatory requirement for individuals in Brunei. It has enabled BruHealth to become a mobile-based digital platform, thus becoming a part of an e-health ecosystem. The proposed framework for representing and examining the BruHealth ecosystem is the unification of two-sided market, value exchange and value network concepts. The framework shows the entities within the ecosystem and the value exchanged between them. The framework also represents BruHealth's core ecosystem. The core BruHealth ecosystem contains the BruHealth platform and the Ministry of Health as the keystone and entities related to its e-health and contact tracing services. BruHealth's development opportunities include creating more features that empower users, giving access to private clinics and granting businesses more value are a few development opportunities to expand the BruHealth ecosystem.

References

Almunawar, M. N., & Anshari, M. (2020). Multi-sided networks of digital platform ecosystem: The case of ride-hailing in Indonesia. *Asia Pacific Journal of Information Systems*, *30*(4), 808–831. https://doi.org/10.14329/apjis.2020.30.4.808

Almunawar, M. N., & Anshari, M. (2021). Digital enabler and value integration: Revealing the expansion engine of digital marketplace. *Technology Analysis & Strategic Management*, *0*(0), 1–11. https://doi.org/10.1080/09537325.2021.1926967

Almunawar, M. N., Anshari, M., & Lim, S. A. (2020). Modelling business ecosystem of digital marketplace using value network. *Journal of Business and Economic Analysis*, *3*(2), 133–150.

Almunawar, M. N., Anshari, M., & Lim, S. A. (2021). A framework for observing digital marketplace. *International Journal of Hyperconnectivity and the Internet of Things (IJHIoT)*, *5*(2), 57–73. https://doi.org/10.4018/IJHIoT.2021070104

Alvarez, R. C. (2002). The promise of e-Health – a Canadian perspective. *EHealth International*, *1*(1), 4. https://doi.org/10.1186/1476-3591-1-4

Amit, R., & Zott, C. (2001). Value creation in E-business. *Strategic Management Journal*, *22*(6–7), 493–520. https://doi.org/10.1002/smj.187

Anggraeni, E., Den Hartigh, E., & Zegveld, M. (2007, October). Business ecosystem as a perspective for studying the relations between firms and their business networks. In *ECCON 2007 Annual meeting* (pp. 1–28).

Anshari, M., Almunawar, M. N., Low, P. K. C., & Al-Mudimigh, A. S. (2013). Empowering clients through e-health in healthcare services: Case Brunei. *International Quarterly of Community Health Education*, *33*(2), 189–219. https://doi.org/10.2190/IQ.33.2.g

Arah, O. A., Westert, G. P., Hurst, J., & Klazinga, N. S. (2006). A conceptual framework for the OECD health care quality indicators project. *International Journal for Quality in Health Care*, *18*(suppl_1), 5–13. https://doi.org/10.1093/intqhc/mzl024

Blau, P. M. (1964). Justice in social exchange. *Sociological Inquiry*, *34*(2), 193–206. https://doi.org/10.1111/j.1475-682X.1964.tb00583.x

Boudreau, K. (2010). Open platform strategies and innovation: Granting access vs. devolving control. *Management Science*, *56*(10), 1849–1872. https://doi.org/10.1287/mnsc.1100.1215

Briscoe, G., Sadedin, S., & Paperin, G. (2007). Biology of applied digital ecosystems. *2007 Inaugural IEEE-IES Digital EcoSystems and Technologies Conference*, 458–463. Cairns, Australia: IEEE. https://doi.org/10.1109/DEST.2007.372015

Clements, M. T., & Ohashi, H. (2004). Indirect network effects and the product cycle: Video games in the U.S., 1994–2002. *SSRN Electronic Journal*. https://doi.org/10.2139/ssrn.500922

de Reuver, M., Bouwman, H., & Haaker, T. (2013). Business model roadmapping: A practical approach to come from an existing to a desired business model. *International Journal of Innovation Management, 17*, 1340006. https://doi.org/10.1142/S1363919613400069

de Reuver, M., Verschuur, E., Nikayin, F., Cerpa, N., & Bouwman, H. (2015). Collective action for mobile payment platforms: A case study on collaboration issues between banks and telecom operators. *Electronic Commerce Research and Applications.* https://doi.org/10.1016/j.elerap.2014.08.004

Stroetmann, K. A. (2018). *Digital Health Ecosystems for African countries–A Guide for Public and Private Actors for Establishing Holistic Digital Health Ecosystems in Africa.* (German) Federal Ministry for Economic Cooperation and Development (Bundesministerium für wirtschaftliche Zusammenarbeit und Entwicklung–BMZ).

Eisenmann, T., Parker, G., & Van Alstyne, M. (2006). Strategies for two-sided markets. *Harvard Business Review, 84*, 92–101+149.

Emerson, R. M. (1976). Social exchange theory. *Annual Review of Sociology, 2*(1), 335–362. https://doi.org/10.1146/annurev.so.02.080176.002003

Evans, D. S., Schmalensee, R., Noel, M. D., Chang, H. H., & Garcia-Swartz, D. D. (2011). *Platform Economics: Essays on Multi-Sided Businesses* (SSRN Scholarly Paper No. ID 1974020). Rochester, NY: Social Science Research Network. Retrieved from Social Science Research Network website: https://papers.ssrn.com/abstract=1974020

Eysenbach, G. (2001). What is e-health? *Journal of Medical Internet Research, 3*(2), e20. https://doi.org/10.2196/jmir.3.2.e20

Fiorina, C. (2000). *The digital ecosystem.* Presented at the In Speech at World Resources Institute Conference, Seattle, Washington. In Speech at World Resources Institute Conference, Seattle, Washington.

Hagiu, A. (2014). Strategic decisions for multisided platforms. *MIT Sloan Management Review, 55*, 92–93.

Han, S. (2020, September 24). BruHealth expands features with appointment bookings, access to medical records. Retrieved March 2, 2021, from The Scoop website: https://thescoop.co/2020/09/25/bruhealth-expands-features-with-access-to-medical-records/

Iansiti, M., & Levien, R. (2004). Strategy as ecology. *Harvard Business Review, 82*(3), 68–78, 126.

Katz, M. L., & Shapiro, C. (1985). Network externalities, competition, and compatibility. *The American Economic Review, 75*(3), 424–440. JSTOR. Retrieved from JSTOR.

Kiesling, L. (2016). *Implications of Smart Grid Innovation for Organizational Models in Electricity Distribution.* https://doi.org/10.1002/9781118755471.sgd043

Koh, T. K., & Fichman, M. (2010). *Multi-Homing Users' Preferences for Two-Sided Exchange Networks* (SSRN Scholarly Paper No. ID 1635615). Rochester, NY: Social Science Research Network. Retrieved from Social Science Research Network website: https://papers.ssrn.com/abstract=1635615

Li, W., Badr, Y., & Biennier, F. (2012, October 28). *Digital Ecosystems: Challenges and Prospects.* 117–122. https://doi.org/10.1145/2457276.2457297

Ministry of Health Brunei Darussalam. (2012). Bru-HIMS. Retrieved March 2, 2021, from http://www.moh.gov.bn/SitePages/Bru-HIMS.aspx

Moore, J. (1993). Predators and prey: A new ecology of competition. *Harvard Business Review*, *71*, 75–86.

Moore, J. F. (2016). *The death of competition: Leadership and strategy in the age of business ecosystems.* HarperCollins.

Nachira, F., Dini, P., & Nicolai, A. (2007). *A Network of Digital Business Ecosystems for Europe: Roots, Processes and Perspectives.* 20.

Pagani, M. (2013). Digital business strategy and value creation: Framing the dynamic cycle of control points. *MIS Quarterly*, *37*, 617–632. https://doi.org/10.25300/MISQ/2013/37.2.13

Pon, B., Seppälä, T., & Kenney, M. (2014). Android and the demise of operating system-based power: Firm strategy and platform control in the post-PC world. *Telecommunications Policy*, *38*(11), 979–991. https://doi.org/10.1016/j.telpol.2014.05.001

Rochet, J.-C., & Tirole, J. (2006). Two-sided markets: A progress report. *The RAND Journal of Economics*, *37*(3), 645–667. https://doi.org/10.1111/j.1756-2171.2006.tb00036.x

Roson, R. (2005). (PDF) Two-sided markets: A tentative survey. Retrieved April 22, 2020, from ResearchGate website: https://www.researchgate.net/publication/24049716_Two-Sided_Markets_A_Tentative_Survey

Spagnoletti, P., Resca, A., & Lee, G. (2015). A design theory for digital platforms supporting online communities: A multiple case study. *Journal of Information Technology*, *30*(4), 364–380. https://doi.org/10.1057/jit.2014.37

Svahn, F., Lindgren, R., & Mathiassen, L. (2015, January 8). *Applying Options Thinking to Shape Generativity in Digital Innovation: An Action Research into Connected Cars.* https://doi.org/10.1109/HICSS.2015.497

Tan, B., Pan, S., University of New South Wales, Lu, X., Fudan University, Huang, L., & Fudan University. (2015). The role of IS capabilities in the development of multi-sided platforms: The digital ecosystem strategy of Alibaba.com. *Journal of the Association for Information Systems*, *16*(4), 248–280. https://doi.org/10.17705/1jais.00393

Tiwana, A., Konsynski, B., & A. Bush, A. (2010). Research commentary—platform evolution: Coevolution of platform architecture, governance, and environmental dynamics. *Information Systems Research*, *21*, 675–687. https://doi.org/10.1287/isre.1100.0323

Torrent-Sellens, J. (2015). Knowledge products and network externalities: Implications for the business strategy. *Journal of the Knowledge Economy*, *6*(1), 138–156. https://doi.org/10.1007/s13132-012-0122-7

Yamakami, T. (2010). A mobile digital ecosystem framework: Lessons from the evolution of mobile data services. *2010 13th International Conference on Network-Based Information Systems*, 516–520. Takayama, Gifu, Japan: IEEE. https://doi.org/10.1109/NBiS.2010.26

3 Examining the digital transformation of intellectual property (IP) infringement services in the Department of Economic Development (DED), Dubai

Jama AlGaizi AlFalasi and Mohammad Habibur Rahman

Introduction

A core objective of any smart government is to achieve digital transformation of the services it offers. In Dubai, public services are currently offered by 28 separate bodies on a single platform. Hence, it is not necessary for users to visit each service to find information or undertake transactions. The Department of Economic Development (DED) is among the bodies making use of this platform to service two core functional elements used by a majority of businesses in the emirate: business registration and licensing, and consumer protection and commercial compliance.

The work of the Consumer Protection and Commercial Compliance sector is undertaken by four separate departments, one of which is the Intellectual Property (IP) Department, whose services relate to the protection of intellectual property rights (IPR). Previously, IP Department procedures were carried out offline, which was costly in terms of time, resources and storage space, and meant that large numbers of users were physically required to visit the offices to gain access to the services offered. Trademark enforcement offers an example of the cumbersome offline procedures previously performed by the IP Department. In this case, users were required to make several visits: first, to ensure the trademark was registered in the protection registry and, thereafter, to open a file for each trademark if they wished to file complaints of infringement. The requirement for users to be physically present in the Department's office was burdensome not only for the trademark owners and/or their representatives but also for staff. Furthermore, as the number of registered trademarks and infringement cases grew over time, an increasing amount of office space had to be dedicated to storing documents.

Smart Dubai (formerly the Dubai Smart Government Department) states that a fully online service must be "provided completely through an

DOI: 10.4324/9781003163824-4

innovative on-line channel, without an offline interaction between the customer and the entity at any stage of accessing, execution, processing, or the delivery of the service." Smart services must also cover transactions which require several interactions, such as requesting or processing approvals or internal investigations (Dubai Smart Government, 2014).

The IP Department now enables users to perform trademark protection procedures remotely, bringing it into line with the overall government strategy of offering e-services. The first version of the IP Gateway went online in 2016 as a means of switching physical services to e-services. The platform allowed forms to be filled in and payments to be made online over several visits. Despite the introduction of this new service, however, the expected savings on time, paper and office space did not materialise. A second version of the IP Gateway was therefore launched two years later, on 2 October 2018. Under this later edition, the previously partial online service was transformed into the fully online one required to meet Smart Dubai's own definition.

Mohammad Lootah, CEO of the Commercial Compliance and Consumer Protection sector in DED, describes the IP Gateway as a means for:

> owners and law firms to file complaints relating to IP rights violation at any time and from anywhere. Complainants can also pay the prescribed fees, track the investigation, monitoring and confiscation processes of DED, as well as obtain data and reports on the action all on the app.
>
> (Ismail, 2018)

That sets the rationale and motivation to investigate the current practices in IPR complaints and examine the benefits stakeholders could derive from online services to determine whether the same transformation should be adopted by other government bodies with responsibility for IP protection, such as the Dubai Police and Dubai Customs on the one hand and whether an integrated digital platform could be a way forward.

Conceptualising IP and digitisation

The World Intellectual Property Organization (WIPO) was set up in 1967 as a specialised agency of the United Nations (UN) with the remit of protecting and promoting IP. It is worth reproducing WIPO's full definition of IP as it is central to the topic addressed in this chapter. For WIPO, IP is "the creation of the mind: inventions, literary and artistic works, symbols, names and images used in commerce" (World Intellectual Property Organization, 2021) and can be categorised as either industrial property or copyright:

> The industrial property includes patents for inventions, trademarks, industrial designs and geographical indications (World Intellectual Property Organization, 2020). The copyright covers: literary works,

films, music, artistic work, and architectural design. Attached to the copyright category, is the rights related to copyright which includes performers and their performances, producers of phonograms in their recording, and the broadcasters in their radio and television programs.

(World Intellectual Property Organization, 2020)

Drahos recognises that the IPR came into existence during the 20th century to protect the rights of ownership to a subject matter (Drahos, 1998). Essentially, IPR such as copyright, patents and trademarks can be viewed like any other property right. By giving legal protection, it allows the owners of IP to benefit from their work or from their investment by giving them the choice as to how their property is used. IP rights have long been recognised within various legal systems (World Intellectual Property Organization, 2020).

As the objective of this chapter is to examine the digital transformation of the procedures to protect trademark IP in Dubai, hence it is imperative to understand the concept of digitisation. The terms digitisation, digitalisation and digital transformation tend to be used interchangeably in the literature. For the purpose of the current chapter, its definition is adapted from Mergel, Edelmann, and Haug (2019) as follows. Digitisation refers specifically to the *downloading* of the forms necessary to fulfil public service obligations; digitalisation refers to the *filling out* of such forms and digital transformation refers to the *complete replacement* of non-digital processes with a new set of fully digital ones which require no physical interaction. There is a global trend in using the digital transformation process in protecting IP trademark.

Global institutional structure in IP protection

The WIPO is responsible for the administration of 26 international treaties which aim to foster and protect human creativity as part of the overall task of nurturing human progress. Moreover, it offers assistance to some developing countries to draft legislation and policies addressing IP and works with bodies such as the World Trade Organization (WTO) to ensure that IP-related agreements are duly implemented.

The first initiative in ensuring creators could protect the IP to their works in other countries was the Paris Convention for the Protection of Industrial Property of 1883 (World Intellectual Property Organization, n.d.), whose signatories are now largely members of the UN. Under the Paris Convention, all signatory states agreed to the mutual protection of the IPRs of their nationals. Trademarks were protected through a six-month right of priority: in other words, whenever a mark was certified by one signatory state, its owner was covered in all other signatory states during that period. The Paris Convention also introduced a set of rules binding on all members addressing patents, marks, industrial design, trade names, indications of source and unfair competition which, together, constitute a clear definition of industrial property rights (World Intellectual Property Organization, 2020).

The common rules enshrined in the Paris Convention in regard to trademarks continue to guide the domestic law of member states in the area of trademark IP registration. Notably, however, conditions for filing and registering marks are not regulated by the Paris Convention, which leaves them at the discretion of each signatory state (World Intellectual Property Organization, 2020).

Under the Berne Convention, minimum standards were stipulated for the protection of rights and duration of works. It laid down that an author had the right to translate, make adaptations and arrangements, perform/recite in public, broadcast, communicate to the public and make reproductions of or use the work as the basis of an audio-visual production. Moral rights were also vested in the author, namely claim to authorship and the right to object to illegitimate use. These protections were to last for 50 years after the author died or, in the case of an anonymous author, from the date of publication. For applied arts and photographic works, protection would last for 25 years from the date of creation (World Intellectual Property Organization, 2020).

Trademark IPR protection: from digitalisation to digital transformation of services

Analyses of changes to service delivery in the public administration literature routinely use the term e-government. A 2019 study by Mergel, Edelmann and Haug sought to determine what was meant by the term 'digital transformation' and how it is understood by today's digital administrators. Their findings suggest that digital transformation is understood to be a comprehensive programme of revision of core governmental processes and services which exceeds traditional digitisation initiatives. Operating along a continuum from analogue to digital, digital transformation requires a holistic review of current policies and processes and a full evaluation of user needs. The ultimate aim is that not only are new digital services created but old services are thoroughly evaluated and revised. A good digital transformation outcome, therefore, entails not just a new mode of delivery but greater satisfaction of user needs (Mergel, Edelmann, & Haug, 2019).

A further outcome of digital transformation should be value creation. In this regard, the authors differentiate between digitisation and digitalisation (as defined above), both of which are required to complete the switch to an entirely online service. However, they add that these two processes alone are insufficient as digital transformation must also take account of the nature and value of the services offered and the underlying processes through which they are devised and delivered (Mergel, Edelmann, & Haug, 2019).

Having offered a comprehensive view of what constitutes digital transformation in the view of respondents, Mergel, Edelmann and Haug turn to what triggers bodies to implement such transformation. They find that digital transformation is largely prompted by external factors (e.g., technological change and demand from the private sector) which expose the need for bodies to leverage technology to deliver fully online public services. Their findings also indicate that the objects of the digital transformation, that is, those which require digital transfer, can be classified as processes, services and products. For today's public administrators, digital transformation requires that when processes are digitised, current processes are re-evaluated and any redundant steps or requirements are eliminated to speed up service delivery. The success of a digital transformation programme can be evaluated by outcomes including improved services, skills, processes and relationships, as well as the evolution of better policies, all of which play important roles in creating and maintaining the best digital infrastructure (Mergel, Edelmann, & Haug, 2019).

International best practices in IP registration and protection

The USA and Singapore both offer models of how IPR registration processes can be digitally transformed. Both have clearly set out to inform trademark owners about the protection they are due. The IPR of the USA is protected by the US diplomatic service: in each of the world's regions, an IP affairs department is attached to a diplomatic mission. Singapore has an international reputation for excellence as regards IP registration and protection, both of which are dependent on the digital transformation of the services offered by the Singaporean IP Centre. Due to their experience in the digital transformation of services both Singaporean and US practices offer useful standards against which to evaluate current IP protection in the UAE, as well as roadmaps towards improvement.

Hogan Lovells brand protection global ranking 2016

Hogan Lovells is an international law firm existing in the field for more than a century. With more than 2,600 lawyers working for the firm, across 24 countries around the world, 11% are practising their duty within the IP field (Hogan Lovells, 2020).

The firm issued in 2016 the Brand Protection Global Ranking, which was based on surveying 55 countries on ten trademark enforcement methods. The research by the firm divided the findings into: Country Scores, Regional and Global Ranking, Heat Maps and Country Reports.

In this section of the literature, the researcher will list and explain the ten trademark enforcement methods and will reflect the rankings of the three countries which had been chosen for this research.

The ten trademark enforcement methods listed by the firm are as follows:

Firstly, *border measures* are the trademark IPR protection by the customs authority. It takes into consideration the cost of recording a trademark with the customs authority, authentication of seized goods by the trademark owner and destroying counterfeit goods – after being confirmed counterfeit – without the need for civil or criminal action implemented on the importer.

The second trademark enforcement method is a *takedown request* "of the listing of an infringing good/service on major online sales platforms."

The third trademark enforcement method is a *cease-and-desist letter*, which is a letter sent from the trademark IPR holder to the infringer, informing them about the infringement and requesting them to stop the infringement.

The fourth method, *interim injunction*, is "a temporary order given by a court of law, which tells someone either to do or not to do something, until an official decision on the case can be made" (Cambridge University Press, 2020).

Fifth is *civil litigation*, taking the infringement matter to a civil court.

Sixth is *criminal prosecution*, complaint for criminal action against the infringer.

Seventh is *trademark opposition*, a service offered by the trademark registrar, after publishing the trademark in the official trademark journal and either before registering the trademark or within limited time after successfully registering the trademark; this service allows a trademark IPR holder to oppose the registration of a trademark which may result in rejection of the trademark application.

Eighth is *trademark cancellation*, a service offered by the trademark registrar, which results in cancelling an existing trademark registration. According to local laws, the cancellation of a registered trademark may be handled by courts and the case may escalate to the supreme court in some cases, which might result in penalties.

Ninth, *raid on premises*, is an action made by a relevant authority based on an infringement complaint to conduct a raid on a premise – such as house, shop, office, warehouse – which holds a matter of trademark infringement.

Tenth, *trade show action*, is an action made against an exhibitor in a fare/show/exhibition if there was a trademark infringement matter.

The listed trademark enforcement methods above shape the main trademark IPR protection in a country. The report made by Hogan Lovells surveyed 55 countries and ranked them according to those enforcement methods.

In the Brand Protection Global Ranking, the USA, Singapore and the UAE had a ranking of 17th, 15th and 28th respectively. Regionally, the USA ranked 1st in the Americas. The UAE ranked 3rd after South Africa and

Jordan in the Middle East and Africa, while Singapore ranked 6th in Asia Pacific after Japan, Hong Kong, South Korea, New Zealand and Australia.

The US protection of trademarks

The body in charge of trademark protection in the USA is the United States Patent and Trademark Office (USPTO). Under USPTO rules, applicants are responsible for enforcing their own rights, while USPTO's task is to ensure that no federal registration similar or identical to that of the applicant, in the same category of goods or services, is made in the name of another party. Hence, it falls to the owner of a trademark to initiate legal action in case of infringement. If an owner suspects current or future infringement of their mark, they should refer it to the US Customs and Border Protection (CBP) for enforcement. This process involves filling out an e-registration application, and an annual fee of US$190 is levied on each file registered (United States Customs and Border Protection, 2021).

It falls to the trademark owner to monitor the marketplace to detect any infringements. If infringements occur, or are suspected, the owners must, in the first place, contract an IP legal expert to contact the alleged offender. The expert will send a cease-and-desist letter, to which the other party may respond or decline to respond or, in some cases, react by filing a lawsuit (United States Patent and Trademark Office, 2019). The Intellectual Property Office (IPO) in the United Kingdom (UK), on the other hand, recommends complainants use ADRs such as mediation and arbitration before filing a suit at a civil court or administrative tribunal.

It is worthy of note that the USPTO requires trademark owners to take responsibility for enforcing their IPR but offers guidance about how they should do so, for example by registering with the CBS or issuing cease and desist letters.

Singapore protection of trademarks

The Intellectual Property Office of Singapore (IPOS), which issues trademark certificates, offers four dispute resolution mechanisms to enforce protection of such certificates. Together, these are known as alternative dispute resolutions (ADRs) as they offer alternatives to litigation. All are confidential, and all are quicker and cheaper than litigation. The first ADR is negotiation, whereby parties negotiate a settlement between themselves, without the involvement of any third party. When one or both disputing parties require a third party to be appointed, one of the other three ADRs is selected, namely, mediation, expert determination or arbitration. If mediation is chosen, the parties meet at the World Intellectual Property Organization Arbitration and Mediation Centre (WIPO AMC), Singapore Mediation Centre or Singapore International Mediation Centre. Choice of location falls to the first party, and the staff at the chosen centre act as facilitators. When parties choose expert determination, an expert from the WIPO AMC is called in to decide the technical issues in the dispute, either as a means to move towards resolution or for later use in arbitration or litigation. Litigation takes place through the IPOS, courts or copyright tribunal, where a judge or hearing officer decides the dispute and outcome. Under arbitration, a specialist third party is asked to decide the disputed issues at either the WIPO AMC or the Singapore International Arbitration Centre. When an ADR is chosen, the disputing parties have more control over outcomes, whereas under arbitration and litigation, it is the third party who determines outcomes (Intellectual Property Office of Singapore, 2019).

In summary, both USPTO and IPOS not only provide an online trademark registration service but are portals to detailed and valuable information for all parties interested in the service and IPR protection more generally. The Findings and Analysis section presents a comparison of the UAE and the compared countries and highlights which practices would be beneficial to the processes of protecting trademark IP in the UAE.

The United Arab Emirates context

When the UAE joined the WIPO in 1974 (World Intellectual Property Organization, 2019), it already had well-established law in the area of IP. Article 121 of the United Arab Emirates Constitution 2011 states that the UAE has "exclusive legislative jurisdiction in the following matters: ... protection of intellectual, technical and industrial property rights; copyright; and printing and publishing rights."

The late former Minister of Finance and Industrial Affairs, His Excellency Dr. Mohammed Bin Kharbash, stated at interview that in 1992 the UAE introduced Federal Laws number 37, 40 and 44 addressing trademarks, the protection of intellectual works and the copyright, organisation and protection of the industrial property of patents, designs and industrial models, respectively. Two years later, the Industrial Property Department was established (BinKharbash, 2000), now known as the Intellectual Property Sector, which encompasses three main departments: Trademarks, International Centre for Patent Registration and Copyright (Ministry of Economy, 2020). Federal Law No. 17 of 2009 adds to the body of IP-related law by regulating the protection of new plant varieties.

IPR protection in the UAE: the institutional role

IPR protection in the UAE falls not only to the MoE but also to local government bodies. In Dubai, these local bodies are the DED, the Dubai Police and the Dubai Customs. Trademarks recorded for protection are also protected in the emirates of Abu Dhabi, Sharjah and Ajman, which handle trademark infringement complaints as a subset of commercial fraud complaints. In the emirates of Ras Al-Khaimah, Umm Al Quwain and Fujairah, the MoE is responsible for dealing with complaints of trademark infringement.

All local government bodies are bound by local laws. In the case of DED, which is the focus of the current research, these are first, Local Law Number 13, 2011, on Practicing Economic Activities in Dubai; and second, Executive Council Resolution Number 13 for the year 2011: Approval of DED Fees.

Different procedures to file IP complaints

Under federal governance such as in the UAE, IP protection varies according to the local law of each state as well as local differences in law enforcement procedures. If an IPR holder wishes to file an infringement case in Dubai, they must record the trademark certificate from the UAE MoE at three local government bodies, namely DED, the Dubai Police and the Dubai Customs.

The IPR protection service provided by the IP Department at DED developed in three distinct phases. First, claimants had to visit the office several times to manually record the trademark file and submit whatever hard-copy documents were required. Meeting these obligations was time-consuming for both complainant and DED staff, given the number of visits required for follow-up and to obtain the inspection report. In the second phase, IPR infringement complaint services were digitalised: soft copies of documents were required rather than hard ones, and users filed complaint forms online. The third phase began with the launch of the IP Gateway, whereby delivering IPR protection against trademark infringement and commercial agency infringement complaints no longer required any physical interaction and could be undertaken anywhere, anytime. IP protection service stakeholders range from commercial agents, brand owners and their advocates and/or their representatives.

The reforms implemented at the DED in the shape of the digital transformation of IP infringement services represent an attempt to introduce the smart services required under the Government of Dubai's paperless transaction strategy and also to ensure more efficient collection of fees, promote speed and accuracy, reduce the burden on operational resources and extend availability. All these outcomes will boost national competitiveness, satisfy domestic businesses and make the country more attractive to foreign investors. In consequence, creativity and innovation will be fostered across all IPR-related fields, including manufacturing, the arts, knowledge generation, invention, media and trademarks.

One strategic need remains unmet in the UAE, including Dubai: a single platform for IP infringements at either local or federal level. There is an opportunity here for the DED to lead by example in the digital transformation of its IP protection service. Hard data is available to prove the benefit to platform users of the impacts of this digitisation and digital transformation, which may inspire local or federal authorities to consider setting up a service of this nature.

The Government of Dubai currently requires that trademarks are enforced through registration with the Dubai Customs, DED and the Dubai Police. Owners suspecting infringement must, similarly, complain to one or more of the three entities, following three different procedures and based on the competency of the entity.

Research findings

This section of the chapter presents findings and analysis. A comparison was drawn between two selected international examples of practice and those seen in the UAE. The purpose of this comparison is to assess the beneficial structure and processes in the USA and Singapore and to their implications for change in Dubai and the UAE.

In the USA, the USPTO attempts to make sure that no other party receives a federal registration similar or identical to the mark being registered in the same class of goods or services. It clearly mentions to the trademark owner applying to register that they are the ones responsible about enforcing the rights of their IPR in the country, and encourages the trademark owners to use the trademark enforcement methods such as sending a 'cease and desist' letter to the infringer or using ADR before taking a legal action for any infringement they might face.

Findings from international best practices indicate that the chosen countries are in a better position regarding knowledge and creation of awareness about the importance of IP, through informative websites of the official registrars. The clarity of the procedure for the applicant starts even before filing for the application and goes through until the last step of receiving the registration and the maintenance actions required for future requirements, such as renewing the registration, changing contact details in the registration and other registration related services.

Singapore offers multiple IP-related services on an online portal. Some of the services are free to be used by the public. Furthermore, its website is considered a comprehensive source of IP information for the country.

In Singapore and the USA, USPTO and IPOS are a separate entity which manages the IP registration. In the UAE, the IP registration is a sector under the Ministry of Economy. Thus, for an applicant, the website is not dedicated to IP registration and protection, and it lacks IP information compared to the USPTO and IPOS websites.

Neither USPTO nor IPOS allows IP infringement complaints to be filed with them or any other government agency, although they allow such complaints to be registered with customs authorities. Both bodies encourage disputants to consider ADRs before undertaking litigation. On the other hand, trademark IP protection in the UAE is enabled by both customs registration and via the relevant specialist authorities, according to the local laws in force in each emirate. Some local administrative bodies have fully online protection services in place which are available remotely to all UAE trademark registration certificate holders.

DED offers two modes of protection: filing an infringement complaint via the IP gateway and market inspection. The market inspection is conducted via qualified inspectors to check all mainland licensed establishments and warehouses and investigate any possible infringements of trademarks recorded in the IP Gateway.

Way forward

The digital transformation of public services facilitates the sharing of databases by multiple government bodies; consequently, interconnection between such bodies is easier than it used to be. Users wishing to log onto a local or federal government website in the UAE can now use a single log-in portal, the "UAE Pass." Hence, users are no longer obliged to create credentials for every application made to a government body or each time they want to access the website of a government entity.

The digital transformation of IP Department services at the DED benefits both customers and the Department itself. Satisfaction rates have increased among users and employees, as infringement complaints can now be resolved more quickly, increasing inspectors' productivity and accuracy. Moreover, the service is available out of traditional office hours, physical visits are no longer necessary, less paper is consumed and there is no need to dedicate storage space to an archive of registration certificates.

On this basis, and as the same customers use the trademark protection services supplied by several governmental bodies, the researchers recommend that a single gateway is created where trademarks can be registered and recorded, infringement complaints can be received and checked against records and infringements can be notified to multiple authorities simultaneously, which will only require front office integration, and back-office integration would not be required due to the difference in the authority and area of specialisation of each of the five entities that are proposed to be in the proposed Government of Dubai IP Gateway shown in Figure 3.1 below.

Figure 3.1 below shows the suggested structure of a gateway which would enable trademark owners and/or their legal representatives to register trademark certificates to enforce and promote protection across all competent authorities in Dubai and enable complaints to be more effectively dealt with (see Figure 3.1). The suggested structure would allow trademark owners and/or their representatives to file a single trademark infringement complaint with multiple authorities. Having reviewed some of the trademark enforcement methods, which are implemented by the competent authorities of the Government of Dubai, it may be hoped that trademark IP protection can be improved by the suggested system.

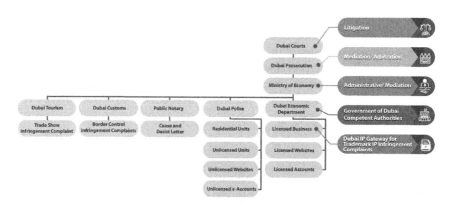

Figure 3.1 A proposed single platform: government of Dubai IP Gateway.

Figure 3.1 lists the enforcement methods available for a trademark owner, and the ADR available to a trademark owner before proceeding to litigation. The proposed Dubai IP Gateway will allow the trademark owner to file an infringement complaint with one or more government entity at the same time and based on the matter of the infringement. In case the defendant didn't cooperate and refrain from infringing the trademark the matter could be escalated to the ministry of economy which is the regulator of IP in the country to issue an administrative action and or mediate between the dispute parties. The public prosecution role comes to mediation and arbitration if the matter had been escalated from the government entities or the ministry of economy. The litigation stage is the highest stage in dispute resolution and Dubai IP Gateway aims to reduce the burden on the litigation system by resolving the infringement complaints.

The proposed Dubai IP Gateway shown in Figure 3.1 above will facilitate the process of registering trademark IP with government bodies and would enable multiple infringement complaints to be filed from a single portal. Under current practice, trademark owners and/or their representatives must register the trademark file at three entities, each of which has its own procedures. Moreover, some government bodies, such as Dubai Customs, charge a fee for registration although no charge is made in the DED's IP Gateway. As noted above, using the proposed gateway will ease the burden on trademark owners and/or their legal representatives. It is recommended that free zones are added to the gateway in the future to enable the emirate to more effectively reduce IP infringements. It may even be possible to incorporate other types of IP infringement complaints to be handled by the relevant authorities.

Furthermore, the proposed gateway will ensure greater accuracy in infringement complaints filed by trademark owners and/or their legal representatives since, unlike the current process, it orders the actions by competent authority. At the moment, complaints can be rejected even after complainants have paid fees because they do not fall under the authority of the entity with which the complaint was filed. In addition, the relevant authorities currently only carry out regular inspections in their areas of specialisation, and the gateway could be used by consumers to notify them of ad hoc trademark infringements and sales of counterfeit goods.

The proposed gateway will also encourage greater awareness of the need to monitor infringements of IP and enable the proper structuring of specialised management. Introducing this type of gateway could bring about radical change in Dubai's IP protection procedures. Each area of management will have its own specialisation and be considered a separate legal entity. Consequently, they will have charge of their own actions and no longer need to undertake time-consuming referrals to other departments or bodies to execute actions. In these circumstances, IP protection will be improved and IP services will run more smoothly, enhancing the satisfaction of applicants and customers.

Under the proposed structure, a mediation and arbitration step can be introduced, so disputing parties are less likely to proceed to litigation. As clearly shown by Singapore's approach to protection, encouraging parties at dispute to use ADRs reduces the burden on the court system, which must otherwise deal with the ensuing litigation. In most cases, a legal cease-and-desist letter is sufficient to persuade an infringer to cease the infringement. If this is not enough, asking the administrative authorities to intervene through the violation scheme could be an effective next step. For example, under current DED practice, a first infringement violation incurs a fine of 15,000 UAE Dirham and seizure of the infringing goods (according to the technical report furnished by the trademark owner). A second violation incurs a fine of 30,000 UAE Dirham in addition to seizure on the same basis, and a third one incurs a fine of 30,000 UAE Dirham, closure of the establishment for between one working day and two weeks (even more, in some cases) and seizure of the infringing goods, as above.[1]

It is worth leveraging the DED's experience of digitally transforming its IP protection services to inform implementation of the same by all government authorities in Dubai dealing with trademark IPR protection, namely the DED, and Dubai Customs and Police. The Government of Dubai enjoys digital infrastructure readiness, and the emirate serves as a regional trade hub. Hence, extending the same basic structure will be of use to service beneficiaries, particularly the addition of the Public Notary, who will seal the cease-and-desist letters potentially used by trademark owners and/or their legal representatives. Moreover, Dubai Tourism is well placed to handle complaints against trade shows and trademark infringements by exhibitors. The body could use its position as regulator of events to facilitate trademark IP protection but does not do so currently.

Smart Dubai could lead the operationalisation of the proposed structure by adopting the IP Gateway currently used by the DED. At the moment, different procedures are observed across different government bodies for the registration of trademarks and infringement complaints, even though all require the same documents and serve the same complainants. Provision of a single platform would cut down on duplication of procedures and clarify to trademark owners and/or their legal representatives the means available to protect their trademark IPR. An IPR holder could access the right agency or agencies by entering the type of complaint on the IP gateway interface. For example, under current practice, if an infringement complaint is made about a residential unit in use by counterfeiters selling infringed goods, the trademark owner must file two separate infringement complaints: one with the Dubai Police and the other with the DED. Thereafter, the Police issues a permit for a raid and the two bodies cooperate to resolve the complaint. The proposed gateway would amalgamate complaints based on user type, and users would no longer have to physically visit one office as well as filing a complaint online to another. Rather, logging a single complaint through the integrated IP Gateway would alert both authorities. It should be a relatively simple matter for Smart Dubai to adopt the structure of the DED IP Gateway to bring government bodies together, creating a smart platform for the registration and management of trademark IP complaints. As the UAE Ministry of Justice (MoJ) has no jurisdiction over the IP-related functions of bodies in Dubai, it has been excluded from considerations of the proposed Gateway.

The digital transformation of the Government of Dubai is led by "smart Dubai" which provides the required infrastructure to secure the transformation of services. Thus, the digital transformation of trademark IP protection services in Dubai, will require a decree from the government's executive council which will regulate and organise the interconnection of government bodies after reviewing existing local laws and decrees and abiding to the federal law. The proposed structure is suggested to be used in Dubai, and the Dubai IP gateway could be visioned based on scalability of the existing IP gateway used by DED as it a perfect example that reflects the efficiency of the digital transformation of the trademark IP protection service in terms of the number of days it takes to close the complaint, accuracy of inspection, availability and access to service, and achieving strategic targets that had been set to transform the government bodies into a paperless transactions and smart services providers. It is expected that the efficiency of the digital transformation of the service across the different government bodies will enhance the position of the government of Dubai in overall IP protection services and it could be further scalable to cover other branches of IP. Moreover, it will increase the confidence in the city for foreign investors and creative innovators.

Conclusion

This chapter observes among others the digital transformation of trademark IP Protection services in DED, Dubai and in the UAE from international perspectives. The authorities in neither the USA nor Singapore offer protection services, other than through customs border control. In both countries, trademark owners are encouraged to use ADRs before proceeding to litigation. In the UAE, protection is limited, but offered by both the customs service and administrative authorities, with each local body having its own area of specialisation. The scenario in the UAE is considered preferable; however, as the same users, namely trademark owners and/or their legal representatives, are served by all the authorities involved, it is suggested that they need clarity about protection methods and should have access to a single platform. A comparison of international practices to those in use in the UAE indicates that an independent federal trademark registration and protection sector could be created by hiving off these functions from the MoE. In this way, federal and local efforts can work synergistically, leading to better state-wide IP management. Under federal law, the MoE is responsible for applying IP law and executing IP directives; however, this should not constitute a barrier to the creation of a standalone body reporting to the same ministry. If the IP and Innovation Sector are rendered a federal entity, the Registrar will be far better placed to implement innovative IP management through a dynamic IP affairs unit. This will promote implementation of federal and local laws and expand the role of IP services from the current offer of registration and protection to the acquisition of an education unit, arbitration centre and consultancy in IP management for businesses. Further, it will simplify registration processes and attorneys will no longer be required to service foreign businesses.

The chapter also perceives how the digital transformation of trademark protection services has impacted stakeholders. The previous section found that this transformation led to faster service delivery, more accurate inspection reports, fewer physical visits and higher satisfaction rates among users. Moreover, the policy implication of the suggested structure will require approval from the government of Dubai's executive council and new decree or law to regulate the suggested proposal. On this basis, it is proposed that expanding the IP Gateway as a unified platform for all IP complaints submitted to government bodies in Dubai will enhance user satisfaction, given that the same customers make use of the three different bodies currently providing trademark protection services. This study proposes a strategic single-gateway structure that could offer services including trademark registration, receipt of infringement complaints based on the validity of registered trademarks and simultaneous filing of such complaints with multiple authorities.

Notes

1 All qualitative statements and quantitative figures are obtained from the DED Commercial Compliance and Consumer Protection Sector's Follow-up and Development Department, with consent from the sector's CEO, and through Mr. Adnan Hussain, Senior Manager of the Development Section.

References

BinKharbash, M. K. (2000, May 4). The UAE is excluded from the US watch list for its intensive efforts in protecting intellectual property. (A. Montaser, Interviewer) Abu Dhabi, United Arab Emirates: AlBayan News Paper. Retrieved from https://www.albayan.ae/economy/2000-05-04-1.1050480

Business Performance Improvement Resource Limited. (2020). *Benchmarking for Best practice – BPIR.com.* Retrieved April 12, 2020, from BPIR: https://www.bpir.com/partners/index.php.html

Business Performance Improvement Resource Limited. (2020). *Dubai We Learn.* Retrieved February 29, 2020, from BPIR: https://blog.bpir.com/category/dubai-we-learn/

Cambridge University Press. (2020). *Cambridge Dictionary.* Cambridge: Cambridge University Press.

Drahos, P. (1998). *The Universality of Intellectual Property Rights: Origins and Development.* Retrieved May 19, 2021, from WIPO: https://www.wipo.int/edocs/mdocs/tk/en/wipo_unhchr_ip_pnl_98_1.pdf

Dubai Smart Government. (2014). *Smart Service Definition Policy Document.* Retrieved April 29, 29, from https://www.smartdubai.ae/docs/default-source/policies-standards/ssdefinitionpolicy-v3-0-(en).pdf?sfvrsn=fa6e1150_14

Hogan Lovells. (2020). *Why Us: A Clear Choice.* Retrieved May 5, 2020, from https://www.hoganlovells.com/en/~/media/ff23532fce634aaa9a9c37d998bd51e2.ashx

Intellectual Property Office of Singapore. (2019). *IPOS I Hearings & Mediation.* Retrieved February 10, 2020, from https://www.ipos.gov.sg/protecting-your-ideas/hearings-mediation

Ismail, E. (2018, October 2). DED launches new edition of 'IP Gateway' as multilingual app. Dubai: Emirates News Agency. Retrieved from http://wam.ae/en/details/1395302711527

Mergel, I., Edelmann, N., & Haug, N. (2019). Defining digital transformation: Results from expert interviews. *Government Information Quarterly, 36*(4), 1–16. https://doi.org/10.1016/j.giq.2019.06.002

Ministry of Economy. (2020). *Intellectual Properties Sector.* Retrieved 01 13, 2020, from https://www.economy.gov.ae/english/Ministry/MinistrySectors/Pages/CopyRightSector.aspx

United States Customs and Border Protection. (2021). *U.S. Customs & Border Protection e-Recordation Program.* Retrieved from IPRR INTELLECTUAL PROPERTY RIGHTS e-RECORDATION: https://iprr.cbp.gov/

United States Patent and Trademark Office. (2019). *Been Sued or Received a Cease and Desist Letter or Email? Answers to Common Questions about Trademark Litigation USPTO.* Retrieved April 18, 2020, from https://www.uspto.gov/trademark/been-sued-or-received-cease-and-desist-letter-answers-common-questions-about-trademark

World Intellectual Property Organization. (2019). *Information by Country: United Arab Emirates.* Retrieved May 4, 2020, from https://www.wipo.int/members/en/details.jsp?country_id=2

World Intellectual Property Organization. (2020a). *Summary of the Berne Convention for the Protection of Literary and Artistic Works (1886).* Retrieved March 16, 2020, from https://www.wipo.int/treaties/en/ip/berne/summary_berne.html

World Intellectual Property Organization. (2020b). *Summary of the Paris Convention for the Protection of Industrial Property (1883).* Retrieved March 16, 2020, from https://www.wipo.int/treaties/en/ip/paris/summary_paris.html

World Intellectual Property Organization. (2020c). *What is Intellectual Property?* Retrieved May 19, 2021, from https://www.wipo.int/edocs/pubdocs/en/wipo_pub_450_2020.pdf

World Intellectual Property Organization. (2021). *About IP.* Retrieved from WIPO: https://www.wipo.int/about-ip/en/

World Intellectual Property Organization. (n.d.). *Paris Convention for the Protection of Industrial Property.* Retrieved March 16, 2019, from https://www.wipo.int/treaties/en/ip/paris/

Part 2

People and knowledge management

4 An analysis of the influence of introversion personality on tacit knowledge sharing

Diyana Najwa Ali, Fahmi Ibrahim and Noor Maya Salleh

Introduction

The concept of knowledge has enormous diversity of definitions and means different things to different scholars which has led to the concept of knowledge, and managing knowledge remains elusive (Ibrahim & Reid, 2010). Literature shows that knowledge has two types – tacit and explicit. While explicit knowledge can be transferred with relative ease using advances in information technology, sharing tacit knowledge is more problematic (Armstrong & Mahmud, 2008; Manaf et al., 2017) because tacit knowledge is highly personal and difficult to express as it is a type of knowledge that evolves over a period of time and it is mostly based on an individual's own experiences (Becerra-Fernandez & Sabherwal, 2015).

Tacit knowledge sharing has proved to constitute a crucial part of Knowledge Management (KM) processes in an organisation (Hvidsten, 2016; Ibrahim et al., 2009). Hence, it is critical to examine what constitutes effective tacit knowledge sharing, as well as what motivations, challenges, encouragements and other external and internal factors that influence its diffusion by socialisation. Employee personality traits are one of the factors affecting tacit knowledge sharing. This is due to the personality differences as they have their varying effects on how people perform at work (Judge, Bono, & Locke, 2000) which include their willingness in the aspect of tacit knowledge sharing (Cabrera et al., 2006).

For a number of years, Eysenck (1947) has argued that one of the most important personality dimensions is that of introversion and extraversion. Introversion can be a barrier to tacit knowledge sharing because effective sharing of tacit knowledge by socialisation requires being socially competent, which involves the ability to talk in public and engage in collaborative discussions (Hvidsten, 2016). There have not been much research done on the relationship between introversion and tacit knowledge sharing. It is, however, possible to achieve a better understanding of how the introverted personality traits influence tacit knowledge sharing by reviewing studies on sociopsychological criteria for knowledge sharing and integrating it with literature on introverted personality characteristics. Thus, the aim of this chapter is to investigate the influence of introversion and tacit knowledge sharing.

DOI: 10.4324/9781003163824-6

Literature review

Tacit knowledge sharing

Knowledge sharing is defined as "the willingness of individuals in an organisation to share with others the knowledge they have acquired or created" (Gibbert & Krause, 2002). Within a plethora of knowledge-based theories, concepts and tools, the SECI model is widely acknowledged as a theoretical landmark and adopted as framework for most knowledge management conceptualisation. The model considers knowledge creation as a dynamic process, in which the continuous dialogue between tacit and explicit knowledge generates new knowledge and amplifies it across different ontological levels (individual, organisational, inter-organisational). Knowledge creation and sharing was claimed to occur naturally through organisational meetings with face-to-face conversations (Ibrahim et al., 2009). Such conversations or interactions would encourage individuals to generate and share knowledge through 'socialisation' of SECI model (Nonaka et al., 2001). On the other hand, tacit knowledge can be created and shared through 'internalisation' process of SECI model (explicit to tacit knowledge). It is argued for the purpose of this study that personality traits of introversion and extroversion are closely related to socialisation process. This view was identified as there being no such thing as completely explicit knowledge because all knowledge will remain tacit and therefore resistant to articulation and codification (Newell et al., 2002, p. 7). In other words, there will be an element of tacit knowledge which is still embodied in people.

Tacit knowledge is unformulated, subjective and difficult to communicate and formalise (Becerra et al., 2008; Chen et al., 2018). It is difficult because it is acquired through experience and becomes embedded within the individual (Nonaka & Takeuchi, 1995). Therefore, tacit knowledge sharing in the workplace requires social interaction and behaviours that are influenced by cultural influences (Borges, 2013; Wei & Miraglia, 2017). At the individual level, however, personality traits have been identified as one of the best predictors of knowledge sharing success, behaviours and attitudes (Matzler et al., 2011; Schmitt et al., 2007) because apparently, personality traits are relatively constant over time and form an individual's responses and behaviours. Thus, it is significant to relate tacit knowledge sharing with introversion which was widely viewed as a character flaw (Dossey, 2016).

Defining introversion

Carl Jung popularised the words introvert and extrovert in the 1920s (Rzadkowska, 2015). An introvert is predisposed to concentrate on subjective influences, i.e. his or her internal universe of concepts, emotions and reflections. An extrovert, on the other hand, is more focused on objects and factual evidence in the real world that surrounds him or her and allows his or her consciousness to be driven by these factors (Jung, 1926). Introversion is the state of being preoccupied by one's own mental self. Introverts are often thought to be more relaxed or thoughtful (Rathod, 2019).

Cain (2012, p. 12) describes introversion as "a preference for environments that are not overstimulating" that includes a list of characteristics that are common in introverts. These characteristics are based on established literature on personality types where she claims that while not all introverts are timid, they are mostly viewed as silent and soft-spoken. Introverts dislike multitasking because they are vulnerable to overstimulation. Instead, they like working alone on one single task in detail. Citing from Hvidsten (2016), other psychological constructs are often used in the psychology literature to denote introverted personality characteristics. Openness to experience, conscientiousness and neuroticism are also directly linked to introversion in the Big Five personality characteristics (Cain, 2012). To exemplify this, being exposed to experience means being open-minded, mentally and artistically adventurous and capable of coming up with fresh thoughts on a regular basis.

Introverts in the workplace

According to Dunning (2001), introverts enjoy a relaxed work environment where they can reflect and interpret information without interruptions. Extroverts, on the other hand, tend to communicate, perform and process information with others through verbal cooperation. Cain (2012) asserts that in today's culture, extroverted personality characteristics are regarded as ideal. As a result, the extrovert's interests in terms of job setting and activities are preferred, such as joint brainstorming, open workplace schedules, intensive community work and no time to work alone (Cain, 2012). Possessing social skills and effectively handling social situations at work is therefore a necessary skill set today (Hvidsten, 2016).

According to a study by Lieberman and Rosenthal (2001), a typical introvert has lower social skills than a typical extrovert. Extroverts often have a wider network than introverts (Pollet, Roberts, & Dunbar, 2011), meaning that extroverts are better at social contact with others. Besides, Zack (2010) has created a networking guide for "People who hate networking," and mentioned introverts as part of her target audience. Consequently, the research findings of Feiler and Kleinbaum (2015) and guidebook by Zack (2010) indicate that extroverts have better social skills and enjoy making new acquaintances more than introverts do (Zack, 2010).

Personality trait and socio-psychological factor influences on knowledge sharing

Personality types have a significant impact on the quality of knowledge sharing, meaning that whether the knowledge shared is reliable, timely, accurate and relevant, depends on the personality of the individual who shares the knowledge (Ismail & Yusof, 2010). A study by Bordia et al. (2006) revealed that, fear has shown to have a negative impact on knowledge contribution. Apparently, some employees might fear that their colleagues will ridicule or not appreciate their knowledge-sharing contributions, resulting in reluctance to sharing knowledge. Meanwhile, intrinsic motivation is closely linked to tacit knowledge sharing, as opposed to explicit knowledge sharing, meaning that employees must feel an intrinsic motivation in order to share their tacit knowledge successfully. This factor associates with the fact that knowledge sharing cannot be forced upon employees. Socio-psychological factors, such as motivation, must lay the foundation for knowledge sharing. In addition, Wulandari et al. (2018) stated in their paper that individuals tend to have certain standard of work and achievements and strive to achieve these standards using various strategic actions. The authors also added that the notion that individuals will strive for his/her achievement explains why people have strong motivation may succeed; and utilise it to a specific and hard-to-achieve goals will be more successful than those with unclear or easily-attainable goals.

Integrating tacit knowledge sharing and introversion

The previous section demonstrated how tacit knowledge sharing necessitates socialisation and how introverts are usually less successful in social environments than extroverts. This literature review has also revealed how evidence shows that socio-psychological factors exist. Factors such as personality traits, for example, have a significant effect on knowledge sharing as a KM process, either positively or negatively. These evidences were synthesised by Hvidsten (2016) which may pave the basic groundwork for this study that is investigating how introversion influences tacit knowledge sharing.

The hindrance of introversion in tacit knowledge sharing

Sharing knowledge through socialisation entails a lot of shifting one's attention to the outside world and other individuals. Introverts' fondness for their own world prevents them from really focusing on what is going on around them as they dislike multitasking (Hvidsten, 2016). Clearly, one must multitask by reading social cues while still maintaining a conversation in any social situations. To exemplify this, a study by Lieberman and Rosenthal (2001) revealed that extroverts performed better than introverts when it comes to decoding nonverbal cues during social interactions. Introverts, on the other hand, came out on top when it came to interpreting social cues by listening to tape recordings of conversations. The study's findings show that introverts do well when they can concentrate on a single task. Based on these findings, introverts may be an obstacle to tacit knowledge sharing since they lack the capacity to concentrate on both the knowledge and the social component of knowledge sharing simultaneously (Hvidsten, 2016).

Getting disconnected in a social environment does not benefit knowledge sharing through socialisation, since introverts are less comfortable in social settings, thus making introversion a negative factor in knowledge sharing. However, Hvidsten (2016) stated that introverts prefer to express themselves in writing which may indicate that introverts are good at sharing explicit knowledge rather than tacit knowledge. Having a self-confidence may also contribute to the sharing of knowledge (Yusof & Ismail, 2010, cited in Hvidsten, 2016) than people who are introvert and "security conscious" which indicates that introverts might be an obstacle in tacit knowledge sharing (Hvidsten, 2016).

The positivity of introversion in tacit knowledge sharing

There are many introverted personality traits that facilitate tacit knowledge sharing and improve social interaction. Firstly, introverts excel at establishing and maintaining emotional close relationships with others (Pollet, Roberts, & Dunbar, 2011). Apparently, close emotional relationships are more likely to foster trust and loyalty – both of which have proved to be motivators for knowledge sharing. This indicates that introverts' ability to establish and maintain close relationships therefore facilitates tacit knowledge sharing.

Good communication skills are needed for effective information sharing (Ismail & Yusof, 2010). Certain elements of introverts' communication style may facilitate tacit knowledge sharing. For example, introverts are known to be good listeners, which enables careful processing of new knowledge as argued by Borges (2012) that listening to ideas enables introverts "to discuss them objectively and internalize them," whereas extroverts are more focused on driving the conversation rather than processing what is being said. In addition, listening closely to others helps them feel valued, and making co-workers feel valued can also motivate them (Grant, Gino, & Hofmann, 2010). Consequently, Borges (2012) believes that introverts are more successful than extroverts at sharing and acquiring tacit knowledge (Hvidsten, 2016).

Research methodology

Qualitative approach with in-depth interviews was adopted for this study due to the high degree of theoretical conceptual understanding of the topic. The interview questions were related to participants' personality, behaviour at work and how they share their tacit knowledge with their colleagues. The participants of this study were knowledge workers who work in both public and private sectors with diverse occupations in Brunei

Darussalam. The study consisted of 11 in-depth and semi-structured interviews that lasted 1–2 hours.

The participants comprised of five males and six females whose ages range from 25 to 36 years old. Most of the participants for the interview are recruited from LinkedIn who are connected with the researcher. Participation Invitation was sent through messages on LinkedIn where participants responded and provided consent to participate. In view of gaining an overview of the role of personality on knowledge sharing was significant, this study deployed a personality test by using "Introversion Scale" of James McCroskey (1997) which acts as a screening activity in order to determine whether the participants can be categorised either under the introvert or extrovert spectrum. It also acts as a pre-interview survey before conducting an in-depth interview with the participants which took five minutes for the participants to fill in.

After completing each interview, a memo was written reflecting on how the interview went and what could be improved which is added to during and after the transcribing process. Analysis was used in the analysis aspect of this study. Thematic analysis is described as a method for describing data, but it also involves interpretation in the processes of selecting codes and constructing themes (Kiger & Varpio, 2020). According to Braun and Clarke (2012), thematic analysis is an appropriate and powerful method to use when seeking to understand a set of experiences, thoughts or behaviours across a data set. It is also a method that arguably offers an accessible, theoretically flexible and straightforward approach to analysing qualitative data (McLeod, 2011).

Findings and discussions

In summary, while introversion has always been regarded as an obstacle, the findings of this study demonstrate that there are also other several factors which may influence people in tacit knowledge sharing. From the analytical process literature and synthesis of thematic analysis, a theoretical framework is developed which inductively provides an overview that would facilitate better understanding of significant contributing factors that influence introversion personality in effective tacit knowledge sharing, as shown Figure 4.1. The descriptions and discussions of the framework as explained below.

Capabilities of introverts in tacit knowledge sharing

The findings of this study show that people do share their tacit knowledge through socialisation and networking. This is because it allows individuals to get together to discuss shared interests. Besides, networking has been proved to facilitate knowledge transfer and is therefore an important tacit knowledge-sharing practice (Reagan & Mcevily, 2003). However, the

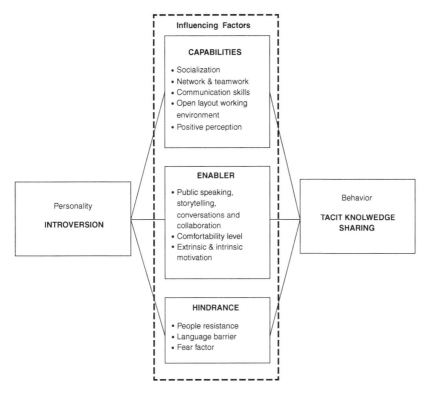

Figure 4.1 Theoretical framework of introverts personality and influencing factors towards tacit knowledge sharing behaviour.

findings from this study may illustrate some contradictions that have been discussed in previous studies. For example, previous research by Lieberman and Rosenthal (2001), as cited in Pollet, Roberts, and Dunbar (2011), has shown that a typical introvert has poorer social skills than a typical extroverted person. However, the findings of this study show that introverts do have the ability to socialise as they believe that networking is very important and they would prefer to socialise in networking events:

> Networking events are crucial for me. Like meeting people with the same job position like mine, but they're from other institution, it's great to know how they operate, how they handle administrative tasks. We also learn how they do their system, dealing with people, stakeholders and so on. And then we'll exchange ideas on how we do our job.
> (Participant 1)
> I prefer socialising … but I would prefer like, if you have your own session, you'll have interaction between yourself with the presenter, so from there will judge people who I want to interact with.

(Participant 8)

I prefer to talk to people! Mingle around with them. That's how I break the ice. That's how I break the awkwardness.

(Participant 9)

This is perhaps because of considering the large amount of collaboration and teamwork in today's workplaces, the level of an employee's contribution in a social work environment is crucial for the professional success of the employee.

In addition, good communication skills are also crucial for successful sharing of knowledge (Ismail & Yusof, 2010). All participants from these findings seem to be having great communication skills, because it was quite convenient to build rapport with them and they were able to respond all the questions with ease. Moreover, when asked about their communication preference to share knowledge, they prefer to share their tacit knowledge through face-to-face communication. This is contradictory to what has been discussed in a study by Hvidsten (2016) where the study revealed that introverts prefer to express themselves in writing rather than verbal communication because social settings might further make introverts even more stressed and withdrawn when having to interact with people.

> I prefer face-to-face communication but I also prefer multi ways of delivering the information for example through phone call, email, but then also depends on the recipients. If they're prompt with communicating through email then I email. Some people prefer business lunch, then I can do that as well.
>
> (Participant 1)
>
> Face-to-face definitely. Because if it's phone calls, sometimes, even myself I'll agree on stuff like "Ah, okay, okay, okay, okay" but then I'm probably daydreaming about something and then after the call ends, I'd be thinking "what did he say just now?" (laughs). So yes, face-to-face...
>
> (Participant 2)
>
> If it's work related, it's better for me to meet them face to face. Email ... it's the slowest way to communicate.
>
> (Participant 5)

They also prefer to work in a team rather than working alone, which is another contradiction to the findings by Hvidsten (2016) who explained that introverts are more uncomfortable in today's common workplace scenarios which require doing brainstorming, group work and little time to work by themselves in peace and quiet. However, the findings of this study discovered that the preference on whether participants prefer to work in a team or alone actually depends on the work scope or tasks which are given to them.

> I can work in team. I can work alone as well. But I would prefer team because team, it's very strong. Because you are gathering brains. And

you have more comments and ideas form different people in your team. … If you are working alone, sometimes it can be stressful…

(Participant 1)

… I prefer working in a team because different people have their own creativity so we can work professionally. Because I'm not that creative, so I need other people's creativity to handle some particular tasks.

(Participant 3)

It's better to work in a team though but it depends on what type of work is given to me. [*Because*] it's much more reliable … and efficient …? Also, better time management.

(Participant 5)

When you're working alone, you only have very little contribution … it's much easier to work in a team because there will be different ideas from different people …

(Participant 7)

Depends on the scope of work. But I … prefer to work alone if I need to focus on something that requires a lot of thinking. Working in a team … you get to have a lot of different opinions from people.

(Participant 8)

In addition, the researcher also asked about the participants' preference of their working environment whether they prefer to have an open-plan office or a private office. All participants prefer to have an open-plan office because they think that having a private office is boring where one participant likened being in a private office to being "in a cave." This has been mentioned by a number of participants:

Because it's much more interactive … You see me now, I'm in my own 'Cave', no team to speak with.

(Participant 1)

Having your own office can be boring … And because my role is to deal with other people, so I need to talk to them …

(Participant 2)

I prefer this open-plan office concept because I want people to approach me easily. I don't like having my own private office because it will be hard for others to approach me.

(Participant 7)

We have open-plan office and I like it that way. It's easy to communicate with my staff and delegate my job openly. Besides, there's no transparency when you're on your own in your private room.

(Participant 8)

Again, this finding is another contradiction to another finding by Dunning (2001) where she advised introverts to seek careers that allow them to take the time they need and to focus on one task in-depth in peace without being disturbed by co-workers. This is corresponding to studies by Taylor (2020) who suggested that quiet places provide introverts clarity (Dossey, 2016) through an opportunity to reflect on thoughts and feelings (Grant, 2014). Some respondents acknowledged that they do not mind to have either open-plan office or private office but there are times when they feel the need to have their own private space to focus on their job:

> I don't mind having a private office or to be in an open plan office but sometimes, it's hard to concentrate. Sometimes, people come into the office and start talking while I have another work that I need to finish.
> (Participant 5)
> Maybe, I'd prefer open-plan office with several number of people ... right now, I'm in one office with my colleague. So, it's just the two of us. Sometimes, she'll talk to me and starts having a conversation with me ... I can't focus on my work, but I feel guilty if I don't talk to her. ... I can't avoid her ... This is the time when I feel like I want a private office. So that I can focus on my work. Because once I get immersed in doing my work, I don't want any distractions.
> (Participant 6)
> There's only two people – me and my colleague ... even though it's just us sharing an office, sometimes I'd prefer to have my own because it's peaceful and I feel like I can focus more doing work when I am alone.
> (Participant 11)

Despite the contradictory findings which have been illustrated in this study, this study also discover similarities of the findings in previous studies. Hvidsten (2016) stated that introverts might be an obstacle in tacit knowledge sharing because of the negative impact of introversion which have been portrayed by several authors. For example, Zelenski (2012, 2013) suggested introversion as a negative and undesirable personality trait perhaps because they are often perceived as quiet and soft-spoken (Cain, 2012). This study discovered that introverts can be perceived as quiet; however, this trait should not be considered as an obstacle because this study revealed that introverts do admit that they can be quiet but it should not be regarded as a negative trait because most of the participants portrayed positive attitude when asked about their behaviour during meetings – how they act in meetings and whether or not they share or contribute their knowledge with others during meetings:

> I like sharing my ideas but normally, I always stay quiet first then observe what other people say during the meeting. ... I think of what I want to share or contribute. I don't feel satisfied if I don't contribute something. My colleagues know this. So, they will ask me in case they feel like I'm being too quiet. They will say things like, "would you like to say something?"
> (Participant 2)

Umm … let's say in a team, the members are all outspoken, I'll be quiet. But, if most of them are all quiet, I'll be the one to talk. I'll encourage the quiet ones to talk and express their ideas. Because you know sometimes people don't want to share. But if I have nothing to share, I wouldn't talk either.

(Participant 3)

If there's someone leading the project, and if that person is good enough, then I'll just keep quiet. But if that person is having a hard time, or having a personal issue, then I will volunteer to take over and lead the meeting.

(Participant 8)

The above responses given by the participants are in accordance with previous literature. Apparently, introverts need more time to reflect on what is being said in the conversation and to prepare what to say next (Hvidsten, 2016) which is why they sometimes prefer to stay quiet before saying anything. This is perhaps due to their nature of personality traits. But this does not mean that they have poor social skills. Although there are some truths in what has been illustrated about introverts in previous literature, there are no such severe issues that introversion should be regarded as an obstacle when it comes to share tacit knowledge. There are, however, other influencing factors that could hinder introverts to share their knowledge as explained in following section.

What facilitates-enables introversion in tacit knowledge sharing

According to Hvidsten (2016), storytelling is a KM mechanism for knowledge sharing and capture. It involves an individual sharing an experience in front of an audience. The tacit knowledge-sharing practices involve social activities such as public speaking, conversations between individuals and collaborative discussions. These activities were mentioned by most of the participants when asked about how they share their tacit knowledge with their peers. However, many have agreed that it also "depends on the crowd" and the "environment" they are in which affects their decision to share their knowledge. For example, Participant 2 suggested that one of the influencing factors for one to share or not to share knowledge actually depends on the individual's role itself:

I've been to many places, so it depends whether people will share about their experience with you. Because, every time I started a new job, it's me myself, bringing my own skill. I guess it depends on your role … when I show my skills to others, and then they find my skills are helpful to them then they would also share their knowledge or skills with me … In my opinion, when people don't want to share their experience or knowledge, it's because they are not skilled enough or they have less knowledge in the field which makes them feel scared to share. Maybe, they're afraid that other people will judge them?

(Participant 2)

Meanwhile, Participant 6 acknowledged that sharing knowledge depends on the level of comfort that she has with her colleagues:

(Participant 6)

Participant 6 also added that sharing knowledge also depends on others' willingness to accept her ideas:

I share whatever I want. Unless it's confidential. But wait, yes … it depends on the people as well whether or not I feel comfortable with them. Because sometimes people don't really want to listen to you and some act arrogant.

(Participant 6)

Another participant has a more or less similar response on the level of comfort with his colleagues. Apparently, having good relationships helps introverts to communicate better which foster tacit knowledge sharing. This is in accordance to a study by Pollet et al. (2011) who suggested that introverts who are good at developing and maintaining emotionally close relationships with other people would make information and knowledge shared between individuals to be reliable. This may also be in line with studies by Skakoon (2015) where the study revealed that introverts like to socialise in small groups and often focus on social energy on close friends and family (Schmidt, 2016).

We treat each other as a family. Issues that we face, no matter personal issue, or work-related issues, we share among each other. Because I notice that if you treat each other as a family, the work productivity will grow better and we can work as a team.

(Participant 8)

We are quite close. We share everything. We gossip too (laugh). And since we are comfortable with each other, it's easy for us to discuss about our work all the time.

(Participant 9)

Both intrinsic and extrinsic motivation also influence introverts to share their knowledge. People can be motivated either extrinsically or intrinsically. If a person is intrinsically motivated, he/she will engage in an action because it is enjoyable and he/she finds it inherently interesting (Deci & Ryan, 1980). On the other hand, an extrinsically motivated individual's actions are driven by a goal (Deci & Ryan, 1980). Exemplifying the intrinsic motivation of an individual is the level of his or her confidence. This has been mentioned by most of the participants.

> If I were to share something through public speaking, like … you need to grab their attention. It's hard. But if it's my passion maybe I'd be able to deliver properly, but of course, I'd still feel nervous, but I know that I can do it. The important thing is confidence. Confidence and being fully prepared will help. But if you're going to give a speech on the topics that is not in your line of work and you're not confident then that is going to be a disaster.
> (Participant 1)

This is in line with a study by Bock et al. (2005) where their study discovered that the more confident a worker is with his or her skills and competencies, the more likely the person is to share his or her knowledge with others. This may also align with the study by Poulsen (2013) where the study found that high intrinsic motivation has a stronger influence on introverts than on extroverts, resulting in introverts being more engaged in knowledge sharing when intrinsic motivation is high. Additionally, some of the participants acknowledged that they expect something in return when they share their knowledge. The participants admitted that they expect to get praised, receive recognition and appreciation whenever he shared something. These expectations are considered to be extrinsic motivation. This may be aligned with a study by Donath (1999) as cited in Hung et al. (2011) where extrinsic benefits were mentioned to be reputation feedback which can lead to active participation and reciprocity, the expectation that an individual's sharing efforts will be reciprocated, thereby ensuring ongoing sharing (Wasko & Faraj, 2005).

> For me, in case I share knowledge to someone, it's because I want him/her to share whatever they know with me. It's a give and take kind of things. Because we're in the same company, so, by right we should take care of each other. And of course, I'm pretty sure everyone needs appreciation.
> (Participant 3)
> I would say … being appreciated. I don't think anyone would give me any presents if I share my knowledge [*laughs*].
> (Participant 4)
> Sometimes I want people to praise whatever I have done [*laughs*]. But it depends on the knowledge I share. If it's something huge and it helps people, of course I would want to be acknowledged for it.
> (Participant 11)

The hindrance of tacit knowledge sharing by introverts

When asked about the potential barriers of sharing knowledge, some of the participants gave different kinds of responses. Some think that there are no barriers to share knowledge at all. However, it seems that there are no such severe issues that may hinder introverts to share their knowledge.

Some of the participants prefer to hide their knowledge when people do not agree with their suggestions. For instance, Participant 1 mentioned that one of the reasons why it is better not to share knowledge was because it is hard to convince people:

> When you have another a peer or peers, to have them to agree with you, it's very hard. Because different people will be having different opinions ... It's hard to convince people.
> (Participant 1)

Language can be considered as a barrier to share knowledge as well, but most participants believed that it is still manageable as long as it is still convenient to communicate and able to have agreement with those who have different mother tongue. Language plays a critical role in articulating, exchanging and assimilating knowledge among knowledge-sharing participants (Tan & Gartland, 2014). This is in accordance with studies by Ellis (1994) and Schomaker and Zaheer (2014) which stated that language is a matter of concern because the proficiency and expressional confidence people enjoy in their native language is usually far superior to that they have in a different language. Different terminologies used in different department within a workplace can be a barrier as well.

> I'd prefer speaking to people with the same language. But then again sometimes, even though you have the same mother tongue people can misinterpret whatever we are saying. I have experienced where people always give me responses that is not what I'm looking for. It's like they have misheard what I've said. [*laughs*]
> (Participant 2)
> Language is definitely a barrier in communicating your ideas to other people. ... there are a lot of foreigners ... I find it hard to express myself ... Sometimes my message or my point is not conveyed to the recipients as I have intended which leads to conflict due to improper usage of sentences or terminology y ... BUT – even though we do have the same language, we don't understand each other sometimes. For example, we came from different organisations before this organisation got merged, so the term that we used are not similar to others from different organisation.
> (Participant 7)

The languages we have – they're not similar. I mean there are different types of terminologies which can be technical sometimes. So, I think that's one of the barriers.

(Participant 9)

Another barrier that was mentioned by some of the participants was fear. For example, Participant 3 explained that knowledge sharing is a good thing but sometimes she fears that she might be sharing the wrong knowledge to the recipient. Participant 9 also mentioned fear of sharing knowledge because she feels shy to express her opinions.

To me sharing knowledge is a good thing. Because it teaches yourself as well. It's just that sometimes I don't feel like sharing my ideas because I'm afraid that I might share things wrongly. Like, if I'm teaching my colleague, I'm afraid that I am actually teaching the wrong thing.

(Participant 3)

I don't feel like sharing when I'm not confident with what I want to contribute. I'm afraid to share especially when I'm not an expert in that certain field or subject.

(Participant 4)

I feel shy to voice out my opinion. I'm afraid that I may not share the correct info or knowledge.

(Participant 9)

The above quotations may align with a study by Bordia et al. (2006) where the study discovered that fear has shown to have a negative impact on knowledge contribution. This is because some employees might fear that their colleagues will ridicule or not appreciate their knowledge-sharing contributions, resulting in reluctance to sharing knowledge as illustrated by Participant 9 above, where she admitted that she "feels shy" to voice out her opinion because she fears that she might be sharing the wrong knowledge. This is perhaps also due to the nature of introversion traits that are described as shy, quiet, withdrawn and reserved (Hvidsten, 2016). This may also be aligned with neuroticism, which is a typical introverted trait. This trait may entail being sensitive to critique from others. Therefore, introverts may avoid contributing to the sharing of both tacit and explicit knowledge as they would not want to risk to be offended by criticism from co-workers (Hvidsten, 2016).

Conclusions

In conclusion, while introversion has been portrayed as a negative personality trait, the findings of this study illustrated several contradictions in previous studies. There are several influencing factors that facilitate introverts to share their tacit knowledge; however, these factors can also be considered as the hindrance or the barriers to tacit knowledge sharing. In theoretical perspective, in order for these factors to work as the facilitators of tacit knowledge sharing, it depends on the role of an individual and the level of comfort they have with the people around them. Nevertheless, these findings will provide practical contribution with the understanding of what motivates introverts to share their knowledge, what influences them not to share their knowledge, to whom do they prefer to share their knowledge with and whether or not they only share their tacit knowledge when they are asked to do so. In essence, the findings provide significant impetus where high intrinsic motivation has a stronger influence on introverts than on extroverts, resulting in introverts being more engaged in knowledge sharing when intrinsic motivation is high. Thus, this study has expanded and enlightened the literature debates on aspects of introversion personality and its influencing factors in tacit knowledge sharing.

References

Armstrong, S. J., & Mahmud, A. (2008). Experiential learning and the acquisition of managerial tacit knowledge. *Academy of Management Learning & Education*, 7(2), 189–208.

Becerra, M., Lunnan, R., & Huemer, L. (2008). Trustworthiness, risk, and the transfer of tacit and explicit knowledge between alliance partners. *Journal of Management Studies*, 45(4), 691–713.

Becerra-Fernandez, I., & Sabherwal, R. (2015). *Knowledge management: Systems and processes*. New York, NY: Routledge.

Bock, Zmud, K., & Lee. (2005). Behavioral intention formation in knowledge sharing: examining the roles of extrinsic motivators, social-psychological forces, and organisation climate. *MIS Quarterly*, 29(1), 87.

Bordia, P., Irmer, B. E., & Abusah, D. (2006). Differences in sharing knowledge interpersonally and via databases: The role of evaluation apprehension and perceived benefits. *European Journal of Work and Organisational Psychology*, 15(3), 262–280.

Borges, R. (2012). Tacit knowledge sharing between IT workers. *Management Research Review*, 36(1), 89–108.

Borges, R. (2013). Tacit knowledge sharing between IT workers: The role of organisational culture, personality, and social environment. *Management Research Review*, 36(1), 89–108.

Braun, V., & Clarke, V. (2012). Thematic analysis. In: Cooper, H., editor. *APA handbook of research methods in psychology. Vol. 2, research designs*. Washington, DC: American Psychological Association, pp. 57–71.

Cabrera, Á., Collins, W. C., & Salgado, J. F. (2006). Determinants of individual engagement in knowledge sharing. *The International Journal of Human Resource Management*, 17(2), 245–264.

Cain, S. (2012). *Quiet: The power of introverts in a world that can't stop talking*. New York: Crown Publishers.

Chen, H., Baptista Nunes, M., Ragsdell, G., & An, X. (2018). Extrinsic and intrinsic motivation for experience grounded tacit knowledge sharing in Chinese software organisations. *Journal of Knowledge Management, 22*(2), 478–498.

Deci, E. L., & Ryan, R. M. (1980). The empirical exploration of intrinsic motivational processes. *Advances in Experimental Social Psychology*, 13, 39–80.

Donath, J. S. (1999). *Identity and deception in the virtual community.* In: Smith, M., & Kollock, P. (Eds.), *Communities in cyberspace.* New York: Routledge, pp. 27–58.

Dossey, L. (2016). Introverts: A defense. *Explore, 12*(3), 151–160.

Dunning, D. (2001). *What's your type of career? Unlock the secrets of your personality to find your perfect career path.* Palo Alto, CA: Davies-Black.

Ellis, R. (1994). *The study of second language acquisition (Oxford applied linguistics).* Oxford: Oxford University Press.

Eysenck, H. (1947). *Dimensions of personality.* NJ: Transaction Publishers.

Feiler, D. C., & Kleinbaum, A. M. (2015). Popularity, similarity, and the network extraversion bias. *Psychological Science, 26*(5), 594.

Gibbert, M., & Krause, H. (2002). Practical exchange in a best practice marketplace. In: Davenport, T. H., & Probst, G. J. B. (Eds.), *Knowledge management case book: Siemens best practices.* Erlangen: Publics Corporate Publishing, 89–105.

Grant, A. (2014). Myths about introverts and extroverts at work. [Online]. Available: www.huffingtonpost.com/adam grant/5-myths-aboutintroverts_b_4814390.html

Grant, A. M., Gino, F., & Hofmann, D. A. (2010). The hidden advantages of quiet bosses. *Harvard Business Review, 88*(12), 28.

Hung, S.-Y., Durcikova, A., Lai, H.-M., & Lin, W.-M. (2011). The influence of intrinsic and extrinsic motivation on individuals' knowledge sharing behavior. *International Journal of Human-Computer Studies, 69*(6), 415–427.

Hvidsten, A. K. N. (2016). Is introversion an obstacle in tacit knowledge sharing through socialization? A study on how personality traits influence knowledge sharing behavior. *Dalhousie Journal of Interdisciplinary Management*, 12 – Spring, djim.management.dal.ca.

Ibrahim, F., & Reid, V. (2010). Integrated use of information technology and people involvement for knowledge management. *International Journal of Technology, Knowledge and Society, 6*(2), 163–180.

Ismail, M. B., & Yusof, Z. M. (2010). The impact of individual factors on knowledge sharing quality. *Journal of Organisation Knowledge Management*, 1–13. Available at https://ibimapublishing.com/articles/JOKM/2010/327569/

Judge, T. A., Bono, J. E., & Locke, E. A. (2000). Personality and job satisfaction: The mediating role of job characteristics. *Journal of Applied Psychology 2000, 85*(2), 237–249.

Jung, C. G. (1926). *Psychological types, or, the psychology of individuation.* London: Routledge & Kegan Paul.

Kiger, M. E., & Varpio, L. (2020). Thematic analysis of qualitative data: AMEE Guide No. 131. *Medical Teacher, 42*(8), 846–854.

Lieberman, M. D., & Rosenthal, R. (2001). Why introverts can't always tell who likes them: Multitasking and nonverbal decoding. *Journal of Personality and Social Psychology, 80*(2), 294–310.

Manaf, H. A., Armstrong, S. J., Lawton, A., & Harvey, W. S. (2017). Managerial tacit knowledge, individual performance, and the moderating role of employee personality. *International Journal of Public Administration, 41*(15), 1258–1270.

Matzler, K., Renzl, B., Mooradia, T., Krogh, G., & Mueller, J. (2011). Personality traits, affective commitment, documentation of knowledge, and knowledge sharing. *The International Journal of Human Resource Management, 22*(2), 296–310.

McLeod, J. (2011). *Qualitative Research in Counselling and Psychotherapy* (Second ed.). Sage Publications.

Newell, S., Robertson, M., Scarbrough, H., & Swan, J. (2002). *Managing Knowledge Work*. New York: Palgrave Macmillan.

Nonaka, I., & Takeuchi, H. (1995). *The knowledge creating company: How Japanese companies create the dynamics of innovation*, New York: Oxford University Press.

Pollet, T., Roberts, S., & Dunbar, R. (2011). Extroverts have larger social network layers: But do not feel emotionally closer to individuals at any layer. *Journal of Individual Differences, 32*(3), 161–169.

Poulsen, C. R. (2013). The interaction between knowledge-sharing ability, motivation and extraversion in a voluntary context [master thesis]. Retrieved from http://www.kb.dk/export/sites/kb_dk/da/kub/lektieronline/PDF/Christian-Romby-Poulsen-The-interaction-between-knowledge-sharing-ability-motivation-and-extraversion-in-a-voluntary-context.pdf

Rathod, V. G. (2019). Personality characteristics of board and non-board students. *IJRAR— International Journal of Research and Analytical Reviews, 6*(2), 411–413.

Reagans, R., & Mcevily, B. (2003). Network structure and knowledge transfer: The effects of cohesion and range. *Administrative Science Quarterly, 48*(2), 240–267.

Reid, F. (2003). Creating a knowledge-sharing culture among diverse business units. *Employment Relations Today, 30*(3), 43.

Riege, A. (2005). Three-dozen knowledge-sharing barriers managers must consider. *Journal of Knowledge Management, 9*(3), 18–35.

Rzadkowska, J. (2015, September 25). Carl Gustav Jung. Store Norske Leksikon. Retrieved from https://snl.no/Carl_Gustav_Jung (from Hvidsten, 2016).

Schmidt, S. (2016). Personality diversity: Extrovert and introvert temperaments. *Journal of Food Science Education*, 15 (3), 73–74.

Schmitt, D. P., Allik, J., McCrae, R. R., & Benet-Martínez, V. (2007). A geographic distribution of big five personality traits: patterns and profiles of human self-description across 56 nations. *Journal of Cross-Cultural Psychology, 38*(2), 173–212.

Schomaker, M. S., & Zaheer, S. (2014). The role of language in knowledge transfer to geographically dispersed manufacturing operations. *Journal of International Management, 20*, 55–72.

Skakoon, J. G. (2015). Introverts rule. *Mechanical Engineering-CIME, 137*(4), 16.

Tan, H., & Gartland, A. (2014). Language, knowledge transfer and firm's strategic assets: the strategic role of language in knowledge transfer to China. *Journal of Chinese Economic and Business Studies, 12*, 63–79.

Taylor, M. (2020). Personality styles: Why they matter in the workplace. *Economic Alternatives, 1*, 148–163.

Wasko, M., & Faraj, S. (2005). Why should I share? Examining social capital and knowledge contribution in electronic networks of practice. *MIS Quarterly, 29*(1), 34–56.

Wei, Y., & Miraglia, S. (2017). Organisation culture and knowledge transfer in project-based organisations: Theoretical insights from a Chinese construction firm. *International Journal of Project Management, 35*(4), 571–585.

Wulandari, F., Ferdinand, A. T., & Dwiatmadja, C. (2018). Knowledge sharing in a critical moment of work: A driver for success? *International Journal of Knowledge Management, 14*(2), 88–98.

Zack, D. (2010). *Networking for people who hate networking*, 1st Edition. San Francisco, CA: Berrett-Koehler Publishers, Inc.

Zelenski, J. M., Santoro, M. S., & Whelan, D. C. (2012). Would introverts be better off if they acted more like extroverts? Exploring emotional and cognitive consequences of counter dispositional behavior. *Emotion, 12*(2), 290–303.

Zelenski, J. M., Whelan, D. C., Nealis, L. J., Besner, C. M., Santoro, M. S., & Wynn, J. E. (2013). Personality and affective forecasting: Trait introverts under predict the hedonic benefits of acting extroverted. *Journal of Personality and Social Psychology, 104*(6), 1092–1108. doi: 10.1037/a003

5 Unveiling the potential mediating role of knowledge sharing in linking job satisfaction and organisational commitment

Md. Zahidul Islam, Wardah Azimah Haji Sumardi and Nurul Amirah Ishak

Introduction

As we progress ahead with the knowledge economy era, effective knowledge management (KM) has emerged as a significant differentiator for many organisations (Suppiah & Sandhu, 2011). The process of developing, sharing and applying knowledge is imperative to achieve and sustain a competitive advantage (Runar Edvardsson, 2007). Among these aspects, the concept of knowledge sharing (KS) is the cornerstone of KM, which plays a crucial part in turning individual knowledge into organisational knowledge (Wang & Wang, 2012). Previous literature has revealed that organisations can benefit greatly when knowledge is shared at the collective level, for instance, improvement in the organisational effectiveness and the innovation capability (Lin, 2007; Wang & Wang, 2012; Yang, 2007).

Nonetheless, the organisation's ability to leverage knowledge for competitive advantage is mostly contingent upon its employees (Malik & Kanwal, 2017). In an organisational setting, it becomes prevalent that employees tend to be less inclined to share their knowledge with other organisational members (Teh & Sun, 2012) when they perceive their knowledge as a valuable asset (Davenport, DeLong, & Beers, 1998). Thus, the lack of willingness of employees to share their knowledge represents a common setback for organisations in managing knowledge. With such a challenge in mind, knowledge sharing has been gaining growing recognition among scholars, particularly when the human factor of KM is emphasised (Yi, 2009).

Correspondingly, as employees have attained strategic importance in the current knowledge-based economy, their perception of their workplace also plays an integral part in keeping the organisations competitive (Jehanzeb & Mohanty, 2019). Most importantly, retaining employees alongside with their valuable skills and expertise is vital since their departure would be a huge loss (Singh & Sharma, 2011; Valaei & Rezaei, 2016). It has been noted that organisations wishing to retain their employees and expecting them to cultivate stronger organisational commitment should foster knowledge sharing among employees through conducive organisational support and policies (Chiu & Chen, 2016). Scholars have affirmed that employee's psychological outcomes related to the organisation such as the employees' commitment

DOI: 10.4324/9781003163824-7

and satisfaction are not only crucial for ensuring the continuance of their membership but also knowledge sharing (Chiu & Chen, 2016).

As such, it would be interesting to explore the interplay between job satisfaction, organisational commitment and knowledge sharing simultaneously. Herein, this chapter aims to propose a framework which integrates knowledge sharing as a potential mediating variable in the association between job satisfaction and organisational commitment. In other words, it is argued that employees' job satisfaction can enhance their knowledge-sharing behaviour, and thereby nurturing their organisational commitment. In retrospect, a substantial body of research exists on examining the impact of job satisfaction and organisational commitment (e.g., Froese & Xiao, 2012; Malhotra, Budhwar, & Prowse, 2007; Mathieu, 1991; Meyer et al., 2002). Similarly, the idea of job satisfaction as a predictor of knowledge sharing is not novel in the literature (Rafique & Mahmood, 2018; Suliman & Al-Hosani, 2014; Teh & Sun, 2012).

However, there has been scant literature on knowledge sharing as the antecedent of organisational commitment (Cheah et al., 2016; Curado & Vieira, 2019; Davoudi & Fartash, 2012). Although those prior studies shed light on the influence of knowledge sharing on organisational commitment, the studies have been mainly restricted to either the affective component of organisational commitment (Cheah et al., 2016; Davoudi & Fartash, 2012) or both affective and normative components of commitment (Curado & Vieira, 2019). As suggested by Meyer and Allen (1997), employees may experience three different forms of commitment (affective, normative and continuance) simultaneously. Furthermore, to the best of our knowledge, no previous study has introduced the mediating role of knowledge sharing in the nexus between job satisfaction and organisational commitment. Hence, this chapter aims to contribute to the current knowledge gap by proposing a framework that depicts knowledge sharing as a potential mediator in linking job satisfaction and organisational commitment.

The organisation of this chapter is as follows. First, the overview of the established link between knowledge sharing (KS), job satisfaction (JS) and organisational commitment (OC) will be presented. The subsequent section will briefly describe the methodology adopted by this chapter. After that, the chapter will deal with OC's conceptualisation into three components (i.e., affective, normative, continuance) and subsequently discuss how KS play a part in developing each of the OC components. Next, the chapter will address the role of job satisfaction in predicting KS. Lastly, the main conclusions and the implications to theory and practice will be presented.

The established link between knowledge sharing, job satisfaction and organisational commitment (OC)

In the literature, there are many studies that examine the links between knowledge sharing (KS), job satisfaction (JS) and organisational commitment (OC), and it is therefore important to acknowledge existing linkages in order to build on this chapter. Most studies (e.g., Cuguero-Escofet et al., 2019; Na-Nan et al., 2020; Teh & Sun, 2012) conceptualised employee attitudes such as JS and OC as antecedents or predictors of KS. It is posited that since the process of KS is controlled by the individual employees, individual attitudes are therefore central to this individual control. As reported by previous studies (e.g., Cuguero-Escofet et al., 2019; Sihombin et al., 2017), individual attitudes such as their level of satisfaction and commitment can either impede or facilitate KS behaviour. In practice, some employees are keen to share their knowledge with others, while others may be reluctant. This may be explained by their individual psychological differences. For example, employees who are happier with their colleagues and their organisation are more inclined to share knowledge (Constant et al., 1994). The clear view here is that high levels of JS (Kucharska & Bedford, 2019) and OC (Swart et al., 2014) are associated with increased KS.

Other studies have also treated job satisfaction (JS) and organisational commitment (OC) as outcomes of knowledge sharing. In particular, there is plenty of empirical evidence that has provided strong association between KS and JS (Hu & Zhao, 2016; Rafique & Mahmood, 2018; Suliman & Al-Hosani, 2014; Teh & Sun, 2012). To explain this, Nonaka and Takeuchi (1995)'s conceptualisation of knowledge sharing is observed to require much social interaction such as face-to-face communication, brainstorming, mentoring and coaching in order to manage the tacit nature of knowledge. Such activities which cater to the social needs of individuals have been linked to job satisfaction. For example, Kianto et al. (2016) found that knowledge management processes in one's working environment is significantly linked with high job satisfaction, with intra-organisational knowledge sharing as the key KM process promoting satisfaction.

As for organisational commitment, despite various studies (Camelo-Ordaz et al., 2011; Swart et al., 2014) claiming organisational commitment (OC) as a precursor of KS or the mediation role of OC in a relationship between many independent constructs and KS, studies exploring the impact of KS on OC are found to be limited. Consequently, the relationship between KS and OC remains unclear and inconclusive, warranting additional inquiry in this research area. On top of this, the literature also made clear that organisational commitment in contemporary organisations is not one dimensional. As suggested by Meyer and Allen (1997), employees may experience three different forms of commitment (affective, normative and continuance) simultaneously at varying degrees. However, most studies have failed to distinguish the different components of commitment and how each type is affected by knowledge sharing. Despite calls for research to further dissect the OC construct into affective, normative and continuance forms when studying knowledge sharing (Swart et al., 2014), most studies (such as Curado & Vieira, 2019; Jayasingam et al., 2016; Naim & Lenka, 2017) are often restricted to affective commitment and/or normative commitment only.

Taken together, though the accumulation of research on the relationship between knowledge sharing (KS), job satisfaction (JS) and organisational commitment (OC) has provided useful insights, the prevailing gap mentioned above stimulates the interest in researching this relationship widely. Henceforth, often explored as antecedent or outcome, given the above inquiry, this chapter proposes the potential role of knowledge sharing as a mediating factor between job satisfaction and organisational commitment.

Methodology

A systematic literature review was conducted by adopting the recommendations of Shahbaznezhad et al. (2019), which consisted of three stages: (i) perform literature search, (ii) select and apply appropriate criteria for inclusion and exclusion of papers and, finally, (iii) develop a framework grounded in the literature.

The literature search was conducted using Google Scholar and four academic university databases (Emerald Insight, SAGE, ScienceDirect, Jstor). To identify the relevant articles, multiple terms and combinations of search queries were used such as "knowledge management," "knowledge sharing," "job satisfaction," "organisational commitment," "affective commitment," "continuance commitment," "normative commitment." Also, through manual searches, several articles were identified using backwards and forward searches. The search was also limited to articles written in English language published between 2000 and 2021. Only peer-reviewed journal articles, as well as selected books were included. Other forms of publications such as working papers and theses were excluded from the review. Specifically, studies determining the relationship or correlation between KS, JS and OC were selected which resulted in 75 distinctive papers.

Review findings and discussions

This section presents the key prepositions concerning the mediating role of knowledge sharing between job satisfaction and organisational commitment. In essence, this chapter proposes a causal link leading from (1) employee's job satisfaction (2) would promote their knowledge-sharing behaviour, which in turn (3) instil their commitment towards the organisation. The subsequent section will first present the conceptualisation of organisational commitment (OC) as affective commitment (AOC), normative commitment (NOC) and continuance commitment (COC), respectively. After that, the proposed relations of knowledge sharing (KS) with all the three components of OC will be addressed, followed by a discussion on job satisfaction (JS) as a precursor of KS, which subsequently contributes to the development of OC.

Conceptualising organisational commitment (OC)

Collectively, most definitions describing OC refer to a psychological link between an employee and the organisation. Nonetheless, according to Allen and Meyer (1990), OC can be defined as a psychological state that binds an employee to the organisation that affects his or her decision to stay within the same organisation. While there are various conceptualisations of OC, this chapter aligns itself with the widely accepted Meyer and Allen's (1991) Three-Component Model (TCM). Based on this TCM model, there are three components of OC – *namely, affective, normative and continuance.* This three-component model of organisational commitment shows the cumulative strength of individuals' attachment to an organisation because (i) they want to (affective), (ii) they ought to (normative) and (iii) they need to (continuance) remain in the organisation (Meyer & Allen, 1991). Specifically, affective commitment (AOC) indicates an individual's emotional attachment (e.g., identification, involvement) to the organisation. On the other hand, normative commitment (NOC) relates to an individual's moral obligation to remain as part of the organisation. Finally, continuance commitment (COC) refers to the individuals' realisation of the benefits of continued membership with the organisation as opposed to the perceived cost of leaving. Furthermore, aligning with the TCM model, the chapter appreciates that these three components of commitment can be experienced simultaneously at a varying degree (Meyer & Allen, 1997). The following section of this chapter will further discuss how these three components of OC can be established by knowledge sharing (KS).

Knowledge sharing (KS) and organisational commitment (OC)

Before reflecting on how knowledge sharing (KS) could affect employees' organisational commitment (OC), it is useful to first briefly describe the concept of knowledge sharing. Broadly, when studying the concept of knowledge sharing (KS), previous literature reveals two varying lenses – *unidirectional and bidirectional.* According to the unidirectional perspective, KS entails the transmission of knowledge in a single direction from a knowledge provider to a knowledge recipient (Yi, 2009), placing a dominant role on the knowledge provider as opposed to the knowledge recipient. In such cases, knowledge sharing is observed to take place only at the individual level (Tangaraja et al., 2016). In contrary to the earlier approach, the bidirectional perspective asserts that KS involves an active exchange of knowledge between individuals through two central processes – *knowledge donation and knowledge collection* (Tangaraja et al., 2016; van de Hooff & de Ridder, 2004).

In essence, 'knowledge donation' entails active communication with others about what one knows, and the 'knowledge collection' involves consulting others to share what they know (van den Hooff & de Ridder, 2004). The active role of both parties, therefore, takes KS beyond the individual level. In this regard, for KS to take place, both parties should be active and willing to send/supply/provide or receive/request/demand knowledge (Java-dpour & Samiei, 2017). Therefore, if one party hesitates to share knowledge, the other will lose out and ultimately, the organisation will be at a disadvantage. Various scholars such as Swart et al. (2014), Tangaraja et al. (2015) and Rahman et al. (2017) have supported this two-way process of knowledge sharing. Henceforth, conceptualising KS from this bidirectional viewpoint, KS herein can be defined as the act of actively exchanging knowledge between entities (e.g., individuals, groups), whereby the role of contributing and seeking knowledge can be borne by both parties interchangeably.

Within the current literature, it is worth acknowledging that the role of knowledge sharing (KS) in determining organisational commitment (OC) has been established by past research (Li et al., 2015; Ouakouak & Oue-draogo, 2019; Rasdi & Tangaraja, 2020). The clear view here is that high levels of OC are associated with increased KS (Goh & Sandhu, 2013; Yesil, 2014). However, contrary to those previous scholarly work, this chapter attempts to explore the links between KS and OC. In essence, the association between KS and OC can be apprehended by taking into consideration Non-aka and Takeuchi's (1995) SECI model of knowledge creation. As visualised in Nonaka's knowledge creation model, the mnemonic SECI signifies the four modes of knowledge conversion between tacit and explicit knowledge (Nonaka & Takeuchi, 1995) – *socialisation, externalisation, combination and internalisation.*

Scholars such as Curado and Vieira (2019) have advocated that the so-cialisation process (S) among individuals helps develop trust through social interactions. Then, the externalisation (E) and combination (C) processes necessitate converting tacit knowledge into explicit knowledge, which is then shared from the level of individual to group and, successively, disseminated to the organisational level. Finally, the internalisation process (I) involves the embodiment of explicit knowledge into tacit form, from the organisational level to the individual level. As individuals use and learn organisational knowledge, it will eventually be internalised in their minds, thereby shaping their (tacit) practices. For instance, reading and reflecting on (explicit codified) documents such as role profiles, enables the employees to know how they are expected to behave in terms of behavioural competencies and uphold the organisation's core values. Consequently, this could promote the alignment of their objectives with those of the organisation. Along this line of thought, scholars asserted that this internalisation process could further instigate employee's action and behaviour, which may come in the form of organisational commitment (Curado & Vieira, 2019).

Collectively, based on the above arguments, it can be argued that the sharing of knowledge that takes place in groups or with individuals provides further insights for employees about the different aspects of their organisations and provides the opportunity to align their own objectives in line with the organisational objectives – thereby forming their organisational commitment. In the extant literature, there have been several scholarly evidences suggesting KS as the precursor of OC (Cheah et al., 2016; Curado & Vieira, 2019; Davoudi & Fartash, 2012). Nevertheless, it should be emphasised that those extant studies could not demonstrate the broader implications of how KS affects all three components of organisational commitment (affective, normative, continuance). Henceforward, the following subsections will address the relationship between KS and each component of organisational commitment.

Knowledge sharing and affective organisational commitment (AOC)

In essence, affective organisational commitment (AOC) refers to the employee's emotional attachment to the organisation (Meyer et al., 2002). Employees with a strong AOC have a strong emotional attachment to the organisation and are willing to help the organisation achieve its goals. Among the three types of OC, AOC is the most studied in KS studies (such as Ikechukwu & Callystus, 2018; Jayasingam et al., 2016; Naim & Lenka, 2017). In a study by Jayasingam et al. (2015), knowledge-sharing culture is reported to have a significant association with affective commitment. As summed up by Curado and Vieira (2019), several empirical studies have corroborated the positive influence of KS on AOC. For instance, Nonaka (1994) found that the active social interactions brought about by KS link employees to the organisation allowing employees to align their values with the organisation. On the other hand, a study by Davoudi and Fartash (2012) observed that the additional information and knowledge gathered from KS enhances employees' satisfaction, which subsequently fosters a sense of security and identification towards the organisation.

In addition to that, Mergel et al. (2008) view KS as a helping behaviour that can enhance employee's commitment to the organisation. Similarly, Benson and Brown (2007) found that knowledge workers develop an emotional attachment with organisations that nurture a supportive environment for knowledge sharing, thereby promoting teamwork and facilitating a close relationship between organisational members. Henceforth, it can be argued that the greater the knowledge shared among employees, the greater their affective commitment towards the organisation (AOC) (Cabrera & Cabrera, 2002). Given the relevance of KS in the development of affective organisational commitment (AOC) put forward by the studies mentioned above, it can thus be proposed that:

P1. Knowledge sharing contributes to the development of employees' AOC.

Knowledge sharing and normative organisational commitment (NOC)

On the other hand, normative organisational commitment (NOC) reflects a perceived obligation to remain in the organisation (Meyer et al., 2002).

Typically, employees with strong NOC are likely to stay in the organisation because they feel they have to. Arguably, in any organisation setting, there is a set of normative pressures that might influence the employees' sense of duty to share knowledge (Meyer et al., 2002), consequently enhancing their NOC. Acknowledging the lack of coverage on the mechanism for explaining or linking the KS-NOC relationship in the literature, this chapter takes into account Curado and Vieira's (2019) use of the SECI model to comprehend the relationship. It is suggested that during the socialisation process in creating knowledge, the frequent interactions which facilitate knowledge exchange (Nonaka & Konno, 1998) lead employees to view knowledge-sharing behaviour as a moral obligation, which in turn increases their NOC.

Arguably, the trust engendered from the socialisation process from KS, in particular, enhances their NOC. Further to this notion, the trust relationships reciprocated among employees are believed to foster a sense of moral obligation to stay in the organisation based on shared values and beliefs (Lewick, 2015). Moreover, when viewed using the social exchange theory, reciprocity can be interpreted as employees' moral obligation to stay in the organisation, given the amount of organisational knowledge used and learned from the organisation. As such, employees perceived a moral obligation to stay with the organisation. Despite the above arguments, some argue that people generally tend to display loyalty and commitment towards an institution such as family, marriage and employment organisation (Davoudi & Fartash, 2012). As such, ascribed with a moral obligation mindset to engage in conduct indicating duty and loyalty in every social circumstance (Cohen, 2007), this could cultivate their commitment's normative component (NOC). Considering the above arguments, it can be proposed that:

P2. Knowledge sharing contributes to the development of employees' NOC.

Knowledge sharing and continuance organisational commitment (COC)

Last but not least, continuance organisational commitment (COC) refers to the employees' identification of the costs involved in leaving the organisation (Meyer et al., 2002). It is understood that employees with strong COC remain in the organisation because they do not want to incur those costs. Accordingly, they tend to extend their effort on behalf of the organisation as they see it to be in their interest to do so. It is assumed that employees are more likely to share their knowledge in an organisation if they realise that those activities could benefit the organisation (Cheah et al., 2016). Once they are heavily invested in doing so, this could enhance their COC, thereby making it difficult for them to leave the organisation (Allen & Meyer, 1990).

In spite of this assumption, past research has not fully reflected on the effect of KS on continuance commitment (Cheah et al., 2016; Curado & Vieira, 2019; Davoudi & Fartash, 2012). Henceforward, following the SECI model, we can assume that KS requires a great deal of interaction and socialisation among individuals to be successful. As such, some scholars (Davoudi & Fartash, 2012; Dunham et al., 1994; Mowday et al., 1982) contend that this close working relationship with co-workers can be viewed as a form of personal non-transferable investment that is distinctive to an organisation. As a result of this investment (Allen & Meyer, 1990), it can be expected that KS could also instil employees' continuance commitment towards the organisation (COC). Taking this view, it can be proposed that:

P3. Knowledge sharing contributes to the development of employees' COC.

The subsequent section will discuss job satisfaction as an antecedent that could contribute to the knowledge-sharing behaviour which in turn foster the three dimensions of organisational commitment (i.e., affective, normative and continuance).

Job satisfaction (JS) and knowledge sharing (KS)

Given the centrality of individuals in sharing knowledge, its success mainly depends on the behaviour of employees (Teh & Sun, 2012). Organisations need employees' support to share their knowledge voluntarily with other employees within the organisation (Lin & Hwang, 2014; Rafique et al., 2020). However, fostering knowledge-sharing behaviour is not a straightforward task. Despite various initiatives taken by organisations, employees remain reluctant to share knowledge, often associated with one's natural tendency to protect knowledge and/or to be apprehensive of the knowledge shared by others (Welschen et al., 2012). Several studies have recorded acts of knowledge withholding behaviour such as knowledge hiding (intentional withholding) and knowledge hoarding (unintentional withholding) (Webster et al., 2008). Consequently, such misbehaviours have pushed researchers and practitioners to further investigate the factors that contribute to knowledge-sharing behaviour among employees. In the literature, three factors have been identified that could affect knowledge sharing in general. This includes individual factors (Lee & Choi, 2003), organisational factors (Lin, 2007) and technology factors (Taylor & Wright, 2004). Nonetheless, to date, studies examining KS and individual factors (e.g., Cuguero-Escofet et al., 2019; Li et al., 2015; Shihabeldeen et al., 2020; Sihombin et al., 2017; Teh & Sun, 2012) have proliferated, suggesting the importance of changing employee attitudes supportive of knowledge sharing. Hislop (2003) echoed similar conclusions in his review study, highlighting employee attitude as the most significant factor influencing knowledge sharing. In the context of this chapter, it is argued herein that individual attitudes such as job satisfaction could have a substantial effect on employee tendency to share knowledge.

Broadly, the concept of job satisfaction (JS) can be referred to as the positive or negative emotional state resulting from the appraisal of one's job or work (Locke, 1969). In essence, job satisfaction involves one's subjective evaluation of a broad range of work-specific variables that are either intrinsic (e.g., career advancement, recognition, achievement, work itself) or extrinsic (e.g., compensations, work relationships, supervisor relations) (Herzberg, 1966; Saridakis et al., 2018). Saeed (2016) contends that employees are more likely to be satisfied when their job expectations are less or equal to what the job delivers. On the contrary, the employees' lack of satisfaction occurs when their expectations are higher compared to what they actually attained from their job. Within the current literature, various researchers have theorised and proven the relationship between job satisfaction (JS) and knowledge sharing (KS). For instance, a recent systematic review by Rafique and Mahmood (2018) reveals a strong positive association between JS and KS (see Lin, 2015; Rehman et al., 2014; Suliman & Al-Hosani, 2014). Scholars have contended that higher levels of JS could promote employees' willingness to share knowledge with others (Kianto et al., 2016). In this vein, Walder (2012) contended that managers should focus on enhancing employees' satisfaction with their work if the management yearns to promote KS in the organisation.

In essence, the JS-KS association is believed to be extended from the satisfaction-performance relationship (Petty et al., 1984; Wright & Cropanzano, 2000). Theoretically, the rationale behind satisfaction-performance connection was believed to be drawn upon human-relations theory, which can be best comprehended by linking it to social exchange theory (Organ, 1977). Based on the premise of social exchange, performance is regarded as an appropriate form of reciprocation to the organisation in exchange for job satisfaction experienced by an employee. Specifically, with regard to the JS-KS relationship, KS behaviour can be viewed as a possible form of reciprocation to the organisation in exchange for job satisfaction.

Within the current literature, several studies such as Naz et al. (2019), Chai et al. (2012), Teh and Sun (2012) and Ma and Agarwal (2007) have used the norm of reciprocity used to explain how employees' job satisfaction could contribute to knowledge sharing. Extending from the norm of reciprocity, this chapter refers to Blau's (1964) Social Exchange Theory (SET) to account for the influence of JS on KS, which entails unspecified obligations between two parties. In other words, when one party contributes to the other party, the other will receive the value and subsequently develops a sense of obligation to reciprocate. However, as Blau (1964) noted, one has to trust others to discharge the obligations. Thus, it can be argued that trust serves as the basis of an individual's non-contractual actions. Relating it to KS, it is human nature that employees can have strong ownership over their possession, including their knowledge. As their trust develops, employees are more likely to engage in KS behaviour to reciprocate job satisfaction achieved at the workplace.

Notwithstanding, it should be acknowledged that there are also prior studies which looked at knowledge sharing (KS) as a predictor of job satisfaction (JS) (e.g., Kianto et al., 2016; Saeed, 2016), whereas a recent review by Rafique and Mahmood (2018) has revealed a positive relationship between KS and JS and vice versa. Nonetheless, this chapter in particular takes the view of organisations focused on building a KS culture, by promoting KS behaviour among the employees. In such a context, employees' JS is argued to have a stronger effect on KS. Following the above rationale, hence it can be proposed that:

P4. Employee's job satisfaction can influence their knowledge-sharing behaviour, which subsequently nurtures their commitment (i.e., affective, normative, continuance) towards the organisation.

The proposed framework: the mediating role of knowledge sharing

Building upon the literature discussed in the preceding sections, a conceptual framework introducing the potential mediating role of knowledge sharing (KS) in linking job satisfaction (JS) and organisational commitment (OC) is illustrated in Figure 5.1. By adopting Meyer and Allen's (1991) Three-Component Model (TCM) and Blau's (1964) Social Exchange Theory as the theoretical lens, the framework postulates that KS has a mediating effect in fostering OC (e.g., affective, normative, continuance). In developing knowledge sharing, the chapter includes job satisfaction into the conceptual framework. However, when proposing this framework, it remains essential to highlight that a substantial body of research has already demonstrated a direct relationship between job satisfaction and organisational commitment. Notwithstanding, it is argued herein that KS could serve as the crucial key mechanism that makes satisfied employees committed to their organisations. To reiterate, there remains a paucity of evidence on knowledge sharing as the precursor of organisational commitment (Cheah et al., 2016; Curado & Vieira, 2019; Davoudi & Fartash, 2012). Furthermore, these existing studies have only focused on the influence of knowledge sharing on either the affective component of organisational commitment (Cheah et al., 2016; Davoudi & Fartash, 2012) or both affective and normative commitment (Curado & Vieira, 2019).

Based on Meyer and Allen's (1991) Three-Component Model (TCM), the chapter reviews the influence of KS on the three components of OC (i.e., affective, normative, continuance), which are as follows: Firstly, the active social interaction enabled by knowledge sharing allows employees to align their values with the organisation (Curado & Vieira, 2019), which subsequently could promote their affective commitment (AOC). Secondly, as employees are ascribed with a moral obligation mindset to engage in conduct indicating duty and loyalty in every social circumstance (Cohen, 2007), this could develop the normative component of their commitment (NOC). Lastly, from the employees' perspective, knowledge-sharing behaviour can be viewed as a form of investment in terms of their time, effort as well as the perceived value of knowledge. Though past research has not fully reflected

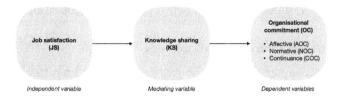

Figure 5.1 The proposed framework.

the effect of KS on continuance commitment (Cheah et al., 2016; Curado & Vieira, 2019; Davoudi & Fartash, 2012), it can be expected that KS could also increase their continuance commitment (COC) towards the organisation (Allen & Meyer, 1990).

On the other hand, the influence of employee's job satisfaction on knowledge sharing is drawn from aspects of social exchange (Blau, 1964) and the norm of reciprocity (Gouldner, 1960). Former studies have demonstrated JS as a strong predictor influencing knowledge sharing (Rafique & Mahmood, 2018; Suliman & Al-Hosani, 2014; Teh & Sun, 2012). Based on the lens of social exchange and the norm of reciprocity, the employees' knowledge-sharing behaviour can be viewed as a means of reciprocation to the organisation in exchange for satisfying their needs and goals (Teh & Sun, 2012).

Conclusion and implications

Taken together, this chapter proposes a framework that introduces knowledge sharing as the potential mediating variable in the relationship between job satisfaction and organisational commitment. As suggested in the framework, it is posited that job satisfaction can be beneficial for promoting employee's knowledge-sharing behaviour. Moreover, the framework proffers that knowledge-sharing behaviour can be used to instil their organisational commitment.

From an academic standpoint, this chapter is expected to contribute to extant literature of both knowledge management and organisational behaviour. Contrary to existing studies, the proposed framework demonstrates a distinct approach by situating knowledge-sharing behaviour as a potential mediator in the linkage between job satisfaction and organisational commitment. Further, following a study by Curado and Vieira (2019), this chapter addresses the gap that existed in literature by conceptualising commitment into three components (affective, normative, continuance).

In terms of practical significance, the proposed framework takes into account the crucial constructs that are imperative for organisational success in the current knowledge era. For this reason, managers and practitioners might benefit from the proposed framework by providing a job and work environment that fulfil and satisfy the employees' need to encourage knowledge-sharing behaviour among employees, and by harnessing such behaviour as a vehicle to nurture their organisational commitment.

Limitations and future research avenues

Though this chapter could contribute to the existing literature, it still has limitations that suggest avenues for future research. This proposed framework is developed based on a systematic review of past literature and has not been tested with observed data, thereby warranting empirical investigation across various contexts. More specifically, future research should consider alternative methods of collecting data. Given the dominance of quantitative methods among the 75 articles reviewed in this chapter, this methodological limitation opens up opportunities for other data collection methods to complement self-report surveys. Perhaps, the deployment of qualitative methods (i.e., interviews, in-depth case studies) as a supplementary method may be highly valuable in advancing knowledge in this field. Aside from methodological opportunities, much more can be taken to advance our theoretical insights. For instance, future research may expand the proposed model by conceptualising job satisfaction into various facets according to Herzberg et al.'s (1959) hygiene and motivator factors (such as working conditions, achievement and responsibility, interpersonal relations, pay and security) to provide a more holistic picture.

References

Allen, N. J., & Meyer, J. P. (1990). The measurement and antecedents of affective, continuance and normative commitment to the organization. *Journal of Occupational Psychology*, *63*(1), 1–18.

Ajzen, I. (1991). The theory of planned behavior. *Organizational behavior and Human Decision Processes*, *50*(2), 179–211.

Amayah, A. T. (2013). Determinants of knowledge sharing in a public sector organisation. *Journal of Knowledge Management*, *17*(3), 454–471.

Benson, J., & Brown, M. (2007). Knowledge workers: What keeps them committed; what turns them away. *Work, Employment and Society*, *21*(1), 121–141.

Blau, P. M. (1964). *Exchange and power in social life*. New Brunswick, NJ: Wiley.

Cabrera, A., & Cabrera, E. F. (2002). Knowledge-sharing dilemmas. *Organization Studies*, *23*(5), 687–710.

Camelo-Ordaz, C., Garcia-Cruz, J., Sousa-Ginel, E., & Valle-Cabrera, R. (2011). The influence of human resource management on knowledge sharing and innovation in Spain: The mediating role of affective commitment. *The International Journal of Human Resource Management*, *22*(07), 1442–1463.

Chai, S., Das, S., & Rao, H. R. (2011). Factors affecting bloggers' knowledge sharing: An investigation across gender. *Journal of Management Information Systems*, *28*(3), 309–342.

Cheah, C. S., Chong, V. S. W., Yeo, S. F., & Pee, K. W. (2016). An empirical study on factors affecting organizational commitment among generation X. *Procedia-Social and Behavioral Sciences*, *219*, 167–174.

Chiu, C. N., & Chen, H. H. (2016). The study of knowledge management capability and organizational effectiveness in Taiwanese public utility: The mediator role of organizational commitment, *SpringerPlus*, *5*(1), 15–20.

Cohen, A. (2007). Commitment before and after: An evaluation and reconceptualization of organizational commitment. *Human Resource Management Review*, *17*(3), 336–354.

Constant, D., Kiesler, S., & Sproull, L. (1994). What's mine is ours, or is it? A study of attitudes about information sharing. *Information Systems Research*, *5*(4), 400–421.

Cugueró-Escofet, N., Ficapal-Cusí, P., & Torrent-Sellens, J. (2019). Sustainable human resource management: How to create a knowledge sharing behavior through organizational justice, organizational support, satisfaction and commitment. *Sustainability*, *11*(19), 5419.

Curado, C., & Vieira, S. (2019). Trust, knowledge sharing and organizational commitment in SMEs. *Personnel Review*, *48*(6), 1449–1468.

Curtis, M. B., & Taylor, E. Z. (2018). Developmental mentoring, affective organizational commitment, and knowledge sharing in public accounting firms. *Journal of Knowledge Management*, *22*(1), 142–161.

Davenport, T. H., De Long, D. W., & Beers, M. C. (1998). Successful knowledge management projects. *Sloan Management Review*, *39*(2), 43–57.

Davoudi, S. M. M., & Fartash, K. (2012). The impact of knowledge sharing on organizational commitment of employees: Case study of Iranian manufacturing companies. *Pacific Business Review International*, *5*(2), 1–10.

Dunham, R. B., Grube, J. A., & Castaneda, M. B. (1994). Organizational commitment: The utility of an integrative definition. *Journal of Applied Psychology*, *79*(3), 370–380.

Froese, F. J., & Xiao, S. (2012). Work values, job satisfaction and organizational commitment in China. *The International Journal of Human Resource Management*, *23*(10), 2144–2162.

Goh, S. K., & Sandhu, M. S. (2013). Knowledge sharing among Malaysian academics: Influence of affective commitment and trust. *Electronic Journal of Knowledge Management*, *11*(1), 38–48.

Gouldner, A. W. (1960). The norm of reciprocity: A preliminary statement. *American Sociological Review*, *25*(2), 161–178.

Herzberg, F. (1966). *Work and the nature of man.* New York: World Publishing.

Herzberg, F., Mausner, B., & Snyderman, B. (1959). *The motivation to work.* New York: Wiley.

Hislop, D. (2003). Linking human resource management and knowledge management via commitment: A review and research agenda. *Employee Relations*, *25*(2), 182–202.

Ikechukwu, D., & Callystus, A. (2018). Knowledge management and organizational commitment. *International Journal of Business and Management Invention (IJBMI)*, *17*(3), 19–24.

Javadpour, A., & Samiei, S. (2017). Motivation and barriers to participation in virtual knowledge-sharing communities of practice. *Management Science Letters*, *7*(2), 81–86.

Jayasingam, S., Govindasamy, M., & Singh, S. K. G. (2016). Instilling affective commitment: Insights on what makes knowledge workers want to stay. *Management Research Review*, *39*(3), 266–288.

Jehanzeb, K., & Mohanty, J. (2019). The mediating role of organizational commitment between organizational justice and organizational citizenship behavior. *Personnel Review, 49*(2), 445–468.

Kianto, A., Vanhala, M., & Heilmann, P. (2016). The impact of knowledge management on job satisfaction. *Journal of Knowledge Management, 20*(4), 621–636.

Kucharska, W., & Bedford, D. A. (2019). Knowledge sharing and organizational culture dimensions: Does job satisfaction matter? *Electronic Journal of Knowledge Management, 17*(1), 1–18.

Lee, H., & Choi, B. (2003). Knowledge management enablers, processes, and organizational performance: An integrative view and empirical examination. *Journal of Management Information Systems, 20*(1), 179–228.

Li, J., Yuan, L., Ning, L., & Li-Ying, J. (2015). Knowledge sharing and affective commitment: The mediating role of psychological ownership. *Journal of Knowledge Management, 19*(6), 1146–1166.

Lin, H. F. (2007). Knowledge sharing and firm innovation capability: An empirical study. *International Journal of Manpower, 28*(3/4), 315–332.

Lin, X. (2015). How does procedural justice climate influence individual outcomes? An affective perspective. *Asia Pacific Journal of Management, 32*(3), 771–800.

Lin, H., & Hwang, Y. (2014). Do feelings matter? The effects of intrinsic benefits on individuals' commitment toward knowledge systems. *Computers in Human Behavior, 30*, 191–198.

Locke, E. A. (1969). What is job satisfaction? *Organizational Behavior and Human Performance, 4*(4), 309–336.

Ma, M., & Agarwal, R. (2007). Through a glass darkly: Information technology design, identity verification, and knowledge contribution in online communities. *Information, 18*(1), 42–67.

Malhotra, N., Budhwar, P., & Prowse, P. (2007). Linking rewards to commitment: An empirical investigation of four UK call centres. *The International Journal of Human Resource Management, 18*(12), 2095–2128.

Malik, M. S., & Kanwal, M. (2018). Impacts of organizational knowledge sharing practices on employees' job satisfaction. *Journal of Workplace Learning, 30*(1), 2–17.

Mathieu, J. E. (1991). A cross-level nonrecursive model of the antecedents of organizational commitment and satisfaction. *Journal of Applied Psychology, 76*(5), 607.

Mergel, I., Lazer, D., & Binz-Scharf, M. C. (2008). Lending a helping hand: Voluntary engagement in knowledge sharing. *International Journal of Learning and Change, 3*(1), 5–22.

Meyer, J. P., & Allen, N. J. (1991). A three-component conceptualization of organizational commitment. *Human Resource Management Review, 1*(1), 61–89.

Meyer, J. P., & Allen, N. J. (1997). *Commitment in the workplace: theory, research, and application*. Newbury Park, CA: Sage Publications.

Meyer, J. P., Stanley, D. J., Herscovitch, L., & Topolnytsky, L. (2002). Affective, continuance, and normative commitment to the organization: A meta-analysis of antecedents, correlates, and consequences. *Journal of Vocational Behavior, 61*(1), 20–52.

Naim, M. F., & Lenka, U. (2017). Linking knowledge sharing, competency development, and affective commitment: Evidence from Indian Gen Y employees. *Journal of Knowledge Management, 21*(4), 885–906.

Na-Nan, K., Kanthong, S., Joungtrakul, J., & Smith, I. D. (2020). Mediating effects of job satisfaction and organizational commitment between problems with performance appraisal and organizational citizenship behavior. *Journal of Open Innovation: Technology, Market, and Complexity*, 6(3), 64.

Nonaka, I. (1994). A dynamic theory of organizational knowledge creation. *Organization Science*, 5(1), 14–37.

Nonaka, I., & Konno, N. (1998). The concept of "Ba": Building a foundation for knowledge creation. *California Management Review*, 40(3), 40–54.

Nonaka, I., & Takeuchi, H. (1995). *The knowledge-creating company: How Japanese companies create the dynamics of innovation*. New York: Oxford University Press.

Ouakouak, M. L., & Ouedraogo, N. (2019). Fostering knowledge sharing and knowledge utilization. *Business Process Management Journal*, 25(4), 757–779.

Petty, M. M., McGee, G. W., & Cavender, J. W. (1984). A meta-analysis of the relationships between individual job satisfaction and individual performance. *Academy of Management Review*, 9(4), 712–721.

Rafique, G. M., Khalid, F., & Idrees, H. (2020). Impact of knowledge sharing on job satisfaction of university librarians in Pakistan. *Library Philosophy and Practice (E-journal)*, 4532. https://digitalcommons.unl.edu./libphilprac/4532

Rafique, G. M., & Mahmood, K. (2018). Relationship between knowledge sharing and job satisfaction: A systematic review. *Information and Learning Science*, 119(5/6), 295–312.

Rahman, S., Islam, M. Z., & Ahad Abdullah, A. D. (2017). Understanding factors affecting knowledge sharing: A proposed framework for Bangladesh's business organizations. *Journal of Science and Technology Policy Management*, 8(3), 275–298.

Rasdi, R. M., & Tangaraja, G. (2020). Knowledge-sharing behaviour in public service organisations: Determinants and the roles of affective commitment and normative commitment. *European Journal of Training and Development*. https://doi.org/10.1108/EJTD-02-2020-0028

Rehman, M., Mahmood, A. K., Salleh, R. & Amin, A. (2014). Job satisfaction and knowledge sharing among computer and information science faculty members: A case of Malaysian universities. *Research Journal of Applied Sciences, Engineering and Technology*, 7(4), 839–848.

Runar Edvardsson, I. (2008). HRM and knowledge management. *Employee Relations*, 30(5), 553–561.

Saeed, M. S. (2016). The impact of job satisfaction and knowledge sharing on employee performance. *Journal of Resources Development and Management*, 21, 16–23.

Saridakis, G., Lai, Y., Muñoz Torres, R. I., & Gourlay, S. (2018). Exploring the relationship between job satisfaction and organizational commitment: An instrumental variable approach. *The International Journal of Human Resource Management*, 31(13), 1739–1769.

Shahbaznezhad, H., Rashidirad, M., & Vaghefi, I. (2019). A systematic review of the antecedents of knowledge transfer: An actant-object view. *European Business Review*, 31(6), 970–995.

Shihabeldeen, H., Babiker, N., & Ahmed, N. (2020). Tacit knowledge sharing: The role of individual factors. *Management Science Letters*, 10(10), 2343–2350.

Singh, A. K., & Sharma, V. (2011). Knowledge management antecedents and its impact on employee satisfaction: A study on Indian telecommunication industries. *The Learning Organization*, 18(2), 115–130.

Suliman, A., & Al-Hosani, A. A. (2014). Job satisfaction and knowledge sharing: The case of the UAE. *Business Management and Economics*, 2(2), 24–33.

Suppiah, V., & Sandhu, M. S. (2011). Organisational culture's influence on tacit knowledge-sharing behaviour. *Journal of Knowledge Management, 15*(3), 462–477.

Swart, J., Kinnie, N., Van Rossenberg, Y., & Yalabik, Z. Y. (2014). Why should I share my knowledge? A multiple foci of commitment perspective. *Human Resource Management Journal, 24*(3), 269–289.

Tangaraja, G., Rasdi, R. M., Ismail, M., & Samah, B. A. (2015). Fostering knowledge sharing behaviour among public sector managers: A proposed model for the Malaysian public service. *Journal of Knowledge Management, 19*(1), 121–140.

Tangaraja, G., Rasdi, R. M., Samah, B. A., & Ismail, M. (2016). Knowledge sharing is knowledge transfer: A misconception in the literature. *Journal of Knowledge Management, 20*(4), 653–670.

Taylor, W. A., & Wright, G. H. (2004). Organizational readiness for successful knowledge sharing: Challenges for public sector managers. *Information Resources Management Journal (IRMJ), 17*(2), 22–37.

Teh, P. L., & Sun, H. (2012). Knowledge sharing, job attitudes and organisational citizenship behaviour. *Industrial Management & Data Systems, 112*(1), 64–82.

Valaei, N., & Rezaei, S. (2016). Job satisfaction and organizational commitment: An empirical investigation among ICT-SMEs. *Management Research Review, 39*(12), 1663–1694.

van den Hooff, B., & de Ridder, J. A. (2004). Knowledge sharing in context: The influence of organizational commitment, communication climate and CMC use on knowledge sharing. *Journal of Knowledge Management, 8*(6), 117–130.

Wang, Z., & Wang, N. (2012). Knowledge sharing, innovation and firm performance. *Expert Systems with Applications, 39*(10), 8899–8908.

Webster, J., Brown, G., Zweig, D., Connelly, C. E., Brodt, S., & Sitkin, S. (2008). Beyond knowledge sharing: Withholding knowledge at work. In J. J. Martocchio (Ed.), *Research in personnel and human resources management* (pp. 1–37). Bingley: Emerald Group Publishing Limited.

Welschen, J., Todorova, N., & Mills, A. M. (2012). An investigation of the impact of intrinsic motivation on organizational knowledge sharing. *International Journal of Knowledge Management (IJKM), 8*(2), 23–42.

Wright, T. A., & Cropanzano, R. (2000). Psychological well-being and job satisfaction as predictors of job performance. *Journal of Occupational Health Psychology, 5*(1), 84–94.

Yang, J. T. (2007). The impact of knowledge sharing on organizational learning and effectiveness. *Journal of Knowledge Management, 11*(2), 83–90.

Yesil, S. (2014). Exploring the links among organisational commitment, knowledge sharing and innovation capability in a public organisation. *European Journal of International Management, 8*(5), 506–527.

Yi, J. (2009). A measure of knowledge sharing behavior: Scale development and validation. *Knowledge Management Research and Practice, 7*(1), 65–81.

6 Establishing mentoring and coaching mechanisms for preserving indigenous knowledge

Hardo Firmana Given Grace Manik,
Andy Susilo Lukito-Budi and Nurul Indarti

Introduction

According to the United Nations, indigenous people are inheritors and practitioners of unique culture and seek recognition for their identities, ways of life, rights to their traditional lands and natural resources. The word "indigenous" is highly related to political framing (Hart, 2010). To be called "indigenous people," the original peoples of a territory must have been first subjected to a coloniser/state-making construct (or development) of some sort and create the dichotomy of "non-indigenous" and "indigenous" as a result. Thus, it insulates the socio-fabric of the communities from an encroaching capitalism-driven world culture ("development") and its related norms and lifestyles, such as Indonesia from Dutch settlement, Malaysia from British settlement and so on.

A literature review conducted by Chua *et al.* (2019) regarding studies of various indigenous communities in several Southeast Asian countries revealed various important findings: passing indigenous knowledge across generations results in community resilience. Forms of community resilience obtained from preserving indigenous knowledge are experienced, for example, the ethnic Brao community located on the Laos–Cambodia border as well as the ethnic Negrito community in Malaysia, which uses its geographical knowledge to avoid invaders or authorities who want to change their authentic, traditional way of life (Baird, 2010; Lye, 2013). Other examples are the ethnic *Kelabit* communities in Indonesia, which use traditional ecological knowledge to manage their natural resources and survive; indigenous communities in North Vietnam use agricultural knowledge to ensure their livelihood needs (Blanchet-Cohen & Urud, 2017; Bonnin and Turner, 2012). Considering the significant benefits of indigenous knowledge, as mentioned above, efforts to preserve indigenous knowledge are vital.

Furthermore, various indigenous communities in Southeast Asia have carried out the endeavour to preserve indigenous knowledge. The preserve action goes through storytelling by the traditional elders to younger generations about various artefacts and traditional practices that constitute communities' identities, such as rituals, folksongs to communicate such folk tales and myths, local languages, traditional dances, etc. (Chua *et al.*, 2019). This storytelling method, which is one of the personalisation strategy models, makes

DOI: 10.4324/9781003163824-8

sense because indigenous communities use a knowledge management system based on collective wisdom and memory, oral literature and cultural activities (Jasimuddin, Klein, & Connell, 2005; Yeo, Zaman, & Kulathuramaiyer, 2013). This process is different from the knowledge management system of business organisations, which is predominantly based on information technology/databases (Yeo, Zaman, & Kulathuramaiyer, 2013). However, the main challenge in this storytelling process is the reluctance of today's younger generations to consider themselves indigenous people as well as their tendency to prefer urban life and leave their indigenous communities (Chua *et al.*, 2019). Therefore, the mentoring and coaching method needs to be discussed and formulated to make the indigenous knowledge storytelling process more formal, planned and participatory and involve indigenous communities' younger generations to overcome this problem (Chua *et al.*, 2019; Medeni, 2006).

Mentoring refers to the process of transferring knowledge and wisdom (know-why) between the mentor and mentee; it aims to change the mentee's mindset and behaviour (Zentgraf, 2020). In indigenous communities, those who act as mentors are indigenous elders or knowledgeable adults, while mentees are younger people or less knowledgeable adults (Iseke, 2013). Meanwhile, *coaching* is the process of sharing idiosyncratic know-how that indigenous peoples possess and passed forward through traditional skill-intensive activities (Benyei, Arreola, & Reyes-García, 2020; Torri, 2012).

From an entrepreneurial perspective, indigenous community members who establish community-owned enterprises or traditional knowledge-intensive small and medium enterprises (SMEs) can benefit from the exchange of traditional knowledge through mentoring and coaching processes (Yokakul & Zawdie, 2011). Thus, considering the urgency to preserve indigenous knowledge more systematically, we aim to contribute a conceptual framework about mentoring and coaching mechanisms in indigenous communities by synthesising some concepts from the knowledge management literature.

The rest of this chapter follows the following outline. The first section presents the introduction as the motivation of this chapter. The second section discusses the process of indigenous knowledge formalisation by using some established concepts, such as the knowledge management cycle, the knowledge management maturity framework and the SECI model. The third section elaborates the mentoring and coaching mechanisms by integrating know-why and know-how into the dynamic process of knowing. Finally, this chapter presents a summary of the discussion.

The importance of incorporating knowledge management to preserve indigenous knowledge

Studying indigenous knowledge fundamentally shifts the mindset that knowledge not only comes from the West, universities, companies and modern non-profit organisations, but it can also come from the East, traditional elders, traditional weaving craftsmen, traditional musicians and other important local actors (Hart, 2010; Love, 2019). Indigenous knowledge[1] is idiosyncratic knowledge owned by an indigenous community that is rooted in perpetual ancestral traditions. Indigenous knowledge is accumulated through interdependent interactions between nature, culture and humans, and its use includes holistic aspects of life (Hart, 2010; Ngulube, 2002). Indigenous knowledge is local, oral and experiential and disseminated through narrative or metaphorical forms of storytelling. It could be symbolised by the form of various artefacts such as clothing, tools and weaponry as well as traditional know-how knowledge practice forms such as myth, customary law, local languages, traditional skills (e.g. sewing traditional clothes, expertise in traditional cuisines), etc. (Bolhassan, Cranefield, & Dorner, 2014).

In this chapter, we classify the elements of indigenous knowledge into two majors, yet inseparable, parts: know-why and know-how. Know-why represents the philosophically basic explanation of indigenous knowledge and the stories for building this knowledge and history to define the knowledge identity (e.g., history, folklore, language, etc.). In contrast, know-how epitomises the skills required to use knowledge philosophy or manifest it in a material/product/service (e.g., traditional handicrafts, traditional medicine, etc.).

Indigenous knowledge is, in fact, vulnerable because of the possibility of it being forever lost if not formally documented and preserved through established knowledge management activities (Hart, 2010). Indigenous knowledge is vitally important because the world needs knowledge diversity that can be contextually used to solve local problems (De Long & Fahey, 2000; Ngulube, 2002). Knowledge management concepts that are rapidly developing in this knowledge economy era can then be applied to preserve indigenous knowledge (Bolisani & Bratianu, 2018).

One of the knowledge management concepts that can help manage indigenous knowledge more formal and systematic is the knowledge management cycle, which starts with knowledge creation/acquisition, knowledge sharing, knowledge storage and knowledge protection (Dalkir, 2005). *Knowledge creation*, or *knowledge capture*, identifies and codifies knowledge and skills that exist in a community and/or from external sources (Dalkir, 2005). Significant indigenous people's knowledge is elders and senior craftsmen who have high levels of traditional skills (Iseke, 2013). *Knowledge sharing* is the process of exchanging or disseminating indigenous knowledge through various mediums, ranging from high-touch ones, such as internships, mentoring and coaching, to high-tech ones, such as sharing on social media. Finally, *knowledge protection* is a process for ensuring that unauthorised parties do not easily acquire the knowledge held by indigenous peoples. Rao (2006) stated that the intellectual property rights of indigenous knowledge have become a major issue that needs to be resolved immediately to gain legal protection and international recognition regarding the authenticity of a heritage.

Furthermore, the extent to which the development and application of indigenous communities' knowledge management cycles can be assessed using the knowledge management maturity metric (KMM) (Pour, Manian, & Yazdani, 2016). KMM incorporates three key process areas: knowledge management (i.e., people), process and technology (DeTienne *et al.*, 2004;

Pee & Kankanhalli, 2009). The *people* aspect is culture, strategy and policy; the *process* aspect refers to key knowledge management activities, such as knowledge creation, sharing and protection and the *technology* aspect (Pee & Kankanhalli, 2009). Table 6.1, adapted from Pee and Kankanhalli's study (2009), contains KMMs for indigenous peoples' knowledge management.

As described in Table 6.1, five key phases function as a blueprint for seeing the commitment and efforts of indigenous communities in formalising their indigenous knowledge: initial, aware, defined, managed and optimising. When at the initial level, the indigenous community has little or no willingness to formally manage its indigenous knowledge; preserving indigenous knowledge has not become the community's main discourse. At the awareness stage, the indigenous community has realised the importance of managing its indigenous knowledge. The trigger is the awareness of some community members who lack of know-how to do this. Further, many indigenous communities actively promote knowledge management and initiate technological infrastructures to support knowledge management at the defined level. The creation, sharing and protection of knowledge have been designed and implemented at this level. Indigenous communities in the managed phase have used knowledge management as the main foundation for all activities, have begun to measure the quantitative and qualitative and beneficial impacts of knowledge management and have adopted an established knowledge management system. Finally, this knowledge management system has been sustainably institutionalised in indigenous communities and their knowledge management systems at the optimising stage.

Another relevant framework for managing indigenous knowledge is the SECI model proposed by Nonaka and Takeuchi (1995). The model describes the interaction between tacit and explicit knowledge via four main activities, i.e., socialisation, externalisation, combination and internalisation (SECI). Socialisation is the process of creating and sharing tacit knowledge, which indigenous peoples do naturally through face-to-face conversations, storytelling, music, dance and apprenticeships. Externalisation is converting tacit knowledge to explicit information where people who have traditional knowledge manifest their knowledge into documents, paintings, pictures, inscriptions and various other artefacts so that other people can access that knowledge. Nonetheless, many cases can capture the culture into written language related to the colonialisation era, such as Christian missionaries or central "stated-force education." Originally, many indigenous people do not have the ability per se to record their culture or purposefully keep themselves from having written/artistic artefacts as means of fleeing from the state (Scott, 2009). The change from tacit knowledge to explicit knowledge, called combination, occurs when various codified knowledge produces new traditional knowledge. Finally, internalisation is converting explicit knowledge into tacit knowledge, which occurs through experiencing traditional values and philosophies or learning by practising traditional skills. In sum, the concept of the knowledge management cycle and the SECI model join together as the building blocks of an indigenous community's mentoring and coaching mechanisms. The next section explains these mechanisms.

Table 6.1 Knowledge management maturity metric to formalise the management of indigenous knowledge

Maturity level	General description	Key process areas		
		People	*Process*	*Technology*
1 Initial	Little or no attention to formally managing indigenous knowledge	Indigenous community is not aware of the need to formally manage knowledge resources	There are no formal processes within indigenous peoples to acquire, share and reuse organisational knowledge	There is no specific knowledge management infrastructure or technology (e.g. online applications, online information systems) that is utilised by indigenous peoples
2 Aware	Indigenous community is aware of and have the intention of managing their organisational knowledge, but may not know-how to do it	Indigenous community is aware of the need to carry out knowledge management	Knowledge indispensable for carrying out indigenous activities and traditional skills are being documented (for example, archiving ancient documents)	Knowledge management technology pilot project initiated by a handful of people in indigenous peoples (not necessarily by the elders)
3 Defined	Indigenous community has equipped basic infrastructure to support knowledge management (e.g. computers, internet access, etc.)	a Traditional elders are aware of their role in promoting knowledge management b Basic training for indigenous community on knowledge management is provided c A knowledge management strategy is designed d The individual roles of each member of indigenous community to support knowledge management are elaborated	a The processes for management of information and knowledge content are carried out. b Quantitative and qualitative metrics are used to measure the increase in productivity and the smooth running of indigenous community's activities driven by knowledge management	a The basic infrastructure for knowledge management is provided in indigenous community, such as computers, Wi-Fi, server systems, etc. b Several knowledge management technology projects have been initiated (for example, the use of big data, cloud computing, etc.)

(*Continued*)

Maturity level	General description	Key process areas		
		People	Process	Technology
4 Managed	Knowledge management initiatives are well established in indigenous community	General knowledge management approaches and strategies have been standardised in indigenous community as indicated by the existence of regularly updated documents, videos, etc.	There are quantitative and qualitative measures of the impact of knowledge management processes (e.g. using productivity metrics) on indigenous community	Fully available indigenous knowledge management systems based on digital technology
5 Optimising	a Knowledge management is fully integrated within indigenous community and continues to be improved b Knowledge management is an automatic component in any organisational process of indigenous community	There is a culture of sharing knowledge between people in indigenous community and with external parties	a Knowledge management processes are constantly being reviewed and improved b Existing knowledge management processes can easily be adapted to meet external environmental challenges	Indigenous knowledge management systems/infrastructures are continuously improved and innovated

Source: Adapted from Pee and Kankanhalli (2009).

Coaching and mentoring mechanisms

Theoretical basis, definition and approaches

Mentoring and coaching are learning activities known as the soft aspects of knowledge management (Dalkir, 2005). Argyris and Schon (1978) differentiated learning into two types: single-loop learning and double-loop learning. *Single-loop learning* is learning to improve things without changing the system or order. In contrast, *double-loop learning* aims to change status quo and challenge underlying assumptions and values or, in other words, to question things that are "taken for granted" (Argyris & Schon, 1978). Single-loop learning generally manifests itself in operational management activities, such as working on instructions from higher-ups in the social hierarchy, monitoring daily performance, making sure others are motivated to work on tasks and supplying missing skills or improving existing ones. Double-loop learning represents in the activities of creating new paradigms, processes and products, adapting to external environmental shocks and acting to change the existing order.

There is a fundamental difference between mentoring and coaching. Mentoring is the process of transferring knowledge, which is dominant in the know-why dimension. It aims to assist mentees in finding their own life goals and solving problems (Clutterbuck, 2005). In contrast, coaching refers to the process of transferring technical know-how and focuses on mastering a certain level of expertise (Zentgraf, 2020).

With their conceptual elucidation, Brockbank and McGill (2006) describe several mentoring models: functionalist, engagement and evolutionary. *Functionalist mentoring* is an approach that encourages juniors/mentees to adapt to the context of a hierarchical structure (i.e., older mentors have power over their mentees). The learning process in functionalist mentoring is more about the transmission of knowledge by giving advice and directions. *Engagement mentoring* is a more dialogical approach than the functionalist one. Engagement respects the mentee's views, emotions and motivations in a more nurturing way. The learning outcome of these two mentoring models is compliance and conformity to the structure, system and identity of the organisation/community, or in other words, maintaining the status quo. Finally, *evolutionary mentoring* is an approach centred on developing a mentee's critical mind (i.e., a significant change in perspective) and aims to realise organisational/community transformation as a learning goal. Functionalist and engagement mentoring is single-loop learning, while evolutionary mentoring is double-loop learning (Brockbank & McGill, 2006). The functionalist and engagement mentoring approaches are prominent in describing the learning process in indigenous communities because the obligation to respect ancestors and maintain a long-established socio-cultural order is the main learning goal (Brockbank & McGill, 2006; Haines *et al.*, 2017) (Table 6.2).

Table 6.2 Summary of mentoring approaches

Approaches	Key points		
	Purpose	*Process*	*Learning outcome*
Functionalist mentoring	Maintaining status quo or conformity to community order/systems	Directive, less dialogic or paying less attention to mentee's views	Personal mindset and behaviour improvement
Engagement mentoring	Maintaining status quo or conformity to community order/systems	Respects mentee's subjective worldview, more dialogic	Personal mindset and behaviour improvement
Evolutionary mentoring	Changing the world	Critical dialogue, empowering the mentees	Community order transformation

Source: Adapted from Brockbank and McGill (2006).

The mentoring process in indigenous communities goes through storytelling about identity, ranging from their history, traditions, folklore, customary law and noble philosophies via cultural activities or indigenous community-operated schools (Fernández-Llamazares & Cabeza, 2018; Swap *et al.*, 2001). The indigenous elders or knowledgeable adults act as mentors/storytellers and the less knowledgeable younger generations are the mentees (Cropper, Luna, & McLean, 2015; Haines *et al.*, 2017; Iseke, 2013). In contrast to state-owned and private schools that use government curriculum outline (mainstream national education), indigenous community-owned schools are generally self-funded and the curricula are based primarily on the experiential learning of traditions that are more independent from knowledge and worldviews outside its culture (Shizha, 2013).

To adapt to technological developments and ensure the acceptance of mentoring among the millennial and post-millennial generations of indigenous communities, Willox, Harper, and Edge (2013) further propose adopting the concept of digital storytelling in indigenous community-owned schools. Nowadays, digital technology can record every mentoring activity process in indigenous schools, such as using a mobile smartphone application (Hidayat *et al.*, 2016). It allows for more real-time mentoring and storytelling and ensures that shared knowledge is not lost because it is stored on an internet server and can reach a wide range of people, regardless of time and geographic constraints (Davis, 2011).

Involvement in group meeting can also increase the participation of indigenous people. They can share their personal stories about their traditions in the meeting (Whyte & Classen, 2012). Furthermore, Inuit communities in Canada are examples of how they have successfully practised digital storytelling (Cunsolo Willox, Harper, & Edge, 2013). A transdisciplinary team of indigenous and non-indigenous researchers in Canada developed a

Table 6.3 Summary of coaching approaches

Approaches	Key Points		
	Purpose	*Process*	*Learning outcome*
Functionalist coaching	Maintaining status quo or conformity to established skill standards in community	Directive, paying less attention to coachee's initiative to develop new or modified skills	Skill improvement
Engagement coaching	Maintaining status quo or conformity to established skill standards in community	Respects coachee's initiative, coach and coachee have good relationship	Skill improvement
Evolutionary coaching	Innovating the community's standard and procedure	Fostering transformative thinking, adopting new technological updates	Creative and innovative skill developments

Source: Adapted from Brockbank and McGill (2006).

digital platform that allowed the Inuit elders and Inuit community members to share stories about their lives in a participatory manner. The result is a powerful and rich source of data related to the life of the Inuit community, which can be accessed and used for mentoring and is enjoyed by community members and even the wider community outside the Inuit community (Cunsolo Willox, Harper, & Edge, 2013).

The next discussion is about coaching. Like mentoring, the coaching process is divided into functionalist, engagement and evolutionary (Brockbank & McGill, 2006). *Functionalist coaching* emphasises the process of enhancing a person's certain skills, with the coach as the central actor of conformity to established procedures and skill standards. *Engagement coaching* has the same learning outcome as functionalist coaching but is about creating a good interpersonal relationship with the coachee. Lastly, *evolutionary coaching* involves the coach building a close relationship with the trained person and fostering critical and transformative thinking that s/he can use to develop creativity and innovation in skills development. In indigenous communities, the functionalist coaching approach and engagement arguably are more prominent because traditional skills are considered a noble heritage and must be preserved and cannot be tampered with (Table 6.3).

Furthermore, the community's practitioners carry out the coaching process of indigenous skills, such as the traditional-handicraft craftsman community, the traditional culinary community and the traditional music community. Referring to the knowledge management literature, these communities can be called indigenous CoPs because they contain three required elements: domain, community and practice (Medeni, 2006; Wenger,

McDermott, & Snyder, 2002). *Domain* in indigenous CoPs reflects a common identity or interest and shared competence that differentiates its members from other people. The shared skills exemplified above are examples of domains. *Community* describes a sense of "commune" or togetherness and solidarity, engagement in joint activities and volunteering to share information and knowledge. Indigenous communities own and do these activities because they comprise of cohesive networks. Finally, *practice* indicates that an indigenous CoP is a collection of practitioners/coaches that develop shared experiences, tools and ways of dealing with problems. An indigenous CoP is a living repository of traditional know-how (Wenger, McDermott, & Snyder, 2002).

Wenger, McDermott, and Snyder (2002) further describe the life cycle of a CoP, which can be contextualised to explain the staging process of an indigenous CoP: potential, coalescing, maturing, stewardship and transformation.

☐ Stage 1: *Potential.* Informal groups usually begin to form when several traditional practitioners (coaches) in indigenous communities frequently discuss certain topics and share insights, stories and techniques. This loose network is an embryo of a CoP, as people start to see their relationship in the shared domain. The more people discussing this potential community experience significant benefits, the lesser the energy needed to sustain this community. The organisers of this potential indigenous CoP then need to define the community's focus on the topics' scopes and the problems that are worth sharing about and build good relationships between members. These organisers are usually an indigenous CoP's well-respected coaches/practitioners.

☐ Stage 2: *Coalescing.* It is the official stage for launching the CoP's events and communicating them to all the indigenous communities' members and external parties. This recognition is important for creating a sense of familiarity among various parties regarding this CoP. In other words, the held events; such as traditional skills training or regularly sharing about practical problems, are the heartbeat of a CoP. Another important issue in this stage is maintaining the energy that has been available since the first stage. A CoP is increasingly valuable for its members when senior practitioners/coaches actively initiate and create a comfortable learning climate, and junior practitioners/coachees respond passionately.

☐ Stage 3: *Maturing.* After starting an indigenous CoP community, the next crucial stage is sustaining it. The stability of the relationships between the CoP's members is dynamic because it contains a relationship hierarchy; the arrival of new members/coachees can disrupt existing interactional patterns and the existence of embedded subgroups. Certainly, various adjustments take place so that the community's harmony is maintained, such as listing the expectations of each new member/coachee and administering which coach/senior practitioner will be the new members/coachees' companion. The coaches/senior practitioners will explain the community's objectives, history, scope of activities and interaction norms so that new members/coachees can immediately move from being peripheral actors to central actors. Lave and Wenger (1991, p. 40) term this process "legitimate peripheral participation."

More specifically, at this third stage, another major challenge is to redefine the community's focus, roles and boundaries. The CoP is shifting from predominantly sharing practical/simple tips to developing a body of knowledge and designing a knowledge repository. Referring to the level of knowledge management maturity, this stage is called the "managed" level. It is a level when the indigenous CoP has designed and managed its knowledge management system with digital technology support.

☐ Stage 4: *Stewardship*. The main objective of this stage is to maintain the solidity of indigenous CoPs. The challenge of achieving the goal of this stage is having a strong sense of ownership in their domain (e.g., the developed ideas, the established norms and regulation in written guidelines, etc.) from both senior and junior practitioners/coaches. The bond disrupts the community's relationship dynamics due to a strong sense of belonging or reluctance to share knowledge. The CoP organiser should possess a sufficient sensitivity level on this situation and immediately enact the necessary tactical solutions. One way is that the CoP organiser can organise a renewal workshop to solidify the CoP. This workshop aims to remind all members that the nature of and motivation for the formation of indigenous CoPs is "knowledge/skill transfer is power" instead of "having knowledge/skill is power." This workshop can redefine whether the community's activity process remains informal or more systematically designed while redefining community boundaries in terms of accepting new members/coachees. Apart from holding this rejuvenation workshop, indigenous CoPs can also refresh themselves by inviting people and groups outside the community (e.g., other indigenous CoPs, associations and academics). The invitees are the ones who have the same desire to talk, share experiences and help build new knowledge and approaches. This method can also be of significant help because external parties can enlighten indigenous CoPs by bringing new perspectives and ideas.

☐ Stage 5: *Transformation*. Transformation. As the life cycle is the world's natural law, indigenous CoPs can also experience an end. Some of the reasons are that CoPs can lose energy; also, members become bored and need new available skills in other communities. In this situation, the old indigenous CoPs become just a social club. Stopping the old indigenous CoP and making a new one is not a problem when all junior practitioners/coachees have mastered the traditional know-how according to the indigenous community's established standards that have been passed from generation to generation. Also, all processes experienced by indigenous CoPs, from its formation throughout its transformation, should be documented as being the best practices by the indigenous CoP organiser and other indigenous communities can adopt that.

Detailed implementation of mentoring and coaching in an indigenous community

Kram (1988) states four phases of a mentor/mentee relationship: initiation, cultivation, separation and redefinition. Initiation is the phase in which the mentor and mentee find matching backgrounds and mutual interests and, together, begin to grow shared enthusiasm. Clutterbuck (2005) terms this process as "rapport building." Cultivation is the phase in which the emotional bond between the mentor and mentee becomes stronger as the interactions between them increase. Separation is the stage when a mentor evaluates the relationship's added value, and the mentee shows a desire to learn independently. This phase is also called "winding down" (Clutterbuck, 2005). The final phase is redefinition, in which the mentor and mentee redefine their relationship and begin to build an equal or peer-like relationship.

Reflecting on the behavioural patterns of these four phases, there are three relationship patterns that emerge as follows: first, the mentees have a dependent relationship with the mentor during the initiation and cultivation

Table 6.4 Stages of the mentoring relationship in indigenous communities

Phase	Definition	Turning points
Initiation	A period of six months to a year when the relationship begins	a Expectations and chemistry are met; the elders or mentors provide teaching and tasks; mentees provide technical assistance, respect and desire to be mentored. b There are opportunities for interaction around works tasks.
Cultivation	A period of two to five years when the maximum psychosocial functions are provided	a Both mentor and mentee continue to benefit from the relationship. b Opportunities for meaningful and more frequent interaction increase. c Emotional bond deepens and intimacy increases.
Separation	A period of six months to two years after a significant change in the structural role relationship and/or in the emotional experience of the relationship.	a Mentee no longer wants specific guidance but rather the opportunity to learn more autonomously. b Mentor is less available to provide mentoring functions.
Redefinition	Redefining relationship, making it a more peer-like friendship.	a Stresses of separation diminish, and new relationships are formed. b The mentor relationship is no longer needed in its previous form. c Peer status is achieved.

Source: Adapted from Kram (1988).

Table 6.5 The flow model of coaching process

Stages	Key activities
Establishing relationship	Building shared commitment, discussing duration of coaching in CoP
Recognising openings	Coachee's difficulties in practising certain skills trigger a personalised recognition
Observation and assessment	Exploring coachee's history and desire about the dreamed skills
Enrolment	Coaching is started
Coaching conversations	Practising and improving skills

Source: Adapted from Flaherty (1999).

phases, second, an independent relationship in the separation phase and third, an interdependent relationship in the redefinition phase (Table 6.4).

Following the logic of a functionalist approach and engagement closer to an indigenous CoP's situation, Brockbank and McGill (2006) propose using the FLOW model from Flaherty (1999) to depict a CoP's coaching process. The FLOW model consists of five steps, i.e., establishing the relationship, recognising an opening theme for coaching, observing/assessing, enrolling the coachee and having coaching conversations. The first stage is to establish a CoP-related relationship based on shared commitment, mutual trust, mutual respect and freedom of expression. The functionalist and engagement coaching approaches allow for building relationships based on historical identity in indigenous traditions. The second stage is recognising openings. The basic idea is that the coaching process is opened and offered to the CoP. Usually, these steps are triggered by recognising certain difficulties or problems faced in the jobs. In the third stage, the coach conducts observations and assessments to explore the coachee's concerns, interests, history, desires, skills and qualities. The next stage is when the coachee agrees to begin a coaching project in the CoP. The last stage is coaching conversations, which involve the process of practising and developing skills (Table 6.5).

Mentoring and coaching as an integrated mechanism

An indigenous community member is expected to master indigenous knowledge to confirm his/her cultural identity or to not become uprooted, to understand a rite of passage in his/her culture, to honour his/her ancestors and to contribute to a world order that is more pro-environmental and pro-sustainable human development (Dweba & Mearns, 2011). At this point, the individual can be called a hero who can prevent the destruction of indigenous knowledge.

The individual learning process starts from the mentoring process or focuses on learning the know-why dimension of indigenous knowledge.

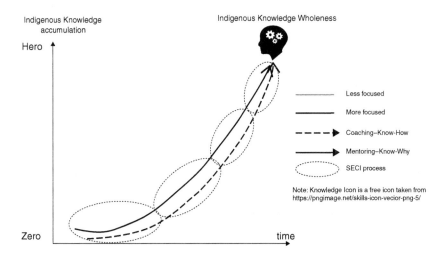

Figure 6.1 Illustrates the integrated process of mentoring (focusing on the know-why) and coaching (focusing on the know-how) of indigenous knowledge.

The know-why dimension is about philosophy and values/worldview, ancestral history, traditional language, traditions, spirituality, economics and the social, cultural, agricultural, maritime and environmental. This know-why is fundamental knowledge that must be studied so that individuals in indigenous communities can comprehensively recognise their own identity. As time goes by and the accumulated know-why is absorbed, internalised and applied by an individual, the next process is learning about the know-how.

The dimension of indigenous knowledge know-how is about the skills required to make unique and authentic artefacts (e.g., traditional handicrafts, traditional tools and weapons, traditional clothing, etc.), tangible symbols or identities of an indigenous community. These artefacts function for least two objectives: (a) as tools used in everyday life and (b) as commodities that are traded or sold (Dweba & Mearns, 2011).

In Figure 6.1, the shape of the concave or convex curves of the mentoring and coaching mechanisms reflects the stages that each mechanism should endeavour. In other words, this represents the interactive learning curve experienced by the mentor and mentee as well as by the coach and coachee. We hypothesised that the interactive process is not yet intensive at the introductory interaction stage but will rise dramatically when both parties share mutual understanding and agreement.

As illustrated in Figure 6.1, the SECI process occurs during the dynamics of mentoring and coaching. Nonaka and Takeuchi (1995) developed the SECI model by combining explicit and tacit knowledge and resulting in four activity cycles: socialisation, externalisation, combination and internalisation.

Socialisation is the conversion of knowledge from tacit to tacit. The socialisation occurs when face-to-face meetings transpire between mentors and mentees in an indigenous community-owned school or via a coach with his/her coachees in an indigenous CoP. The mentee/coachee absorbs the mentor/coach's knowledge by observing and imitating the mentor's exemplary attitudes and behaviour. This process is also known as social learning (Bandura, 1977).

Externalisation is the conversion of knowledge from tacit to explicit, which mentors and coaches can do by making tutorial documents or videos about their knowledge from which the mentee/coachee can learn. Mentees and coachees can also produce similar documents and videos about knowledge descriptions and the practice of making certain traditional artefacts they learned about during the mentoring and coaching process.

Combination is the conversion of knowledge into explicit knowledge, manifested in the mentor and coach's efforts to synthesise various explicit knowledge in documents and videos to produce new or advanced traditional knowledge for the mentees/coaches to learn. Mentees/coachees can also carry out similar activities so that mentors/coaches can evaluate the growth of their accumulated knowledge.

Finally, *internalisation* is the conversion of knowledge from explicit to tacit. Mentors and coaches can apply the new, explicit knowledge they have acquired to further learning material for mentees/coachees in this process. Mentees and coachees can apply explicit knowledge directly in documents and videos that were synthesised during the combination stage. The knowledge spiral that continues to grow in the SECI cycle means that every individual who follows the mentoring and coaching process diligently will acquire a holistic accumulation of indigenous knowledge (i.e., know-why and know-how) from day to day, month to month and year to year. The end of the spiral will ideally achieve the wholeness of tacit and descriptive forms of the targeted indigenous knowledge.

Summary

This chapter is an initial attempt to anticipate the threat of indigenous knowledge of becoming oblivion and to stimulate further discourse by using some of the established concepts in the literature on knowledge management and mentoring/coaching. We contribute by depicting a detailed process or mechanism through which an indigenous community member can master indigenous knowledge in its wholeness (i.e., know-why and know-how).

The next important note that must be paid attention to by an indigenous community is the tension between innovation and tradition. Indigenous communities indeed act as custodians of traditional knowledge, but they cannot close themselves to the rapidly changing conditions of human society and technology. This tension must be mitigated by re-examining mentoring and coaching approaches that maintain the status quo (e.g., functionalism and engagement) and by starting to adopt an evolutionary mentoring and coaching approach to a level that does not destabilise an indigenous community's harmonious life. Investigating this issue is an appealing research agenda.

This chapter also contributes to generating ideas for further studies in this area. For instance, the coaching and mentoring mechanisms of specific indigenous knowledge reveal a new research avenue for investigating how these two mechanisms interact; we can compare the mechanisms' interactions to more established knowledge transfers cases. This chapter also brings new insight into details about the knowledge transfer process through an organisational learning framework. A question such as "Can these two mechanisms follow the established timeline of a framework, or would there be necessary adjustments?" would be a good spark for explorative research. In light of this, the indigenous knowledge arena can strengthen its position among other fields in the knowledge management domain.

Note

1 Scholars use various terms when referring to indigenous knowledge, such as local knowledge, rural people's knowledge and traditional knowledge (Hart, 2010). This chapter uses the terms indigenous knowledge and traditional knowledge interchangeably.

References

Argyris, C., & Schon, D.A. (1978). Organizational learning: A theory of action perspective. Reading, MA: Addison-Wesley.

Bandura, A. (1977). *Social learning theory.* Prentice Hall.

Benyei, P., Arreola, G., & Reyes-García, V. (2020). Storing and sharing: A review of indigenous and local knowledge conservation initiatives. *Ambio*, 49(1), 218–230.

Bolhassan, R., Cranefield, J., & Dorner, D. (2014). Indigenous knowledge sharing in Sarawak: A system-level view and its implications for the cultural heritage sector. Proceedings of the Annual Hawaii International Conference on System Sciences, 3378–3388.

Bolisani, E., & Bratianu, C. (2018). *Emergent knowledge strategies.* Cham: Springer International Publishing.

Brockbank, A., & McGill, I. (2006). *Facilitating reflective learning through mentoring & coaching.* London: Kogan Page.

Chua, R.Y., Kadirvelu, A., Yasin, S., Choudhry, F.R., & Park, M.S.A. (2019). The cultural, family and community factors for resilience in Southeast Asian indigenous communities: A systematic review. *Journal of Community Psychology*, 47(7), 1750–1771.

Clutterbuck, D. (2005). Establishing and maintaining mentoring relationships: An overview of mentor and mentee competencies. *SA Journal of Human Resource Management*, 3(3), 2–9.

Cropper, A.D., Luna, R.E., & McLean, E.L. (2015). Scientific storytelling: From up in the clouds to down to earth... A new approach to mentoring. ISEC 2015-5th IEEE Integrated STEM Education Conference, 252–257.

Cunsolo Willox, A., Harper, S.L., & Edge, V.L. (2013). Storytelling in a digital age: Digital storytelling as an emerging narrative method for preserving and promoting indigenous oral wisdom. *Qualitative Research*, 13(2), 127–147.

Dalkir, K. (2005). *Knowledge management in theory and practice.* Boston, MA: Elsevier Inc.

Davis, D. (2011). Intergenerational digital storytelling: A sustainable community initiative with inner-city residents. *Visual Communication*, 10(4), 527–540.

De Long, D.W., & Fahey, L. (2000). Diagnosing cultural barriers to knowledge management. *Academy of Management Executive*, 14(4), 113–127.

DeTienne, K.B., Dyer, G., Hoopes, C., & Harris, S. (2004). Toward a model of effective knowledge management and directions for future research: Culture, leadership, and CKOs. *Journal of Leadership & Organizational Studies*, 10(4), 26–43.

Dweba, T.P., & Mearns, M.A. (2011). Conserving indigenous knowledge as the key to the current and future use of traditional vegetables. *International Journal of Information Management*, 31(6), 564–571.

Fernández-Llamazares, Á., & Cabeza, M. (2018). Rediscovering the potential of indigenous storytelling for conservation practice. *Conservation Letters*, 11(3), 1–12.

Flaherty, J. (1999). *Coaching evoking excellence in others.* Elsevier Inc.

Haines, J., Du, J.T., Geursen, G., Gao, J., & Trevorrow, E. (2017). Understanding elders' knowledge creation to strengthen indigenous ethical knowledge sharing. *Information Research*, 22(4), 8.

Hart, M.A. (2010). Indigenous worldviews, knowledge, and research: The development of an indigenous research paradigm. *Journal of Indigenous Voices in Social Work*, 1(1), 1–16.

Hidayat, E., Lukman, Noprisson, H., Sensuse, D.I., Sucahyo, Y.G., & Putra, E.D. (2016). Development of mobile application for documenting traditional knowledge in Indonesia. 2016 IEEE Student Conference on Research and Development (SCOReD), 1–5.

Iseke, J. (2013). Indigenous storytelling as research. *International Review of Qualitative Research*, 6(4), 559–577.

Jasimuddin, S.M., Klein, J.H., & Connell, C. (2005). The paradox of using tacit and explicit knowledge strategies to face dilemmas. *Management Decision*, 43(1), 102–112.

Kram, K. (1988). *Mentoring at work.* Lanham: University Press of America.

Lave, J., & Wenger, E. (1991). *Situated learning legitimate peripheral participation.* Cambridge University Press.

Love, T.R. (2019). Indigenous knowledges, priorities and processes in qualitative organization and management research: State of the field. *Qualitative Research in Organizations and Management: An International Journal*, 15(1), 6–20.

Medeni, T.D. (2006). Living tradition of "Yaren Talks" as an indigenous community of practice in today's knowledge society. In E. Coakes & S. Clarke (Eds.), *Encyclopedia of communities of practice in information and knowledge management* (pp. 353–356). London: Idea Group Publishing.

Ngulube, P. (2002). Managing and preserving indigenous knowledge in the knowledge management era: Challenges and opportunities for information professionals. *Information Development*, 18(2), 95–102.

Nonaka, I., & Takeuchi, H. (1995). *The knowledge-creating company.* New York: Oxford University Press.

Pee, L.G., & Kankanhalli, A. (2009). A model of organisational knowledge management maturity based on people, process, and technology. *Journal of Information and Knowledge Management*, 8(2), 79–99.

Pour, M.J., Manian, A., & Yazdani, H.R. (2016). A theoretical and methodological examination of knowledge management maturity models: A systematic review. *International Journal of Business Information Systems*, 23(3), 330–352.

Rao, S.S. (2006). Indigenous knowledge organization: An Indian scenario. *International Journal of Information Management*, 26, 224–233. https://doi.org/10.1016/j.ijinfomgt.2006.02.003

Shizha, E. (2013). Reclaiming our indigenous voices: The problem with postcolonial Sub-Saharan African school curriculum. *Journal of Indigenous Social Development*, 2(1), 1–18.

Swap, W., Leonard, D., Shields, M., & Abrams, L. (2001). Using mentoring and storytelling to transfer knowledge in the workplace. *Journal of Management Information Systems*, 18(1), 95–114.

Torri, M.C. (2012). The jamu system: Linking small-scale enterprises, traditional knowledge and social empowerment? *International Journal of Entrepreneurship and Small Business*, 15(4), 488–501.

Wenger, E., McDermott, R., & Snyder, W.M. (2002). *Cultivating communities of practice: A guide to managing knowledge.* Harvard Business School Press.

Whyte, G., & Classen, S. (2012). Using storytelling to elicit tacit knowledge from SMEs. *Journal of Knowledge Management*, 16(6), 950–962.

Yeo, A.W., Zaman, T., & Kulathuramaiyer, N. (2013). Indigenous knowledge management in the kelabit community in eastern Malaysia: Insights and reflections for contemporary KM design. *International Journal of Sociotechnology and Knowledge Development*, 5(1), 23–36.

Yokakul, N., & Zawdie, G. (2011). The knowledge sphere, social capital and growth of indigenous knowledge-based SMEs in the Thai dessert industry. *Science and Public Policy*, 38(1), 19–29.

Zentgraf, L.L. (2020). Mentoring reality: From concepts and theory to real expertise and the mentor's point of view. *International Journal of Mentoring and Coaching in Education*, 9(4), 427–443.

7 Determinants of knowledge sharing behaviours among merchant navy officers

Capt. Shankar A Govindasamy and Omkar Dastane

Introduction

In the fast changing business world today, knowledge has become the backbone of every organisation for survival in competitive environment (Fullwood, Rowley, & McLean, 2019). Thus, systematic and effective knowledge management (KM) strategy has been recognised as an innovative way to capture, store and disseminate useful knowledge in the organisation (Dong, Bartol, Zhang, & Li, 2017). Though KM involves various processes, knowledge sharing (KS) is the primary process that impacts the success of KM (Amayah, 2013). The positive impacts of KS have been associated with organisational effectiveness in achieving competitive advantage (Mueller, 2012), firm innovation capability (Lin, 2007b) and increased productivity (Linm, 2007c). Additionally, KS is also beneficial for individual performances (Fullwood, Rowley, & Delbridge, 2019), individual creativity, skill development (Dong, Bartol, Zhang, & Li, 2017), team effectiveness and enhancements (Mueller, 2012). Despite being the most important KM process, KS is the most difficult process to implement because knowledge resides in employees' minds and does not come naturally for certain individuals. Previous studies have highlighted that organisations often fail to capture what employees know due to lack of understanding of which factors influence the dissemination of knowledge in an organisation (Fullwood, Rowley, & Delbridge, 2019). Therefore, the ultimatum is to determine what motivates and encourages employees to share their knowledge with others.

Shipping, the lifeline of world economies, is perhaps the most international and oldest industries of all the world's greatest industries (UNCTAD, 2018). In Malaysia, the shipping industry is a significant contributor to the Malaysian Economy. In 2019, Malaysia's total trade was RM1.835 trillion and of these 98.4% of trade is carried by sea (MATRADE, 2019). In spite of that, with globalisation and uncertainty in market situation, the shipping companies are facing tremendous pressures on their business strategies and operations (Ha & Seo, 2017). The entire industry is experiencing numerous challenges concerning environmental regulation, changes in trade patterns, security risks, rising cost and high mobility and turnover of employees

DOI: 10.4324/9781003163824-9

(Shemon, Hasan, & Kadir, 2019). According to the Marine Department Malaysia (MARDEP), high mobility and shortage of seafarers has caused a loss of RM30 million outflow a month (MARDEP, 2016). This has made shipping companies to realise that the traditional business practices concentrating on short-term financial profit will no longer guarantee survival (Luu, 2014).

Shipping companies are required to improve their knowledge and competencies in a closer relationship within organisation and also the entire maritime cluster (Fei, Chen, & Chen, 2009). Knowledge resource and innovation are crucial to build an enduring competitive advantage and uphold their capability to create distinctive competitive advantage. In addition, losing critical business knowledge has become an issue for the entire industry. In such dire situation, the shipping industry must engage on knowledge management strategy and motivate the officers to embrace sharing and transferring knowledge, with aim to retain the tacit knowledge within the company. As a result, the negative effects of brain drain due to officers leave the organisation can be minimised (Abdelwhab Ali, Panneer selvam, Paris, & Gunasekaran, 2018).

Knowledge and competency transfer to crew members is critical in ship management process. The skill, experience, knowledge that every individual working on board vessel is invaluable resource of a ship management organisation (Lee, 2010). An effective strategy to retain these valuable knowledges is through systematic knowledge management system. KM enables value creation through a structured process of KS where senior officers can pass their skill, knowledge and operational experience on to cadets and junior officers. Moreover, human error in the shipping industry could be reduced by improving the knowledge of officers on board and systematic information and KS (Chan, Hamid, & Mokhtar, 2016). For this reason, KS among seafarers is seen as an avenue to reduce human errors in shipping industry incidents.

Shipping industry is a data and information rich industry which requires knowledge within the industry to be managed appropriately for sound decision making (Caesar, Cahoon, & Fei, 2020). Research on KM and its practices have been widely discussed and applied across numerous sectors but dearth of studies in the context of shipping industry (Yang, Marlow, & Lu, 2009). Specifically, no empirical study of KM practices has been conducted in shipping or maritime related industries in the setting of Malaysian shipping industry. Given these factors, it is the aim of this study to examine key elements that influence knowledge sharing behaviour of merchant navy officers in the context of Malaysian shipping industry. The following research questions are addressed. (1) Do individual factors (trust, intrinsic motivation) encourage knowledge sharing behaviour among Merchant Navy Officers? (2) Do organisational factors (organisation culture, organisation rewards) encourage knowledge sharing behaviour among Merchant Navy

Officers? (3) Does the use of ICT facilitate knowledge sharing behaviour among Merchant Navy Officers?

Literature review

Knowledge is fact, information or skill gained through education or experienced from practical or theoretical understanding of a subject (Bolisani & Bratianu, 2018). Knowledge Management (KM) is the systematic methods employed by organisations to create, assemble, store and distribute information in the organisation (Islam, Hasan, & Rahman, 2015). Knowledge management researchers have used numerous terms to define knowledge sharing (KS) such as knowledge exchange, distribution and transaction. KS is the action of dissemination of useful 'know-how' (experienced based knowledge), 'know-what' (task related knowledge) or information among individuals, groups, teams, departments and organisations (Akhavan, Rahimi, & Mehralian, 2013).

Riege (2005) categorises factors affecting KS into three main domains, namely personal or individual factors, organisational factors and technological factors. Individual factors originate from people's behaviour, perception and actions that can relate to either individuals, groups within or between departments. Individual factors that influence knowledge sharing behaviour includes personal characteristics (age, gender), trust, interpersonal skills, intrinsic motivation, communication skill, personality, attitudes and values, time, experience and power of knowledge (Lin, 2007c). This study investigates two individual dimensions that affect knowledge sharing behaviour, namely trust and intrinsic motivation.

Organisational context refers to the conducive corporate environment and condition that supports the process of sharing. This includes leadership, management support, organisational structure, organisation culture, organisation reward system, policy and work process (Amayah, 2013). This study focuses on the influence of organisation culture and organisation rewards in facilitating knowledge sharing behaviour. Information and communication technology (ICT) has the ability to offer instant access to large amount of data and information by enhancing work processes and innovation in an organisation (Abdelwhab Ali, Panneer selvam, Paris, & Gunasekaran, 2018). Also, technology acts as a facilitator to encourage and support knowledge sharing process by making it easier to share easily and effectively (Lin & Lee, 2004; Riege, 2005). Technology aspects that involve KS include ICT availability, ICT literacy and expectations to use ICT.

One of the earliest studies in relation to KM in shipping industry was by Yang, Marlow, and Lu (2009) for shipping in Taiwan. The study confirmed organisational structure and KM culture to have significant positive relationship on organisational performance aspects such as financial performance, customer service and innovation. Lee (2010) studied Korean maritime transport companies and suggested that knowledge resource and KM strategy is not an option but necessity. Fei (2011) in his study in China found significant positive relationship between perceived effectiveness of ICT and knowledge sharing. Previous research in the shipping industry also indicates that one of the most important elements to shipping performance is the tacit knowledge of officers (Lee & Song, 2015).

Nevertheless, although past research has pointed out the importance of knowledge resource in shipping industry, they have not specifically emphasised what influence for the knowledge to be disseminated or shared (Luu, 2014). Nonetheless, in an industry like shipping which involves working in isolation, knowledge can be still hoarded rather than being disseminated. Therefore, it is essential for organisations to investigate what motivates knowledge to be shared. Thus, this study is expected to integrate the gap by exploring to what extend people, organisational and technological factors influence knowledge sharing behaviour of merchant navy officers in the context of Malaysian shipping industry. The following knowledge sharing framework as displayed in Figure 7.1 is built upon previous knowledge sharing research, to investigate how people, organisational and technology factors influence knowledge sharing behaviour among Merchant Navy Officers in the context of Malaysian shipping industry.

Trust has been acknowledged as the most influential determinant of KS (Asrar-ul-Haq & Anwar, 2016). Trust is an antecedent to KS with broad concept and has many dimensions and definitions (Chiu, Hsu, & Wang, 2006). In this study, only interpersonal trust will be discussed being the trust that exists between people (colleagues). In organisations, trust is the mutual belief and assurance between and among employees in terms of purpose and manner (Samadi, Wei, & Wan Yusoff, 2015). Past research indicates that

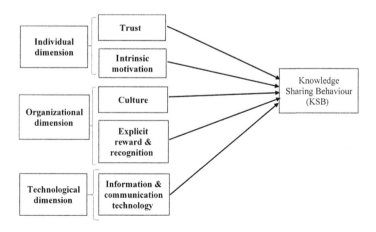

Figure 7.1 Conceptual framework.

mutual trust between employees has a significant positive impact on KS (Pangil & Chan, 2014). In a study conducted on 150 software developers in Sri Lanka, Wickramasinghe and Widyaratne (2012) found that interpersonal trust has significant positive effects on KS. Likewise, Pangil and Chan (2014) in their cross-sectional study conducted in a multinational company in Malaysia revealed that interpersonal trust is significantly related to KS. When trust occurs between two parties, a close relationship is built, hence creating commitment to share knowledge (Wickramasinghe & Widyaratne, 2012). Individuals may initiate and share their precious tacit knowledge more freely only when there is mutual trust among them (Rahman, Osmangani, Daud, & AbdelFattah, 2016). Therefore, the following hypothesis is proposed:

H1: The level of trust has positive relationship with knowledge sharing

As KS is not obligatory, motivation plays significant role in ensuring successful KS (Huang, Chiu, & Lu, 2013). Intrinsic motivation such as knowledge self-efficacy and enjoyment in helping others are related to an individual engaging in an activity out of interest or for the pleasure of sharing their experience (Lin, 2007c). Knowledge self-efficacy is the judgement of individuals that their knowledge and experience is beneficial in solving organisation related problem (Lin, 2007c). Likewise, enjoyment in helping others is the pleasure gained by employees when helping others by sharing their knowledge (Olatokun & Nwafor, 2012). Past research has revealed that intrinsic motivation plays significant role in increasing employees' willingness to share their knowledge with their colleagues, particularly tacit knowledge which is more difficult to share (Huang, Chiu, & Lu, 2013). De Almeida, Lesca and Canton (2016) in their study aimed to bring better understanding of motivated behaviour of telecommunication related company found out that intrinsic motivation is the key component for KS and therefore recommended that sustaining intrinsic motivation as fundamental to the success of KS. These findings indicated that intrinsic motivation is a key component in determining knowledge sharing behaviour. Thus, the following hypothesis is proposed:

H2: Intrinsic motivation has a positive relationship with knowledge sharing

Organisation culture has been widely discussed by scholars as a notable factor being influential towards knowledge sharing behaviour (Islam, Jasimuddin, & Hasan, 2015). Organisation culture involves beliefs, values, norms, assumptions, interpretation and identity built in an organisation that characterise the characteristics of the organisation (Nooshinfard & Nemati-Anaraki, 2014). There are many dimensions of organisation culture such as innovative, competitive, collaborative, bureaucratic, learning and development and top management support. This study particularly focuses on collaboration, learning and development. Collaborative culture or a sense of collaboration refers to how employees in an organisation actively assist and support each other in solving daily work-related task (Nooshinfard & Nemati-Anaraki, 2014). Numerous studies have supported that organisational culture positively influence tacit knowledge sharing in organisations (Cavaliere & Lombardi, 2015; Islam, Jasimuddin, & Hasan, 2015). For instance, Al-Alawi, Al-Marzooqi, and Mohammed (2007) confirmed the positive impact of organisation culture on knowledge sharing in organisations in Bahrain. Organisations that encourage KS work environment provide harmonious atmosphere for members to share ideas and insights. In this context, KS is seen as a natural part of their job function, rather than being forced to share ideas and knowledge. Hence, the following hypothesis is posited:

H3: There is a positive relationship between organisation culture in organisations and knowledge sharing

Reward and recognition system in organisations are developed in order to encourage employees to achieve organisational goals through appropriate behaviour and performance (Šajeva, 2014). The topic of reward and recognition system in an organisation can be discussed in terms of extrinsic and intrinsic reward. Extrinsic rewards are monetary rewards provided to employees based upon knowledge sharing. Intrinsic rewards include recognition and acknowledgement as a motivating factor for knowledge sharing efforts. This study concentrates on extrinsic reward which comprises of monetary incentives, promotional opportunities, job security, training and development that offered by an organisation. Lin and Lo (2015) conducted a research on 180 respondents from healthcare organisation in Taiwan and found reward systems to be a significant facilitator for KS. Similarly, numerous research echoed the findings (Jiacheng, Lu, & Francesco, 2010). Such rewards can be used to stimulate KS activities in the initial stage, nonetheless not beneficial in creating the culture of KS in organisations (Islam, Jasimuddin, & Hasan, 2015; Tohidinia & Mosakhani, 2010). Therefore, introducing a proper reward system is essential to promote continuous KS in organisations. This study expects that if employees are rewarded accordingly, it will have a positive effect on KS. Hence, the following hypothesis is proposed:

H4: There is positive relationship between organisation reward system and knowledge sharing

Organisations have long recognised the use of information and communication technology (ICT) as a facilitator for KM processes such as creation, storage, transfer and application of the knowledge. The use of ICT refers to information technology infrastructure, outfits and arrangements, platforms and computerised solutions that facilitate and help organisations to share and transfer knowledge effectively (Pee & Kankanhalli, 2016). Current studies have also highlighted other KS tools such as dynamic websites, content repositories, social networking tools (Facebook, Twitter, Wikis, blogs) as critically important in KS (Archer-Brown & Kietzmann, 2018). The discussion about the role of ICT in KS includes the availability of ICT in an organisation, literacy and willingness of staff to use ICT and expectation to use ICT systems. In this study, the availability of ICT in facilitating KS will be discussed. Researchers have emphasised that active use of ICT mediums such as internet, intranet, emails, databases and knowledge repositories enhances the process of effective KS (Islam, Hasan, & Rahman, 2015). Besides, tacit knowledge needs to be codified (turning tacit knowledge to explicit knowledge) before being shared with others. In this case, technology enables knowledge codification and accelerates new knowledge application through workflow automation (Wamitu, 2015). Numerous studies have supported the use of ICT in accelerating KS (Abdelwhab Ali, Panneer selvam, Paris, & Gunasekaran, 2018; Archer-Brown & Kietzmann, 2018). Therefore, the following hypothesis is posited:

H5: There is positive relationship between the use of ICT systems and knowledge sharing behaviour

Methodology

The present research adopts positivist paradigm with deductive orientation to maximise the research outcome. The quantitative method is chosen since it allows hypothesis testing across a wide variety of variables and the results are applicable to a wider range of people or setting (Hair et al., 2006). This study employed self-administered close-ended questionnaire distributed through online platform using google form link. The questionnaire was tagged to seafarers' community at Facebook and other social media groups and blogs such as LinkedIn. Snowball sampling was employed to recruit respondents through referrals. In total, 272 questionnaires were returned, producing a response rate of 50%. One major reason for low response rate is due to limited internet bandwidth on board the ships. Respondents were only able to complete the questionnaire when vessels are in port limit or coasting near land. In addition, the survey was conducted from January 2020 till March 2020 where most countries were experiencing 'lockdown' due to pandemic Covid-19. The target population of this study are all Merchant Navy Officers registered with Marine Department Malaysia (MARDEP). Anonymity and confidentiality of the data collected from the survey is ensured by complying with Personal Data Protection Act 2010. Also, data collected is purely for academic purpose only.

This study uses a survey instrument to indicate responses. According to Zikmund (2003), effectiveness of survey relies on the quality of questionnaire. Definition of crucial terms is provided to give better understanding of the overall purpose of the survey. In general, all questions in the survey

Table 7.1 Constructs, selected items and sources

Variables		Adapted items	Source
Knowledge sharing behaviour	1	I am willing to share work related knowledge whenever required by my colleagues	Ling, Sandhu and Jain (2009)
	2	I like to mentor new colleagues by sharing my knowledge with them	Suppiah and Sandhu (2011)
	3	I find sharing knowledge with colleagues is a valuable experience for me	Bock and Kim (2002)
	4	I share my knowledge with colleagues in appropriate and effective way	Bock and Kim (2002)
	5	I share my experience with my colleagues to prevent them, repeating same mistakes I made.	Suppiah and Sandhu (2011)
	6	I freely share my knowledge and experience in meetings	Suppiah and Sandhu (2011)
B		Determinants to knowledge Sharing People dimension	
Trust (reliability of knowledge source and recipient)	1	My colleague and I consider each other to be trustworthy.	
	2	I can trust the colleagues I work with to lend me a hand if I needed it.	Al-Alawi, Al-Marzooqi and Mohammed (2007)
	3	Most of my colleagues can be relied upon to do as they say will do.	Noorderhaven and Harzing (2009)
	4	I believe that my colleagues have adequate work-related knowledge.	
Motivation (*Intrinsic motivation- knowledge self-efficacy & enjoyment in helping others*)	1	I have the confidence in my ability to provide knowledge that my colleagues consider useful.	Lin (2007)
	2	I have the experience needed to provide useful knowledge for the shipping community	
	3	I provide useful knowledge as well as other colleagues in my organization	
	4	I enjoy sharing my knowledge with colleagues.	Huang, Chiu and Lu (2013)
	5	I feel satisfied helping my colleagues by sharing my knowledge.	
	6	Sharing my knowledge with my colleagues is pleasurable.	

Organizational dimension			
Organization reward	1	I expect to receive monetary rewards in return for sharing knowledge with my colleagues.	*He and Wei (2009)*
	2	I expect to be rewarded with an increased job security in return for sharing knowledge with my colleagues.	*Bock and Kim (2002)*
	3	I expect to be considered for interesting and prestigious projects when engaging in knowledge sharing activities	
	4	I expect to learn from others in return for knowledge shared with my colleagues.	
Organization culture (Collaboration, learning and development)	1	My organization emphasizes and creates opportunity for the communication of ideas, knowledge and experiences among colleagues.	*Cavaliere and Lombardi (2015)*
	2	Relationship between my colleagues are considered to be collaborative rather than competitive	
	3	There are opportunities to undertake professional development training in my organization	
	4	There are informal and/or formal activities to cultivate knowledge sharing in my organization	
Technological dimension			
Use of ICT infrastructure to support KS	1	There are latest technologies in my organization ICT to support knowledge sharing practices	*Yang, Marlow and Lu (2009)*
	2	My organisation has a user-friendly central knowledge repository.	
	3	I use the technologies provided to share my knowledge inside my organization.	
	4	ICT systems and work processes are well integrated to facilitate share of knowledge.	

instrument were close-ended taking into consideration the nature of survey being self-administered. All items in the questionnaire were measured using a seven-point Likert scale ranging from 1 to 7 with scale 7 indicating 'strongly agree' and scale 1 indicating 'strongly disagree.' The instrument is divided into two parts. The first part covers respondent's general demographic information such as gender, age, professional competency qualification, rank on board, vessel trading limit, type of vessel and working experiences in the industry. In the second part, respondents were asked their opinion on statements related to the construct namely knowledge sharing behaviour, trust, intrinsic motivation, organisation culture, organisation reward and information communication technology. Based on the literature review, the questionnaire was developed by adapting concepts and items from prior studies to enhance validity. In total, data were collected to measure six constructs. Items of the construct and its source of adaption is summarised as Table 7.1.

Based on the research objective of this study which requires theory testing and confirmation, this study intends to use Statistical Package for Social Science (SPSS) and Analysis of Moment Structure (AMOS). The statistical procedures ranged between simple descriptive statistics, reliability, normality and validity test. To ensure the overall fit of the measurement model and whether the theoretical model is supported by sample data, structural equation modelling (SEM) was established using AMOS.

Results and discussion

Demographic analysis

Shipping industry is one of those few industries 'male dominated' which has the lowest number of women workforces (maritimeinfo.org, 2019). Therefore, majority of respondents consist of male, 256 (94.12%) as compared to female 16 (5.88%). As for the age group distribution, mostly are 31–40 years old (43.01%), followed by 41–50 years old (35.66%) and 19–30 years (16.18%). Most officers (69.12%) have obtained a minimum certificate of competency, a professional qualification required by the Marine Department Malaysian to sail on board Malaysian vessels. Others have additional qualification such as diploma (15.44%), master's degree (8.09%), bachelor degree (6.62%) and associate degree (0.74%). Most respondents have working experience of more than five years on board ship. Mainly, the vessel's crew has two types of seafarers, namely officers and ratings. This survey only focuses on officers whose rank ranges from Master to junior officers/engineers. 32.35% of this survey's respondents are Master (Captain), the supreme authority of a merchant vessel. This is followed by Chief Engineer (20.96%), Chief Officer and Second Officer (10.29%) and other. Most of the respondents' sail on foreign going vessels trading worldwide (91.91%) such as gas carrier (55.9%), oil tanker (11.0%), chemical tanker (7.72%), bulk carrier (3.68%) and others.

Normality assessment

Kline (2011) in his study discovered that skewness and kurtosis index below three and ten, respectively, does not indicate serious data deviation from normality. Based on the normality assessment, 26 out of 28 items are negatively skewed. This is corresponding to the mean scores where most mean scores are close to 6 or above 6. It is found that the kurtosis value for most items is within the range except KSB 1, KSB 2, KSB 3, KBS 5, RR 4, OC 1 and OC 4 are beyond the acceptable range. Further normality assessment using Histogram and boxplot found outliers in those items. To determine if these outliers are genuine and not just errors, a cross-check with the original questionnaire was conducted. However, these outliers showed that the responses were accurate data point with genuine scores.

Reliability test

Internal reliability explains the extent to which all items in a test measure of the same concept or construct, thus connected to inter-relatedness of the items within the test (Hair et al., 2006). The results revealed overall Cronbach alpha scoring of 0.856. Dependent variable indicated a score of 0.826. Four out of five independent variable outcomes ranged between 0.802 and 0.862. One variable achieved exceptional high reliability of 0.921. As such, all items reflect good reliability and internal consistency and up to the par with the rule of thumb as mentioned above.

Confirmatory factor analysis

The initial measurement model for this study includes 28 items describing six latent constructs: knowledge sharing behaviour (KSB), trust (T), intrinsic motivation (IM), organisation culture (OC), organisation reward (RE) and information and communication technology (ICT). For the initial model, factor loading ranges from 0.471 to 0.960. However, based on the rule of thumb for factor loadings, latent construct must load a minimum acceptable level of 0.5 to keep the model fit (Hair et al., 2006). As such, a re-run of CFA was conducted to ensure the fitness of the model by removing poor factor loading items.

In order to find the better model fitness for the confirmatory factor analysis, items with factor loading lower than 0.5 and modification indices greater than 15 were either removed as suggested by (Hair et al., 2006) which resulted in acceptable model fit as displayed in Figure 7.2. The overall model fit is measured with three model fitness categories, namely absolute fit, incremental fit and parsimony fit as shown in Table 7.2. The model value of CMIN/DF is 1.908, which is deemed acceptable as it is below the accepted value of 3.00. The GFI, CFI, NFI and TLI values in above are, respectively, 0.900, 0.957, 0.914 and 0.948. Two of the values are above 0.900, which are

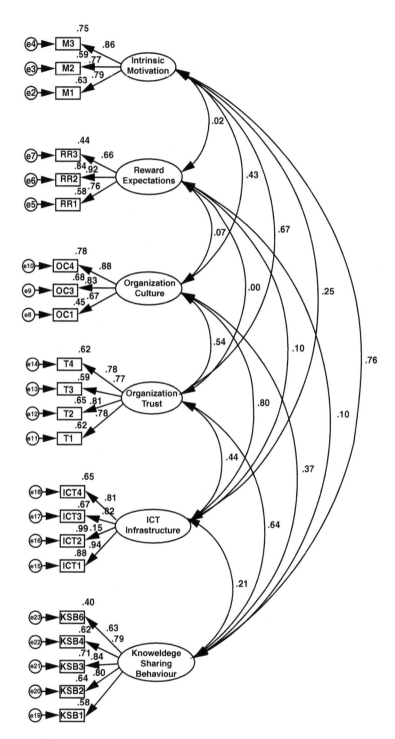

Figure 7.2 Final measurement model.

Table 7.2 Model-fit indices for measurement model

Category	Index	Level of acceptance	Index value	Comments
Absolute fit	Chi-square	P-values > 0.05	0.000	Supported
	RMSEA	< 0.08	0.056	Acceptable
	PCLOSE	> 0.00	0.113	Acceptable
	GFI	> 0.90	0.900	Acceptable
Incremental fit	AGFI	> 0.80	0.867	Acceptable
	CFI	> 0.90	0.957	Acceptable
	TLI	> 0.90	0.948	Acceptable
	NFI	> 0.90	0.914	Acceptable
Parsimonious fit	Chisq/df	< 3.0	1.908	Acceptable

Table 7.3 Convergent and divergent validity assessment

Construct	Loadings	CR	AVE
IV1	> 0.7	0.932	0.776
IV2	> 0.7	0.851	0.657
IV3	> 0.7	0.828	0.621
IV4	> 0.7	0.838	0.636
IV5	> 0.7	0.866	0.618
DV	> 0.6	0.878	0.591

CFI and NFI. Consequently, they are accepted fit. However, GFI and TLI are just on the borderline to the value 0.900. Finally, the RMSEA value for CFA final run is measured at 0.056 in Table 7.2 and is deemed accepted as fit since it is lesser than 0.08. All the model-fit indices exceed the respective common acceptance level, therefore demonstrating the measurement model exhibited a fairly good fit with the data collected.

Validity assessment

There are three types of validity assessed for this measurement model, namely convergent validity, construct validity and discriminant validity. The recommended value of convergent validity is when factor loadings are more than 0.5 and Average Variance Extracted (AVE) shared between constructs and measures are more than 0.5 (Hair et al., 2006). From Table 7.3, it is evident that factor loading for all items exceeds the recommended level of 0.5. The values are also statistically significant at $p < 0.001$ which gives the model a suitable convergent construct.

Based on the recommendation of Hair et al. (2010), the discriminant validity test was conducted to ensure if the factors differed among themselves at an adequate level of statistical significance. Table 7.4 demonstrates the correlation between each pair of latent exogenous constructs. It is evident

Table 7.4 Discriminant validity assessment

	CR	AVE	MSV	MaxR(H)	IV1	IV2	IV3	IV4	IV5	DV
IV1	0.932	0.776	0.648	0.954	0.881					
IV2	0.851	0.657	0.581	0.86	0.247	0.81				
IV3	0.828	0.621	0.011	0.884	0.103	0.02	0.788			
IV4	0.838	0.636	0.635	0.865	0.805	0.428	0.073	0.798		
IV5	0.866	0.618	0.444	0.867	0.435	0.666	−0.002	0.539	0.786	
DV	0.878	0.591	0.581	0.888	0.212	0.762	−0.099	0.373	0.644	0.769

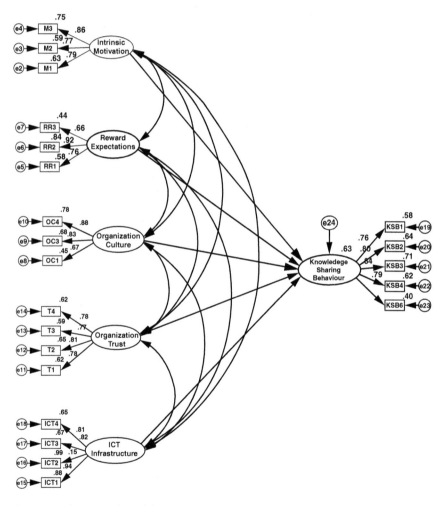

Figure 7.3 Structural model.

that the correlation between each pair of latent exogenous construct is less than 0.85 which indicates that the measurement model is free from redundant items. Therefore, the results demonstrated evidence of discriminant validity for this study.

Structural equation modelling

Structural Equation Modelling or SEM is often used to analyse latent constructs using one or more observed variables and provides structural modelling to impute the relationship between the latent variables. Figure 7.3 depicts the SEM Path Diagram with the revised mapping of the relationship with each variable. This is also in sync with the list of questionnaire items dropped to improvise the modelling.

The structural model testing of this study was constructed using AMOS 22. Table 7.5 illustrates the acceptance level and the results achieved. Therefore, it can be concluded that the model fitted the data well.

The model value of CMIN/DF is 1.908, which is deemed acceptable as it is below the accepted value of 3.00. The GFI, CFI, NFI and TLI values in above are, respectively, 0.900, 0.957, 0.914 and 0.948. Two of the values are above 0.900, which are CFI and NFI. Consequently, they are accepted fit. However, GFI and TLI are just on the borderline to the value 0.900. Finally, the RMSEA value for CFA final run is measured at 0.056 in Table 7.2 and is deemed accepted as fit since it is lesser than 0.08. All the model-fit indices exceed the respective common acceptance level, therefore demonstrating the measurement model exhibited a fairly good fit with the data collected.

Results of hypothesis testing

After the CFA of the measurement model, this study applied SEM approach by using standardised estimation of the structure model to test the proposed hypothesis. SEM allows assessing the relationships of the multiple dependence relationship (Hair et al., 2006).

Table 7.5 Model-fit indices for structural model

Category	Index	Level of acceptance	Index value	Comments
Absolute fit	Chi-Square	P-values > 0.05	0.000	Supported
	RMSEA	< 0.08	0.056	Acceptable
	PCLOSE	> 0.00	0.113	Acceptable
	GFI	> 0.90	0.900	Acceptable
Incremental fit	AGFI	> 0.80	0.867	Acceptable
	CFI	> 0.90	0.957	Acceptable
	TLI	> 0.90	0.948	Acceptable
	NFI	> 0.90	0.914	Acceptable
Parsimonious fit	Chisq/df	< 3.0	1.908	Acceptable

Table 7.6 Hypothesis results

	Dependent variable		Independent variable	SE	P-value	
H1	Knowledge sharing behaviour	<---	Trust	.255	0.002	Supported
H2	Knowledge sharing behaviour	<---	Intrinsic motivation	.591	***	Supported
H3	Knowledge sharing behaviour	<---	Organization culture	.051	0.628	Not supported
H4	Knowledge sharing behaviour	<---	Organization reward	−0.107	0.028	Supported
H5	Knowledge sharing behaviour	<---	ICT infrastructure	−0.075	0.424	Not supported

As shown in Table 7.6, the results of the analysis revealed that hypothesis (H1, H2 and H4 are supported). However, three other hypotheses, H3, H5 and H5 are not supported.

Discussion of findings

As Table 7.6 suggests, level of trust has significant positive influence on knowledge sharing behaviour ($\beta = 0.255$, $p < 0.05$), supporting H1. This finding is in line with numerous researchers who confirmed trust as a belief system in relationship among the members of an organisation (Mueller, 2012; Rahman, Osmangani, Daud, & AbdelFattah, 2016). Intrinsic motivation in H2 focuses on knowledge self-efficacy, a behaviour induced by the need of employees to feel competence and self-determination when dealing with working environment and enjoyment in helping others (Lin, 2007c). Coinciding with previous research, this study found intrinsic motivation to significantly affect knowledge sharing behaviour, thus supporting H1 at ($\beta = 0.591$, $p < 0.001$). Studies have proved that individuals who enjoy helping others are intrinsically motivated and more favourable towards knowledge sharing (Šajeva, 2014). Similarly, Olatokun and Nwafor (2012) confirmed that knowledge self-efficacy, a feeling of competence, positively correlates with willingness to share knowledge.

The perspective of organisational culture in this study concentrates on the role of collaborative culture and learning culture. Surprisingly and contrary to common belief, the results of this study showed that organisational culture is weakly or insignificantly associated with knowledge sharing behaviour. Thus, H3 is not supported in this study, ($\beta = 0.051$, $p > 0.05$). Although most studies indicate a positive impact of organisational culture on knowledge sharing behaviour (Cavaliere & Lombardi, 2015), there are also studies which resulted conversely. The impact of organisational rewards in influencing knowledge sharing behaviour seems rather mixed. Even though some studies have found reward and recognition system to facilitate knowledge sharing in organisations (Wang & Hou, 2015), other studies found no substantial relationship between both (He & Wei, 2009). This study finds significant but negative impact organisational reward in facilitating knowledge sharing behaviour. Hence, H4 is rejected, ($\beta = -.107$, $p < 0.05$). Therefore, this finding is consistent with studies by Tohidinia and Mosakhani (2010) whereby extrinsic reward was found to be ineffective in encouraging people to share knowledge. One possible reason for this could be the shipping work environment which requires working in team. As such, sharing of knowledge within teams is difficult to observe and measured directly and the output can hardly be credited to a particular person (Borges, 2013).

The role of information and communication technology has been identified as a major knowledge sharing enabler (Archer-Brown & Kietzmann, 2018). However, surprisingly, this study did not find any significant relationship between the existence of ICT systems and knowledge sharing. Thus, H5 is not supported ($\beta = -0.075$, $p > 0.05$). The use of ICT systems seems insignificant in facilitating knowledge sharing among the Merchant Navy officers in this study. One logical explanation for this could be lack of ICT usage and exposure such as knowledge management tools and systems on board the ship. Usage of ICT on board is also associated with high cost which refrains many from using this facility on board. Furthermore, working on board ship is a unique environment whereby members work and live on board. As such, officers usually turn to friends and peers to learn relevant knowledge rather than engaging in an extensive search through organisation's knowledge management systems and databases (Caesar, Cahoon, & Fei, 2020) regardless of how efficient the system is.

Conclusion

The result of this study indicates two intrinsic motivational factors, enjoyment in helping others and knowledge self-efficacy in determining the proclivity to share knowledge among Merchant Navy Officers. The finding suggests that engaging in knowledge sharing activities is motivated by emotional benefits such as enjoyment of solving challenging problems and seeking social recognition. Secondly, this study examined the effect of organisation culture and organisation reward such as monetary rewards and recognition in influencing knowledge sharing behaviour. The finding revealed that organisational factors are insignificant in influencing knowledge sharing behaviour. Lastly, research objective three pertains to investigate the impacts of use of information and communication technology (ICT) to facilitate knowledge sharing. It may be considered surprising that no positive relationship was observed between the use ICT and knowledge sharing. Use of ICT was thought to have potential to enable more sharing but somehow considered to be underused.

First, the study demonstrated that knowledge sharing is primarily a self-determined activity and therefore cannot be explicitly or directly rewarded. Findings from this study provide empirical support that interpersonal trust has positive influence on knowledge sharing among the officers. Seafarers work in remote and isolated community often away from ashore for 3–6 months or more at a time. At the same time, the number of people on board is limited and most tasks are carried out as team effort. Thus, this creates a tendency to trust colleagues and co-workers in forming and maintaining social relationship. Therefore, individuals prefer to share their knowledge with whom they appear to be reliable and trustworthy. Next, this study also suggests that employees are more apt to share knowledge with their colleagues and co-workers when they feel confident about their capability to perform the act of knowledge sharing. Likewise, the finding also indicates that employee's intention to share knowledge comes from the simple enjoyment of sharing knowledge with others.

Implications

The outcome of this study offers insights that may assist shipping companies in enhancing their employee's knowledge sharing. First, the findings of this study recommend that to promote knowledge sharing activities in a unique characteristics industry such as shipping, it is vital to create an environment of people-oriented rather than technology oriented. Ship managers should focus on fostering intrinsic reward values such as sense of belongings, competences, respect and recognition to encourage knowledge sharing activities in their organisation. Next, the results also warranted the need for ship managers to examine the availability and usage of information communication technology (ICT) tools and systems on board the ship. While ICT does not guarantee competitive advantage, but lack of it may affect organisation to become less competitive, particularly when considering ICT as a means to foster knowledge sharing. Lastly, although the findings of this study revealed that expected monetary rewards may discourage the formation of positive behaviour towards knowledge sharing, ship managers should not neglect the role of reward as a triggering factor for knowledge sharing.

Limitation of study and avenues for future research

Nevertheless, there are inevitably some limitations to this study. First, although this chapter addresses significant factors to facilitating knowledge sharing, it did not discuss the extent of knowledge sharing practice in the shipping industry. The way how knowledge is acquired and shared is critical for the success of knowledge sharing strategy. Thus, there is a need to explore this issue further in future studies. Second, is the limitation incurred by the scope of the survey. As the survey was conducted among Merchant Navy Officers sailing on board Malaysian registered vessels, care must be taken in generalising the results to the shipping industry of other registered countries. Although issues in relation to shipping companies are universal worldwide, cultural background should be taken into consideration when generalising the results. Thirdly, the definition of organisational culture that was used in this study was generalised. As a matter of fact, organisation culture could be classified with many dimensions and categories. In addition, because the respondents for this research are from multinational background, there are differences in corporate and national culture from one organisation to the other. It can also be expected that there are variances with regard to knowledge sharing behaviours, depending on the nature of the cultural dimension that is practised within a firm. As such, future research could make contributions by examining the effects of other cultural elements on knowledge sharing. Fourth, there is also limitation in the methodology of the study. As such, only quantitative method was applied in this study. The adoption of mixed method, a combination of both quantitative and qualitative studies, would bring a deeper understanding of the issues being investigated.

References

Abdelwhab, A., Panneer, S. and Gunasekaran, P. 2018. Key factors influencing knowledge sharing practices and its relationship with organisational performance within the oil and gas industry, *Journal of Knowledge Management*, 23(9), 1806–1837. doi: 10.1108/JKM-06-2018-0394.

Akhavan, P., Rahimi, A. and Mehralian, G. 2013. Developing a model for knowledge sharing in research centers, Vine. doi: 10.1108/VINE-06-2012-0020.

Al-Alawi, A. I., Al-Marzooqi, N. Y. and Mohammed, Y. F. 2007. Organisational culture and knowledge sharing: Critical success factors, *Journal of Knowledge Management*, 11(2), 22–42. doi: 10.1108/13673270710738898.

de Almeida, F. C., Lesca, H. and Canton, A. W. P. 2016. Intrinsic motivation for knowledge sharing – competitive intelligence process in a telecom company, *Journal of Knowledge Management*, 20(6), 1282–1301. doi: 10.1108/JKM-02-2016-0083.

Amayah, A. T. 2013. Determinants of knowledge sharing in a public sector organisation, *Journal of Knowledge Management*, 17(3), 454–471. doi: 10.1108/JKM-11-2012-0369.

Archer-Brown, C. and Kietzmann, J. 2018. Strategic knowledge management and enterprise social media, *Journal of Knowledge Management*, 22(6), 1288–1309. doi: 10.1108/JKM-08-2017-0359.

Asrar-ul-Haq, M. and Anwar, S. 2016. A systematic review of knowledge management and knowledge sharing: Trends, issues, and challenges, *Cogent Business and Management*, 3(1), 17. doi: 10.1080/23311975.2015.1127744.

Bock, G. W. and Kim, Y. G. 2002. Breaking the myths of rewards: An exploratory study of attitudes about knowledge sharing, *Information Resources Management Journal*, 15(2), 14–21. doi: 10.4018/irmj.2002040102.

Bolisani, E. and Bratianu, C. 2018. Emergent knowledge strategies: Strategic thinking in knowledge management, *Springer International Publishing*. doi: 10.1007/978-3-319-60656.

Borges, R. 2013. Tacit knowledge sharing between IT workers: The role of organisational culture, personality, and social environment, *Management Research Review*, 36(1), 89–108. doi: 10.1108/01409171311284602.

Caesar, L. D., Cahoon, S. and Fei, J. 2020. Understanding the complexity of retention among seafarers: A perspective of Australian employers, *Australian Journal of Maritime and Ocean Affairs*, 1(1), 1–26. doi: 10.1080/18366503.2020.1736242.

Cavaliere, V. and Lombardi, S. 2015. Exploring different cultural configurations: How do they affect subsidiaries' knowledge sharing behaviors?' *Journal of Knowledge Management*, 19(2), 141–163. doi: 10.1108/JKM-04-2014-0167.

Chan, S. R., Hamid, N. A. and Mokhtar, K. 2016. A theoretical review of human error in maritime accidents, *Advanced Science Letters*, 22(9), 2109–2112. doi: 10.1166/asl.2016.7058.

Chen, C. J. and Hung, S. W. 2010. To give or to receive? Factors influencing members knowledge sharing and community promotion in professional virtual communities, *Information and Management*, 47(4), 226–236. doi: 10.1016/j.im.2010.03.001.

Chiu, C. M., Hsu, M. H. and Wang, E. T. G. 2006. Understanding knowledge sharing in virtual communities: An integration of social capital and social cognitive theories, *Decision Support Systems*, 42(3), 1872–1888. doi: 10.1016/j.dss.2006.04.001.

Dong, Y., Bartol, K. M., Zhang Z. X. and Li, C. 2017. Enhancing employee creativity via individual skill development and team knowledge sharing: Influences of dual-focused transformational leadership, *Journal of Organisational Behaviour*. John Wiley and Sons Ltd, 38(3), 439–458. doi: 10.1002/job.2134.

Fei, J. 2011. An empirical study of the role of information technology in effective knowledge transfer in the shipping industry, *Maritime Policy and Management*, 38(4), 347–367. doi: 10.1080/03088839.2011.588259.

Fei, J., Chen, S. Y. and Chen, S. 2009. Organisational knowledge base and knowledge transfer in the shipping industry, *Electronic Journal of Knowledge Management*, 7(3), 325–340.

Fullwood, R., Rowley, J. and Delbridge, R. 2013. Knowledge sharing amongst academics in UK universities, *Journal of Knowledge Management*, 17(1), 123–136. doi: 10.1108/13673271311300831.

Fullwood, R., Rowley, J. and McLean, J. 2019. Exploring the factors that influence knowledge sharing between academics, *Journal of Further and Higher Education*, 43(8), 1051–1063. doi: 10.1080/0309877X.2018.1448928.

Ha, Y. S. and Seo, J. S. 2017. An analysis of the competitiveness of major liner shipping companies, *Asian Journal of Shipping and Logistics*, 33(2), 53–60. doi: 10.1016/j.ajsl.2017.06.002.

Hair, E., Halle, T., Terry-Humen, E., Lavelle, B. and Calkins, J. 2006. Children's school readiness in the ECLS-K: Predictions to academic, health, and social outcomes in first grade. *Early Childhood Research Quarterly*, 21(4), 431–454.

Hair, J. F., Celsi, M., Ortinau, D. J. and Bush, R. P. (2010). *Essentials of marketing research* (Vol. 2). New York: McGraw-Hill/Irwin.

He, W. and Wei, K. K. 2009. What drives continued knowledge sharing? An investigation of knowledge-contribution and -seeking beliefs, *Decision Support Systems*, 46(4), 826–838. doi: 10.1016/j.dss.2008.11.007.

Huang, M. C., Chiu, Y. P. and Lu, T. C. 2013. Knowledge governance mechanisms and repatriate's knowledge sharing: The mediating roles of motivation and opportunity, *Journal of Knowledge Management*, 17(5), 677–694. doi: 10.1108/JKM-01-2013-0048.

Islam, M. Z., Hasan, I. and Rahman, M. H. 2015. Factors affecting knowledge transfer in public organisation employees, *Asian Social Science*, 11(4), 223–233. doi: 10.5539/ass.v11n4p223.

Islam, M. Z., Jasimuddin, S. M. and Hasan, I. 2015. Organisational culture, structure, technology infrastructure and knowledge sharing: Empirical evidence from MNCs based in Malaysia, 45(1), 67–88. doi: 10.1108/VINE-05-2014-0037.

Jiacheng, W., Lu, L. and Francesco, C. A. 2010. A cognitive model of intra-organisational knowledge-sharing motivations in the view of cross-culture, *International Journal of Information Management*, 30(3), 220–230. doi: 10.1016/j.ijinfomgt.2009.08.007.

Lee, E. S. 2010. Knowledge resource in maritime transport industry: A case analysis, *Asian Journal of Shipping and Logistics*. doi: 10.1016/S2092-5212(10)80007-0.

Lee, E. S. and Song, D. W. 2015. The effect of shipping knowledge and absorptive capacity on organisational innovation and logistics value, *International Journal of Logistics Management*, 26(2), 218–237. doi: 10.1108/IJLM-01-2013-0011.

Lin, H. F. 2007a. Effects of extrinsic and intrinsic motivation on employee knowledge sharing intentions, *Journal of Information Science*, 33(2), 135–149. doi: 10.1177/0165551506068174.

Lin, H. F. 2007b. Knowledge sharing and firm innovation capability: An empirical study, *International Journal of Manpower*. doi: 10.1108/01437720710755272.

Lin, H. F. 2007c. Knowledge sharing and firm innovation capability: An empirical study, *International Journal of Manpower*, 28(3–4), 315–332. doi: 10.1108/01437720710755272.

Lin, H. F. and Lee, G. G. 2004. Perceptions of senior managers toward knowledge-sharing behaviour, *Management Decision*, 42(1), 108–125. doi: 10.1108/00251740410510181.

Lin, S. W. and Lo, L. Y. S. 2015. Mechanisms to motivate knowledge sharing: Integrating the reward systems and social network perspectives, *Journal of Knowledge Management*, 19(2), 212–235. doi: 10.1108/JKM-05-2014-0209.

Ling, C. W., Sandhu, M. S. and Jain, K. K. 2009. Knowledge sharing in an American multinational company based in Malaysia, *Journal of Workplace Learning*, 21(2), 125–142. doi: 10.1108/13665620910934825.

Luu, T. 2014. Knowledge sharing and competitive intelligence, *Marketing Intelligence and Planning*, 32(3), 269–292. doi: 10.1108/MIP-05-2013-0077.

Mueller, J. 2012. Knowledge sharing between project teams and its cultural antecedents, *Journal of Knowledge Management*, 16(3), 435–447. doi: 10.1108/13673271211238751.

Noorderhaven, N. and Harzing, A. W. 2009. Knowledge-sharing and social interaction within MNEs, *Journal of International Business Studies*, 40(5), 719–741. doi: 10.1057/jibs.2008.106.

Nooshinfard, F. and Nemati-Anaraki, L. 2014. Success factors of inter-organisational knowledge sharing: A proposed framework, *Electronic Library*, 32(2), 239–261. doi: 10.1108/EL-02-2012-0023.

Olatokun, W. and Nwafor, C. I. 2012. The effect of extrinsic and intrinsic motivation on knowledge sharing intentions of civil servants in Ebonyi State, Nigeria, *Information Development*, 28(3), 216–234. doi: 10.1177/0266666912438567.

Osmangani A. M., Daud, N. M., Chowdhury A. H., and Hassan, H. 2015. Trust and work place spirituality on knowledge sharing behaviour: Perspective from non-academic staff of higher learning institutions, *Learning Organisation*, 22(6), 317–332. doi: 10.1108/TLO-05-2015-0032.

Pangil, F. and Chan, J. M. 2014. The mediating effect of knowledge sharing on the relationship between trust and virtual team effectiveness, *Journal of Knowledge Management*, 18(1), 92–106. doi: 10.1108/JKM-09-2013-0341.

Pee, L. G. and Kankanhalli, A. 2016. Interactions among factors influencing knowledge management in public-sector organisations: A resource-based view, *Government Information Quarterly*, 33(1), 188–199. doi: 10.1016/j.giq.2015.06.002.

Rahman, M. S. and Hussain, B. 2014. The impact of trust, motivation and rewards on knowledge sharing attitudes among the secondary and higher secondary level students' evidence from Bangladesh, *Library Review*, 63, 637–652. doi: 10.1108/LR-06-2013-0072.

Rahman, M. S., Osmangani, A. M., Daud N. M. and AbdelFattah, F. A. M. 2016. Knowledge sharing behaviors among non-academic staff of higher learning institutions: Attitude, subjective norms and behavioral intention embedded model, *Library Review*, 65(1–2), 65–83. doi: 10.1108/LR-02-2015-0017.

Šajeva, S. 2014. Encouraging knowledge sharing among employees: How reward matters, *Procedia – Social and Behavioral Sciences*. 156(April), 130–134. doi: 10.1016/j.sbspro.2014.11.134.

Samadi, B., Wei, C. C. and Wan Yusoff, W. F. 2015. The influence of trust on knowledge sharing behaviour among multigenerational employees, *Journal of Information and Knowledge Management*, 14(4), 1–9. doi: 10.1142/S0219649215500343.

Shemon, W. S., Hasan, K. R. and Kadir, A. 2019. Human resources competitiveness in shipping industry: Bangladesh perspective human resources competitiveness in shipping industry, *Bangladesh Perspective* Paper ID: ICBM-19-0323, (June).

Suppiah, V. and Sandhu, M. S. 2011. Organisational culture's influence on tacit knowledge-sharing behaviour, *Journal of Knowledge Management*, 15(3), 462–477. doi: 10.1108/13673271111137439.

Tohidinia, Z. and Mosakhani, M. 2010. Knowledge sharing behaviour and its predictors, *Industrial Management and Data Systems*, 110(4), 611–631. doi: 10.1108/02635571011039052.

Wamitu, S. N. 2015. Tacit knowledge sharing in public sector departments in Kenya, *Open Journal of Business and Management*, 3(1), 109–118. doi: 10.4236/ojbm.2015.31011.

Wang, W. T. and Hou, Y. P. 2015. Motivations of employees' knowledge sharing behaviors: A self-determination perspective, *Information and Organisation*, 25(1), 1–26. doi: 10.1016/j.infoandorg.2014.11.001.

Wickramasinghe, V. and Widyaratne, R. 2012. Effects of interpersonal trust, team leader support, rewards, and knowledge sharing mechanisms on knowledge sharing in project teams, *Vine: The Journal of Information and Knowledge Management Systems*, 42(2), 214–236. doi: 10.1108/03055721211227255.

Yang, C. C., Marlow, P. B. and Lu, C. S. 2009. Knowledge management enablers in liner shipping, *Logistics and Transportation Review*, 45(6), 893–903. doi: 10.1016/j.tre.2009.05.003.

Zhang, P. and Ng, F. F. 2012. Attitude toward knowledge sharing in construction teams, *Industrial Management and Data Systems*, 112(9), 1326–1347. doi: 10.1108/02635571211278956.

Part 3

Information and knowledge management

8 Value co-creation in the social media platform

The perspectives of organisations and prosumers

Shahidul Islam, Nazlida Muhamad, Vai Shiem Leong and Wardah Hakimah Sumardi

Introduction

Value creation for organisation, customer and society is an integral element of overall business strategy (Dwivedi et al., 2020; Kao, Yang, Wu, & Cheng, 2016). In traditional product-centric views, value is considered a benefit added to a product or service derived via exchange of goods or services. According to service-dominant (SD) logic, value may be generated by an interactive process where both employees and customers are involved in a value-creating process, known as value co-creation (Edvardsson, Tronvoll, & Gruber, 2011). Due to the information and communication technology (ICT) evolution, the process of value co-creation, for both customers and organisations, has changed profoundly (Xie, Wu, Xiao, & Hu, 2016).

Social media, a component of innovative digital communication technologies, has become an essential part of everyday life for people across the world. In 2020, over 3.6 billion people are using social media worldwide, a number projected to increase to almost 4.41 billion in 2025 (Clement, 2020). In contrast to traditional computer-mediated communication technologies like e-mail, teleconferencing, intranets, decision-support systems and instant messaging, social media refers to a group of Internet-based technologies, such as Facebook, YouTube, LinkedIn, Twitter, Instagram, Wikipedia, blogs that allow users (including service providers and customers) to easily create, edit, evaluate and/or link to content or to other creators of content (Majchrzak, Faraj, Kane, & Azad, 2013). Social media usage influences how service entities, including organisations, employees and customers, interact and maintain relationships with social media users. Consequently, scholars underscore value co-creation through effective utilisation of social media for building efficient knowledge management and customer relationship management and improving organisational, customer and societal value (Dhanesh & Duthler, 2019; Nisar, Prabhakar, & Strakova, 2019).

Digitalisation capabilities offer organisations access to a wide range of knowledge on consumer behaviour, predict patterns about consumers and markets, which may push significant organisational change and adoption

DOI: 10.4324/9781003163824-11

in order to realise competitive advantage (Roblek, Bach, Meško, & Berton-celj, 2013; Xie et al., 2016). Brey (2019) indicates that good understanding of social media and its environment help to devise social media marketing (SMM) strategies and create effective social media content that co-create value. Influence of social media in designing marketing strategies becomes an important force for successful SMM (Dwivedi et al., 2020). Furthermore, Cheung, Pires, Rosenberger, Leung, and Ting (2020) note that literature on SMM and value co-creation is still limited. They find evidence that effective SMM strategies lead to the strengthening of value co-creation, consumer-brand engagement and repurchase intention in the context of China and Hong Kong. In line with this, the first objective of this study is to identify and illustrate organisational push strategy (effective use of SMM and social media content) that generates co-created value for organisation, customer and society, especially in the context of Asian countries.

Next, ICT has revolutionised many aspects of consumers' information access, which facilitate and allow them to create or use different applications/features and virtual communities with an unprecedented level of freedom of opinion sharing, knowledge sharing and persuading others. Eventually, consumers who manage to become knowledgeable consumers or online users of social media (software application) for interaction and collaboration turn into *prosumers*, who have "the ability to participate in a product or service conception, design, execution, and/or testing and have a certain influence on their social network" (Seran (Potra) & Izvercian, 2014). This new consumer who actively participates in online knowledge sharing, e-WOM (electronic word of mouth) and gradually gets involved with online brand community, and organisation social media fan groups has been termed as prosumers (Tapscott & Williams, 2008). To enhance competitive strategies and market success, organisations are interested into a new approach oriented towards prosumer inclusion in organisational model (Seran (Potra) & Izvercian, 2014). Social media offers a wide range of opportunities for organisation to incorporate prosumers into organisational value co-creation model.

However, significant challenges exist in using prosumer creativity in managing customer solutions in strategic value co-creation activities. Organisations should be involved in this value co-creation process by identifying motivators and deterrents in facilitating prosumer value co-creation. Therefore, understanding prosumer value co-creation process and how organisation integrate resources aiming to facilitate prosumer inclusion in corporate activities are needed to enhance brand awareness, customer relationship management and product/service development effectively and efficiently (Chepurna & Rialp Criado, 2018). The second research objective is to identify and exemplify organisational pull strategy (effective use of prosumer value co-creation) that generates co-created value for organisation, customer and society, especially in the context of Asian countries.

Despite the ever-increasing role of social media in facilitating new and innovative ways of knowledge conversations and collaboration between organisations and customers that co-created value for parties involved in a social media ecosystem, past literature does not sufficiently provide a holistic understanding of the process itself. Given the importance of effective utilisation of social media for value co-creation, this chapter demonstrates push and pull approaches through which organisation gets involved into value co-creation through social media, and offers a conceptual model of prosumer motivation to value co-creation through social media. Specifically, this paper answers the following research questions:

RQ1: How can we explain push strategy (organisation develops social media content) to value co-creation through social media in the Asian context?
RQ2: How can we apply pull strategy (organisation incorporates prosumers) to value co-creation through social media in the Asian context?

Methodology

The chapter is a qualitative conceptual analysis of literature and uses several frameworks to illustrate cases from the Asian context. First, the paper discusses the theoretical foundation of value co-creation through social media. Next, the paper proposed two strategies in order for organisation to involve in value co-creation through social media: push strategy and pull strategy based on the theoretical backdrop and insights from the literature. To further describe how organisation can utilise social media to accomplish the objectives, the paper exemplified Brey's (2019) social media value co-creation framework and Seran (Potra) and Izvercian's (2014) prosumer creativity and focus model in the context of Asian countries. Then, the paper proposes a conceptual model on prosumer motivation to co-create value with firms and other customers by integrating knowledge from several leading papers on customer value co-creation (Yi & Gong, 2013), and employee motivation to co-create value (Amin, Shamim, Ghazali, & Khan, 2021). The study clarifies the prosumer value co-creation process in the social media environment and presents pertinent discussion to provide an understanding of the theoretical backdrop of the model and future research directions. Finally, the theoretical and managerial implications of the paper are discussed.

Theoretical foundation: value co-creation through social media

Value co-creation is an interactive process between organisation and customers – the process includes several stages through which value is generated or value is co-created (co-created value) (Kao et al., 2016). Generally, value refers to benefits or gains against the sacrifices or costs. However, the typical co-created value includes relationship value, experiential value, positive emotions/absence of negative emotions, information (knowledge and learning), symbolic/expressive value and community or societal value. Since both organisation and customers actively participate in value co-creation process, both parties become benefitted from the process of value co-creation (Grönroos & Voima, 2013).

Building on the ideological and technological foundations of Web 2.0, social media allows the creation and exchange of both user-generated content (UGC) and marketer-generated content (MGC) (Goh, Heng, & Lin, 2013). Social media offers an unparalleled platform for its users with multiple directions of communication, and richer interactions with larger audience size and scope (Kao et al., 2016). As a result, scholars argue that social media content (which is relatable) can speak to the needs and interest of customers and co-create value for the customers (Brey, 2019). On the other hand, value co-creation is an interactive process and in service system, value co-creation is service interaction between service provider and customers (Grönroos & Voima, 2013). Hence, organisation can involve in value co-creation through social media in two major ways: creating MGC that co-create value for both the provider and customers (Brey, 2019) and facilitating or enabling customers to create UGC and engage in the co-creation process (Grönroos & Voima, 2013).

Organisation creates and presents content in social media for carrying out marketing and promotional activities, e.g., SMM. Unlike traditional online marketing, creating and processing social media content requires understanding of social media environment and its platforms, social media users and the influence of social media on organisational changes and adaption. Social media is an interactive and open network system, where anyone can participate or share knowledge freely and openly. Hence, literature indicates that insights from social media if appropriately extracted and processed to form marketing knowledge, social media become distinctive resource for value creation (Cheung et al., 2020). The SD logic notes that organisation can facilitate customer value co-creation by integrating resources and developing a collaborative service ecosystem, whereby customer create value with the organisation and also with other customers (Grönroos & Voima, 2013). In this regard, customers who play an active role in value co-creation are the organisation's focal point. In social media world, customers who gain the knowledge and ability to participate in a product or service design and improvement are defined as virtual prosumers. Hence, organisation should find ways to incorporate (facilitate or engage) prosumers as such they will work as free ambassador and value co-creator for the organisation.

Previous studies on value co-creation have theorised various models as theoretical lenses for investigating value co-creation using social media platforms. Prahalad & Ramaswamy (2004) proposed building blocks of interactions between firms and customers, i.e., Dialogue, Access, Risk assessment, and Transparency (DART) model that facilitate co-creation experience.

Hargrave and Van De Ven (2006) introduced a collective action model of institutional innovation which states that change and innovation come from participants' interactions and the dialectical process. Maglio et al. (2009) devised five stages, whereas Kietzmann et al. (2011) proposed seven building blocks also known as social media honeycomb model to illustrate how firms should engage with social media. Kao et al. (2016) outlined IEPAR (Interact-Engage-Propose-Act-Realize) of utilising social media as a co-creation platform with customers. Ge & Gretzel (2018) established taxonomy of value co-creation transpiring in firm-customer interactions on social media. Seran (Potra) & Izvercian (2014) provided an enriching approach regarding managerial decision to make efficient use of prosumer innovative potential in value co-creation. Prosumers actively seek potential ways to involve in value co-creation with firms.

Discussion and findings

Influence of SM on organisation: a push strategy to value co-creation

Social media has offered both organisations and customers with many new opportunities. Social media has provided customers with an unprecedented level of freedom to express their thoughts, share their knowledge and influence others' behaviour. Eventually, social media becomes a significant component of daily lives of global population and "media of choice" across the whole world. At the same time, organisations are enforced to introduce new and competitive business models aligning with social media and to build relationship with customers of greater reach using marketing and branding strategies (Dwivedi et al., 2020). Social media has pushed organisation to become value co-creation facilitator (Brey, 2019). Marketing plays a central role in designing strategies of creating value using social media, for both organisation and customers, shifting focus from traditional digital marketing to value co-creation through dyadic conversation between employees and customers.

Roblek et al. (2013) illustrate that social media and its environment provide organisation with access to knowledge in a form of customer intelligence and competitive intelligence that further push organisational changes and adoption of strategies necessary to facilitate customer value creation process (see Figure 8.1). Social media allows organisation to access ideas of disparate actors, who can be "social customer," "creative customers," "social media influencers" and "prosumers" – they are knowledgeable, have ability to influence and are actively creating and disseminating relatable and value-adding contents (Brey, 2019; Dhanesh & Duthler, 2019). These social media users not only share their knowledge but also post their feelings, criticize, inquire and provide feedback about products or service improvements. These sorts of social media contents are a great source of understanding customers' cognitive and emotional assessments, which are high of importance to theorise organisational strategies for social media value co-creation. Therefore, the key consideration of push strategy is to monitor social media conversations, to extract fresh ideas, to relate the insights to the organisation's objectives and, finally, to generate customised posting or content that is relatable to customers' needs and wants (Brey, 2019).

Value co-creation on social media is unique and challenging as it requires understanding of social media content while tackling overall meaningful relationships between an organisation and creative online communities (Beig & Khan, 2018). The push strategy to social media value co-creation is largely driven by content pertaining to customers' wants and needs. Organisation must design for the effective posting that triggers customers to continue their interaction but in a desirable way of improving organisational and customer value. In order to illustrate how organisation can facilitate customers' value co-creation, this chapter adapts Brey's (2019) social media value co-creation framework. Figure 8.1 provides six vertical categories, including respond, transact, educate, awareness, stimulate and entertain.

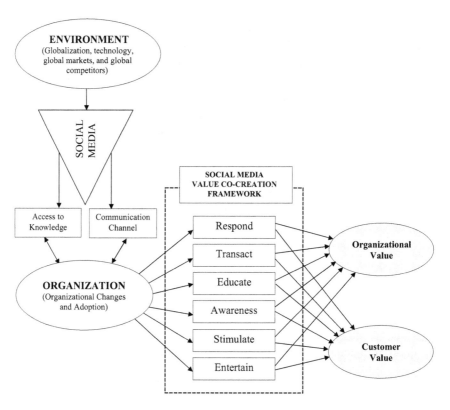

Figure 8.1 Social medial value co-creation framework.

Respond – It is fundamental for organisation to respond to customer's question, concerns or interests. Analysing social media content and its databases is a prerequisite to having a meaningful engagement with customer conversations to address potential concerns or benefits. For instance, a customer expressed disappointment with a restaurant dining experience, by posting on the brands' Facebook page: "I never thought they would send such worst kind of food. I ordered nachos and they sent something like *gravy type masala* with burned chips … it was really awful", while another customer voiced that if the space is wider, then it would be great. This review on social media imparts credibility to the information and customers put trust on the review (Lee, Kim, Chung, Ahn, & Lee, 2016). Management should take additional steps in responding and monitoring social media content in order to rectify the problem via service recovery or to avail new opportunities to deliver organisational value through the public demonstration of customer responsiveness.

Transact – In order to encourage customers to take actions related to buying products, organisation can prepare transact content through social media. In the context of South Korea, Lee et al. (2016) evidence that social media activities influence customers' intention to purchase through social commerce tools. Brey (2019) exemplifies that if a store offers a discounted price for being an active Twitter follower by sharing the offer or ordering through online platform, then organisation will have the co-created value of revenue and exposure and at the same, for the customers, a value proposition and social equity through sharing will be established.

Educate – The aim of educate vertical is to push brand (or product or service) knowledge and its pertinent options/alternatives and features. This strategy intended to increase customer engagement and learning opportunities about products and services. For instance, LifeSpring as a leading community-based mental health institute, through their official Facebook page and YouTube channel, provides a series of mini tutorials about their programs and features. They also used comments and queries posted on their social media in order to customise their tutorials towards customers' needs and benefits. These sorts of content and informative videos and tutorials generate awareness of what makes their service offerings innovative and different while customers also receive useful information, which helps gain understanding of service offerings, and its purchase options, and potential benefits.

Awareness – This strategy is one of the creative ways to make customers familiar with the organisation and its brand by eliciting customers' engagement in dialogue regarding community and societal activities. Awareness content advocates the topics of customers' interests outside of products or services, non-brand information. For instance, a coffee shop enterprise, through their Facebook fan page, initiates environmental care campaigns, positing slogan such as: "Protecting the earth is our responsibility to ourselves and coming generations. What can we do to slow down the speed of global warming?" The firm was successful in creating awareness about the topic and attracting large number of fans and establishing effective community interaction – which is potentially supportive to nurture future business and customer engagement. Customers and community interests were also fulfilled as the events/campaigns match with their value system.

Stimulate – Organisation can facilitate opportunities and stimulate customers to share their service or brand-related experience and stories through social media. The aim of this strategy is to derive customers' emotional attachment with the brand, which helps strengthen brand-customer relationship and engagement. Disparate customers have unique stories to share – which are the potential ways to encourage customers' active engagement and enhance brand reputation. Customers also gain co-created value from participating in this process by building social capital (become famous, new relationship) within the brand community. A non-profit organisation, Child & Old Age Care, for instance, successfully creates deeper emotional attachment among their fans or followers through posting stories of lost children and old aged parents, and appeal their followers to share the post, while encouraging to share new experiences or similar stories.

Entertain – Social media users find entertainment features or content as exciting and gratifying whether the content brand-related or non-brand-related. Beig & Khan (2018) discuss that brand-related humorous content such as witty remarks, jokes, funny photos, animations and short comedy clips are consumed, produced or contributed by social media users to satisfy their needs for relaxation and entertainment. Hence, the use of entertainment content is one of the creative strategies to display brand personality and value proposition and also useful to humanise and generates engagement through strategy supporting similar content. For instance, a professional sports team starts in friendly joking with their opponents using Twitter to gain the competitive spirit outside of the actual game. By initiating share worthy content, organisation pushes its customers (or fans) to make the content viral, allowing fans to actively engage with the brand and developing memorable relationship. In return, customers also gain intrinsic value of relieving mental stress and creating a positive mental association with the idea of the content or in particular the brand. Table 8.1 represents a summary of discussion on push strategy to value co-creation in the social media platforms.

Influence of organisation on SM: a pull strategy to value co-creation

Realising the importance and recognition of social media value co-creation, organisations start to uphold online brand communities and social media public pages (Parveen, Jaafar, & Ainin, 2015). With the opportunity of accessing unprecedented level of freedom of knowledge sharing and influencing others, customers are participating in knowledge conversation using social media and they want to be a part of the brand building and service

Table 8.1 A push strategy to value co-creation in social media

Push strategy	Customers' engagement in social media	Organisation strategy
Respond	Customers put trust on public review on social media.	Organisation should take steps to monitor public review, respond via service recovery or avail new opportunity and improve credibility.
Transact	Social media influence customers' purchase intention. Customers buy through social media.	Organisation should offer discounted price for being an active social media by sharing the offer or ordering through online platform.
Educate	Customers learn from social media.	Organisation should provide useful information, mini tutorials and informative videos in order for customers to gain understanding of service offerings and their benefits and purchase options.
Awareness	Customers show interest in non-brand information and involve in community and social activities using social media.	Organisation should create contents advocating topics of community and society wellbeing, which is potentially supportive for customer engagement.
Stimulate	Customers participate in value co-creation within brand community in social media.	Organisation should create contents to derive customers' emotional attachment with the brand.
Entertain	Social media users find entertainment features or content as exciting and gratifying.	Organisation should create brand-related humorous content and display brand personality and value proposition.

improvement programs (Chepurna & Rialp Criado, 2018). Consequently, organisations are searching for ways to get in touch with a special group of customers, who are prosumers with the ability to participate and influence their social networks. This section highlights organisational strategies to engage prosumers, in order to make them involve in value co-creation, whereby they become enthusiastically attached with brand, brand promoter and free ambassador for the organisation. This study adapted the prosumer creativity and focus model, as proposed by Seran (Potra) and Izvercian (2014), which provides four key strategies through which organisation incorporates prosumers' contribution in product or service achievement.

Customisation – This strategy represents the initial response of the organisation towards consumers' desire of customised products or services. For instance, Pizza Hut Brunei (www.pizzahut.com.bn) offers standard products (and multiple alternative offers) in which consumers could select or combine at ease from an existing and predefined offer. Mobile services have different packages in which customers can choose or order to suit their particular needs. The aim of this strategy is to make strategic use of company's resources to maximise profits and sales. This strategy, also known as mass customisation, provides customers with a range of default choices of service from which they must to pick the desired products or services. Mass customisation limits prosumers role in the design and development of new products and services, whereas value co-creation process provides prosumers with the opportunity or facility of active involvement of sharing ideas and experiences in order for the organisation to innovate new products and services or improvement of existing services (Kristensson, Matthing, & Johansson, 2008).

Crowd sourcing – This organisational strategy represents a way of getting help from the prosumers and benefitting them, who can bring innovative ideas or solution to a problem the organisation faces. For instance, one inspiring case of crowd sourcing was presented by Yadav, Kamboj, and Rahman (2016) is "Crash the Pepsi IPL" – a creation of 30-second advertisement for Pepsi Co. in India. A series of events including creating and uploading ad, registering and sharing the YouTube link, short-listing and finalising the winners, and showing the five winners' ads on TV during Pepsi IPL-2015 was very exciting and successful in engaging customers and creating a feeling among customers, and stimulating their creativity and innovations. These sorts of participations bring entire communities into the value co-creation platforms, a variety of ideas and local and international recognition for the organising company. The crowd sourcing provides company with increased sales and brand value, enhanced customer relationship and improved recommendations and e-WOM (Seran (Potra) & Izvercian, 2014).

Working together – This strategy of working together represents collaboration between prosumers and company, where organisation initiates a shared service system/program (firm-prosumer) – in which prosumer is the centre of value creation/development activities and company becomes the resource integrators or the supplier of prosumers' needs. With few limitations and specifications set by the organisation, prosumers can use the resources to design their products/service delivery, to promote their standpoints and hobbies and to make profits or become famous. The strategic use and management of Facebook, YouTube and other social networking and user-generated content tools is the strategy of working together that shifts the role of consumers as passive recipients into active participants in value co-creation process. Seran (Potra) and Izvercian (2014) cited an example of Ponoko website (www.ponoko.com), where prosumers can design their virtual product with the help of design software and they can get the physical product printed by 3D printing. Prosumers have the legal rights and ownership of the innovative design and product; they can also sell it for profits. Ponoko provides this service for a fee. Another example is No Music Media (www.youtube.com/c/NoMusicMedia) which is a YouTube channel dedicated to remaking of famous Nasheeds (Islamic songs) without music for their non-music fans. The individual producers of the Nasheeds can use the platform for free to accumulate more views from a particular segment and become famous and benefitted.

Kao et al. (2016) proposed IEPAR model (Interact, Engage, Propose, Act, and Realize) of value co-creation with consumers through social media, illustrating a case of Taiwanese franchise (a leading global coffee shop chain). The enterprise uses Facebook fan page for brand management. Through environmental care campaigns, the firm attracts a large number of fans and establishes an effective community interaction, following the similar principles of DART-FB (Dialogue, Access, Risk assessment, Transparency, Fun, and Benefits). The platform supported prosumers' creative thinking without interfering or manipulating any negative comments that were posted by consumers, rather the chief brand manager offered incentive reward to encourage consumer's exchange of ideas – which essentially provided the firm with unexpected insights, from which various proposals could be developed. Through this process of working together, prosumers developed affective engagement (emotional identification) with the online brand community and they were more likely to participate and offer responses for the potential collective innovation. In return, the enterprise gains cost reduction (less or no cost in market surveys and new product development process), expansion of consumer base (consumers' sharing and forwarding it through social media) and service recovery (opportunity to quickly respond to consumers' demands for products and services).

Creative commons – This strategy of creative commons represents a certain perspective which brings together prosumers and connects them in a service. The organisation provides prosumers with a platform or system, where prosumers collaborate among themselves (prosumer-prosumer) or with other consumers (prosumer-customers) in order to co-create value through sharing knowledge, responding and criticising to a problem or solution. In these open source systems of value co-creation, the organisation receives high reputation and sustainable advantage of future profit, whereas prosumers also become famous in their social networks by solving problems and meeting needs (Seran (Potra) & Izvercian, 2014). Examples of such creative commons strategy can be "research gate" (www.researchgate.net) and "Wikipedia" (www.wikipedia.org). These sorts of platforms are built collaboratively by millions of people that fetches a huge and priceless reputation and global recognition for the brand (or the company or the founder), who provided the open system. Disparate actors jointly access the platform, which they do not own or control unilaterally, and using the platform, they hold unique brand associations expanding the potential of brand knowledge (Chandler & Vargo, 2011).

Supporting the brand communities, and encouraging active learning through an organisational design, the organisation manages to create service ecosystems that help benefit from value co-creation of service offerings (co-design) and develop innovative ways to profit from the brand community's co-created value (Seran (Potra) & Izvercian, 2014). Using Prahalad & Ramaswamy's (2004) DART model of value co-creation (Dialogue, Access, Risk assessment, and Transparency), Smaliukiene et al. (2015) analyse service ecosystems and value co-creation process of "Couch Surfing International, Inc." (a non-profit corporation that provides hospitality service platform and social network services) and "TripAdvisor LLC" (a public corporation that provides travel services). These online travel service providers provide platforms that integrate customer-to-customer (guest-to-host) interactions and value co-creation in their platforms. These platforms provide customers with full access to resources on platform. For instance, customers can engage through participation and citizenship behaviour; they can directly involve in dialogue with service providers, customers, friend of friend, destination experts; they have access to ranking, comments, reviews, photos, videos, locations; they have freedom to express positive or negative feedback visible in public. Through this process of value co-creation, prosumers jointly access the platform, where they create value of co-design, know-how exchange, personal interaction and experience sharing through participation and citizenship behaviour. By providing these value facilitations, organisation gains knowledge on creative ideas and innovative design on the trip, and builds sustainable service ecosystem that provides huge brand recognition and extraordinary competitive advantage.

A conceptual model of prosumer value co-creation through social media

As this study regards the customers who want to participate in value co-creation process as prosumers, it is essential for marketers to understand prosumers' resources (e.g., knowledge, skills, social networks and others) and their motivation and attitudes in co-creating value with organisation or with other customers. Since service providers' competencies are important in facilitating a satisfying and appropriate service encounter, at the same way, for organisation, prosumers' motivations, capabilities and experiences are critical resources in value co-creation through social media. Hence, the aim of this section is to offer a conceptual framework to understand prosumers' value co-creation through social media. Figure 8.2 shows that both barriers and motivators play a role in influencing prosumer to co-create value. Islam, Hoque, and Jamil (2020), for instance, found that responsiveness, user's attitude, accessibility and perceived ease of use indicate discriminating role in the usage of online health services in the Asian context. Organisations should involve in this value co-creation process by enabling stimulus to motivate prosumers as free ambassadors. The conceptual framework also highlights prosumer value co-creation attitude influences value co-creation behaviour, which in turn impacts on social media value co-creation behaviour, as reflected by organisational value, customer value and societal value.

Scholars underscore both motivating factors and inhibiting factors that affect prosumers' participation (e.g., Chepurna & Rialp Criado, 2018). Organisations should find ways to improve customer-centricity by reducing inhibiting factors that negatively affect customers' participation while motivating customers who want to participate in the value co-creation process. For instance, scholars summarise motivating factors including learning benefits, social integrative (new connection or collaboration), personal integrative (own status, self-confidence), hedonic value and incentives as financial benefits (Constantinides, Brünink, & Romero, 2015). Other scholars reveal deterrent factors that negatively affect prosumers' value co-creation including internal deterrence (i.e., lack of trust, technology anxiety, no shared values with brand, scepticism, technology perceived ease of use and inertia) and external deterrence (task layout, no offline meeting and personal availability) (Chepurna & Rialp Criado, 2018). Organisations should understand these determinants and incorporate necessary resource in order to facilitate both prosumers' value co-creation process.

The theoretical backdrop of the relationship pertaining to the framework includes theory of planned behaviour (TPB) model (Ajzen, 1991; from Chepurna & Rialp Criado, 2018), and Stimulus-Organism-Response (S-O-R) framework (Jacoby, 2002; from Kamboj et al., 2018). TPB explains that a number of factors including motivating factors or inhibiting factors determine or guide individual's attitude, which in turn influence behaviour intentions and then actual behaviour. Amin et al. (2021) show the evidence of this motivation-attitude-behaviour (MAB) theory in modelling employee value co-creation behaviour. Kamboj et al. (2018) also reveal that customers' motivations for participation in social networking sites (i.e., building interpersonal relationships, entertainment, information seeking, brand likeability and incentives) positively influence customer participation, which in turn significantly affects brand trust and brand loyalty. Subsequently, both brand trust and brand loyalty positively influence branding co-creation in brand communities on social media.

Amin et al. (2021) found three dimensions including interaction attitude, responsive behaviour and knowledge sharing to reflect employee value co-creation attitude. The framework of this study also suggests adding "brand experience attitude" to reflect prosumer value co-creation attitude. This is because prosumers are from the customers, who are being targeted by the marketing and brand promotional activities.

The outcomes of prosumer value co-creation are more collective and appealing to wider community. The proposed framework, hence, links prosumer value co-creation behaviour to outcomes such as organisational value, customer value and societal value. As identified in different places of the previous discussion, the proposed framework summarises co-create value or major consequences (e.g., Brey, 2019; Kao et al., 2016) including *organisational value* (e.g., increase revenues or moves customers through the purchase funnel, demonstrate customer responsiveness, establish credibility

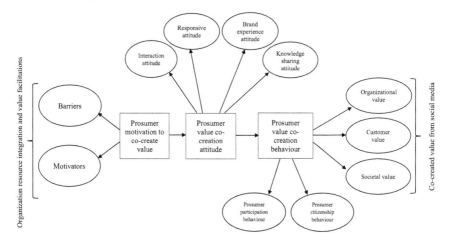

Figure 8.2 A proposed model of prosumer value co-creation through social media.

and trust, sustainable competitive advantage and e-WOM), *customer value* (e.g., highlight voice of customers, value-based customer service, gain insights into products/services, knowledge or learning related to community and social interest and social capital and social network) and *societal value* (e.g., social and community concerns are addressed, new and innovative approach to solve common interests and receive opportunities to nurture creative community's needs and wants).

Theoretical and managerial implications

This paper makes three theoretical contributions to the existing value co-creation literature. First, this research is the first one to design and exemplified push and pulls strategies for value co-creation using social media platforms. In attending the influence of social media, this study discusses organisational change and adaptation in order to apply push strategy to value co-creation through social media. In doing so, this study has used Brey's (2019) social media value co-creation framework and illustrated the framework's application using examples from the Asian context. The pertinent discussion presents understanding social media contents that co-create value. Second, this study has used Seran (Potra) and Izvercian's (2014) the prosumer creativity and focus model in order to discuss pull strategy to value co-creation, citing cases from the Asian context. Hence, this paper provides new insights into organisational push and pulls strategies of value co-creation and extends the existing knowledge on value co-creation through social media in the Asian context. Third, this is the first paper, so far, to propose a conceptual model of prosumer value co-creation through social media. In proposing the model, this paper identify key motivators and inhibitors that may affect prosumer motivation to co-create value, key dimensions that have the potential to reflect prosumer value co-creation attitude and potential outcomes pertaining to organisational value, customer value and societal value. The conceptual model is expected to offer a new lens of studying prosumers value co-creation in digital platform like social media and opens opportunities for further empirical investigation.

This study finding has various managerial and societal implications. Firstly, this paper provides insights on how can organisations utilise social media as a resource of creative ideas, trending news or concerns and innovative knowledge and insights. Consequently, in order to push customers to engage in value co-creation with service providers, managers and marketers should utilise social media as resource integrators and generate important contents that co-create value. For instance, in an empirical study, Parveen et al. (2015) explored that social media usage positively impacted on organisational performance in customer relationship management and improved information accessibility and cost reduction concerning marketing and customer service. Secondly, the study notes that prosumers' participation in social medial value co-creation is highly important in building brand community and maintaining customer relationship in the long run. Hence, for creating a collaborative platform between organisation and prosumer, managers should actively follow pull strategies, including customisation, crowd sourcing, working together and creative commons. Since organisation is looking for ways to customer-centric approach, managers may approach the strategies to make prosumer to be involved in value co-creation, whereby they become enthusiastically attached with brand, brand promoter and free ambassador for the organisation. This phenomenon has changed consumer behaviour and how organisations conduct their business (Dwivedi et al., 2020). Nisar et al. (2019) illustrate that the effective utilisation of social media within an organisation (for instance, in community of practice-based discussion groups) positively affects organisational performance through increasing information richness and informal and social communication. Thirdly, this study reveals that prosumers' value co-creation behaviour in social media potentially exerts significant influence on organisational value, customer value and societal value. This study also informs manager about motivators and inhibiting factors that affect prosumer attitude towards value co-creation and thus help organisations in designing customer-driven value co-creation practices through social media platforms. By understanding prosumers' sphere of value co-creation, managers may create and nurture a co-creation culture in social media and gain huge reputation and customer-based brand equity.

Conclusions and future research directions

This paper builds on previous studies to develop a general approach towards push and pull strategy to value co-creation that can be applied across social media channels. Following the push strategy, organisation understands social media influence and its data or contents, and develops social media content to co-create value. In contrast, following the pull strategy, organisation incorporates prosumers' role and creativity into strategic corporate co-creation activities. The chapter highlights practical examples from the Asian context to provide detailed solutions and specific guidelines for applying of model and relevant strategies. Hence, the chapter helps understanding the shifting marketing strategies from traditional digital marketing to new and innovative marketing strategies such as social media marketing, content marketing, value co-creation, e-WOM and free brand ambassador. This chapter also offers a conceptual model of prosumer value co-creation through social media. The discussion further provides necessary shreds of evidence in order for organisation to facilitate prosumers value co-creation through social media. Thus, this chapter is expected to help researchers to formulate measures for organisational performances in handling potential problems and concerns posed by employees and prosumers while involving in value co-creation. This chapter systematises the ways prosumer can engage in ongoing participative and citizenship knowledge conversations/ value co-creation behaviour using social media. For instance, generative role-taking takes place in social media platform within the organisations in order to argue, complain and share frustrations publicly, and the conceptualisation of generative role-taking can be used to describe the ways prosumers can engage in ongoing participative and citizenship knowledge conversations (i.e., value co-creation) using social media. This chapter offers a conceptual model, which requires further investigation at empirical level. Nonetheless, the proposed model of prosumer value co-creation through social media platform will supplement past research. Future research should consider the successful use and application of the proposed model in the context of Asian digital economy.

References

Ajzen, I. (1991). The theory of planned behavior. *Organizational Behavior and Human Decision Processes*, *50*(2), 179–211. https://doi.org/10.1016/0749-5978(91)90020-T

Amin, M., Shamim, A., Ghazali, Z., & Khan, I. (2021). Employee motivation to co-create value (EMCCV): Construction and validation of scale. *Journal of Retailing and Consumer Services*, *58*(October 2020), 102334. https://doi.org/10.1016/j.jretconser.2020.102334

Beig, F. A., & Khan, M. F. (2018). Impact of social media marketing on brand experience: A study of select apparel brands on facebook. *Vision*, *22*(3), 264–275. https://doi.org/10.1177/0972262918785962

Brey, E. T. (2019). Co-creating value from social media: A framework. *Journal of Creating Value*, *5*(2), 222–236. https://doi.org/10.1177/2394964319869054

Chandler, J. D., & Vargo, S. L. (2011). Contextualization and value-in-context: How context frames exchange. *Marketing Theory*, *11*(1), 35–49. https://doi.org/10.1177/1470593110393713

Chepurna, M., & Rialp Criado, J. (2018). Identification of barriers to co-create on-line: The perspectives of customers and companies. *Journal of Research in Inter-active Marketing, 12*(4), 452–471. https://doi.org/10.1108/JRIM-01-2018-0018

Cheung, M. L., Pires, G. D., Rosenberger, P. J., Leung, W. K. S., & Ting, H. (2020). Investigating the role of social media marketing on value co-creation and en-gagement: An empirical study in China and Hong Kong. *Australasian Marketing Journal* (xxxx). https://doi.org/10.1016/j.ausmj.2020.03.006

Chua, A. Y. K., & Banerjee, S. (2013). Customer knowledge management via social media: The case of Starbucks. *Journal of Knowledge Management, 17*(2), 237–249. https://doi.org/10.1108/13673271311315196

Clement, J. (2020). How many people use social media? Retrieved December 6, 2020, from Statistica website: https://www.statista.com/statistics/278414/number-of-worldwide-social-network-users/

Constantinides, E., Brünink, L. A., & Romero, C. L. (2015). Customer motives and benefits for participating in online co-creation activities. *International Journal of Internet Marketing and Advertising, 9*(1), 21. https://doi.org/10.1504/IJIMA.2015.068346

Dhanesh, G. S., & Duthler, G. (2019). Relationship management through social media influencers: Effects of followers' awareness of paid endorsement. *Public Relations Review, 45*(3), 101765. https://doi.org/10.1016/j.pubrev.2019.03.002

Dwivedi, Y. K., Ismagilova, E., Hughes, D. L., Carlson, J., Filieri, R., Jacobson, J., … Wang, Y. (2020). Setting the future of digital and social media marketing research: Perspectives and research propositions. *International Journal of Infor-mation Management*, (May), 102168. https://doi.org/10.1016/j.ijinfomgt.2020.102168

Edvardsson, B., Tronvoll, B., & Gruber, T. (2011). Expanding understanding of service exchange and value co-creation: A social construction approach. *Jour-nal of the Academy of Marketing Science, 39*(2), 327–339. https://doi.org/10.1007/s11747-010-0200-y

Ge, J., & Gretzel, U. (2018). A taxonomy of value co-creation on Weibo: A commu-nication perspective. *International Journal of Contemporary Hospitality Manage-ment, 30*(4), 2075–2092. https://doi.org/10.1108/IJCHM-09-2016-0557

Goh, K. Y., Heng, C. S., & Lin, Z. (2013). Social media brand community and con-sumer behavior: Quantifying the relative impact of user- and marketer-generated content. *Information Systems Research, 24*(1), 88–107. https://doi.org/10.1287/isre.1120.0469

Grönroos, C., & Voima, P. (2013). Critical service logic: Making sense of value crea-tion and co-creation. *Journal of the Academy of Marketing Science, 41*(2), 133–150. https://doi.org/10.1007/s11747-012-0308-3

Hargrave, T. J., & Van De Ven, A. H. (2006). A collective action model of institu-tional innovation. *Academy of Management Review, 31*(4), 864–888. https://doi.org/10.5465/amr.2006.22527458

Islam, S., Hoque, M. R., & Jamil, M. A. Al. (2020). Predictors of users' preferences for online health services. *Journal of Consumer Marketing, 37*(2), 215–225. https://doi.org/10.1108/JCM-05-2018-2689

Jacoby, J. (2002). Stimulus-organism-response reconsidered: An evolutionary step in modeling (consumer) behavior. *Journal of Consumer Psychology, 12*(1), 51–57. https://doi.org/10.1207/S15327663JCP1201_05

Kamboj, S., Sarmah, B., Gupta, S., & Dwivedi, Y. (2018). Examining branding co-creation in brand communities on social media: Applying the paradigm of stimulus-organism-response. *International Journal of Information Management, 39*(October 2017), 169–185. https://doi.org/10.1016/j.ijinfomgt.2017.12.001

Kao, T. Y., Yang, M.-H., Wu, J.-T. Ben, & Cheng, Y.-Y. (2016). Co-creating value with consumers through social media. *Journal of Services Marketing, 30*(2), 141–151. https://doi.org/10.1108/JSM-03-2014-0112

Kietzmann, J. H., Hermkens, K., McCarthy, I. P., & Silvestre, B. S. (2011). Social media? Get serious! Understanding the functional building blocks of social media. *Business Horizons, 54*(3), 241–251. https://doi.org/10.1016/j.bushor.2011.01.005

Kristensson, P., Matthing, J., & Johansson, N. (2008). Key strategies for the successful involvement of customers in the co-creation of new technology-based services. *International Journal of Service Industry Management, 19*(4), 474–491. https://doi.org/10.1108/09564230810891914

Lee, Y. K., Kim, S. Y., Chung, N., Ahn, K., & Lee, J. W. (2016). When social media met commerce: A model of perceived customer value in group-buying. *Journal of Services Marketing, 30*(4), 398–410. https://doi.org/10.1108/JSM-04-2014-0129

Lucia-Palacios, L., Pérez-López, R., & Polo-Redondo, Y. (2020). How situational circumstances modify the effects of frontline employees' competences on customer satisfaction with the store. *Journal of Retailing and Consumer Services, 52*(August 2019), 101905. https://doi.org/10.1016/j.jretconser.2019.101905

Maglio, P. P., Vargo, S. L., Caswell, N., & Spohrer, J. (2009). The service system is the basic abstraction of service science. *Information Systems and E-Business Management, 7*(4), 395–406. https://doi.org/10.1007/s10257-008-0105-1

Majchrzak, A., Faraj, S., Kane, G. C., & Azad, B. (2013). The contradictory influence of social media affordances on online communal knowledge sharing. *Journal of Computer-Mediated Communication, 19*(1), 38–55. https://doi.org/10.1111/jcc4.12030

Nisar, T. M., Prabhakar, G., & Strakova, L. (2019). Social media information benefits, knowledge management and smart organizations. *Journal of Business Research, 94*(May 2018), 264–272. https://doi.org/10.1016/j.jbusres.2018.05.005

Parveen, F., Jaafar, N. I., & Ainin, S. (2015). Social media usage and organizational performance: Reflections of Malaysian social media managers. *Telematics and Informatics, 32*(1), 67–78. https://doi.org/10.1016/j.tele.2014.03.001

Prahalad, C. K., & Ramaswamy, V. (2004). Co-creation experiences: The next practice in value creation. *Journal of Interactive Marketing, 18*(3), 5–14. https://doi.org/10.1002/dir.20015

Roblek, V., Bach, M. P., Meško, M., & Bertoncelj, A. (2013). The impact of social media to value added in knowledge-based industries. *Kybernetes, 42*(4), 554–568. https://doi.org/10.1108/K-01-2013-0014

Seran (Potra), S., & Izvercian, M. (2014). Prosumer engagement in innovation strategies the prosumer creativity and focus model. *Management Decision, 52*(10), 1968–1980. https://doi.org/10.1108/MD-06-2013-0347

Smaliukiene, R., Chi-Shiun, L., & Sizovaite, I. (2015). Consumer value co-creation in online business: The case of global travel services. *Journal of Business Economics and Management, 16*(2), 325–339. https://doi.org/10.3846/16111699.2014.985251

Tapscott, D., & Williams, A. D. (2008). *Wikinomics: How mass collaboration changes everything*. Portfolio, New York, NY.

Xie, K., Wu, Y., Xiao, J., & Hu, Q. (2016). Value co-creation between firms and customers: The role of big data-based cooperative assets. *Information and Management, 53*(8), 1034–1048. https://doi.org/10.1016/j.im.2016.06.003

Yadav, M., Kamboj, S., & Rahman, Z. (2016). Customer co-creation through social media: The case of 'Crash the Pepsi IPL 2015.' *Journal of Direct, Data and Digital Marketing Practice*, *17*(4), 259–271. https://doi.org/10.1057/dddmp.2016.4

Yi, Y., & Gong, T. (2013). Customer value co-creation behavior: Scale development and validation. *Journal of Business Research*, *66*(9), 1279–1284. https://doi.org/10.1016/j.jbusres.2012.02.026

9 The use of big data technology to support the transformation of public content management towards knowledge management

Ahmad Budi Setiawan, Ari Cahyo Nugroho, Karman and Bambang Mudjiyanto

Introduction

A research paper titled "Spreading True and Fake News Online" published in Science in March 2018 revealed a surprising discovery: "Fake news spreads much faster than actual news." In this study, Vosoughi et al. (2018) as scientists analysed a collection of 126,000 rumours (hoaxes) spread by approximately 3 million Twitter account holders between 2006 and 2017. In addition to finding that fictitious messages spread much faster than actual messages, we also analyse them. It also found that fictitious messages were able to reach a larger audiences than factual messages. The distribution of scams typically follows three patterns. First, the information disseminated takes advantage of public confusion and can therefore easily attract public attention; second, signs generally use references to people who are known to the public, even though the information is often twisted, cut out and even fabricated; third, the spread of hoax spills over into syndication by disseminating information via various social media.

The existence of hoax as internet negative content is increasingly becoming a problem in the midst of relatively low levels of information and political literacy in society. In fact, if you use rationality, people can recognise hoax from common features, such as often from unclear sites. It could also be that the title and body of information are often unrelated, and the sources cited are difficult to verify or even no sources at all. The information conveyed also targets the feelings of the reader so that it often gives a provocative and tendentious title as reported on *Kompas* magazine (Kompas, 25/8/08 2017, p. 15).

The rapid development of technology supports the emergence of new data whose development is also rapid in number. The data is supported by the existence of personal data that can be generated by individual data sharing activities (volunteered data), personal activities (observed data), as well as data from the relationship between the two (inferred data). The effects of the growing data are felt by social media companies like Facebook, LinkedIn,

DOI: 10.4324/9781003163824-12

Google, Microsoft or Yahoo search engines. The data is irregular, varied, structured or unstructured and has different formats. These data sets are commonly known as Big Data (Krishnan, 2013; Seref, 2013).

Indonesian Internet Network Providers Association (APJII) releases the Internet Users Survey and believes that internet users' penetration is the biggest contributor to hoaxes (APJII, 2017). Until 2017, the number of internet users in Indonesia was 143.27 million (more than 50% of Indonesia's population). The ease of internet access coupled with the presence of social media has increased the spread of hoaxes in society. The 2017 APJII survey identified that the highest media for spreading hoax was social media as much 92.4% (APJII, 2017). The behaviour of social media users is not supported by adequate digital literacy capabilities (post-truth era). This causes the spread of hoax to increase.

On the other hand, along with the massive presence of hoax in the community, Big Data technology is currently present along with the development of web 2.0 technology. Through Big Data technology, a large amount of data and large volumes of data are increasingly being explored. This is not limited to a collection of data that is processed, processed and used in processing a business process. Starting from the massive data, the information generated is able to make a radical contribution to the mindset and way of looking at a problem (Schonberger & Cukier, 2013).

When it comes to information, Big Data is able to present more complete data, not only in one-way or two-way relationships. For example, on Facebook, relationships that occur between users have more and more opportunities, ranging from friendship, work, hobbies or friends from school. A relationship is ultimately needed to solve certain problems (Associates, 2014). One of the characteristics of Big Data is that it contains unexpected, hidden and mass information that does not necessarily come from the usual data mining process. This information is the reason why Big Data becomes a very important thing for an organisation or enterprise.

The company's goals can be achieved if the IT department can work together with management. Therefore, we need supervision and management of IT functions so that they are able to make the most of IT resources (ISACA, 2012). Big Data is one of the new phenomena in the IT world that can benefit organisations. For the use of Big Data to bring benefits to the organisation, everyone got involved in Big Data integration process must be carried out properly and reliably and must not be partial (Zhang & Huang, 2013). An analogy to this theory is presented as the blind and elephants, where each part has a non-holistic interpretation. In other words, each part of the organisation only understands its part and thus has the ability to present biased information. Big Data in this case is seen as an integrated system of the organisation in order to find benefits.

On the other hand, Knowledge Management (KM) plays a fundamental role in supporting the symbiosis of tacit and overt knowledge in business, which can be used to make valuable decisions for the success of the organisation. These decisions are extremely important when it comes to preventing crises through strategy and reinvention. Big data can be used to analyse and organise the vast amount of available data in the form of knowledge in order to filter out the best and most valuable information, thus giving the organisation a competitive advantage. This chapter aims to understand the relationship between big data and KM, as well as how big data can serve as a factor in efficient data management.

Managing data that is very diverse and very large in number will require an efficient way to process it, especially if the information generated from the data is needed to support decision makers' decisions, it will take time to convert the data into information. Therefore, the principle of Big Data is very suitable to applications, where the principle of Big Data is to be able to manage a lot of different data and turn it into desired information in a very short time. In addition, the concept of Knowledge Management transforms information disseminated on social media into knowledge that needs to be managed. Given the very wide use of social media, this is something that needs to be considered, especially for the general public to see.

The duties and functions of media supervision are a very important part of the Ministry of Communication and Information of Republic Indonesia. This is in line with Presidential Instruction (Inpres) Number 9 of 2015 concerning Public Communication Management, in which the Ministry of Communication and Information Technology is responsible for reviewing information that is being developed, as well as monitoring and analysing media content. In carrying out these duties and functions, the Ministry of Communication and Information Technology of Indonesia entrusts them to the Media Monitoring Section of the Directorate of Media Management, Director General of Information and Public Communication. This division currently requires the use of Big Data technology in managing public issues circulating in society through digital media. This division is responsible for monitoring and processing the public media on a daily basis. In addition, their job is to collect information from government public relations in the regions and process it again. Apart from online and print media, social media is also one of the things that needs to be monitored.

Based on the problems described above, the use of Big Data technology in the management of public issues originating from digital media is needed in order to support the policy-making process. In addition, the integration of Big Data technology with the concept of Knowledge Management allows all data and information processed through big data machines to become knowledge and wisdom for the government. In the end, this knowledge and wisdom will greatly assist in the decision-making process and policy making for the whole Indonesia Government, so that the policies issued are effective and appropriate for the community. Thus, the research focuses on problems discussed in this study are how to implement the concept of Big Data which is integrated with the concept of Knowledge Management in issue management and public communication to support the government policy-making process.

Literature review

Big data technology

Big Data is defined as tools, processes and procedures that enable an organisation to create, manipulate and manage very large, diverse and fast data sets. Big Data is an organisational resource, i.e., information the use and processing of which is useful for improving knowledge and decision-making processes (Milton, 2009; Schmarzo, 2013). Gartner describes the Big Data dimension as 3V, namely Volume, Velocity, Variety (Gartner, 2009). As Big Data grows, it not only covers 3V, but expands to 5V, namely Volume, Velocity, Value, Veracity and Variety. Technically speaking, Big Data is a large set of both structured, semi- and unstructured data so that it cannot be processed with the usual relational database tools (Firat & Keane, 2013; Krishnan, 2013; Sawant & Shah, 2013; Zikopoulos et al., 2013; Schell, 2013; Seref & Duygu, 2013). Based on this understanding, Big Data is the terminology of huge data that is very large, fast, diverse, complex and capable of providing information that is very important and crucial. Big Data is a prediction consisting of artificial intelligence, machine learning and other features supporting the prediction process (Prajapati, 2013; Zaiying Liu, 2013). The emerging data has a chance to provide a political guide without prior implementation (Milton, 2009; Schonberger, 2013).

In addition to offering a big leap in organisational decision management and decision making, Big Data integration comes with several implementation challenges and risks. Big Data has capabilities beyond the mere processing of databases due to the characteristics of Big Data, which include data volume, speed, data variety/type and structure, data volatility/variability and value (Zikopoulos et al., 2013). Therefore, implementing Big Data requires a framework. To get the right framework, first define the Big Data features to apply as follows:

- amount and processing of data and possibilities
- variety of data/data sources
- required speed and timeliness
- targeted services, products, solutions and applications
- presentation of data, applications and interpretations and
- privacy, error handling and security.

Big Data emerges from all the things that are related in this world, very large, complex, at high speed. Big Data is a technological trend for new approaches to understanding the world and making business decisions (Muhtaroglu et al., 2013; Ohlhorst, 2013). These decisions are made on the basis of very large amounts of structured, unstructured and complex data (e.g., tweets, videos, commercial transactions). According to Bill Schmarzo, the Big Data integration process in an enterprise has a business maturity index consisting of several phases (Bill, 2013): Business Monitoring, Business Insights, Business Optimisation, Data Monetisation, Business Metamorphosis.

Characteristics of big data

Big Data is one of the new phenomena in the IT world and is able to provide benefits to organisations. For the application of Big Data to have benefits in the organisation, all involved in the Big Data integration process must be carried out appropriately and thoroughly and may not be partial (Zhang, 2013). The analogy of this theory is illustrated as blind people and elephants, where each part has a non-holistic interpretation. In other words, each part of the organisation only understands its part so that it has the opportunity to produce biased information.

Big Data in this case is seen as an integrated system of an organisation in order to find its benefits. A data is not categorised as "Big Data" just because of the large amount of data, but there are several characteristics that distinguish Big Data from other systems. Some characteristics of Big Data, namely, Big Data Systems have a VOLUME of very large data, which usually exceeds ordinary servers in general and this data will continue to grow every day. The amount of data can reach more than 100 TB and is usually stored in external infrastructure (not maintained alone). In addition, not only is the amount of data that many, Big Data also has a variety of data (VARIETY), with the format and type of data that is very diverse so that it requires a special process to be able to process it. In addition to the large and varied amount of data, Big Data must also be able to process the data in a very fast time (VELOCITY) so that the data can be useful not only because of the information generated but also because of the speed needed to process it. The fourth characteristic of Big Data is the truth of the data itself (VERACITY). For information that is processed from these data in order to become useful and trustworthy information, we also have to look at the source of the data used. Therefore, for the Big Data, the truth of the data is one thing that must be considered as well.

Knowledge management

Knowledge management is a formatted and directed system and process developed within an organisation to create, seek, collect, select, organise, document, store, maintain and disseminate information and knowledge in order to support the needs of each individual in companies so that they can be used in making good decisions to support business strategies. Knowledge management is used in the management of organisational knowledge to create value and produce competitive advantage or excellent performance. The combination of human knowledge in organisations will produce different organisational knowledge. However, organisations that have a lot of quality knowledge are not necessarily able to produce goods or services of the same quality. Therefore, it is important for a company to have Knowledge Management in order to get the maximum benefit from knowledge.

According to Short (2000), Knowledge Management is an effort to achieve organisational goals, through strategies to motivate and facilitate knowledge-workers to develop, and to improve their ability to interpret data and information using available information sources, experience, expertise, culture, character, personality, feelings and so on so that they can give meaning to others.

Davenport et al. (1998) state that Knowledge Management is a systematic, firm and deliberate effort to build, update and apply knowledge in order to maximise the effectiveness of knowledge linkages in the company and store it as knowledge assets to be updated on an ongoing basis to create creation and innovation. Meanwhile, Robert and James (1997) argue that a Knowledge Management concept is a process of creating, capturing and using knowledge to improve organisational performance. Knowledge Management is often associated with two types of activities. The first activity is to document and determine the appropriate individual knowledge and then disseminate it through the company database. KM also includes activities to facilitate the exchange of human knowledge via groupware, e-mail and the internet.

On the other hand, along with this, Laudon and Laudon (2004, 2008) state that knowledge management is a series of processes developed within an organisation to create, collect, maintain and disseminate knowledge of the organisation. Meanwhile, according to Turban et al. (2005), knowledge management is a process that helps organisations identify, select, organise, find and transfer important information and expertise that is already structured in organisations and knowledge in organisations that are not yet structured.

Knowledge management is a process of planning and controlling the performance of activities regarding the formation of a knowledge process, namely a process that helps an organisation or institution in obtaining, selecting, disseminating (distribution) and transferring information that is considered important and information obtained from a person's various expertise such as information appear during discussions to solve organisational problems, dynamic learning, strategic planning and decision-making processes. According to Wijaya (2014), knowledge management has a flow cycle known as the General Knowledge Model (GKM) as depicted in Figure 9.1.

The explanation of the General Knowledge Model is as follows:

1   Knowledge Creation, is a process of creating new knowledge, can be done through a process of development, discovery or capture of knowledge.

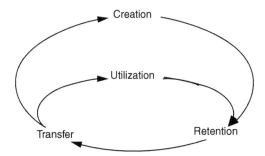

Figure 9.1 General knowledge model.

2   Knowledge Retention (knowledge storage) is a process that aims to maintain and retrieve existing knowledge.
3   Knowledge Transfer is a process for transferring knowledge from one party to another, including the process of communication, translation, modification and also sorting. Knowledge Transfer can also be understood as Knowledge Sharing.
4   Knowledge Utilisation is a process related to the use of existing knowledge.

Knowledge management is used to facilitate the collection, recording, organising, filtering, analysis, retrieval and dissemination of explicit and implicit knowledge and can demonstrate a very clear strategic function. The function of a knowledge management application is as an intermediary for the transfer of knowledge between providers and seekers of knowledge from the mind of the owner to an external storage place and vice versa, knowledge retrieval from external storage which is filtered according to needs and easily understood by users.

In the Knowledge Management process, knowledge can become a wisdom to support the decision-making process. In this case, according to Dewiyana (2006), the level of knowledge management can be described as a pyramid below (Figure 9.2).

The explanation for each level of knowledge management in the image above is as follows:

1   Level 1: Distributed data is transformed by processing (data processing) into information. At this level, it is usually called document management, namely managing the content of information (content management), organising and distributing information. Users can access and retrieve documents online in the database.
2   Level 2: Data is analysed and applied so that it becomes information. Users can contribute information to the system, create new content and

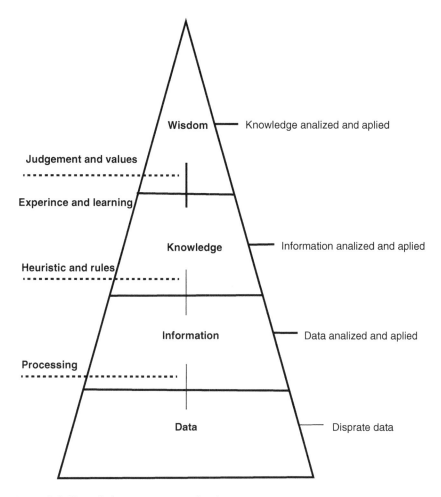

Figure 9.2 Knowledge management level.

develop knowledge databases. Users can read documents online, download, complete them and then send them to the desired destination. Thus, the information can be updated continuously.

3   Level 3: Information is analysed and applied so that it becomes knowledge. This requires an understanding of the input and output of information to support organisational activities. Knowledge is built by organisations through the process of acquiring, distributing, collaborating and communicating as well as creating new knowledge.

4   Level 4: Knowledge is analysed and applied so as to make people wise. At this level, enterprise intelligence is developed by building a network of experts, interaction with operational databases and performance support, where new knowledge is generated, added to the system.

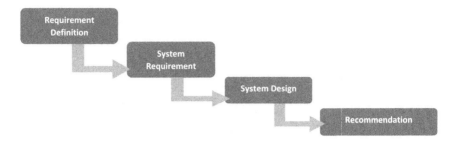

Figure 9.3 Modified waterfall method.

Research methods

This study uses a qualitative approach to try to explore the existing needs. To find alternative implementation options, this study uses the Modified Waterfall method. Although this method was originally used in the field of software engineering, this method is suitable for exploring various alternative options for implementing Big Data (Figure 9.3).

This study does not specifically discuss the whole stages of system implementation of Big Data Technology to support the transformation of public content management. Therefore, if it refers to the Modified Waterfall method, this study deals with only at the System Design stage. This research will go through four stages:

1   Formulation of System Requirements: At the beginning of the research will formulate the requirements needed by the Big Data System to monitor various public media. At this stage, interviews are conducted with officials related to public information managers at the Directorate General of Information and Public Communication to obtain information about business processes in managing public information.
2   Alternative System Design Options: After formulating the needs of the Big Data System, the next step is designing appropriate alternative choices to be applied to the Big Data System. At this stage, interviews are conducted with technical executing employees related to public information managers at the Directorate General of Information and Public Communication to obtain information on technical aspects and conditions.
3   Data Collection: Stages of data collection is carried out through the Focus Group Discussion (FGD) process to obtain Expert Judgment from relevant experts. This stage is carried out by discussions with experts from both big data and data science practitioners as well as academics

in the Information Technology field who have expertise in the field of data science.

4 Strengthening alternative choices: FGD results and surveys will be used to reinforce alternative implementation options that were previously designed.

5 Formulation of Recommendations: After that, a recommendation will be made to implement the Big Data system based on alternative choices that have been generated from this research.

Results and discussions

Formulation of system requirements

Before defining a Big Data model, which would be appropriate for use in handling negative content, we must first be able to define what Big Data system needs to handle negative content. The formulation of this need will be specified in the Business Process to make it clear what the process of Big Data system operations looks like with negative content, especially in media monitoring. Of these two tasks, the government simply wants to see if there is a "gap" between issues circulating in the media and public opinion by looking at government policies and programmes so that the government can predict that it will fill the "gap," for example by providing information related to the topic, review of the program of activities, etc. Public Issue Monitoring (MIP) is an activity consisting in media monitoring based on news headlines. The header that was displayed was for messages that were frequently used in other messages. Based on the data collected with the help of the FGD that has been carried out, the extensive Media Monitoring carried out using the Big Data system in the field of media monitoring gives two routine results, namely Public Issue Monitoring (MIP) and Monitoring Content Analysis (MCA) (Figure 9.4).

Meanwhile, Monitoring Content Analysis (MIP) is the activity of monitoring the media by viewing the content of the message. The message body displayed is the message with the most headers. By creating MIP reports, the use of sentiment analysis can speed up the news analysis process in conjunction with social network analysis (SNA), enriching the analysis results with information such as linking one number to other media. Unlike MIP, which only sees the message headers, at this stage, the analysis is more generated based on the message content.

System planning

Initially, in the management of public information content by the Directorate General of Public Information and Communication, public information content originated from the electronic format of printed media news or

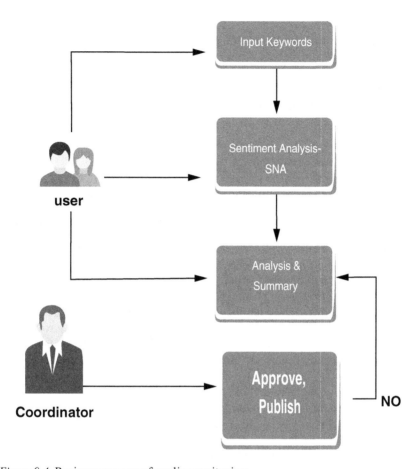

Figure 9.4 Business process of media monitoring.

news from electronic media in text format. Therefore, the data that is built is a structured data model and is a relational database such as MySQL, Oracle and others. In an increasingly massive technological development, the data is not only in the form of text document format but also in the form of image, sound and even video formats. Then, along with this, a business intelligence system was also built that used a structured and relational database with systems such as Cognos, Pentaho and others. The development of Big Data technology which has big data processing capabilities, enables data management of public information content with different technologies such as map reduction, high-performance computing clusters and many more. This means, in theory, that Big Data technology is part of Business Intelligence, and Big Data can be used to create an organisation that has a large source of information to support decision making. However, in this case, there are several things that differ in volume, not only big data, but the data growth is very fast so that in a short time the data can grow very

Table 9.1 Big data system characteristics

Components	Traditional data	Big data
Architecture	Centralised	Distributed
Data volume	Terabytes	Petabytes to exabytes
Data type	Structured or transactional	Unstructured or semi-structured
Data relationships	Known relationship	Complex/unknown relationship
Data model	Fixed schema	Schema-less

fast and big and the existing data has very large differences (diversity), of course, in large data sets itself, especially in the creation of a data warehouse, multiple transformation load extraction to handle various data. Big Data technology can become a standard that is both cleaned of various noise, also transformed so that it is much more compatible with existing or operating business processes for multiple organisations.

In implementing a decision-making system based on the management of public information content, Big Data Business Intelligence also requires technology that can support the business processes that exist within business intelligence itself so that it can function as expected. Therefore, it is necessary to build the right infrastructure and meet the needs of large data sets, one of which is very fast data processing, even though at the same time the data is large and growing rapidly. We will recognise the need for infrastructure to sustain Big Data technology (Table 9.1). In Big Data technology itself, infrastructure has different characteristics from traditional data.

Problems and challenges in the process of decision-making systems based on the management of public information content are in the process of data acquisition, data recording, extraction, cleaning, annotation, integration, aggregation, representation, analysis, modelling, interpretation and visualisation. Big data itself has applications and benefits for various fields as mentioned above. For this reason, there are two relevant technologies in Big Data infrastructure, namely:

1   High-Performance Computing Cluster (HPCC) or can be referred to as Data Analytics Supercomputer (DAS)
2   Hadoop Platform (Map Reduced-Based Platform)

From the two technological approaches, there are significant differences in terms of function and there are similarities in the processes that run within them. The similarity of the two technologies is that they both use more than one computer in the process of retrieving information or processing various information or even both can be seen using the concept of clusters in the technology architecture used. Basically, the two of them can also be well integrated to support each other.

High-Performance Computing Clusters (HPCC) itself basically builds a supercomputer consisting of more than one computer with certain

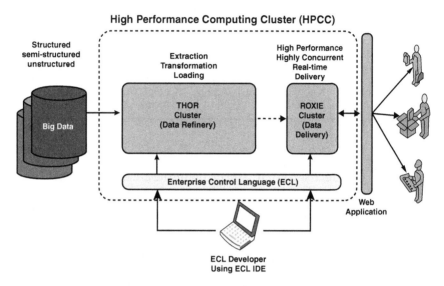

Figure 9.5 High-performance computing clustering.

specifications (usually the same) to help each other, or share tasks with each other so that they can collectively process data, especially in terms of data search. Large processes that usually run on their own, such as Extract, Transform and Load, are then analysed to obtain information that is more in line with the organisation's business needs. HPCC Technology uses a declarative, data-centric programming language, called Enterprise Control Language (ECL), to allow a team of programmers to process big data across a high-performance computing cluster without the programmer being involved in many of the lower level, imperative decisions (Figure 9.5).

Meanwhile, the Hadoop Platform itself is a technology project developed by Apache in managing large data so that it is far more effective and efficient. Hadoop itself consists of various components; even Hadoop itself has its own distributed file system called Hadoop File System (HDFS). The advantages of HDFS itself are (Figure 9.6):

- Fault tolerance and implemented on inexpensive hardware
- Write Once, read many, is a simple coherence, and moreover the framework that is built in Hadoop when we will use Hadoop, using Java technology.
- Moving computing/processes faster than moving data.
- Similar to Google File System, but HDFS divides files into blocks in distributed cluster nodes.
- Core components: master vs. slave, name node vs. data node, job tracker vs. task tracker.

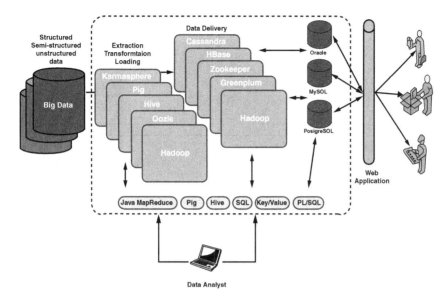

Figure 9.6 Hadoop platform.

Here's an overview of the Hadoop Platform:

In the implementation of the Big Data system in the context of managing public information content by the Directorate General of Information and Public Communication, the two technology architecture concepts are integrated. Here is one integration architecture between HPCC and Hadoop platforms (Figure 9.7):

There are differences in the database management system for public information content by the Directorate General of Information and Public Communication, which basically has a correlation between structured or organised data and database management system tools. Where the database management system used is software commonly used to manage database systems such as MySQL, Oracle, PostgreSQL and others. Based on the results of the discussion regarding system requirements, at this time, there are other needs for database management with the implementation of the big data concept into a Big Data management system in the context of managing public information content. The following are the requirements for implementing the Big Data Management system:

1   Not all data processing problems in public information management can be best resolved using the traditional relational DBMS system.
2   Conventional DBMS is not enough for big data because of; access speed (volume issue), simplicity of setup, the need for looser representation of structures/schemes (variety issues), the different data management needs and Distributed architecture needs (scale out).

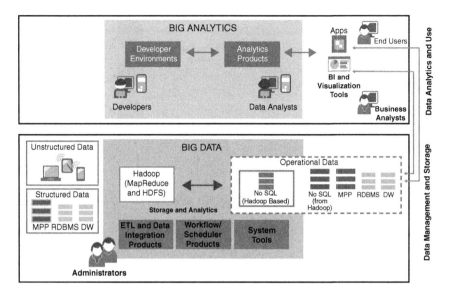

Figure 9.7 Integrated architecture of HPCC and Hadoop.

Based on some of those prerequisites for implementing the Database Management System, it can be seen that there are fundamental differences in each Database Management System because big data is the orientation of each database management system. In the developed system, the database management system for Big Data used is NoSQL. The NoSQL system has the distinction of being an unrelated database, in that it does not require the previously mentioned linkages, and is usually distributed and scaled. Without a special scheme so that it is softer with this scheme, and the use of an Application Programming Interface that is simpler in the use of manipulation or data processing.

The most famous technology for the NoSQL system itself is Hadoop with a reduction map between versions 1.0 and 2.0 which has significant differences, especially in the framework model, the second is Document Oriented which has a hierarchical concept in document data, and usually documents are encapsulated and encoded in XML standard, JSON, YAML and others. Meanwhile Graph Oriented is a DBMS which represents a data graph model that shows the interconnection between data.

In the mining process (data mining) in the database management system for public information content by the Directorate General of Information and Public Communication, the existence of big data itself is very much needed because in the datamining process it requires a lot of data processing with various characteristics resulting in a much more complex but needed model high degree of accuracy. Through this big data technology, datamining itself is required to accept the challenge of how to do datamining on a very large scale and distributed with a very varied variation of data. So, it is hoped that the use of the right technology infrastructure from Big Data to be able to support the business process of managing public information content by the existing Directorate General of Public Information and Communication will be much better, especially in the process of information and knowledge retrieval and in the end it will be used to support the policy-making process and systems decision making in the organisation of the Directorate General of Information and Public Communication in particular and for the Ministry of Communication and Information Technology in general.

Implementation of integrated big data and knowledge management

The application of Big Data and Knowledge Management in the management of public information can be interpreted as a repository of all information databases, news and policy knowledge that an organisation has. In terms of managing public information and controlling negative news content, the Ministry of Communication and Information Technology processes information circulating in the public from various media channels then selects which news content has negative content and which news has positive content to ward off negative news.

The application of knowledge management carried out by the Directorate of Information Management, Directorate General of Information and Public Communication in its information system departs from the fact that information is spread in various media and information needs by various levels of society as well as the need to make policies based on public opinion through developing media. The concept of this idea is also accompanied on the basis of the rapid development of information technology. This shows that there is a social reality that is outside the human will. The fact is that the development of technology and information today can no longer be stopped by humans. This is a social fact that is external in nature and has the power to compel the consciousness of each individual.

On the other hand, knowledge is defined as the belief that a phenomenon is real and that they have certain characteristics. In this case, the Directorate of Information Management, Directorate General of Information and Public Communication takes the role of awareness of their knowledge of social reality, namely by implementing knowledge management in its information system by creating an integrated concept between Big Data and Knowledge Management System as an effort to provide effective and effective information services efficient to society as well as the basis for policy making by the Government.

For this reason, by utilising Big Data technology combined with the concept of Knowledge Management, useful information is collected and then processed into tacit knowledge that can be disseminated to the public. The implementation of this concept refers to the concept model proposed by Hijazi (2017), as can be seen in Figure 9.8.

Useful information generated from positive content is then further processed into knowledge and then used as a support for public policy making.

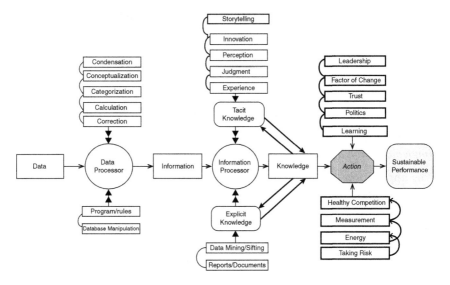

Figure 9.8 Integrated big data system and knowledge management.

The information which later becomes knowledge is used not only for internal purposes but also for other government agencies according to their respective sectors. Knowledge can enable the organisation to develop and exploit other tangible and intangible resources better than the competitors can, even though the resources themselves might not be unique. Knowledge, especially context-specific tacit knowledge, tends to be unique and therefore difficult to imitate. Moreover, unlike most traditional resources, it cannot easily be purchased in a ready-to-use form.

As a recommendation of the research team in implementing the integration of the Big Data and Knowledge Management System systems. As a tool to see the successful implementation of knowledge management, it is necessary to measure organisational performance by measuring the balance score card (financial aspects, customer aspects, internal process aspects and learning and growth perspective) periodically as an annual evaluation and can further categorise the levelled knowledge management system implemented. The recommendations for levelling the implementation of the knowledge management system are described in Table 9.2.

Thus, the parameters used as indicators of the successful implementation of Knowledge Management are:

a   Knowledge inventory & acquisition includes: knowledge capturing, E-Library, Knowledge centre.
b   Knowledge activity, which includes: newsmaker forum, policy-maker and analyst forum, innovation forum, problem-solving-collaboration sharing discussion forum.

Table 9.2 Knowledge management system implementation level

Knowledge management implementation level	Information
Level 1. *Initiate*	Knowledge Management implementation must start from an internal organisation supported by related parties and then spread this initiative to the entire community.
Level 2. *Develop*	The development stage began with newsmaker groups to spearhead the emergence of various groupware to share knowledge.
Level 3. *Standardise*	The stage where the various processes and approaches needed to develop knowledge begin to be developed.
Level 4. *Optimise*	The stage where the success of implementing Knowledge Management is measured for its effectiveness.
Level 5. *Innovate*	The stage where the organisation has been able to take advantage of the application of Knowledge Management and has become a culture in stabilising every decision and policy taken.

Planning the application of knowledge management is a long-term strategy that includes three components in value creation, including quality, efficiency and growth, with an internal objective strategy. Meanwhile, the four main pillars that support the implementation of the Knowledge Management concept and system are:

1   Leadership/Management consists of strategy, values, decision-making process, prioritisation, resource allocation, promote system thinking, integrative management roles.
2   Organisation consists of operational aspects: functions, processes, structures, control and measurements support system technology, utilisation.
3   Technology consists of various IT products that support the collaboration and codification.
4   Learning consists of various learning forums, principles and behaviours and promote collaborative learning environments.

Although the proposed integrated big data and knowledge management system implementation framework is expected to benefit from big data systems and cloud computing concepts, there are relevant challenges and limitations that need to be addressed. The main concern in implementing this integrated system is facing the challenges of technical problems. Due to the rapid development of technology and sophistication for a process of collecting and managing large amounts of data, frameworks need to find ways to handle large volumes of diverse data and time-consuming data processing.

Often data is too diverse to analyse and extract value for effective decision making. Another related issue is poor data governance which acts as an important factor in limiting efforts to extract value from big data. At the same time, moving away from traditional data management techniques and producing efficient analytical algorithms for processing structured and unstructured data appears to be a challenge.

Conclusion

The Integrated Big Data System and Knowledge Management can support the public communication process through the media monitoring process. So, with the help of this concept, it is possible to overcome the shortcomings that exist in the analysis of sentiments from different news content from different media channels and strengthen it. The sentiment analysis methods used in the Big Data System should be combined with the analysis of social networks in order not only to stop at monitoring the media but also to find key people or actors affected by the problem. This is very important to maximise the Big Data functionality for implementation. As it would be very unfortunate, if the large resources allocated to a Big Data implementation were only used for monitoring, it would be better to do a predictive analysis to estimate how big the problem might be. The concept of the Knowledge Management System, which is integrated with the Big Data system, then transforms the content of the information received into very valuable knowledge so that it can later be used as a support in making decisions in shaping government policy in various sectors. In addition, it can also be used to handle negative information content, thanks to which in the future, the Ministry of Communications and Information Technology together with other government agencies will be able to react faster to problems forecasted by the Big Data system integrated with the Knowledge Management System, which may become large before the problem becomes an uncontrolled problem. By simplifying the processes taking place in the Big Data system that will be implemented, they can be divided into three categories: Input, Process and Output. The recommended combination of methods is in the process step. So, we hope that thanks to this recommendation, apart from the possibility of maximising the Big Data function to be implemented, it will not significantly change the Media Monitoring function. In the case of Big Data implementation, it is better to use the option of building a partial system so that important parts of the system, such as Corpus, can be owned by themselves, and the built system can be designed and monitored as needed. This option can reduce the government's dependence on other parties as well as reduce the annual spending of large funds on paying suppliers.

In implementing knowledge management that is integrated with Big Data at the Directorate of Public Information Management, Directorate General of Information and Public Communication, the successful implementation of knowledge management in the context of managing public information needs to be supported by four components which include: technoware, humanware, infoware and orgaware. There are five stages of Knowledge Management implementation, namely: (1) creating a knowledge map in the organisation; (2) planning the application of knowledge management; (3) compiling a map of knowledge management strategies; (4) implementing knowledge management and (5) measuring knowledge management activities.

References

Asosiasi Penyelenggara Jasa Internet Indonesia, APJII. (2017). Survei Penetrasi dan Perilaku Pengguna Internet Indonesia tahun 2017. Asosiasi Penyelenggara Jasa Internet Indonesia. Jakarta. Access from: https://apjii.or.id/content/read/39/342/Hasil-Survei-Penetrasi-dan-Perilaku-Pengguna-Internet-Indonesia-2017

Associates, S. K. (2014). Introduction to Big Data: Challenges, Opportunities and Realities. IEEE 47th Hawaii International Conference on System Science American University, USA, 728.

Avita Katal, M. W. (2013). Big Data: Issues, Challenges, Tools and Good Practices. IEEE Conference Publications, Department of CSE, Graphic Era University, India, 404–409.

Chanmin Park, T. W. (2013). Big Data and NSA Surveillance – Survey of Technology and Legal Issues. IEEE International Symposium, Multimedia, Law Offices of Kim, Lee & Park, Beverly Hills, California, Department of Computer Science, California State University Northridge, California, 516–517.

Christian Seebode, M. O. (2013). BIG DATA Infrastructures for Pharmaceutical Research. IEEE International Conference on Big Data, ORTEC Medical, Berlin, Germany, 59–63.

Cresswell, J. W. (2008). *Research Design: Qualitative, Quantitative, and Mixed Methods Approaches*, Third Edition. SAGE Publications Inc.

Davenport, T. H., and Prusak, L. (1998). *Working Knowledge: How Organizations Manage What They Know.* Harvard Business School Press.

Dewiyana, H. (2006). Kompetensi dan Kurikulum Perpustakaan: Paradigama Baru dan Dunia Kerja di Era Globalisasi Informasi. *Jurnal Studi Perpustakaan dan Informasi*, 2(1).

Firat, T., and Keane, J. A. (2013). "Big Data Framework". IEEE International Conference on Systems, Man, and Cybernetics, School of Computer Science, The University of Manchester, Manchester, UK, 1494–1499.

Gartner. (2009). Big Data. Gartner.

Hijazi, Sam. (2017). "Big Data and Knowledge Management: A Possible Course to Combine them Together". 2017 ASCUE Proceedings, 49–58.

Hyejung Moon, H. S. (2013). Big Data and Policy Design for Data Sovereignty: A Case Study on Copyright and CCL in South Korea. IEEE Conference, National University of Science and Technology Seoul, Republic of Korea, 1026–1029.

ISACA. (2012a). *COBIT 5 – A Business Framework for the Governance and Management of Enterprise IT.* USA: ISACA.

ISACA. (2012b). *COBIT 5 Enabling Information.* USA: ISACA.

ITB. (2013). Big Data Untuk Pembangunan. Big Data Seminar 29 November 2013, ITB, Bandung.

Krishnan, K. (2013). *Data Warehousing in the Age of Big Data*. USA: MK Publications.

Laudon, K. C., and Laudon, J. P. (2004). *Management Information Systems* (8th ed.). Upper Saddle River, NJ: Pearson Education.

Laudon, K. C., and dan Laudon, J. P. (2008). *Sistem Informasi Manajemen*. Jakarta: Salemba Empat.

Luna Dong Xin, D. S. (2013). Big Data Integration. IEEE 29th International Conference on Data Engineering (ICDE), AT&T Labs–Research, Florham Park, NJ, USA, 1245–1248.

Milton, M. (2009). *A Brain-Friendly Guide: Head First Data Analysis*. USA: O'Reilly.

Minelli, M., Chamber, M., and Dhiraj, A. (2013). *Big Data, Big Analytics: Emerging Business Intelligence and Analytic Trends For Today's Businesses*. USA: John Wiley & Sons, Inc. ISBN: 9781118147603, 111814760X

Muhtaroglu, C. P., Demir, S., Obali, M., and Girgin, C. (2013). Business Model Canvas Perspective on Big Data Applications. IEEE International Conference on Big Data, Bilgem, Turkey, 32–37. DOI: 10.1109/BigData.2013.6691684.

Ohlhorst, F. J. (2013). *Big Data Analytics: Turning Big Data Into Big Money*. Wiley & Sons, Inc.

Paul, C., and Zikopoulos, D. (2013). *The Power of Big Data: The IBM Big Data Platform*. USA: McGraw Hill.

Prajapati, V. (2013). *Big Data Analytics with R and Hadoop*. Birmingham, UK: Packt Publishing.

Richard Chew, K. G. (2013). Impacts of Big Data Impact and Benefit. ISACA White Paper.

Robert, J. T., and James, J. H. (2006). *Optimal Knowledge Management, Wisdom Management, System, Concept, and Application*, Published in the United States of America by Idea Group Publishing (an imprint of Idea Group Inc.).

Sawant, N., and Shah, H. (2013). *Big Data Application Architecture Q&A: A Problem-Solution Approach*. APress, New York: Springer Science+Business Media.

Schell, R. (2013). Security: A Big Question for Big Data. IEEE International Conference on Big Data University of Southern California, USA.

Schmarzo, B. (2013). *Understanding How Data Powers Big Business*. USA: John Wiley & Sons, Inc.

Schonberger, V.-M., and Cukier, K. (2013). *Big Data: A Revolution that will Transform How we Live, Work, And Think*. New York, USA: Houngthon Mifflin, Harcourt Publishing.

Seref, S., and Duygu, S. (2013). Big Data: A Review. IEEE International Congress on Big Data: Gazi University, Department of Computer Engineering, Faculty of Engineering, Ankara, Turkey, 42–47.

Short, T. (2000). *Components of Knowledge Strategy: Keys to Successful Knowledge Management*. NJ: Information Today.

Soumendra Mohanty, M. J. (2013). *Big Data Analytics*. New York, USA: Springer Science+Business.

Turban, E., Aronson, J. E., and Liang, T-P.(2005). *Decision Support Systems and Intelligent Systems*, 7th Edition. New Delhi: Prentice Hall.

Vosoughi, S., Roy, D., and Aral, S. (2018). The spread of true and false news online, *Science* 09 Mar 2018, 359(6380), 1146–1151, DOI: 10.1126/science.aap9559

Wijaya, A. E. (2014). Model Penerapan Knowledge Management System untuk Penyusunan Tugas Akhir Berbasis Teknologi Mobile Menggunakan J2ME (Studi Kasus STMIK SUBANG). Seminar Nasional Informatika UPN Veteran Yogyakarta.

Wu, X. Zhu, X., Wu, G.-Q. and Ding, W. (2014). Data Mining with Big Data. *IEEE Transactions on Knowledge and Data Engineering*, 26(1), 97–107.

Zaiying Liu, P. Y. (2013). A Sketch of Big Data Technologies. Seventh International Conference on Internet Computing for Engineering and Science, School of Information Science and Technology, Shanghai Sanda University Shanghai, China, 26–29.

Zhang, D. (2013). Inconsistencies in Big Data. IEEE Conference, Department of Computer Science, California State University Sacramento, CA, USA, 61–67.

Zhang, J., and Huang, M. L. (2013). 5Ws Model for Big Data Analysis and Visualization. IEEE 16th International Conference on Computational Science and Engineering, School of Computer Software, University of Technology, Sydney Australia, Tiajin University Tiajin China, 129–134.

Zikopoulos, P., deRoos, D., Parasuraman, K., Deutsch, T., Giles, J., and Corrigan, D. (2013). *Harness the Power of Big Data: The IBM Big Data Platform*. USA: The McGraw-Hill.

Additional reading

Mergel, I. (2011). The Use of Social Media to Dissolve Knowledge Silos in Government, In R. O'Leary, S. Kim, & D. VanSlyke (Eds.), *The Future of Public Administration, Public Management, and Public Service Around the World*, 177–183. Washington, DC: Georgetown University Press.

Rafizan, O., and Kusumasari, D. (2017). Studi Implementasi Sistem Big Data Untuk Mendukung Kebijakan Komunikasi Dan Informatika, *Jurnal Masyarakat Telematika dan Informasi*, 8(2), 81–96.

Subiakto, H., and Rachmad, I. (2014). *Komunikasi Politik, Media dan Demokrasi (Cetakan Kedua)*. Jakarta: Kencana Prenadamedia Group.

10 Implication of knowledge management systems adoptions

Higher education institutions context

Fadzliwati Mohiddin, Mohammad Khanafi Jumat, Heru Susanto, Fahmi Ibrahim, Desi Setiana, Didi Rosiyadi and Alifya Kayla Shafa Susanto

Introduction

Research background

Knowledge Management (KM) concept in today's organisations has become a very important area. Undoubtedly, knowledge management systems were one type of technology used in the operation of the organisation. Higher education organisations whose knowledge operations must also adapt to this type of technological advancement not only to meet their academic goals, but also for the administration purposes of the institution. In higher education organisations, therefore, administrative units are very important as educators and students usually engage to satisfy their needs with various administrative departments (Susanto et al., 2021; Susanto et al., 2021; Susanto et al., 2021; Susanto et al., 2021)".

Several gaps have been recognised as to why this study is required based on the literature reviews. First, the literature review of higher education knowledge management demonstrates that KM practices based in Higher Education Administrative Departments are an unexplored study area inclusively. Research on the application of KM in Higher Education (HE) has also been discovered to be limited in the South East Asian region (Sharimllah Devi, Chong, & Ismail, 2009; Sohail & Daud, 2009; Susanto & Almunawar, 2015; 2016; 2018).

Secondly, in present study developments, the implications of knowledge management are discovered to be a rapidly evolving sector. Researchers have many distinct views on knowledge management implications. Studies investigating the importance for KM in Higher Education Institutions (HEIs) in the scope of Brunei Darussalam are still to be discovered.

Problem statements

Data and technology are now growing rapidly, triggering the conversion of data into helpful information, referred to as knowledge. People are realising the value of knowledge and methods of acquiring, recognising, capturing,

DOI: 10.4324/9781003163824-13

retrieving, using or measuring, managing and collaborating knowledge and experience in order to share understanding without losing it. For this purpose, the word "Knowledge Management" (KM) is developed. KMS provides the technical support to enable knowledge capture and exchange across the many different stakeholders in organisations to take place freely, readily and openly. KMS also gives each user a platform for acquiring, documenting, transferring, creating and applying knowledge to fulfil the knowledge objectives of the organisation (Debowski Shelda, 2006).

In Brunei Darussalam, KMS is a new field especially in HEIs. It is necessary to understand what KM and KMS are before implementation. A study conducted by Sam Hijazi and Lori Kelly (2003) showed that higher learning institutions and the business environment have some challenges in acknowledging KM's engagement as a new business process support model. Therefore, there is a need to understand what KM is. Furthermore, the knowledge is all around us and has not been systematically collected, co-ordinated and managed particularly in the Brunei Darussalam HEIs. HEIs not only provide learners with knowledge, but they need to also manage and cooperate with present knowledge for future reference. The present greater educational organisations abroad have therefore adjusted to their evolving position in a knowledge-based culture (Kostas Metaxiotis, John Psarras, 2003) and recognised the importance of their intellectual capital to their continued position in culture (Rowley, 2000).

Research objectives

This study will also attempt to develop a knowledge management systems implication framework to apply to the HEIs. With this research also, it could give enhancement to the quality of the overall work of the institute through a systematic and relevant study of administration needs, current practice, new developments and successful ways of establishing those developments and managing them.

The main objectives to conduct this study are:

- To identify and analyse the KMS tool used on the organisational level within Politeknik Brunei.
- To identify and study the obstacles or permit to the use of ICT in work, learning and teaching environment which could encourage greater use of KMS within the context of Politeknik Brunei.
- To identify what the perceptions and practices of KMS were, within this context.
- To collect and bring together all the findings and key points from a review of a significant part of the available literature associated with staffs' integration of ICT into their daily work, both for administration and teaching purposes, hence developing a conceptual framework of the user behaviour factors affecting KMS practices in HE administration.

Literature review

The present is the era of information technology, in which the information is considered as an essential asset to increase the competitive advantage of organisations. Due to the confrontation of this challenge, companies are seeking new ways to improve their competitive edge. In the past, different departments of an organisation work in an isolated manner, without coordinating with each other (Kwong, 2016). Most writers define knowledge in the field of knowledge management by distinguishing the meaning between data, information and knowledge. Data relates commonly to the raw facts and numbers (Alavi & Leidner, 2001; Bhatt, 2001), whereas information is considered to be data placed in context or processed (Alavi & Leidner, 2001; Bollinger & Smith, 2001) which can reside in computers. Meanwhile, Bhatt (2001) sees knowledge as a collection of structured information. Hence, when information is combined with experience and judgment, it will become knowledge. Knowledge is authenticated data (Alavi & Leidner, 2001) and relates to the understanding, consciousness or knowledge obtained through study, research, observation or experience (Bollinger & Smith, 2001) and serves as a fundamental basis for the information that an individual requires in order to undertake a task (Bartol & Srivastava, 2002). According to Alavi and Leidner (2001), knowledge is also personalised data linked to facts, processes, concepts, interpretations, ideas, observation and judgment in the minds of people. McMurray (2002) describes knowledge as a mix of experience, values, expert and contextual information that helps individuals or organisations evolve and absorb new experiences.

KMS gives a new era for academic environment across the world by transforming the way in which Higher Education Institutes (HEIs) disseminate information and knowledge to society for further growth. With KMS, conferences and seminars at national and International level can be held. Nowadays, many international universities and other institutions are actively participating in KMS for educational activities and doing research. It is now becoming popular in the education field due to the need to disclose the intellectual power available in institution for sharing experiences. Poonam and Jennifer (2017) researched that universities in Mauritius do not have KM strategy or policy in place, but the research participants know well with KM concepts which include knowledge creation, sharing and transfer. Their case study represents KM initiative and solution through identifying the barriers which need to be addressed in supporting universities contribution to the development of the Mauritian economy.

The objective of knowledge management is to utilise the knowledge and enhance the knowledge sharing so that the overall competitiveness and the innovation capabilities of the organisation. The learning organisations are those organisations in which every employee makes continuous efforts for the learning and development (Du Plessis, 2007). The knowledge development and the learning organisations are interlinked terms. The process in the knowledge management must be focused on the human resources, training and development and information technology of the organisation. The human resource planning refers to the holistic development of the employees working in the organisation. The personal training of the employees refers to the classification, accumulation, sharing and propagation of the information so that knowledge management can be achieved. Several organisations are focused on developing a learning type of organisation; however, it requires a radical change in the culture of the organisation.

KMS models and frameworks in HEIs

There have been several efforts to explain and evaluate current frameworks for knowledge management. Frameworks can either be categorised as prescriptive, descriptive or a mixture of both. Prescriptive frameworks provide guidance on the sort of KM process (Rusli Abdullah et al., 2008), focusing on the element of individuals, technology, culture and material (Ali A. Zahrawi & Yazrina Yahya, 2009). In the conduct of knowledge management, prescriptive frameworks also prescribe methodologies to be pursued. Descriptive frameworks, on the other part, characterise or define KM (Rusli Abdullah et al., 2008) and usually focus on the delivery of KM strategy elements (Ali A. Zahrawi & Yazrina Yahya, 2009). Descriptive frameworks seek to characterise the essence of knowledge management, either the entire knowledge management phenomenon or targeting a particular phenomenon. Frameworks combining prescriptive and descriptive frameworks merge both physical execution and KM development policy elements (Ali A. Zahrawi & Yazrina Yahya, 2009).

This study utilises Handzic's (2001) grouping, which categorised KM frameworks into descriptive frameworks and prescriptive frameworks. Handzic (2001) also puts together a distinct knowledge management viewpoint and provides a unifying study structure by interpreting and synthesising current methods. Handzic's model is portrayed in Figure 10.1 and introduces three interrelated model elements, i.e. the ideas of working knowledge, knowledge processes and knowledge enablers.

The basis of this framework is the theory of working knowledge, identified as knowledge that should be possessed and used by an organisation to maintain excellence. This involves the tacit and explicit knowledge with the aspect of know-what and know-how. Another element of the model is three generic kinds of knowledge processes – generating, transferring and applying. The model also provides two types of socio-technological variables as knowledge enablers. These include the organisational environment and technological infrastructure, covering variables such as organisational structure, leadership and culture, as well as a large variety of information and communication technologies and systems providing the basis for supporting knowledge.

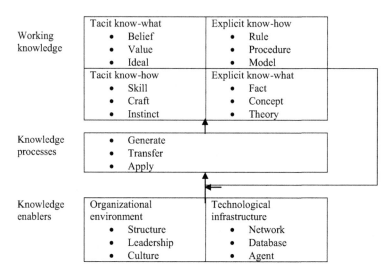

Figure 10.1 A unifying knowledge management research framework (Handzic, 2001).

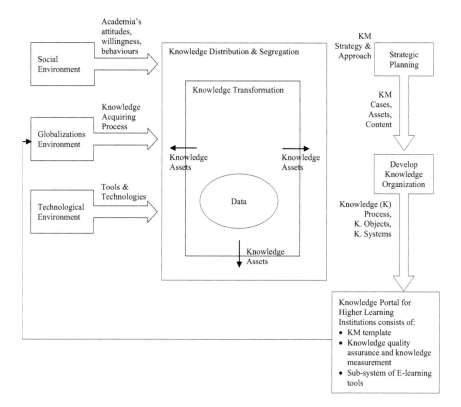

Figure 10.2 Knowledge management framework for higher learning institution (Maizatul Akmar Ismail & Chua, 2005).

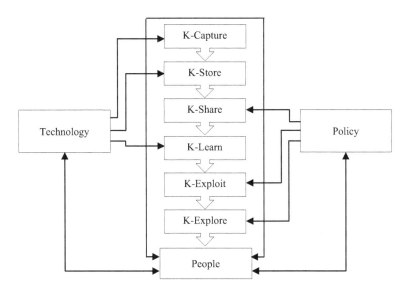

Figure 10.3 A dynamic model of knowledge management (Chen & Burstein, 2006).

Maizatul Akmar and Chua (2005), based on Handzic's model, suggested a model for deployment in a setting appropriate to higher education institutions. Figure 10.2 presents this model.

Chen and Burstein (2006) created another model for the implementation of knowledge management for higher education organisations. Their model involves six operations to manage knowledge, i.e. to capture, store, share, learn, explore and exploit. To contribute to effective execution of KM, this model is associated with suitable technologies, strategies and procedures. Figure 10.3 shows this model. People are the variable that drives everything in KM initiatives; according to Chen and Burstein (2006), strategies promote a suitable culture to effectively execute KM, and technologies promote KM operations.

Proposed conceptual framework

Brunei Darussalam higher education institution

Higher Education Institute in Brunei Darussalam is the responsibility of the Ministry of Education (MOE) under the Office of Permanent Secretary (Higher Education), Higher Education Division. The Higher Education Division was established on 1 April 2008, with a mission "To provide an environment that enhances the quality of higher education and responsive to national development needs" and a vision "Quality Division towards Higher Education Excellence." The establishment marks excellence in Brunei Darussalam's development by the emergence of institutions of higher learning 30 years ago. This accomplishment is very significant and paved the way for the higher education industry to develop further in an attempt to define the country's higher education path and further growth.

At the Higher Education level, Brunei Darussalam consists of five Higher Education institutes, namely: Universiti Brunei Darussalam, Universiti Teknologi Brunei, Universiti Islam Sultan Sharif Ali, Kolej Universiti Perguruan Ugama Seri Begawan and Politeknik Brunei. For this study, Politeknik Brunei has been selected as the subject of interest by the researcher.

Conceptual framework

Knowledge and knowledge management are not new concepts, and with that Politeknik Brunei's attempt to use ICT innovation to suit within the

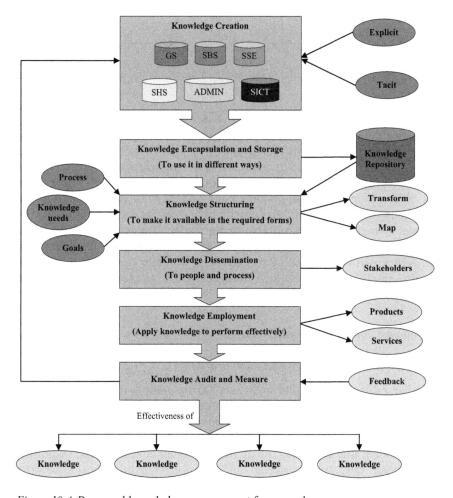

Figure 10.4 Proposed knowledge management framework.

schools. This section puts forward a structure for knowledge management systems for Politeknik Brunei that will therefore create complete use of information communication technologies in a beneficial manner to complement knowledge management in line with Politeknik Brunei's mission and vision. The framework shown in Figure 10.4 is an outline illustration of Politeknik Brunei's suggested structure for KM implementation.

The framework structure acts as the basis and provides the fundamental of KM to be implemented in Politeknik Brunei and could be to other higher education institution. This KM framework has been created by Mamta Bhusry and Jayanti Ranjan (2011).

The structure includes identifying the current gap in the needs of knowledge of the organisation and offers an iterative mechanism to close the gap. It focuses on identifying the strategic requirement by the higher education institution which is based on organisational goals and objectives, hierarchical organisational structure, stakeholders and processes. Once this has been accomplished, it is essential to determine the degree of the organisation's current KM – what and how much helpful knowledge is effectively gathered and reused in the appropriate ways. The next stage is to determine the gap in the knowledge and the factors creating this gap. Therefore, there is a need to close the gap towards goals and objectives for the effective use of organisational knowledge.

Methodology

Research design

This study is approached using a mixed methodology. As Johnson has defined in his study, mixed methods is the category of study that incorporates both the qualitative and quantitative method, and is selected as it is believed that this method could make up for each other's flaws so that information obtained will be more valid and reliable (Moore, 2016). The qualitative methods in this study are used when the open-ended questions are given to the PB staff and lecturers to understand their reason and opinions in more elaborate ways, without restricting them with limited options when carried out with close-ended questions. It is done by giving the open-ended questions in the online questionnaires provided to the PB staff and lecturers and by analysing the data obtained from the secondary data of the relevant authorities.

Research participants

A total of 245 questionnaires have been emailed to all Politeknik Brunei management staff and lecturers from the schools and management departments; 104 responded and participated in this study. The schools involved are from School of Business (SBS), School of Health and Science (SHS), School of Information Communication and Technology (SICT), School of

Science and Engineering (SSE) and General Studies (GS). Meanwhile, the management departments that participated in this research include Administration, Strategic Management Unit, Registrar Office, Human Resource Department, Estate Management, Finance Services, Information and Communication Technology Department, Quality Assurance, International and Public Relation Department (IPRD), Industry Service, Students Affairs, Centre for Innovative Teaching and Learning (CiTL), Library/Learning Centre, Academic Department, Centre for Students Development and Innovation (CSDI) and Research and Development. They were all sharing their experiences, opinions and information to contribute in gathering the data through the online questionnaire given to them.

Findings

Background of the respondents

a   Number of years work experience of the respondents:

Table 10.A

A	Years	Total respondents (N = 104)	100%
1	1–5 years	54	52
2	6–10 years	35	34
3	11–15 years	5	5
4	16 years above	10	10

More than half of the respondents were in the working experience between 1 and 5 years. 34% were between 6 and 10 years work experience, while 15% of the respondents were above 11 years work experience (see Table 10.A).

b   Name of Department or School of the respondents:

Table 10.B

B	Department/schools	Total respondents (N = 104)	100%
1	School of business (SBS)	23	22
2	School of health and sciences (SHS)	11	11
3	School of information and communication technology (SICT)	10	10
4	School of science and engineering (SSE)	30	29
5	Department of general studies (GS)	13	13
6	PB administrations	17	16

Majority of the respondents are from School of Business and School of Science and Engineering. These two schools have the greatest number of lecturers and staff in total compared to the other two schools and PB administrative department. For other schools, more than half of the lecturers participate in this study; meanwhile, for PB administration, less than half of the staff responded to the questionnaires given (Table 10.B).

Individual findings

In this section of the survey, the researcher aimed to establish how many respondents from various departments and schools within Politeknik Brunei had adopted a definition for KM, and what the elements and perceptions of knowledge were.

From Table 10.1, a big proportion of respondents (71%) regarded knowledge to be information technology, but KM academics (Davenport and Prusak, 2000a; Bixler, 2005; Serban and Luan, 2002a; Wiig, 1998) believe that KM includes much more than IT alone. Brixler (2005) argues that the recent developments in information and communication technology can facilitate processes such as channelling, storing or distribution of information; however, the ultimate responsibility is on the manager or knowledge employee to convert this information into actionable knowledge that enhances efficiency (Bixler, 2005).

In addition, knowledge that is viewed as a tool and methodology obtained a feedback percentage of 51%, that indicate more than half of participants seen awareness of tools and methodologies as a knowledge sharing needs tools. And, relying on tools alone will not generally provide a reaction. Fifty percent of participants perceived that organisational knowledge could be generated and disseminated within the institutions. It is known that PB is

Table 10.1 KMS user perceived knowledge in Politeknik Brunei

A2	Knowledge in institution	Total respondents [N = 104]	
		N	%
1	Information technology	74	71
2	Organisational knowledge	52	50
3	Tacit knowledge	45	43
4	Knowledge creation, dissemination	42	40
5	Tools and methodology	53	51
6	Individual knowledge	50	48
7	Explicit knowledge	54	52
8	Core competence	47	45
9	Intellectual capital	45	43
10	Organisational learning	44	42

Table 10.2 Perception on elements of knowledge in Politeknik Brunei

A3	Elements of knowledge	Total respondents [N = 104]	
		N	%
1	Personal experience	84	81
2	Action based	46	44
3	Objects or facts	46	44
4	Personal	56	54
5	Difficult to share	39	38
6	Tacit knowledge	36	35
7	Conceptual	42	40
8	Intellectual process	43	41
9	Impersonal	47	45
10	Easy to share	41	39
11	Explicit knowledge	51	49
12	Cultural	31	30
13	Subjective	35	34
14	Context independent	28	27
15	Interaction and networking	53	51
16	Objective	29	28
17	Context dependent	26	25

an academic institution, where it consists of different schools and administrative departments with different disciplines and areas of study, and considering the concept of academic tribes and fiefdoms by Becher and Trowler (2001), the literature expected that the greatest response would be to see knowledge as individual as well as explicit. Thus, 52% viewed knowledge as explicit and individual; however, it was considered by more participants as organisational knowledge rather than individual knowledge.

On the perception of the elements of knowledge components, more than half of the participants (Table 10.2) stated that the elements of knowledge within the PB relied on personal experience (81%), and that combination both explicit and tacit (84%) knowledge, that they were extracted from an intellectual process (41%) and the knowledge exchange was engaged in this process. Furthermore, less than half of the participants stated that knowledge was both objective (44%) and subjective (34%). 38% said that sharing knowledge was difficult; 30% thought that knowledge had a cultural component to it.

Organisational culture

Kidwell et al. (2000) claim that culture is a key component of the ability of an institution to embrace KM. They describe this culture as the "beliefs, values, norms, and behaviours that are unique to an organisation" (Kidwell et al., 2000). It is said that a strong culture has a high degree of similarity between organisational members' values and goals, hierarchical integration and strategies (Sporn, 1996). Sporn (1996) seeks to describe weak cultures as those with comparatively closely connected subunits or cultures that may contradict each other. This part of the questionnaire was intended to determine the type of culture of knowledge sharing prevailing within Politeknik Brunei.

Results from this research revealed that culture has been rated as one of the main issues for successful implementation of knowledge management systems. Knowledge Management Systems' culture to support for

Table 10.3 KM organisational culture in Politeknik Brunei

	Organisational culture	Strongly disagree						Strongly Agree		NA	
		1		2		3		4		5	
		N	%	N	%	N	%	N	%	N	%
B1	Facilitate knowledge sharing	5	5	17	16	53	51	29	28	0	0
B2	Transfer of knowledge to new workers	5	5	17	16	53	51	29	28	0	0
B3	Dialogue is encourage and facilitated	6	6	16	15	57	55	24	23	1	1
B4	Network of common interest	8	8	23	22	50	48	23	22	0	0
B5	KM activity encouragement	7	7	22	21	44	42	31	30	0	0
B6	Staff share knowledge – regular updating database	7	7	19	18	47	45	31	30	0	0
B7	Staff share knowledge – preparing written documentation	2	2	20	19	43	41	39	38	0	0

Table 10.4 Knowledge sharing facilities in Politeknik Brunei

B8	Knowledge sharing facilities	Total respondents [N = 104]	
		N	%
1	Multimedia presentation	72	69
2	Reflective learning processes	52	50
3	Workshop	86	83
4	Forums	26	25
5	Video conferences	8	8
6	Handovers	31	30
7	Creativity techniques	29	28
8	Training needs analysis	38	37
9	Mentoring and coaching	86	83
10	Team briefings	65	63
11	Others	2	2

Table 10.5 KM encouragement in Politeknik Brunei

B9	KM encouragement	Total respondents [N = 104]	
		N	%
1	Top-down management	42	40
2	Top-down enforcement	39	38
3	Individual encouragement	64	62
4	Group encouragement	75	72
5	Others	1	1

Table 10.6 KM practices in Politeknik Brunei

B10	KM practices	Total respondents [N = 104]	
		N	%
1	A responsibility of Top Management	73	70
2	A responsibility of Academics	71	68
3	A responsibility of the knowledge officer or knowledge management unit	59	57
4	Explicit criteria for assessing worker performance	28	27
5	Others:	2	2

implementation is the one which values knowledge and encourages its creation, sharing and application. It was noticeable from the research that the development of such culture maintained to be one of the greatest challenges for the KMS initiatives, particularly in Higher Education Institutions. Knowledge management includes knowledge sharing. The research tried to determine how knowledge was shared within Politeknik Brunei. Sharing knowledge was noticeable mainly through workshops (83%), mentoring and coaching (83%), multimedia presentation (69%), team briefings (63%) and reflective learning processes (50%) where knowledge sharing (Table 10.3) was facilitated (Table 10.4).

Furthermore, Knowledge Management was supported and encouraged in a top-down model (40%) and was encouraged rather than implemented (Table 10.5). It was also encouraged on a group basis (72%) and on an individual basis (62%). In the current KM practices (Table 10.6), it was responsibility of Top Management (70%) and followed by responsibility of Academics (68%).

Technologies, products, models and processes

Most firms make their first moves with KM in the domain of technology (Davenport & Prusak, 2000a). The survey aimed to understand the level of integration of the various information systems between functional areas within Politeknik Brunei. When information systems are not integrated on some level, data capturing, storing and retrieval inefficiencies and duplication of effort, are inevitable. Meanwhile, e-learning, content management, collaboration tools, document management, portals, business intelligence, knowledge bases, search engines, customer relationship management, data mining, workflow and creativity techniques were tools listed in this study as being used within Politeknik Brunei to support KMS.

The survey revealed (Table 10.7) that 43% of the PB responded that they had integration with some functions. Thirty-seven percent had very little integration and only 23% indicated that they had a fully integrated system.

Another aspect of this survey was to investigate the KM technologies used within the HEI context and to establish the most common technologies used to support and enable the KM agenda. The survey revealed (Table 10.8) that E-Learning (74%) was the most common technological tool used to support KM, which is not surprising as it enables training support to the student at anytime, anywhere. Content Management (44%), "the ability to manage content over the web" (Luan & Serban, 2002, p. 89), and document

Table 10.7 Information systems integration in Politeknik Brunei

C1	Level of integration	Total respondents [N = 104]	
		N	%
1	Fully Integrated system	24	23
2	Integrated within some functions	45	43
3	Very little integration	38	37
4	No integration	12	12
5	Do not know	20	19

Table 10.8 Technology usage in Politeknik Brunei

C2	Technology usage	Total respondents [N = 104]	
		N	%
1	Business intelligence	33	32
2	Knowledge base	35	34
3	Collaboration	37	36
4	Content management	46	44
5	Documentation management	49	47
6	Portals	44	42
7	Data mining	14	13
8	Creativity techniques	33	32
9	Workflow	22	21
10	Search	6	6
11	E-Learning	77	74
12	Other	1	1

management (47%) were listed as technologies used to support KM, which Luan and Serban (2002) contend are key to a sound KM infrastructure.

Responsibility for knowledge management practices

The survey aimed to understand whether KM required certain people to drive and implement it, and whether certain roles within the institution were responsible for KM.

It was interesting to note that the main drivers of a KM strategy (Table 10.9) were perceived to be Information Communication and Technology Department (61%), Head of School/Assistant Head of School (61%), Centre

Table 10.9 Persons responsible for KM in Politeknik Brunei

D1	Persons responsible for KM	Total respondents [N = 104]	
		N	%
1	Director/assistant director	44	42
2	Academic programme	39	38
3	CiTL	62	60
4	CSDI	28	27
5	Estate management	13	13
6	Finance services	29	28
7	Head of school/assistance head of school	63	61
8	Human resource department	26	25
9	Industrial services	27	26
10	ICT	63	61
11	International and public relation	19	18
12	Lecturers	55	53
13	Library/learning centre	35	34
14	Quality assurance	16	15
15	Registrar	22	21
16	Research and development	39	38
17	Strategic management unit	43	41
18	Student affairs	13	13
19	Others:	1	1

Table 10.10 Formal persons responsible for KM in Politeknik Brunei

D2	Formal person responsible for KM	Total respondents [N = 104]	
		N	%
1	Head of strategic management unit	28	27
2	Head of ICT	56	54
3	Registrar	13	13
4	Head of academic programme	36	35
5	Head of library	20	19
6	No one person assigned this role	41	39

for Innovation in Teaching and Learning Department (60%) and PB lecturers (53%), whereas the formal persons responsible for KM were listed
as the Head of Information Communication and Technology Department
(Table 10.10).

Benefits and challenges

HEIs have several advantages to gain from implementing an institution-wide
KM strategy (Hamre & Pickette, 2002; Kidwell et al., 2000; Metcalfe, 2006;
Serban & Luan, 2002a). Kidwell outlines the benefits of administrative services, the strategic planning process, the research process and the curriculum development process for student services and alumni services. Kidwell
et al. (2000) further argue that an institution-wide strategy to KM can contribute to progress in both explicit and tacit knowledge sharing and the subsequent increase in advantages.

Literature suggests several benefits for KMS implementation, but how do
PB perceive the benefits of KMS? Five benefits that yielded the highest frequency of responses in the survey were (Table 10.11):

* Improved management learning (93%);
* Improved efficiency (87%);
* Improved quality of services (75%);
* New and improved processes (66%);
* Improved organisational learning (65%).

Perceptions of benefits of KM within PB seem to be linked mainly to quality,
improvement and learning rather than as a tool to reduce operating costs;
however, PB are expected to be innovative, creative and entrepreneurial
in their search to attract additional funding, especially given the financial
pressure and constraints within which they need to work. Politeknik Brunei
are not for profit institutions, and the external pressure for PB to account

Table 10.11 KMS benefits

E1	KMS benefits	Total respondents [N = 104]	
		N	%
1	Improved efficiency	90	87
2	Improved management learning	97	93
3	New and improved processes	69	66
4	Improved organisational learning	68	65
5	Reduced operating costs	64	62
6	Improved quality of services	78	75
7	No known benefits	6	6
8	Others:	1	1

Table 10.12 KMS challenges

E2	Challenges in KM	Total respondents [N = 104]	
		N	%
1	Lack of an appropriate IT infrastructure	74	71
2	Cultural issues	44	42
3	Politics and resistance to organisational change	52	50
4	Diversity of the internal constituency and their needs	34	33
5	Lack of appropriate software tools	56	54
6	Lack of KM strategy	71	68
7	Power issues	41	39
8	Organisational structure	35	34
9	Lack of support from senior management	56	54
10	No central unit taking responsibility to drive the KM agenda	51	49
11	No known challenges	17	16
12	Others:	2	2

for their quality of services and products, could possibly account for this emphasis in quality.

The survey (Table 10.12) revealed six main challenges contributing to difficulties in the implementation of KM within the Politeknik Brunei:

- Lack of an appropriate IT infrastructure (71%)
- Lack of KM Strategy (68%)
- Lack of appropriate software tools (54%)
- Lack of support from senior management (54%)
- Politics and resistance to organisational change (50%)
- No central unit taking responsibility to drive the KM agenda (49%).

Development within the institution

Serban (2002) argues that there are several factors for knowledge management to emerge and grow. Serban and Luan (2002) argue that some of the factors include information overload and chaos, data congestion, segmentation and specialisation of data and skills, mobility and retention for the workers and competition. This part of the study directed at understanding how knowledge management within Politeknik Brunei evolved, and what external or internal variables affected the development of knowledge management.

Table 10.13, Knowledge Management type activities, emerged within Politeknik Brunei as a supporting mechanism to an existing institution development process (48%). The fact that Knowledge Management emerged primarily within Politeknik Brunei as a supporting mechanism to an existing institution development process does mean that substantial work

Table 10.13 KMS development in Politeknik Brunei

F1	KM development	Total respondents [N = 104]	
		N	%
1	As part of an IT project	30	29
2	As part of a change management programme	36	35
3	As a supporting mechanism to an existing institution development process	50	48
4	As part of the service planning process	17	16
5	As part of a corporate knowledge management or other strategy	33	32
6	As a side effect of another strategy or initiative	39	38
7	Other:	4	4

within the field of KM at an administration level is still required. Knowledge management processes work best when driven by effective, easy-to-use techniques; however, the emphasis on technology alone will make little advancement towards knowledge management (Serban & Luan, 2002b) and institutions will need to confirm that other elements of knowledge management, such as teaching, organisational problems and problems of management (Stankosky, 2001), are adopted.

Organisations are usually motivated or affected by inner and/or external factors to include perceived management tools that can help and enhance their company strategy. In this regard, higher education institutions are not distinct, as they are also affected by inner and external forces to enhance services and products.

Some of the external factors (Table 10.14) influencing the decision to start thinking about including KM type activities in Politeknik Brunei were:

- Availability of funding (43%);
- Criticism from external (or internal) stakeholders (38%) and
- Pressure from government for better accountability (37%).

Some of the internal factors (Table 10.15) listed as influencing the implementation of KM activities were:

- Internal pressure to collaborate (59%);
- An organisational culture that values and supports sharing and re-use (54%) and
- The availability of IT software to facilitate it (50%).

Factors influencing KM inclusion

The survey revealed that there is positive feedback from the respondents in the implementation of KMS for Politeknik Brunei (Table 10.16).

Table 10.14 External forces influence emergence of KMS in Politeknik Brunei

F2	External forces	Total respondents [N = 104]	
		N	%
1	Competitive markets	32	31
2	Pressure from government for better accountability	38	37
3	Availability of funding	45	43
4	Demands for more openness/transparency	27	26
5	Criticism from external (or internal) stakeholders	39	38
6	Other	12	12

Table 10.15 Internal forces influence emergence of KMS in Politeknik Brunei

F3	Internal forces	Total respondents [N = 104]	
		N	%
1	The availability of IT software to facilitate it	52	50
2	Embedded processes that facilitated sharing and organisational learning	48	46
3	Internal pressure to collaborate	61	59
4	An organisational culture that values and supports sharing and re-use	56	54
5	Other	9	9

Table 10.16 Reasons using KMS in Politeknik Brunei

G	Reasons using KMS	Strongly disagree						Strongly agree		NA	
		1		2		3		4		5	
		N	%	N	%	N	%	N	%	N	%
G1	Improve competitive advantage	0	0	0	0	44	42	55	53	5	5
G2	Integrate knowledge	0	0	1	1	38	37	65	63	0	0
G3	Capture and use knowledge from outside	0	0	7	7	29	28	68	65	0	0
G4	Share & transfer of knowledge	0	0	4	4	25	24	66	63	9	9
G5	Increase efficiency	0	0	8	8	32	31	64	62	0	0
G6	Protect from loss of knowledge	0	0	1	1	36	35	67	64	0	0

G	Reasons using KMS	Strongly disagree						Strongly agree		NA	
		1		2		3		4		5	
		N	%	N	%	N	%	N	%	N	%
G7	Staff training	0	0	1	1	45	43	58	56	0	0
G8	Staff acceptance of innovations	0	0	9	9	33	32	62	60	0	0
G9	Improve staff retention	3	3	14	13	33	32	41	39	13	13
G10	Identify and protect strategic knowledge	4	4	11	11	36	35	49	47	4	4
G11	Ease collaborative work or project	1	1	8	8	24	23	64	62	7	7
G12	Promote share of knowledge with stakeholders	1	1	15	14	16	15	67	64	5	5

Discussion

Contributing factors that hinder or promote KMS implementation

- Lack of IT infrastructure

  One of the main factors contributing to the hindrance of KMS implementation is lack of an appropriate IT infrastructure (71%) and also lack of appropriate software tools (54%). Evidence from the respondent on the level of satisfaction in the use of technology to facilitate knowledge sharing and transfer within Politeknik Brunei. Respondents were asked "How satisfactorily does the use of technology facilitate knowledge sharing and transfer within your institution," 46% responded as being very unsatisfactory while 12% were unsure. This study also found that "Existing knowledge groups or communities of practice (interest) are supported by technology tools," about 48% of the responses disagreed with the current practices which is less reinforcement on technology tools.

- Lack of KM strategy, Lack of support from senior management and Politics and the resistance to change received the next highest responses

  The KM strategy in Politeknik Brunei have contribute to impede the use of KM (68%), which relates to lack of support from the senior management (54%) and may be from political and the resistance to change (50%) added to the difficulty of KM implementation. With KM strategy, it would guide and enhance the thinking of KM within the institution. Most institutions implement KM, formally addressing KM which was incorporated into the Information Strategy.

- PB incentives to motive staff and lecturers to increase KM.

The perception was that Politeknik Brunei required certain incentives or catalysts to motivate staff and lecturers to increase or include KM activities. Participants listed a number of incentives needed to motivate them to increase KM activity:

- Any organisation development initiative should be initiated, collaborated, facilitated, supported and reinvigorated by the top level management;
- Create more functions in the existing Knowledge Management Systems like an e-library for PB to store documents. Easier for others to refer. Re-design the whole Knowledge Management System to a more user friendly system. Should be encouraged to use as a main sharing platform;
- Develop clear vision of the objectives and benefits of the KM;
- Availability of experts and funding;
- Better knowledge management and facilities, hence leading to ease of doing work and faster information retrieval;
- Employees must realise that management values their contribution, which will eventually lead to improvement of organisational performance as well as fulfil the employee expectation. Management's display of equal, if not more, concern for Human Capital as compared to that of Financial Capital, will trigger the use of creative potential of employees through organisational knowledge management system;
- Give more training and awareness programmes on knowledge management practices;
- Lecturer should focus on teaching. Other admin work should be handled by admin staff. Too much responsibilities cause lecturer to neglect main role to help students (admin work having deadline, difficult to reach goal to prepare effective teaching materials – make lecturer prone to lose their innovativeness as no time to prepare);
- Ministry's and top management support including financial, in-kind, etc.;
- Motivating employees include communicating to them, modelling expected behaviours, establishing standard goals to be included in all performance plans, monitoring and reporting on progress against organisational goals, recognising those who demonstrate desired behaviours, providing incentives for meeting objectives and rewarding outstanding performance;
- Provide town hall and coffee talk sessions conducted by senior leaders, notes from senior leaders to employees who contribute reusable content, standardised performance goals, monthly progress reports and awards for those who set the best example of sharing their knowledge and
- "The best way is through inspirational leadership" – communicating regularly, setting clear expectations, monitoring performance,

regularly thanking and praising and most important, leading by example. But you can also motivate people through goals and measurements, recognition and rewards, gamification and badging and positive incentives and negative incentives.
- Quality improvement.
- Recognition.
- Rewards and recognition.
- Special incentives.

Conclusions

This research study suggests that it could assist to give better understanding between knowledge management systems and the institution, and provide important input to the development of the theory of knowledge management systems and Politeknik Brunei, such that the research study:

- Presents a basic theory on knowledge management systems as applied in Politeknik Brunei;
- Presents a substantive conceptual framework on knowledge management systems applied on Politeknik Brunei;
- Provides an overview on knowledge management as a management tool within Politeknik Brunei;
- Provides factors that influence knowledge management use on a systematic level;
- Identifies the practices and current state of KM implementation in Politeknik Brunei.

The results from this research show several possible implications to manage and improve Knowledge Management Systems practices in Politeknik Brunei. Encouraged by the way knowledge is shared in organisation and the benefits of adopting such a KMS, the way forward now is to work deeper into this conceptual framework for Politeknik Brunei to develop a KMS. If the framework is enforced, it will bring more advantages to enhance the quality of information sharing and use. Such implementations should be managed properly, however. The establishment of a KMS should be correctly scheduled and implemented as to the Politeknik Brunei's requirements. On the other hand, among the Politeknik Brunei population, the theoretical and conceptual definition of knowledge management should be commonly understood.

Acknowledgements

Heru Susanto, as main contributor. Fadzliwati Mohiddin, Mohammad Khanafi Jumat, Fahmi Ibrahim, Desi, Setiana, Didi Rosiyadi as contributors. All authors reviewed and approved final version of this manuscript.

References

Alavi, M., & Leidner, D. E. (2001). Knowledge Management and Knowledge Management Systems: Conceptual Foundations and Research Issues. *MIS Quarterly*, 25(1), 107–136.

Chen, F., & Burstein, F. (2006). A Dynamic Model of Knowledge Management for Higher Education Development. Paper Presented at the International Conference on Information Technology Based Higher Education and Training (ITHET).

Coukos-Semmel, E. (2003). Knowledge Management in Research University: The Processes and Strategies. Paper Presented at the American Educational Research Association 2003 Annual Meeting, Chicago, IL.

Cronin, B. (2001). Knowledge Management, Organizational Culture and Anglo-American Higher Education. *Journal of Information Science*, 27(3), 129–137.

Darroch, J., & McNaughton, R. B. (2002). Examining the Link between Knowledge Management Practices and Types of Innovation. *Journal of Intellectual Capital*, 3(3), 210–222.

Dasgupta, M., & Gupta, R. K. (2009). Innovation in Organizations: A Review of the Role of Organizational Learning and Knowledge Management. *Global Business Review*, 10(2), 203–224.

Davenport, T. H., & Prusak, L. (1998). *Working Knowledge: How Organizations Manage What They Know*. Boston, MA: Harvard Business School Press.

Deshpande, R., & Farley, J. U. (2004). Organizational Culture, Market Orientation, Innovativeness and Firm Performance: An International Research Odyssey. *International Journal of Research in Marketing*, 21, 3–22.

Du Plessis, M. (2007). The Role of Knowledge Management in Innovation. *Journal of Knowledge Management*, 11(4), 20–29.

Microsoft. (May 2000). Digital Dashboard: Business Process Assessment Guide. Available from http://www.microsoft.com/business/digitaldashboard/ddbpag.asp

Mohd Ghazali Mohayidin, Nor Azirawani, Man Norfaryanti Kamaruddin, & Mar Idawati Margono (2007). The Application of Knowledge Management in Enhancing the Performance of Malaysian Universities. *The Electronic Journal of Knowledge Management*, 5(3), 301–312.

Mum Wai, Y., & Dominic, L. H. C. (2008). Top Management Leadership: Success Factors of Knowledge Management Implementation in Tunku Abdul Rahman College (TARC) in Malaysia. Paper presented at the International Conference on the Roles of the Humanities and Social Sciences in Engineering 2008, Perlis, Malaysia.

Petrides, L. A., & Nodine, T. R. (2003). *Knowledge Management in Education: Defining the Landscape*. Half Moon Bay, CA: Institute for the Study of Knowledge Management in Education.

Shelda, D. (2006). *Knowledge Management*. Australia: John Wiley & Sons Australia. Ltd.

Susanto, H., & Almunawar, M. N. (2015). Managing Compliance with an Information Security Management Standard. In *Encyclopedia of Information Science and Technology*, Third Edition (pp. 1452–1463). IGI Global.

Susanto, H., & Almunawar, M. N. (2016). Security and Privacy Issues in Cloud-Based E-Government. In *Cloud Computing Technologies for Connected Government* (pp. 292–321). IGI Global.

Susanto, H., & Almunawar, M. N. (2018). *Information Security Management Systems: A Novel Framework and Software as a Tool for Compliance with Information Security Standard*. CRC Press.

Susanto, H., Fang Yie, L., Mohiddin, F., Rahman Setiawan, A. A., Haghi, P. K., & Setiana, D. (2021). Revealing Social Media Phenomenon in Time of COVID-19 Pandemic for Boosting Start-Up Businesses through Digital Ecosystem. *Applied System Innovation*, *4*(1), 6.

Susanto, H., Hamid, H., Mohiddin, F., & Setiana, D. (2021). Role of Learning Technology Strategies among People With Disabilities: A Job Opportunities Barrier. In *Handbook of Research on Analyzing IT Opportunities for Inclusive Digital Learning* (pp. 215–248). IGI Global.

Susanto, H., Ibrahim, F., Nazmudeen, S. H., Mohiddin, F., & Setiana, D. (2021). Human-Centered Design to Enhance the Usability, Human Factors, and User Experience within Digital Destructive Ecosystems. In *Global Challenges and Strategic Disruptors in Asian Businesses and Economies* (pp. 76–94). IGI Global.

Susanto, H., Yie, L. F., Rosiyadi, D., Basuki, A. I., & Setiana, D. (2021). Data Security for Connected Governments and Organisations: Managing Automation and Artificial Intelligence. In *Web 2.0 and Cloud Technologies for Implementing Connected Government* (pp. 229–251). IGI Global.

Susanto, H., Yie, L. F., Setiana, D., Asih, Y., Yoganingrum, A., Riyanto, S., & Saputra, F. A. (2021). Digital Ecosystem Security Issues for Organizations and Governments: Digital Ethics and Privacy. In *Web 2.0 and Cloud Technologies for Implementing Connected Government* (pp. 204–228). IGI Global.

Thorn, C. A. (2001). Knowledge Management for Educational Information Systems. What Is the State of the Field? *Educational Policy Analysis Archive*, 9(47), 17–36.

Part 4

Technology for information and knowledge management

11 Strengthening artificial intelligence implementation of security business management in time of digital economy innovation

Heru Susanto and Alifya Kayla Shafa Susanto

Introduction

To keep up with the technology evolution and the industrial revolution 4.0, businesses need to keep stay alert and look forward to any new technologies that may emerge that can become a competitive advantage or benefit to their company. Various technologies had emerged that can assist businesses in achieving their organisational goals such as the Internet of Things (IoT), Artificial Intelligence (AI), Blockchain, Augmented Reality (AR) and more. Artificial Intelligence is one of the technologies that can open up new opportunities for businesses to grow. And, recently for the past few years across the globe, there has been a lot of research and focus on AI. According to Regalado (2018), AI and machine learning "can improve processes and increase efficiency" in varying parts of the organisation and open up new opportunities for businesses to grow or build. And, according to Huawei GCI Report (2018), Artificial intelligence had allowed "digital transformation" to affect "market competitiveness, productivity, and innovation" more positively. Where business management is the act of planning, organising, directing, coordinating and controlling business activities, this is where AI implementation plays an important part in improving business management that can help the businesses to grow. Thus, this research is to study how AI can be implemented in business management, and how businesses in Brunei can benefit from implementing AI in the organisation's business management.

The aim of this study is to reveal and manage AI-related applications to boost business management in Brunei Darussalam. However, the main objectives of this study are as follows:

- To find out the current state of effectiveness and efficiency of traditional business management against using AI in the business management.
- To find out the level of AI adoption in Business Management in Brunei Darussalam.
- To reveal and manage the challenges in implementing AI in business management in Brunei.

DOI: 10.4324/9781003163824-15

Moreover, the study will help to uncover the current state of Brunei's business management. This will be beneficial for businesses to understand that there is room for improvement in their business management and to help them understand what AI can do to help boost their business management. The study will also reveal and manage any AI-related applications. From these findings, business management will be easier and more efficient for business owners/managers. This will further improve business management in Brunei Darussalam. Therefore, AI's help in the boosting of business management, in turn, will allow Brunei's businesses to be able to compete in the Asian market.

The paper is structured in as follows. Firstly, the literature review section will give the background knowledge on business management, artificial intelligence, the implementation of AI, the frameworks on Resource Dependency Theory and Transaction Cost Economics. Then, we discuss the research method to collect data and the limitation that had been encountered in this research. Next is the presentation of data in the illustrations of charts and tables that had been collected through the survey. After that are the discussion, critical thinking and recommendations of the research questions and hypothesis. Finally, the conclusion of the overall research study and the references that had been used for this research are given.

Literature review

According to Gartner (2018), only 4% of companies already have invested and deployed AI initiatives, whereas 25% in the short-term planning and actively experimenting with AI and 21% in medium- or long-term planning while 35% put AI on the radar but no action has been planned yet and 14% had no interest in implementing AI. Artificial Intelligence is working its way into a lot of organisation's workplaces that are augmenting human performance through Virtual Personal Assistant (VPN) and various forms of a chatbot which according to survey conducted by Gartner, by 2021, 70% of the organisation will integrate AI to assist their employees' productivity. AI implementation among enterprises grew 270% in the past four years (Gartner, 2019) and the number tripled in the past year. AI implementation was considered rare four years ago as only 10% of the enterprise responded that they had implemented AI or do so shortly. 10% raised up to 37% by 2019, showing that if enterprises don't start implementing AI in their organisation, chances are high that their competitors will implement AI to gain advantages. So, this will be a concern for businesses that do not implement AI. Thus, it is no longer out of question for small businesses to start integrating AI. Narrative Science (2016) listed out six top choices of business and technology executives that they believe are the most important benefits that AI should provide business. At the top of the list, 38% beneficial on predictions on activity related to machines, customers or business health. The second place is the automation of manual and repetitive tasks at 27%.

At third place, monitoring and alerts to provide assessments on the state of your business at 14%. Fourth is to increase the quality of communication with customers at 10% and for recommendations related to internal issues or customer-facing efforts at 7%. And lastly, 4% are for other benefits.

AI implementations in business management

In business management, AI played behind the scene's role to manage handling or assisting with regular aspects and functions of the business functions. In business information, artificial intelligence can give huge benefits by helping businesses to manage their data through deep analysis. And, there are plenty of industries benefitting from AI in their operations. Artificial Intelligence can be applied to numerous different sectors and industries. The healthcare industry used and tested AI for dosing drugs and different kinds of treatment for patients and also for surgical procedures in the operating room. In the financial industry, Artificial Intelligence is used to detect and flag activity such as unusual and suspicious debit card usage and large account deposits. This will help the bank's fraud department in detecting any malicious activity that may affect the bank reputations.

In the logistics sector, Artificial Intelligence can help to predict and determine an efficient travel route based on its ability to source information from several places including weather, average fuel consumption, traffic and other elements for the companies that use freight trucks or flights. Thus, predicting the most efficient route to use can increase efficiency, lower cost and time consumption. Moreover, artificial intelligence shifting paradigm of the way how business processes works, especially in decision making, human resource management, cybersecurity, customer relations and marketing are some of the management that can be benefited from this (Susanto & Almunawar, 2015; Susanto & Almunawar, 2016; Susanto *et al.*, 2021". Below are some of the examples that use the application of AI in business operations.

Human resource departments and staffing agencies (Chrisos, 2018) are using Artificial Intelligence technologies to assist them to find the best talent from resume submissions. AI can match the best applicants with job positions based on keyword functionality and AI's ability to gather and analyse information from several sources co-currently. Thus, this will reduce the amount of time to shortlist candidates that are suitable for the job rather than checking each application submissions which are usually in large quantity that requires a lot of time to be checked.

In Decision Making, Artificial Intelligence is used to assist managers in making the best decision. For example, an energy management system that collects data from various sensors, which are contextualised by machine learning algorithms. From the result, the decision-makers would be able (Mills, 2018) to understand the energy usage and the maintenance demands in order to make the right choice. In the marketing and advertising area where Artificial Intelligence is used to reach the company targeted customer base (Mills, 2018; Susanto, Ibrahim, et al., 2021) by showing them the ads that suited with their interests. AI was able to achieve this by analysing their customer's data to have a better understanding of their customer preference and behaviours.

Success stories of AI integration

Unilever is one of the companies that had successfully able to integrate Artificial Intelligence into their business operations. The company managed to streamline its hiring and onboarding as well as take advantage of their extensive amounts of data through AI (Susanto et al., 2021; Susanto et al., 2021; Yie et al., 2021). Unilever observed that the origins of their data were coming from various interfaces and APIs. This means that access to the data is prevented, thus making the data unreliable. To counter this problem, Unilever had developed its own platform where it can collect data from both internal and external sources and then store the data and most importantly, their employees can access those data. The company used the data for varying purposes such as demand forecasts to marketing analytics. Amazon is another example of a company that had applied AI in its business operations. The company had used machine learning to optimise their inventory management and delivery (Esposito, 2019; Mohiddin & Susanto, 2021; Mohiddin et al., 2021). Due to the AI-empowered system, the company was able to successfully enter into the food industry through the acquisition of Whole Food that now uses Amazon delivery services. Both Unilever and Amazon are exemplary as both used readily available technology to solve their problems. Indeed, these two companies are large corporations with deep pockets. However, Esposito (2019) believes that businesses should be thinking about AI realistically and strategically so that they can achieve their goals.

Esposito (2019) emphasises that the purpose of AI technologies is to improve society and not to displace workers. In order to abate the fear of job loss, business owners can address the problem by creating new and more functional jobs. As technologies will improve efficiencies and create new insights. As a result, new jobs will emerge due to those improvements. Esposito (2019) believes that people and machines need to cooperate together. However, we should not let machines make a decision on our behalf.

Methodologies

Research strategy

The research strategy will provide the direction as well as help in choosing the correct methodology for collecting and analysing the data. Two main strategies can be applied to the research study, namely qualitative and quantitative. The qualitative research strategy will give insights into research problems. The methods include interviews, observations and open-ended surveys, whereas quantitative data implies to look at the pattern in numeric data that can be analysed using statistics. The methods can be used to include the questionnaire and polls. This research study will use both primary and secondary sources. Primary sources are raw information and first-hand evidence which include interviews and surveys. On the other hand, secondary sources provide second-hand information and commentary from other researchers which include journal articles, reviews and academic books. Secondary sources describe, interpret, analyse or synthesise primary sources.

Research method

There is one research method that will be used in this research study. The method is through questionnaires. This method is used to collect both qualitative and quantitative data. The responses will later be analysed using a statistical technique to generalise the whole population. However, the limit of questionnaires is that they could not get the level of detail in qualitative responses compared to a questionnaire conducted in an interview. The type of questionnaire used will be a self-completed questionnaire. This means that the subject will complete it themselves. And, the questionnaire will be completed through a web-based survey. In this case, Google Forms will be used. This application will make administering the survey much quicker and easier as well as cheap compared to face-to-face interviews.

The target audience of the survey are local business owners, managers or support staff who can represent their company. A pilot test is conducted to ensure that the respondents will be able to answer the questions. Five businesses are selected to answer the questionnaire and to give feedback on their experience on answering the survey and to give suggestions on how the survey can be made easier to answer. Thus, if, there are any difficulties in answering the survey and suggestions were given, the survey will be amended to help respondents able to answer the questions more easily.

Findings

The types of organisations that were involved in answering this survey were 62.5% proprietorship companies, 25% partnership companies and 12.5% private companies. As shown in Figure 11.1, the respondents are from varying sizes of organisation, which were 54.2% from micro-enterprise, 29.2% from small enterprise and 16.7% from medium enterprise. The survey was also able to gather data from varying business sectors as shown in Table 11.1. Most of the respondents are from the wholesale and retail trade at 33.3% and least at 4.1% from transportation, manufacturing, education and cosmetic sectors. So, the data collected are not only limited to the same group of businesses which means that different views and opinions can be collected.

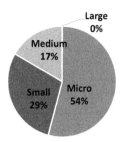

Figure 11.1 Size of enterprise.

Table 11.1 List of business sectors

No.	Sector	Number of companies (%)
1	Wholesale and retail trade	33.3
2	Agriculture, forestry and fishery	12.5
3	Transportation and storage	4.2
4	Manufacturing	4.2
5	Information and communication	4.2
6	Education	4.2
7	Hospitality and tourism	8.3
8	Food and beverages	12.5
9	Beauty, cosmetics & healthcare	4.2
10	Creative industry	12.5

Utilisation of information systems

Based on whether these companies had utilised their Information System, 66.7% of the respondents agree that they utilise the organisation's Information System, while 33.3% does not utilise the organisation's Information System. Twenty percent of companies that had not utilised the organisation's Information System were from the micro-enterprises, 8% were from small and 4% were from medium enterprise. Based on these, the micro- and small enterprises that do not utilise IS, may not utilise it due to lack of awareness on the importance of having a proper IS or having no proper personnel to manage (Figure 11.2).

Table 11.2 shows that the most encountered security breaches are system failure and/or data corruption follows by infection from viruses or malicious software. The main cause of the security breaches that these companies had encountered is likely due to human errors/failures.

Based on Table 11.3, the most involved business processes using the IS are payment processing, corporate email and data storage. This means that if the mentioned processes are affected by security breaches, it could lead to interruption of business operations.

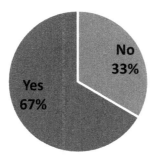

Figure 11.2 Utilisation of information system.

Table 11.2 Information security breaches encountered

No.	Security breaches	Number of companies (%)
1	System failure/data corruption	52
2	Infection by viruses or malicious software	20
3	Theft or fraud involving computers	8
4	Attack by an unauthorised outsider/system hacked	4
5	Misused of authorisation access	16

Table 11.3 Business processes that are involved by using the information system

No.	Processes	Number (%)
1	Corporate website	11.3
2	Corporate email	13.7
3	Payments processing	16
4	Payroll processing	8
5	Sales and/or marketing	9
6	Customer transactions processing	10
7	Finance and accounting	9
8	Office tools (e.g. Word processing)	9
9	Data storage	13.7

DBI adoptions

Figure 11.3 shows that most businesses do not introduce DBI in their company. Only 8.3% had introduced DBI in their company while the other 91.7% did not introduce DBI. One of the main causes of this is due to the lack of awareness of the company on any new innovative technology that may become a competitive advantage for them, and they lack talent/personnel that can manage and understand these new technologies.

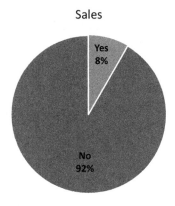

Figure 11.3 Introduction of DBI in the company.

Table 11.4 shows the comparison of DBI implementation based on two companies. The mode of exercising the DBI was through business process re-engineering department and through information technology department. Company A had used the first method while company B used the second method. The core processes of company A had been affected after exercising DBI while company B had been affected on both their core and generic processes.

Both companies had launched their core process when implementing DBI, and these processes were changed by bringing in new technology, using software solution, and both companies did not hire any external consultant for DBI.

Based on the extent of how much has there been reduction of cost in the company after DBI had been introduced, company A stated that 1there had been 1–20% of reduction while company B stated that there had been less than 10% of reduction in cost. Based on the extent of the increase in revenue the company had after implementing DBI, company B stated that there had been 21–30% increase in revenue, while company A stated that there had been an 11–20% increase in revenue. Based on the extent of number of customers that had increased after implementing DBI, both companies had agreed that there had been more than 30% increase in the number of customers. This means that DBI had managed to improve the company's cost reduction, revenue and number of customer after being implemented in both companies. However, there has been difference in the improvement of cost reduction and revenue for both companies (Table 11.5).

Both of the respondents agree that the roles that IT has played in the newer processes under DBI exercise were analytical and knowledge management. And, company A stated that the roles IT has played in the newer processes under DBI exercise were transactional, geographical, sequential,

Table 11.4 Comparison of Company A and B on DBI implementation

No.	Item	Company A	Company B
1	How was the DBI exercise undertaken?	Through business process re-engineering department	Through information technology department
2	Which new processes were launched when DBI was implemented?	Core process	Core process
3	Did DBI exercise in your Company effect the following processes?	Core	Both, core and generic.
4	Were the above processes changed by bringing in technology?	Yes	Yes
5	Was any Software Solution being used for the DBI?	Yes	Yes
6	Did your company hire external consultants for DBI?	No	No
7	What type of cost has been affected due to introduction of DBI?	Operating cost	Operating cost
8	To what extent there has been reduction in the cost in the company after DBI has been implemented?	11 to 20%	less than 10%
9	To what extent the revenue of the company had increased after DBI has been implemented?	11 to 20%	21 to 30%
10	To what extent number of customer have increased after DBI has been implemented?	More than 30%	More than 30%

Table 11.5 Role IT play in the newer processes under DBI exercise

No.	Role of IT	Company A	Company B
1	Transactional	/	
2	Informational		
3	Geographic		/
4	Sequential	/	
5	Analytical	/	/
6	Automation		/
7	Tracking		/
8	Knowledge management	/	/

automation and tracking. Meanwhile, neither stated that the IT's role played in the newer processes under DBI exercise was informational.

Adoption level of AI

Based on Figure 11.4, 45.8% of the respondents had stated that they had not adopted AI and had no plan to do so in the future. Another 45.8% state that they had not adopted AI but plan to do so in the future. And, 8.3% stated that AI had been incorporated in some part of the business management. Meanwhile, 0% had one or more AI pilot projects and had incorporated AI extensively in their business management.

Based on the two companies that had adopted AI, both companies agree that the reason that they had adopted AI was to automate processes/operations. And, company B had also agreed that the reasons that they had adopted AI were to obtain or sustain a competitive advantage, current competition will likely to use AI and there's pressure to reduce cost that requires the company to use AI, while neither of the company stated that AI will allow them to move into new businesses and due to new organisation using AI will enter their market (Table 11.6).

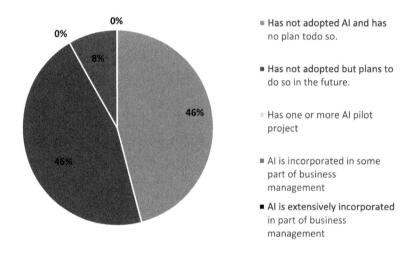

Figure 11.4 AI adoption level.

Table 11.6 Reason for adopting AI between Company B and C

No.	Reason(s)	Company B	Company C
1	AI will allow us to obtain or sustain a competitive advantage	/	
2	AI will allow us to move into new businesses		
3	New organisations using AI will enter our market		
4	Current competitors will use AI	/	
5	The pressure to reduce costs will require us to use AI	/	
6	To automate processes / operations	/	/

Table 11.7 Comparison between Company B and C on adoption of AI

No.	Question(s)	Company B	Company C
1	AI technology/tool(s) used?	Formstack	Sage
2	Did any of the technologies listed above boost your business management's performance?	Yes	Yes
3	Did your company encounter any difficulties when implementing these technologies?	Yes	Yes
4	Challenges/difficulties that your company faced?	Designing interface for customer friendly use	Technical difficulties
5	How did your company overcome the problem stated previously?	By trial and error	Re-do

According to Table 11.7, AI technologies/tools that the two companies had used are Sage and Formstack. Both companies had agreed that using these technologies had boosted their business management's performance. These companies had also encountered difficulties when using these technologies, which were technical issues when designing the interface. And, these difficulties were overcome through trial and error and redoing it again.

The main reason why the companies currently did not adopt AI but they plan to do in the future is due to the lack of talent to manage and understand AI technology followed by due to the lack of fund/investment to adopt AI technology. This shows that the companies do want to adopt AI but due to these factors they could not. And, some companies do not see any significant benefit of adopting AI for now but will adopt it if there's significant benefit to be gained. And, the least contributing factor for not adopting AI now is due to organisational culture (Figure 11.5). Listed below is the compiled list of what the companies expected to get when they adopt AI in their company:

1   Improve decision making
2   Increasing efficiency and effectiveness
3   To ease and automate business operation/processes
4   Improving customer satisfaction and attracting new customers
5   Decreasing risks and human errors/improving security
6   To forecast and boost sales

The main reason for these companies to not adopt AI and had no plan to do so in the future was due to no significant benefits that were to be obtained from adopting AI followed by insufficient funds and lacking in talents to manage and understand such technologies. The other reason why the companies do not want to adopt was due to the primary strength of the company is on individual's soft skills instead of focusing on AI technology (Figure 11.6).

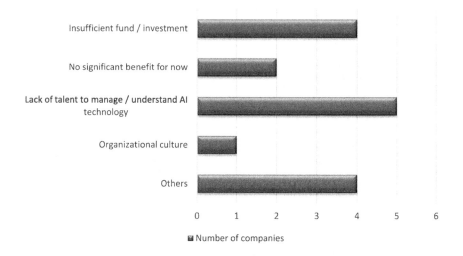

Figure 11.5 Reason(s) for not adopting AI but plan to.

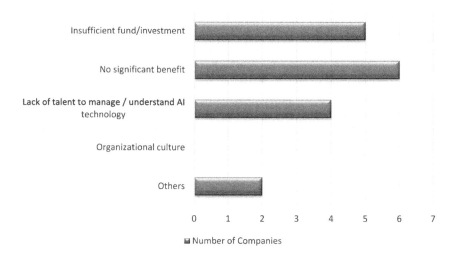

Figure 11.6 Reasons for not adopting AI and will not invest in it.

Based on Figure 11.7, 100% of the respondent stated that AI will bring positive impact to business management, although 48.5% had no plan to adopt AI in their companies. The companies still agree that AI technologies can bring positive impact. This shows that if the reasons why the companies do not adopt AI can be addressed, there're high chances that these

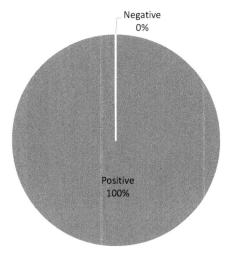

Figure 11.7 Opinion on impact of AI.

companies will adopt AI in their company. Listed below is the compilation of reasons why they think AI can give positive impact:

1   Improve marketing and sales
2   Improve security
3   Time saving
4   Improve efficiency and effectiveness
5   Minimise amount of work and leave more room for creativeness
6   Very useful for bigger corporation to manage more efficiently

Effectiveness and efficiency of AI

Figure 11.8 shows the opinion of the respondents on the level of effectiveness in business management when using AI and when without using AI. The trends from without using AI to using AI in business management were showing that the satisfactory level was increasing while the dissatisfactory level was decreasing. This means that, according to the respondent's opinion, using AI in the business management can improve the satisfactory level of effectiveness in business management.

However, it shows the opinion of the respondents on the level of efficiency in business management when using AI and when without using AI. The trends from without using AI to using AI in business management were also showing that the satisfactory level was increasing while the dissatisfactory level was decreasing. This means that, according to the respondent's

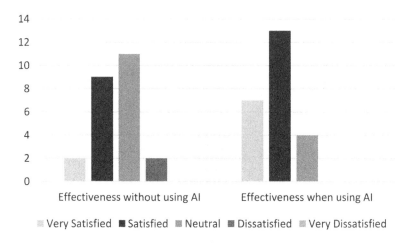

Figure 11.8 Comparison of effectiveness.

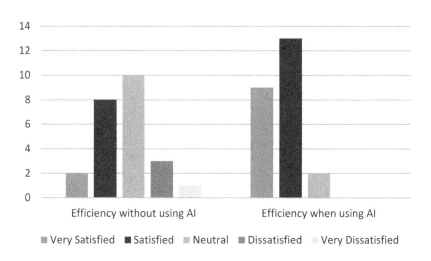

Figure 11.9 Comparison of efficiency.

opinion, using AI in the business management can improve the satisfactory level of efficiency in business management (Figure 11.9).

Discussions

In terms of the effectiveness, chart 8 shows the opinion of the respondents on the level of effectiveness in business management when using AI and when without using AI. The conversion from without using AI to using AI in business management was showing that the satisfactory level was increasing while the dissatisfactory level was decreasing. This means that, according to the respondent's opinion, using AI in the business management can actually improve the satisfactory level of effectiveness in business management. Meanwhile, in terms of efficiency, chart 9 shows the opinion of the respondents on the level of efficiency in business management when using AI and when without using AI. The conversion from without using AI to using AI in business management had also showed that the satisfactory level was increasing while the dissatisfactory level was decreasing. This means that, according to the respondent's opinion, using AI in the business management can improve the satisfactory level of efficiency in business management. Thus, the first research question and the objective of the research were accomplished, where it shows the level of effectiveness and efficiency between the traditional method versus modern method through using AI based on the respondent's opinion.

However, measuring the level of effectiveness and efficiency between the traditional method versus modern method through using AI through the opinion of the respondents alone is not enough. There should be a measurement using monetary value or through the measurement of how fast task/project can be completed satisfactorily with the help of AI and compare this data with data of before using AI, which should also be considered.

The level of AI implementations

According to AITI[1]'s ICT[2] Business Report in 2019 that consisted of 814 businesses that are represented by either executive, manager or support staff. The figure above shows the adoption of emerging technology where one of the technologies is Artificial Intelligence. Based on this figure, AI adoption was only 2.4% compared to the other emerging technologies. And based on Chart 4, 8.3% of the businesses stated that AI had been incorporated in some part of the business management (Figure 11.10).

As mentioned in previous section, AI can assist businesses to be more efficient and effective in their management of business as AI can overcome the bottleneck of human efficiency and removing the repetitive and standardised works. This is where the growth of AI can be seen as displacing jobs; however, it is the other way around as AI had also created new jobs/positions. According to the report from the World Economic Forum, AI had caused 75 million jobs to be deposed by 2020; however, in the next few years, AI could create 133 million new roles which is a net of 58 million new jobs. Thus, with the growth of AI, people should be prepared for the emerging roles and keep up-skilling themselves and their employees with relevant

---

1 Authority for Info-communications Technology Industry.
2 Information and Communication Technology.

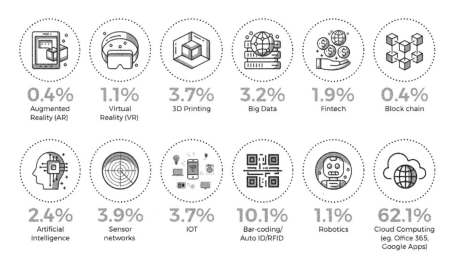

Figure 11.10 Adoption of emerging technology.

skills that will be useful for the company's future if they want to grab this opportunity to grow and be more relevant in this fast face technology evolution as the businesses should not only keep watch on AI but also on other emerging technologies.

However, according to Chart 4, 8.3% state that AI had been incorporated in some part of the business management. Based on the two companies that had adopted AI, both companies had agreed that the reasons that they had adopted AI was to automate processes/operations. And, company B had also agreed that the reason that they had adopted AI was to obtain or sustain a competitive advantage; current competition will likely to use AI and there's pressure to reduce cost that requires the company to use AI. According to Table 11.7, AI technologies/tools that the two companies had used were Sage and Formstack where both companies had agreed that by using these technologies, it had boosted their business management's performance.

The charts and the real business situations had showed that AI can be applied in varying parts of business operations. The adoption of AI will bring about change that can be beneficial to the businesses. Also, management's main objective is to achieve business goal and to ensure that business operation is functioning smoothly and through AI, business management will be able to run more efficiently and effectively. The adoption of AI in businesses can help in improving the businesses to be able to contribute more to the economic growth which eventually will help Brunei in achieving one of the visions in Wawasan 2035. Therefore, the second research question on what Brunei businesses can gain benefit from adopting AI is answered as some of the benefits that had been mentioned previously and not only businesses alone can be benefitted from this, the nation can also gain benefit from it. Thus, the hypothesis was accepted as AI can improve effectiveness and efficiency of BM as well as SMEs can also able to gain benefit from AI.

Business transformation: AI approaches

The phenomenon of AI approaches for business processes is quite interesting. Here, the AI solution/tools that Company B and C used were Formstack and Sage. Listed below are several other AI tools that are available that can transform businesses. Firstly, Formstack will provide aid to businesses to create powerful online forms that allow businesses to collect information, payments, registration and more in one central location within minutes. Secondly, Sage provided several AI solutions for any size of business. In other hand, the study found that for several industries such as manufacturing, wholesale, professional services, education and non-profits. The solutions are for several business needs such as accounting, enterprise management, payroll, HR and CRM. Third, Textio, which can aid organisations to write better job listing as it analyses every word and makes it worthwhile to the potential applicants who use predictive technology. Companies that had used this tool are such as Twitter, Microsoft, Square and Starbucks.

Fourth is DigitalGenius which uses AI and natural language processing to carry out human-like conversations with customers via calls and SMS. This tool will make use of predictive automation to analyse the question asked and then to find the right answer. This will aid businesses in improving their customer service operations as it analyses customer service logs, understands the everyday transaction and chooses the best response.

Fifth is Quill. This tool can help small businesses to automate writing documents such as reports through converting certain specific sets of data. Sixth is Recorded Future, which acts as a threat to intelligence system. This can help businesses to anticipate any future threats and thus lower threat risks. It makes use of machine learning to detect any kind of external threat to the company at a much faster rate. Last is DataRPM, which makes use of the predictive method to anticipate various things such as assets failure and analysing factors that can cause frequent repairing. This tool can help businesses to reduce their operational cost.

Moreover, related to RDT is the study that is based on the principle that an organisation interacts with other organisations that they had a transaction with, in order to acquire resources. This transaction will be beneficial or create a dependency on the organisation. Based on Table 11.5, Company B had depended on external organisation to provide them the service for DBI implementation. The relationship between company B and the external company will be unequal if the resources are scarce, or being controlled by an uncooperative organisation that had created an unequal exchange of power, authority and access to the resources. Thus, in order to avoid this situation of dependency, Company B should develop a strategy that can enhance their bargaining power in their relationship, for example, developing links with other organisations.

On the other hand, TCE is when cost was incurred during an economic exchange which can be used as determinant when making decision. Based on Table 11.5, the core processes of company A had been affected after exercising DBI and had launched their core process when implementing DBI; these processes were changed by bringing in new technology, using software solutions and the company did not hire an external consultant for DBI. Based on the extent of how much has there been a reduction in cost in the company after DBI had been introduced, company A stated that it had been 11–20% reduction. Based on the extent of the increase in revenue the company had after implementing DBI, company A stated that there had been an increase of 11–20% increase in revenue. Based on the extent of the number of customers had increased after implementing DBI, the company had agreed that more than 30% increase in the number of customers.

This means that DBI had managed to improve the company's cost reduction, revenue and the number of customers after being implemented in the company. Thus, the cost incurred by Company A can be used in making the decision on whether the DBI that had been implemented was successful or if they should stop its operation. And, since there had been an improvement for the company processes and cost reduction, the company should consider continuing with using the services.

AI as driver to cope with Covid-19

Covid-19 is putting heavy implications towards businesses across the world and there are several ways AI helps businesses in coping with this pandemic. First is through the AI-powered sales performance solution. This solution can identify which customers are more likely to buy a product or services from the business. So, this can help the sales teams to improve productivity and effectiveness by choosing the right customer to prioritise. Moreover, with this pandemic, understanding and collecting the demand of consumers will be harder and more critical as consumer stays at home and the interaction had shifted from personal to digital, thus creating new, unstructured data that is difficult to comprehend by a human. This is where AI comes in to analyse this data into producing data that the businesses need to know what consumers need and want.

Second is the ability to match demand and supply. AI solutions can help in analysing the demand and supply which is critical in these circumstances. On the positive side is the fact that there is an increasing amount of external data that is available on-demand where the demand measures depended upon the external data that are being used to match up with what their supply chain can produce. So, with the AI solution, it ensures that no extra production occurs nor unsatisfied demand happens. However, AI typically relies on data from the past; meanwhile, Covid-19 is new and unprecedented. So, companies had to make sure that they use representative data.

Last is the ability to respond faster. For example, the recent incident with consumer panic buying had led to supply chain disruption, which leaves manufacturers struggling to meet the spiking demands. Moreover, some factories are not in operation in this pandemic, making it harder to meet the demands. So, companies that had adopted AI had responded with faster speed in sourcing, producing and shipping their products. This means that the company that had already integrated AI in their organisation will be able to respond much faster than those that did not. Moreover, with the current unstable circumstances, companies can use AI to do forecasting that can model different kinds of scenarios and able to do tests and come up with possible responses to any situation that may arise.

Conclusion

In conclusion, in order to keep up with the fast pace of evolving technologies, businesses need to stay alert and keep on a lookout for any new technologies that may be beneficial to them if they want to grab the opportunity to grow. One of these technologies is AI, which can help businesses to gain competitive edges against their competitors. And, one of the important aspects in keeping the organisation organised is the business management; so, in order to improve efficiency and effectiveness of BM, businesses should consider implementing AI in their business management. This study will analyse the state of business management in Brunei Darussalam, to find out what are the benefits that businesses, not only large firms but also the small and medium enterprises, can gain benefit from, to understand what are the challenges that prevent businesses from implementing AI in their company. A survey was conducted to collect responses from business owners, managers or support staff on behalf of their company. A total of 24 responses were collected from various sectors and sizes of the organisation. From this investigation, it reveals that 48.5% had not adopted AI and had no plan to do so; another 48.5% also had not adopted AI but plan to do so in the future, while 8.3% had adopted AI in some part of their business management. The investigation also showed that the effectiveness and efficiency of traditional against using AI in business management had shown an increasing level of satisfaction in both categories. While AI implementation in Brunei is quite low in comparison, this may be because of several reasons such as lack of fund, lack of proper staff and lack in belief that AI can help benefit their company and due to organisational culture. The benefits that these business can gain from adopting AI are improvement of business management that can transform the business, such as prediction of threats, forecasting sales, automation of works and many more.

References

Frankenfield, J. (2020, January 22). How artificial intelligence works. Retrieved from https://www.investopedia.com/terms/a/artificial-intelligence-ai.asp

Gerner, M. (2020, April 17). 7 ways AI can help businesses during COVID-19. Retrieved May 4, 2020, from https://www.raconteur.net/technology/covid-19-ai-solutions

Gupte, V. (2019, June 18). News: AI tech's impact on project professionals. Retrieved from https://www.peoplemattersglobal.com/amp-skillup-ai-techs-impact-on-project-professionals-22057

Hillman, A. J., Withers, M. C., & Collins, B. J. (2009). Resource dependence theory: A review. *Journal of Management*, 35(6), 1404–1427.

Leu, F. Y., Liu, C. Y., Liu, J. C., Jiang, F. C., & Susanto, H. (2015). S-PMIPv6: An intra-LMA model for IPv6 mobility. *Journal of Network and Computer Applications*, 58, 180–191.

Mohiddin, F., & Susanto, H. (2021). Three parties engagement of learning management system: students-lecturer technology evidence from Brunei. In *Handbook of research on analyzing IT opportunities for inclusive digital learning* (pp. 130–153). IGI Global.

Mohiddin, F., Susanto, H., & Ibrahim, F. (2021). Implications of knowledge management adoption within higher education institutions: business process reengineering approach. In *Handbook of research on analyzing IT opportunities for inclusive digital learning* (pp. 307–351). IGI Global.

Leu, F. Y., Susanto, H., Tsai, K. L., & Ko, C. Y. (2020). A channel assignment scheme for MIMO on concentric-hexagon-based multi-channel wireless networks. *International Journal of Ad Hoc and Ubiquitous Computing*, 35(4), 205–221.

Rebecca. (2019, November 15). Business applications for artificial intelligence: What to know in 2019: Harvard Professional Development: Harvard DCE. Retrieved from https://www.extension.harvard.edu/professional-development/blog/business-applications-artificial-intelligence-what-know-2019

Roby, K. (2020, April 16). COVID-19: How artificial intelligence can help companies plan for the future. Retrieved May 4, 2020, from https://www.techrepublic.com/google-amp/article/covid-19-how-artificial-intelligence-can-help-companies-plan-for-the-future/

Rouse, M. (2019, December 31). What is artificial intelligence (AI)? Retrieved from https://searchenterpriseai.techtarget.com/definition/AI-Artificial-Intelligence

Susanto, H., & Almunawar, M. N. (2015). Managing compliance with an information security management standard. In *Encyclopedia of information science and technology*, Third Edition (pp. 1452–1463). IGI Global.

Susanto, H., & Almunawar, M. N. (2016). Security and privacy issues in cloud-based E-Government. In *Cloud computing technologies for connected government* (pp. 292–321). IGI Global.

Susanto, H., & Almunawar, M. N. (2018). Information security management systems: A novel framework and software as a tool for compliance with information security standard. 1st Edition. *CRC Press*.

Susanto, H., Fang Yie, L., Mohiddin, F., Rahman Setiawan, A. A., Haghi, P. K., & Setiana, D. (2021). Revealing social media phenomenon in time of COVID-19 pandemic for boosting start-up businesses through digital ecosystem. *Applied System Innovation*, 4(1), 6.

Susanto, H., Hamid, H., Mohiddin, F., & Setiana, D. (2021). Role of learning technology strategies among people with disabilities: A job opportunities barrier. In *Handbook of research on analyzing IT opportunities for inclusive digital learning* (pp. 215–248). IGI Global.

Susanto, H., Ibrahim, F., Nazmudeen, S. H., Mohiddin, F., & Setiana, D. (2021). Human-centered design to enhance the usability, human factors, and user experience within digital destructive ecosystems. In *Global challenges and strategic disruptors in Asian businesses and economies* (pp. 76–94). IGI Global.

Susanto, H., Yie, L. F., Rosiyadi, D., Basuki, A. I., & Setiana, D. (2021). Data security for connected governments and organisations: Managing automation and artificial intelligence. In *Web 2.0 and cloud technologies for implementing connected government* (pp. 229–251). IGI Global.

Susanto, H., Yie, L. F., Setiana, D., Asih, Y., Yoganingrum, A., Riyanto, S., & Saputra, F. A. (2021). Digital ecosystem security issues for organizations and governments: Digital ethics and privacy. In *Web 2.0 and cloud technologies for implementing connected government* (pp. 204–228). IGI Global.

Talwar, R. (2018, March 7). How SMEs can harness the power of AI for maximum impact. Retrieved May 4, 2020, from https://disruptive.asia/smes-harness-ai/

Yie, L. F., Susanto, H., & Setiana, D. (2021). collaborating decision support and business intelligence to enable government digital connectivity. In *Web 2.0 and cloud technologies for implementing connected government* (pp. 95–112). IGI Global.

Uzialko, A. C. (2019, April 22). How artificial intelligence is transforming business. Retrieved from https://www.businessnewsdaily.com/9402-artificial-intelligence-business-trends.html

Williamson, O. E. (1970, January 1). Transaction cost economics. Retrieved from https://link.springer.com/chapter/10.1007/978-3-540-69305-5_4

Young, S. (1970, January 1). Transaction cost economics. Retrieved from https://link.springer.com/referenceworkentry/10.1007/978-3-642-28036-8_221#howtocite

Young-Ybarra, C., & Wiersema, M. (1999). Strategic flexibility in information technology alliances: The influence of transaction cost economics and social exchange theory. *Organization Science*, 10(4), 439–459.

12 Expanding and enhancing knowledge using Artificial Intelligence (AI) in the Asian agro-industrial sector

Rindra Yusianto, Marimin Marimin, Suprihatin Suprihatin and Hartrisari Hardjomidjojo

Introduction

The world population continues to grow, so the demand for food tends to increase faster than supply. By 2030, the global population will increase to 8.5 billion people. Therefore, the need for food is estimated to increase by 60% (UN DESA, 2019). This increase has a significant impact on sustainable food security and could increase poor and hungry people.

Furthermore, the SARS-CoV-2 (COVID-19) pandemic began to hit many countries in Asia at the end of 2019, as well as having an impact on food security, including the stability of food availability and access to food (Peng & Berry, 2019). Most agro-industry players have felt the effects of COVID-19, such as difficulties in obtaining raw material supplies, marketing and high price fluctuations. This pandemic has caused a significant increase in demand for food, which will lead to a global hunger crisis. Based on the Global Hunger Index (GHI), the score for hunger in Southeast Asia in 2020 ranges from 9.9 to 20.1, where the level of severe hunger in Indonesia and the Philippines is 20.1. Meanwhile, Myanmar (19.8), Vietnam (15.5) and Malaysia (13.1) were in the moderate category, and Thailand (9.9) was in a low category. South Asia has the highest malnutrition rate (14.7%) and the most significant hunger in Asia, with 30.9. These include Afghanistan, Bangladesh and India (FAO, IFAD, UNICEF, 2020).

According to the International Labor Organization (ILO), in the 2012–2022 period, there was a decrease in the number of productive age people in Asia who worked in the agro-industrial sector from 1.33% to 8.85%. The most significant decline was in Thailand, from 42.14% to 33.29%, then Vietnam 47.86% to 41.87%, the Philippines 31.16% to 26.99%, Indonesia 35.93% to 31.82% and Malaysia 12.70% to 11.37%. The reduction in the productive workforce, coupled with the complexity and uncertainty in decision making, and demands for environmental sustainability, has given birth to innovative adaptive technology (Prause, 2019). Adaptive smart technology that is implemented massively in this sector is Artificial Intelligence (AI) which utilises the Internet of Things (IoT) (Shanmugapriya et al., 2019; Saiz-Rubio & Rovira-Mas, 2020). This innovation makes the

DOI: 10.4324/9781003163824-16

agro-industry an essential role in economic development in several countries in Asia, with an average contribution of 13.5% to Gross Domestic Product (GDP) (Dahiri & Fitri, 2020). PwC research results showed that the most significant economic gain from AI will be in China (26% increase in GDP by 2030), equivalent to $10.7 trillion and accounts for nearly 70% of the global economic impact (Mayers, 2017). Asian economic growth will be able to emphasise solving the problem of supply and demand imbalances.

In response to global food security trends, modern logistics has attracted the attention of many agro-industry players (Borsellino et al., 2020; Kurbatova et al., 2020). Modern logistics related to agricultural raw materials processing are called agro-logistics. The main problem of agro-logistics is the characteristics of agricultural products with high vulnerability, complexity and uncertainty. The perishable nature of commodities, sensitivity to climate change and high price fluctuations are the causes of this problem. Quality decreases rapidly after harvest, so the potential for post-harvest losses is up to 40% (Hsiao et al., 2018; Yusianto et al., 2019). Therefore, logistical transparency is needed to improve sustainable agro-industry with a supply and demand balance that considers the characteristics of the agricultural product.

Potatoes (*Solanum tuberosum L.*) are commodities that can support sustainable agro-industry (Devaux et al., 2019). Potatoes are the essential horticultural food after wheat, rice and maize. Potatoes produced around 370 million tons, or an increase of 10.9% from the production volume in 2010 (FAO, IFAD, UNICEF, 2020). Production increases by 4.5% per year, with the highest average output in Asia, 144.6 million tons (FAO, 2019). China has the most increased production in Asia with 96 million tons/year. Meanwhile, Indonesia is in 10th position with a total output of 1.3 million tons/ year and an average growth of 8.4%.

This research aims to increase the potato agro-industry competitiveness by predicting the harvest number using IoT, determining optimal logistics routes using AI and tracking and tracing potato commodities in Asia, especially Indonesia. The research focus is the use of AI and IoT to develop a sustainable agro-industry. The research contribution elaborates a sustainable agro-industry using remote sensing with a multi-thresholding and synergy spatial perspective based on AI.

Literature review

Many agro-industrial companies in Asia are already using AI to automate their business processes (Das et al., 2019). The goal is to make things fast, practice, integrated and adaptive. They use AI for the best real-time decision making, such as combing thousands of routes, selecting the best route, tracking the fastest delivery, managing effective delivery schedules and reducing the risk of delivery failure (Wisskirchen et al., 2017).

To improve sustainable agro-industry, the supply and demand balance that considers potato characteristics within the logistical transparency approach is this research focus. Logistics transparency starts from predicting harvest number, tracking and tracing logistics and planning distribution and transportation routes.

Based on potato growth rates in Asia (Table 12.1), China has the highest production with 96 million tons/year. Japan has the best productivity, namely 30.6 tons/hectares, where the planted area of 0.08 million hectares has produced 2.45 million tons/year. Meanwhile, Indonesia is in 10th position with 1.3 million tons/year and average growth of 8.4%.

Predicting the potato harvest number

In the Asian agro-industrial sector, the AI application to precision agriculture has been overgrown (Antony et al., 2020). In this sector, the World Bank projects world economic growth from South and East Asia and the Pacific, with an average increase of up to 4% in 2021 (Ignacio, 2021). However, the lack of information regarding supply and demand imbalances makes AI very dominant in helping raw materials in the Asian region. AI can predict the available raw materials by considering cropland suitability. As a commodity that can support sustainable agro-industry, potatoes in Asia are concerned about world agro-industry players. Currently, China still dominates world potato production (Figure 12.1).

Cropland suitability is a factor that needs to be influential at the on-farm level. The cropland suitability measures how the quality of land units corresponds to specific land-use requirements (Al-taani et al., 2020). Therefore,

Table 12.1 Potatoes growth rates in Asia

Region/Country	2016–2018			Growth rate		
	Production	Area	Yield	Production	Area	Yield
	(1000 tons)	*(1000 ha)*	*(tons/ha)*	*%*	*%*	*%*
China	96.136	4.942	19.45	3.2	2.4	0.8
India	46.395	1.82	25.49	6.3	3.4	2.9
Bangladesh	9.435	411	22.96	5.3	7.6	6.5
Pakistan	3.802	170	22.36	n.a.	n.a.	n.a.
Nepal	2.817	195	14.45	n.a.	n.a.	n.a.
Uzbekistan	2.453	116	21.15	n.a.	n.a.	n.a.
Japan	2.452	80	30.65	n.a.	n.a.	n.a.
North Korea	1.909	149	12.81	2.7	3.3	3.0
Kyrgyzstan	1.321	85	15.54	n.a.	2.6	n.a.
Indonesia	1.316	67	19.64	8.4	5.3	2.9

Source: FAO (2019).
n.a. = not available.

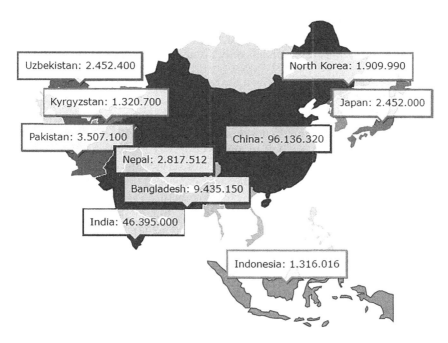

Figure 12.1 Spatial distribution of potatoes production in Asia (Modified from FAO, 2019).

cropland suitability evaluation can estimate the suitability of agricultural land for various alternative uses. This evaluation compares the growth requirements, characteristics and quality of land for a particular service by utilising the potentially available resources. Cultivating potatoes on suitable cropland can increase productivity, reduce the risk of crop failure and reduce post-harvest losses (Yusianto et al., 2020a). Rykaczewska (2015), in their research, explained that rainfall and temperature in an area affect cropland suitability. However, they did not discuss physical and spatial conditions.

Cropland suitability methods are becoming increasingly complex, where standard statistical techniques are unable to solve this problem. So, in predicting the potatoes harvest number, it requires innovative technology based on AI using IoT (Marimin et al., 2017). The IoT platform can optimise precision agriculture, manage production and maximise the potato crop quality (Marcu et al., 2019). Remote sensing takes data and then feeds it into a machine learning algorithm (Tervonen, 2018). However, it did not discuss the type of sensor used.

Foughali et al. (2019) have developed the IoT-based Decision Support System (DSS). They used the IoT MCU platform, the DHT11 humidity and a temperature sensor. Kiani & Seyyedabbasi (2018) have developed other related research. Rad et al. (2015) explained intelligent monitoring that the Cyber-Physical System with precision agriculture. Kamalakkannan et al. (2020) have also researched IoT applications in the agro-industry. However, most of the previous research has only discussed IoT implementations.

Determining logistics routes

The ASEAN Economic Community (AEC) in 2015 has encouraged countries in the ASEAN region to develop strategies to win the competition. The contribution of ASEAN GDP to global GDP is 3.2%, with a total population of 8.7% (Wan & Zhan, 2011). Logistics services in the agro-industrial sector are considered the key to business success in this competition. AEC has opened up great opportunities for this sector in the Asian region. The Asian agro-industry has excellent potential, but inefficiency is massive, reaching 40% of the product value (UNESCAP, 2017). Using AI, industrial logistics can play an essential role in a distribution chain.

Innovative technology development has made AI performance, accessibility and costs more profitable. The advent of AI has transformed the fragmented logistics market following the same route. AI has become an integral part of any future agro-industrial logistics system. AI plays a vital role in saving time, reducing costs and increasing productivity (Wisskirchen et al., 2017). In addition, AI can improve efficiency, affect warehousing operations and reduce logistics costs. Inefficiency in the transportation sector being 20.43%, it is increasingly convincing that the agro-industrial logistics sector needs to implement AI along its supply chain beginning from post-harvest (Suarez, 2012). At present, post-harvest loss is an increasingly exciting issue. When farmers have improved on-farm handling, and advanced harvesting innovative technology, the researchers began to focus on post-harvest logistical problems.

In the Asian region, such as Japan, Singapore, Korea, China, Thailand and Vietnam, countries have a reasonably high international logistics performance index (LPI). Japan has the highest LPI score, namely 4.03 with logistics competence 4.09, and tracking and tracing 4.05 (Table 12.2). Japan consistently carried out its logistics system improvement package, namely the efficiency process using innovative technology, environmentally friendly and security (Hao et al., 2020). Based on the latest research results from Savills World Research, China and Korea are still the most significant market leaders in the logistics sector (Macdonald, 2019). However, in contrast to China, the potential in India is not supported by good manufacturing. The logistics penetration rate in India is relatively low at only 3.6%.

Previous studies related to logistics in Asia have focused on selecting the best route. Bozyigit et al. (2017), in their research, stated that the Dijkstra algorithm is the most widely used to solve logistics route problems but is inefficient for the route on public transportation. In Peyer et al. (2009), Dijkstra's algorithm can be generalised for selecting the shortest

Table 12.2 The International logistic performance index in Asia

Rank	Country	LPI score	Logistics competence	Tracking and tracing
1	Japan	4.03	4.09	4.05
2	Singapore	4.00	4.10	4.08
3	United Arab Emirates	3.96	3.92	3.96
4	Korea, Rep.	3.61	3.59	3.75
5	China	3.61	3.59	3.65
6	Taiwan	3.60	3.57	3.67
7	Qatar	3.47	3.42	3.56
8	Thailand	3.41	3.41	3.47
9	Vietnam	3.27	3.40	3.45
10	Malaysia	3.22	3.30	3.15
11	India	3.18	3.13	3.32
12	Indonesia	3.15	3.10	3.30
13	Turkey	3.15	3.05	3.23
14	Saudi Arabia	3.01	2.86	3.17

Source: https://lpi.worldbank.org/international/global (2019).

route. They consider routing problems with travel-time criteria. Their research resulted in a significant time efficiency of overall playing time from several days to several hours. The Dijkstra algorithm can determine the shortest route of the ten best tourist destinations in Bali, Indonesia (Fitriansyah et al., 2019). But in their study, they only used distance as a single criterion.

According to Roghanian and Kebria (2017), the optimal route selection must consider multiple attributes, such as distance, time, emissions and risk. They named the multi-attribute Dijkstra, who combined the Dijkstra and TOPSIS. Keser et al. (2016) have developed a multi-criteria route with a heuristic function. They used AHP for multi-criteria aggregation to determine actual costs and heuristics. Their results stated that distance, time, safety and fuel consumption were the selected criteria.

Tracking and tracing of agro-industrial products

In developing sustainable food security, logistical support is needed from potato cultivation to post-harvest, increasing productivity and quality and business institutions and improving post-harvest technology (Klen et al., 2017). On a larger scale, the availability of potatoes is not only fulfilled by domestic production, but the export-import activities of these commodities can also support sustainable food security. If domestic production is insufficient and potato imports are restricted, this will become an obstacle to food security. For example, when Russia, Ukraine and Kazakhstan have announced plans to limit exports, food security concerns extend to China and India. In addition, when Vietnam also temporarily stopped its exports to protect domestic supplies due to the Mekong

Delta drought in the 2020–2025 period, several countries in Asia began allocating their potato supplies from other countries (MRC, 2019). The Philippines has given the US$600 million for its food sufficiency efforts by supplying India and Pakistan. This supply and demand imbalance occurs due to a lack of real-time information, so it is necessary to track and trace logistics using AI.

Logistics traceability is a tool that meets the requirements for food availability. This system is the most effective heuristic function monitoring system. The primary standard is information to determine their suppliers and customers (Gracia et al., 2018). Tracking and tracing can provide transparency at every stage of food management, so they are essential for producers, distributors and consumers in various countries in Asia. Tracking and tracing require the identification of the unit. Identification technologies such as barcode and Radio Frequency Identification (RFID) can be used (Michaelides, 2010). These technologies can serve as differentiation methods and identify what and where there is a problem in their logistics supply chain.

The development of its international ports strongly influences the growth of agro-logistics in Asia. Asia has the top five international ports in the world (Table 12.3).

The connectivity effect between nodes causes the total value generated by transportation agro-industrial logistics services in Asia to be almost 28.1% compared to the average produced by the world. According to the WTO, in 2005, the value of logistics exports in Japan contributed 6.3% of the world's total logistics exports, Korea 4.2%, Singapore 2.7% and China 2.7%. The logistics agro-industry in Asia has the opportunity to become a node in enhancing cooperative relations with the international community.

Integrated statistical methods with spatial analysis using Geographical Information Systems (GIS) can solve complex traceability problems (Baidya et al., 2014). Tracking and tracing can quickly provide information on which areas are experiencing a surplus and the other regions experiencing shortages of potato supply. In agro-industrial logistics, monitoring and tracing allow us to know which countries are surplus and lack; this follows the one up and one down principle. An integrated traceability system using AI will provide sustainable food security quality (Folinas et al., 2012).

Table 12.3 The top five international ports in the world

Rank	Port name	Country	TEUs (million)	Growth rate (%)
1	Singapore	Singapore	232	8.7
2	Hong Kong	China	2242	2
3	Shanghai	China	1808	24.3
4	Shenzhen	China	1620	18.6
5	Pusan	Korea	1184	3

Research method

Based on Table 12.1, the country with the potato's most significant growth rate is Indonesia, namely 8.4 tons/ha. So, in this research, the average production in Indonesia is used with secondary data from several countries in Asia.

Before implementing IoT, we conducted a spatial perspective analysis using spatial analysis and geoprocessing. Then, we collected data from 14 sub-districts in Wonosobo, Central Java, Indonesia to determine a suitable research sample. Sample points determination based on land units and using 1.5 km grid intervals in all regions. So, the number of grids obtained is 16 grids on all land units (Figure 12.2); meanwhile, geoprocessing uses a geo-segregation analyser. The research sample used a random grid based

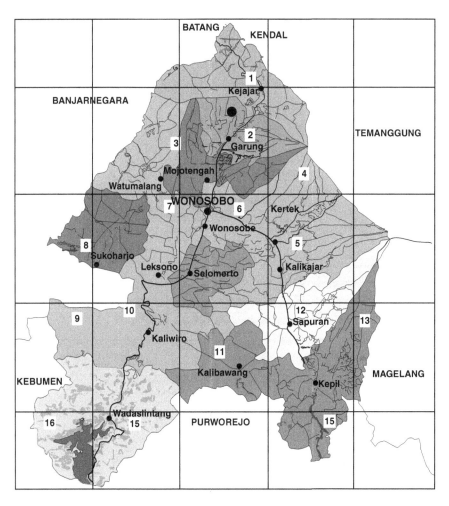

Figure 12.2 The research sample node.

on spatial conditions. We recorded data from a spatial perspective using latitude (X) and longitude (Y) coordinates. We installed temperature and humidity sensors SHT15 and Rain Gauge rainfall sensors at five points in the research. These sensors have provided data regularly per day for 30 days. Calibrate the SHT15 sensor with one digital output chip using an accuracy of $\pm$ 0.4 @ 5–40°C. Rain Gauge sensor-controlled from a mobile device based on the Android operating system with the Raspberry Pi. Data processing obtains maps of temperature, humidity and rainfall.

After determining the most suitable coordinate location, then process the total harvest prediction. This process requires data on the existing full harvest conditions from the obtained coordinates, drone preparation, image processing and image acquisition (Figure 12.3). Then, the prediction results are compared with the current products.

To determine the optimal route, we propose a new algorithm, namely the Spatial Dijkstra Spatial algorithm. This algorithm combines the classic

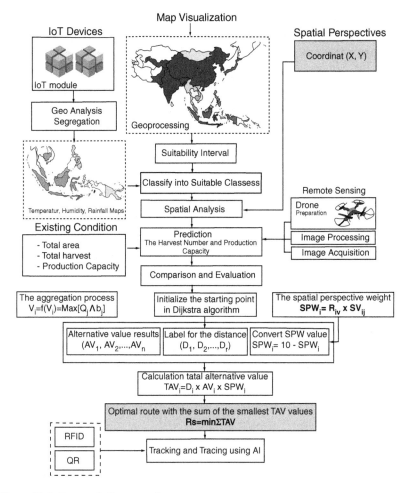

Figure 12.3 Research framework.

Dijkstra Algorithm with the aggregation process of the Multi-Expert Multi-Criteria Decision Making (ME-MCDM) approach and spatial perspective. After determining the optimal route with the smallest Total Alternative Value (TAV), RFID and QR code are used to perform tracing and tracking. The databases used are spatial database, model base and knowledge base. We design the architectural system into three main activities: classify suitable classes, cropland suitability and total harvest and production capacity prediction using IoT (Figure 12.4).

In this research, we were mapping the area using $2.5 \times 2.5\,\text{m}^2$ (Figure 12.5). Based on the land suitability interval, we divided the map into 25 grids with a distance of 1.5 km.

Logistical traceability involves managing traceability data by integrating spatial perspectives and AI, identifying, modelling, processing and presenting. Next, we divide the AI block architecture into three main modules: user management, ISDSS and interfaces (Figure 12.6).

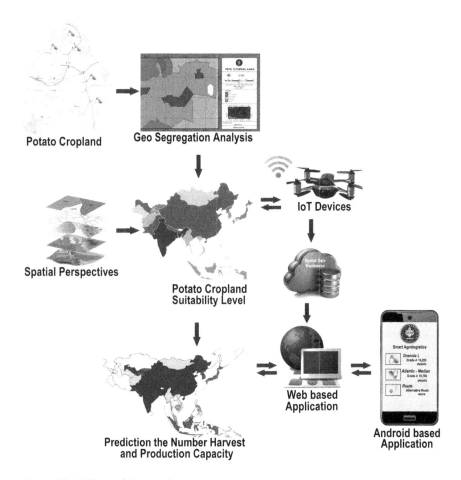

Figure 12.4 The architectural system.

Figure 12.5 Image acquisition data using drone.

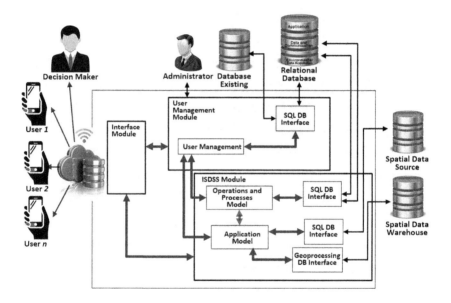

Figure 12.6 AI block architecture.

Result and discussions

Predicting potato harvest in Asia

This research uses a spatial distribution based on the GIS stacking layer covering five spatial perspective maps: altitude, soil texture, slope percentage, rainfall and temperature. Based on the spatial analysis, we obtained an average height of 674.8 m asl. Soil texture is predominantly podzol and regosol. We did not get the latosol texture, while andosol was present in P_1, P_2 and P_3 samples. Average slope is 8–13% (slightly steep) (Table 12.4).

Table 12.4 The spatial analysis results for 16 sample points

Sample code	Altitude m asl	Soil texture	Slope criteria	Rainfall mm/month	Temperature °C
P_1	1.378	Andosol	Bumpy	341.00	19
P_2	1.019	Andosol	Sloping	326.83	23
P_3	860	Andosol	Bumpy	317.75	24
P_4	825	Regosol	Hilly	313.33	22
P_5	815	Regosol	Sloping	351.92	23
P_6	744	Regosol	Flat	306.67	26
P_7	910	Regosol	Bumpy	247.50	24
P_8	400	Podzol	Bumpy	325.91	26
P_9	360	Podzol	Flat	260.75	27
P_{10}	512	Podzol	Bumpy	240.05	26
P_{11}	626	Regosol	Bumpy	350.42	26
P_{12}	760	Regosol	Flat	336.17	26
P_{13}	522	Podzol	Flat	347.08	27
P_{14}	522	Podzol	Bumpy	347.08	27
P_{15}	272	Podzol	Sloping	234.25	29
P_{16}	272	Podzol	Sloping	234.25	29

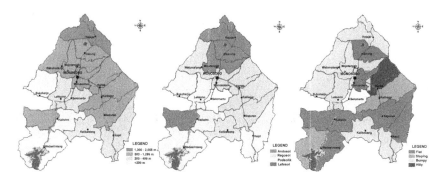

Figure 12.7 Comparison based on altitude, soil texture and slope.

Based on the altitude, only the P_1 sample is most suitable (>1,300 m asl). Meanwhile, based on texture (andosol), the appropriate area for potato plants is in the northern part of the research area. Based on the slope factor (8–13%), the middle part is more suitable, while the north of the site is less suitable because it is >14% (hilly) (Figure 12.7).

The average daily rainfall for all samples is above 300mm/month, and the average temperature is above 20°C (Figure 12.8). Almost all research areas are suitable for potato crops, especially in the eastern and northern parts.

Based on the spatial analysis, the cropland suitability values were 67.21% scattered in the eastern and southern parts of the research area (Figure 12.9).

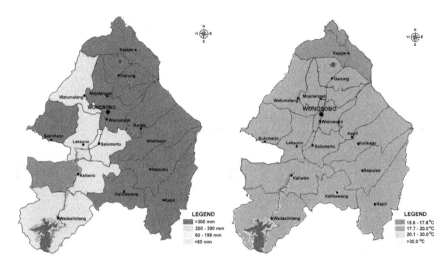

Figure 12.8 Comparison based on rainfall and temperature.

Table 12.5 The result of weighing harvest data

Block	Weight (kg)	Block	Weight (kg)
A1	8.50	D1	9.89
A2	9.67	D2	9.96
A3	8.20	D3	8.10
A4	8.98	D4	9.87
B1	7.70	E1	9.50
B2	7.30	E2	10.10
B3	8.20	E3	9.78
B4	10.50	E4	8.10
C1	8.90	F1	7.20
C2	7.98	F2	7.25
C3	7.20	F3	7.00
C4	7.05	F4	9.96

The most suitable site is 5.85% in the northern part of the study area, with conformity without limiting factors. Based on the validation, this region has the most significant amount of production, namely 447,060 tons/year.

Next, we predict the number of potato harvests. The separation of regions uses the multi-thresholding method, where region 1 is the background image, and region 2 was the potato leaf image. The average sample weight was 8.62 kg or had productivity of 1.38 kg/m^2 (13.79 tons/ha) (Table 12.5).

The average sample weight has a productivity of 13.79 tons/ha (Table 12.6). Comparing existing conditions with predictions using IoT and spatial analysis shows a good level of accuracy.

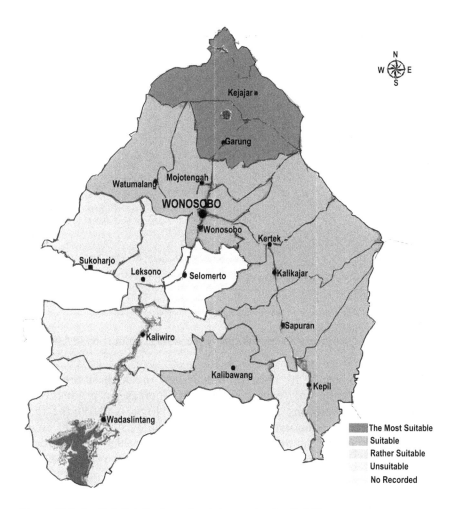

Figure 12.9 Spatial distribution of potato cropland suitability.

Table 12.6 The total harvest comparison

Comparison	Existing condition	Prediction of the potato harvest
Production (tons)	44.61	8.62
Harvested area (ha)	2.89	0.63
Productivity (tons/ha)	15.44	13.79

The system can provide the total harvest predictions with an accuracy rate of 89.35%. We implemented it in five countries in Asia (based on Table 12.1), namely China, India, Bangladesh, North Korea and Indonesia (Figure 12.10).

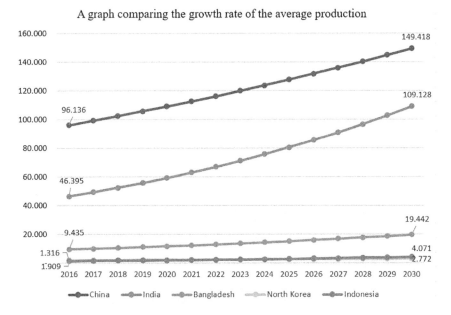

A graph comparing the growth rate of the average production

Figure 12.10 A Comparing the growth rate of the average production in Asia.

Based on Figure 12.10, even though it had the highest production level in 2016, China only experienced a 55% increase in production in 2030, 149.418 million tons. According to the UN DESA (2019), the agro-industrial sector production needs to be increased by 70% in 2030, so using this method, the country that meets the target in 2030 is Bangladesh, with a production increase of 106% from 9,435 million tons to 19,442 million tonnes, with India 135%. Indonesia's most significant production increase was 209%.

The accuracy in this study is 89.35%, so it is feasible and can be used to make predictions. According to Dewi and Muslikh (2013), the accuracy of proper predictions is higher than 80% (Figure 12.11).

Predictions of increased production using IoT are more rational than predictions using growth rates. Using this method until 2030, China will remain the largest producer in Asia, namely 133,505–149,418 million tons. The results showed that the application of intelligent technology, namely IoT in the agro-industrial sector in Asia, especially in the early post-harvest stage, produces accurate predictions with an accuracy rate of 89.35%. In 2030, several countries will meet the target of increasing their agro-industrial production by 70%. Until 2030, China will dominate potato production in Asia (Figure 12.12).

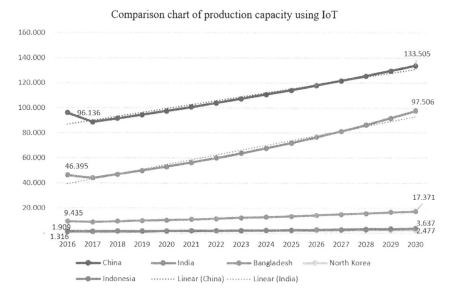

Figure 12.11 A comparison of production capacity using IoT.

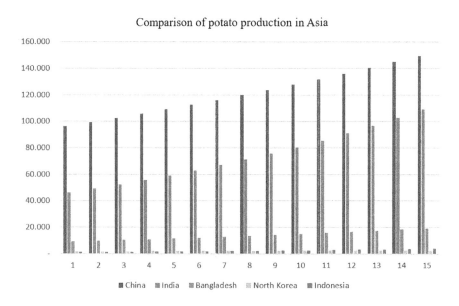

Figure 12.12 A comparison of potato production in Asia.

The highest increase in production was Indonesia by 176%, from 1,316 million tons to 3,637 million tons, followed by India 110%, Bangladesh 84%, China 39% and North Korea 30% (Figure 12.13). The increasingly adaptive role of intelligent technology provides opportunities for the agro-industry sector in Asia to grow better. According to Ravenhill (2006), the trade balance for agro-industrial products has offset the balance in its manufacturing trade for most countries in Asia. This research has approved that an IoT-based can indicate harvest number and productivity with a better accuracy rate. By predicting the total harvest in the future, decision-makers in Asia can quickly, precisely and accurately take policies related to the agro-industrial sector from on-farm, post-harvest, marketing and balancing supply and demand.

It appears that countries such as Indonesia, India and Bangladesh will have a central role in the development of the Asian agro-industry in 2030. China still dominates this sector; apart from having large cultivated land, implementing innovative technology in China went very well. The country is estimated to be left behind in North Korea, increasing only around 30% in 2030. North Korea needs to focus more on implementing IoT for its agro-industrial sector. Meanwhile, based on the average growth in this sector, Indonesia has an excellent opportunity to compete with other countries in Asia.

Optimal logistics routes in potato agro-industry

The rapid growth of the market has made the Asian region connected to the global logistics market. As a result, Asia is now playing an increasingly important role globally (Wu & Cheng, 2008). In this research, we discuss the optimal DSS for determining potato logistics routes using AI. We used

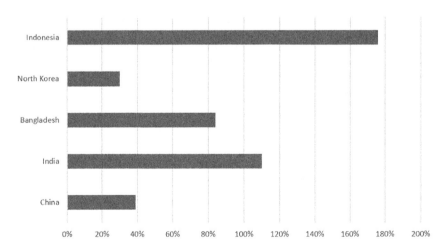

Figure 12.13 Prediction of an increase in the production capacity in 2030.

a spatial Dijkstra algorithm with the Android platform. The route selection by considering the spatial perspective gives a real contribution to the growth of the Asian agro-industrial sector. Perishable characteristics of potato commodities require AI to handle them.

The current condition shows that post-harvest loss in the Asian agro-industrial sector, the initial data, is an average of 3.28% (Yusianto et al., 2020b). The storage has the most significant loss contribution, namely 35.98%. This loss is the result of transportation problems which also contributed to the loss of 20.43%. We use AI to facilitate the selection of the most optimal route. The characteristics of perishable commodities require choosing the shortest route, like the Dijkstra algorithm (Peyer et al., 2009; Marimin & Septiani, 2016). Dijkstra's algorithm divides network nodes into three types: unlabelled nodes, temporarily labelled nodes and marked nodes (Bozyigit et al., 2017). We have combined AI with Dijkstra's algorithm and radian approach with a mobile-based application for Route Guidance Systems (RGS). Many navigation systems have implemented the RGS approach (Keser et al., 2016). This system provides information about which route to select, distance and travel time (Ringhand & Vollrath, 2017).

In this research, we used five nodes to give the code $V = \{V_1, V_2, ... V_5\}$. Each node contains code, name and coordinates. We measure the distance between one node and another node. First, we used the classical Dijkstra algorithm to calculate the shortest potato distribution route. By using the classical Dijkstra's algorithm, the shortest route is obtained. Second, the shortest potato distribution route is determined using a modified Dijkstra algorithm. Google APIs server with coordinates (X, Y) will make it easier to determine the shortest route. Third, the radian approach is applied to display all nodes in the database. We guide user navigation from the point to the node with the shortest route. Finally, the classic Dijkstra algorithm results in comparison to an Android-based navigation system. The network graph used the classical Dijkstra algorithm in this study (Figure 12.14).

Using the classical Dijkstra algorithm, P_1 $(V_1, V_5) = (V_1, V_2, V_5)$ with the shortest distance travelled is 133 km. Furthermore, this navigation system displays the shortest distribution route sequence in dynamic maps using Google Maps. The complexity of its databases, spatial warehouse systems and technology infrastructure in determining logistics routes affect AI applications. This research combines an advanced navigation system based on the Android operating system with navigation technology for RGS. We use AI and the spatial Dijkstra algorithm to determine the optimal route that connects between nodes. The knowledge base represents nodes as international ports owned by several countries in Asia. The system will store the best route in the database; then, the inference engine connected to the Google API will visually display the route between nodes (Figure 12.15).

Based on the network graph in Figure 12.14, the distance from V_1 to V_2 is 14.0 km. So, with this Android-based navigation system, users will be

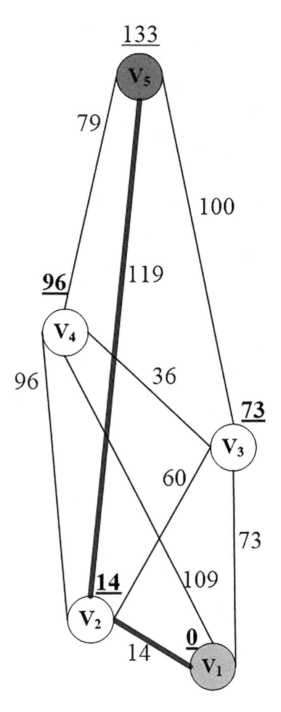

Figure 12.14 Network graph using Dijkstra algorithm.

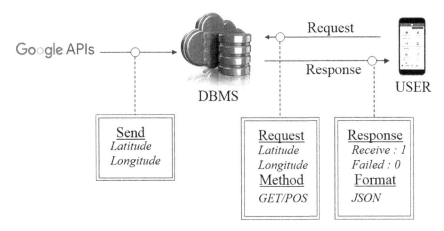

Figure 12.15 The optimal distribution route using Google APIs.

guided using the directions application from Google Maps. This navigation covers a distance of 14.0 km with an estimated travel time of 19.0 minutes. This navigation system proved consistent. So, this method made it easy for decision-makers to distribute their potatoes via the optimal route, whereas the most optimal way using the new approach that we proposed, namely the Spatial Dijkstra, was P (V_1, V_5) = (V_1, V_2, V_3, V_5) with a TAV weight of 1,547 (Figure 12.6). The new method, Spatial Dijkstra, can be verified to get the optimal route by considering multi-alternative with conflicting multi-criteria, suitable for solving the problem of distribution of agro-industrial products. This research has shown that the spatial Dijkstra can provide a more reasonable solution than the classical Dijkstra.

AI has paved the way for increasing the GDP of developing countries in Asia through the agro-industrial sector. According to Zai et al. (2018), technology utility and sustainability are the most decisive success factors in agro-industry logistics at 30%, distribution and transportation at 18%, while logistics costs are only 5%. The speed, accuracy and ease of application in guiding routes are the advantages of AI. So, the utility of adaptive technology greatly influences the success of the logistics sector of the agro-industry in Asia. AI using the spatial Dijkstra algorithm makes a genuine contribution.

Tracking and tracing in the Asian agro-industry logistics

In Asia, China continues to expand its foreign trade, hoping to remain the largest economy in Asia. China implements technology integration and promising cooperation in the agro-industry sector. In addition to using innovative technology, they also strengthen their logistics traceability

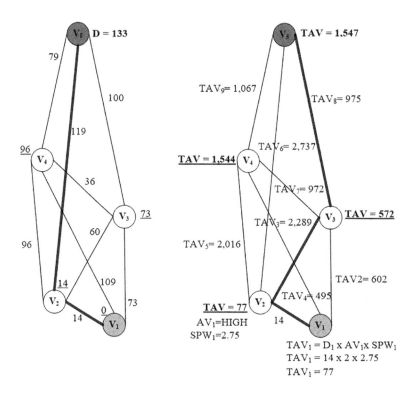

Figure 12.16 Comparison route using classical and spatial Dijkstra.

technology using AI. Singapore and Japan will benefit from establishing themselves as transitional sites for Chinese trade. The development of logistics in Singapore shows that the country has made itself a friendly and comfortable environment to become a transition place for the logistics services of international companies operating in the Asian market. Singapore developed an integrated system capable of tracking and tracing optimally. Wu and Cheng (2008) stated that most producers of agro-industrial products in Asia not only require low-cost services but also require services with precision so that more logistics services in the agro-industrial sector in Asia are of higher quality.

Agro-industry tracking data consists of static and dynamic data. Static data consists of product features that cannot be changed, such as distance and size. In contrast, dynamic data contains elements that can change and are transactional, such as invoice numbers and delivery dates. In agro-industry, traceability that applies AI can usually determine the position or coordinate points using GPS. In this research, tracking and tracing in the logistic agro-industry uses a knowledge base management system, model base and database (Figure 12.17).

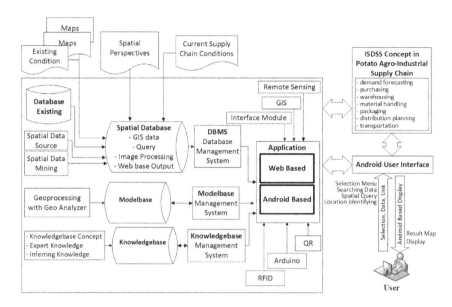

Figure 12.17 The agro-industry logistics traceability model using AI.

The AI configuration in tracking and tracing was developed by involving the model base and DBMS. The knowledge base for logistics activities includes demand forecasting, purchasing, requirements planning, production planning, manufacturing inventory, warehousing, material handling, industrial packaging, finished goods inventory, distribution planning and transportation (Figure 12.18). The AI model uses real-time tracking and tracing in logistic systems using GIS and sensing controls. The AI framework developed is based on the concept of intelligent logistics to ensure sustainable food security. AI optimises the role of RFID in GPS tracking and navigation systems. Product tracking and tracing during distribution delivery can be monitored quickly, accurately and in real-time. AI can answer various logistics and transportation problems by answering four issues, namely congestion, expense, efficiency and traceability.

In this research, we also develop spatial logistics so that it is possible to identify areas with shortages of supply as priority handling so that sustainable food security can be optimal. An integrated intelligent logistics system, where AI involving a knowledge base management system, DBMS and the model base can access real-time logistics systems. Logistics systems, including demand forecasting, purchasing, requirements planning, production, inventory, warehousing, material handling, packaging, distribution and transportation planning, can predict harvest time and determine optimal shipping routes. AI for tracking and tracing in this study can solve the problem of sustainable food security.

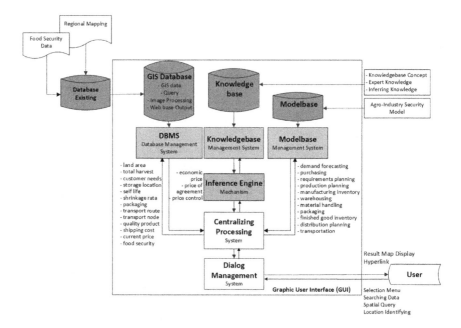

Figure 12.18 Tracking and tracing configuration using AI.

This research result shows that 55% of logistic agro-industry users were satisfied with the presence of AI. Satisfaction is directly proportional to their comfort level, which is 35%, which indicates that AI can positively impact their every activity. In addition, the use of AI helps save where as many as 68% of users agree that the use of AI has been able to reduce costs because of the benefits it provides. This research result shows that the accuracy with tracking and tracing based on an AI is 89.21%. The accuracy of the research results shows that tracking and tracing using AI is a method that can solve the problem of sustainable food security in the Asian region.

Conclusions and implications

Many agro-industrial companies in Asia are already using AI to automate their business processes. They use AI for the best real-time decision making, such as combing thousands of routes, selecting the best route, tracking the fastest delivery, managing effective delivery schedules and reducing the risk of delivery failure. To improve their sustainable agro-industry, the supply and demand balance that considers the characteristics of commodities in a logistics transparency approach is discussed in this research.

The results showed that the spatial perspective, namely altitude (>1,300 masl), soil texture (andosol), slope (8–13%), rainfall (300mm/month) and temperature (17–20°C), affected increase in the potato harvests number. This research has succeeded in predicting the number of the harvest with an accuracy rate of 89.35%. This research also shows that the proposed new method, namely spatial Dijkstra, can provide the most optimal alternative logistic route solution than the classical Dijkstra. This research also established accuracy with tracking and tracing based on an AI of 89.21%. This new approach has demonstrated the supply and demand balance in an adaptive, sustainable agro-industrial model simulation.

Based on the results of this research, it appears that countries such as Indonesia, India and Bangladesh will have a central role in the development of the Asian agro-industry in 2030. China still dominates this sector; apart from having large cultivated land, implementing innovative technology in China went very well. The country is estimated to be left behind in North Korea, increasing only around 30% in 2030. North Korea needs to focus more on implementing IoT for its agro-industrial sector.

The method of predicting the potato harvests number, an optimal DSS for determining logistics routes, and tracking and tracing agro-industrial products can expand and enhance knowledge using AI in the Asian agro-industrial sector. This model needs to be implemented in Asian sustainable agro-industry so that decision-makers can more quickly and accurately recommend a decision.

References

Al-taani, A., Al-husban, Y., & Farhan, I. (2020). Land Suitability Evaluation for Agricultural Use using GIS and Remote Sensing Techniques: The Case Study of Ma'an Governorate, Jordan. *The Egyptian Journal of Remote Sensing and Space Sciences*, *1*(1), 1–9.

Antony, A. P., Leith, K., Jolley, C., Lu, J., & Sweeney, D. J. (2020). A Review of Practice and Implementation of The Internet of Things (IoT) for Smallholder Agriculture. *Sustainability (Switzerland)*, *12*(9), 1–19.

Baidya, P., Chutia, D., Sudhakar, S., & Goswami, C. (2014). Effectiveness of Fuzzy Overlay Function for Multi-Criteria Spatial Modeling – A Case Study on Preparation of Land Resources Map for Mawsynram Block of East Khasi Hills District of Meghalaya, India. *Journal of Geographic Information System*, *6*(12), 605–612.

Borsellino, V., Schimmenti, E., & El Bilali, H. (2020). Agri-food Markets Towards Sustainable Patterns. *Sustainability (Switzerland)*, *12*(6), 1–35.

Bozyigit, A., Alankus, G., & Nasiboglu, E. (2017). Public Transport Route Planning: Modified Dijkstra's Algorithm. *2nd International Conference on Computer Science and Engineering*, *10*(1), 6–9.

Dahiri, & Fitri, H. (2020). Agriculture Sector: Plays a Big Role, Investment Realization Is not Optimal. *Buletin APBN*, *5*(14), 7–11.

Das, K., Wibowo, P., Chui, M., Agarwal, V., & Lath, V. (2019). Automation and the Future of Work in Indonesia. *McKinsey & Company*, *1*(9), 1–28.

Devaux, A., Goffart, J.-P., Petsakos, A., Kromann, P., Gatto, M., Okello, J., Suarez, V., & Hareau, G. (2019). Global Food Security, Contributions from Sustainable

Potato Agri-Food Systems. *The Potato Crop: Its Agricultural, Nutritional and Social Contribution to Humankind, 1*(4), 1–35.

Dewi, C., & Muslikh, M. (2013). Comparison of the Accuracy of Backpropagation Neural Network and ANFIS for Predicting Weather. *Journal of Scientific Modeling & Computation, 1*(1), 7–13.

FAO. (2019). World Food and Agriculture—Statistical Pocketbook 2019. *World Food and Agriculture—Statistical Pocketbook 2019, 1*(1), 1–254.

FAO, IFAD, UNICEF. (2020). The state of food security and nutrition in the world 2020. *Transforming Food Systems for Affordable Healthy Diets, 7*(2), 1–44.

Fitriansyah, A., Parwati, N. W., Wardhani, D. R., & Kustian, N. (2019). Dijkstra's Algorithm to Find Shortest Path of Tourist Destination in Bali. *Journal of Physics: Conf. Series, 1338*(1), 1–7.

Folinas, D., Manikas, I., & Manos, B. (2012). Traceability Data Management for Food Chains. *British Food Journal, 108*(8), 622–633.

Foughali, K., Fathallah, K., & Frihida, A. (2019). A Cloud-IoT based Decision Support System for Potato. *Procedia Computer Science, 160*(1), 616–623.

Gracia, L., Solanes, J. E., Muñoz-benavent, P., Esparza, A., & Valls, J. (2018). Control Engineering Practice Cooperative transport tasks with robots using adaptive non-conventional sliding mode control. *Control Engineering Practice, 78*(1), 35–55.

Hao, J., Shi, H., Shi, V., & Yang, C. (2020). Adoption of Automatic Warehousing Systems in Logistics Firms: A Technology-Organization-Environment Framework. *Sustainability (Switzerland), 12*(12), 1–14.

Hsiao, Y., Chen, M., Lu, K., & Chin, C. (2018). Last-Mile Distribution Planning for Fruit and Vegetable Cold Chains. *The International Journal of Logistics Management, 29*(3), 862–886.

Ignacio, J. (2021). Global GDP Growth in 2021 could be Limited to 1.6% on Vaccine Delay. *S&P Global Market Intelligence, 1*(1), 5–7.

Kamalakkannan, S., Kulatunga, A. K., & Bandara, L. A. D. A. D. (2020). The Conceptual Framework of IoT-based Decision Support System for Life Cycle Management. *Procedia Manufacturing, 43*(2018), 423–430.

Keser, S. B., Yazici, A., & Gunal, S. (2016). A Multi-Criteria Heuristic Algorithm for Personalized Route Planning. *Anadolu University Journal of Science and Technology Applied Sciences and Engineering, 17*(2), 299–313.

Kiani, F., & Seyyedabbasi, A. (2018). Wireless Sensor Network and Internet of Things in Precision Agriculture. *International Journal of Advanced Computer Science and Applications, 9*(6), 99–103.

Klen, A. A. P., Rabelo, R. J., Spinosa, L. M., & Ferreira, A. C. (2017). Integrated Logistics in the Virtual Enterprise: The PRODNET-II Approach. *IFAC Proceedings Volumes, 31*(31), 225–231.

Kurbatova, S. M., Aisner, L. Y., & Vlasov, V. A. (2020). Agrologistics: The Concept, Significance, Types. *IOP Conference Series: Materials Science and Engineering, 918*(1), 1–7.

Macdonald, J. (2019). Leaders and Laggards: The Rise of Online Retail. *Impacts, 1*(1), 1–3.

Marimin, Adhi, W., & Darmawan, M. A. (2017). Decision Support System for Natural Rubber Supply Chain Management Performance Measurement: A Sustainable Balanced Scorecard Approach. *International Journal of Supply Chain Management, 6*(2), 60–74.

Marimin, & Septiani, W. (2016). Intelligent System for Pasteurised Milk Quality Assessment and Prediction. *The 51st Annual Meeting of the International Society for the Systems Sciences, 8*(1), 1–11.

Mayers, D. (2017). What's The Real Value of AI for Your Business and How Can You Capitalise? *Water and Wastes Digest, 56*(9), 1–29.

Michaelides, R. (2010). Optimisation of Logistics Operations using GPS Technology Solutions: A Case Study. *POMS 21st Annual Conference, 5*(1), 1–17.

MRC. (2019). Drought Management Strategy for the Lower Mekong Basin 2020–2025. In *Vientiane: Mekong River Commission Secretariat, 1*(1), 1–86.

Peng, W., & Berry, E. M. (2019). The Concept of Food Security. *Encyclopedia of Food Security and Sustainability, 2*(1), 1–7.

Peyer, S., Rautenbach, D., & Vygen, J. (2009). A Generalization of Dijkstra's Shortest Path Algorithm with Applications to VLSI Routing. *Journal of Discrete Algorithms, 7*(4), 377–390.

Prause, M. (2019). Challenges of Industry 4.0 Technology Adoption for SMEs: The Case of Japan. *Sustainability (Switzerland), 11*(20), 1–13.

Rad, C.-R., Hancu, O., Takacs, I.-A., & Olteanu, G. (2015). Smart Monitoring of Potato Crop: A Cyber-Physical System Architecture Model in the Field of Precision Agriculture. *Agriculture and Agricultural Science Procedia, 6*(1), 73–79.

Ravenhill, J. (2006). Is China an Economic Threat to Southeast Asia? *Asian Survey, 46*(5), 653–674.

Ringhand, M., & Vollrath, M. (2017). Investigating Urban Route Choice as a Conflict between Waiting at Traffic Lights and Additional Travel Time. *Transportation Research Procedia, 25*(5), 2428–2440.

Roghanian, E., & Kebria, Z. S. (2017). The Combination of TOPSIS Method and Dijkstra's Algorithm in Multi-attribute Routing. *Scientia Iranica, 24*(1), 2540–2549.

Rykaczewska, K. (2015). The Effect of High Temperature Occurring in Subsequent Stages of Plant Development on Potato Yield and Tuber Physiological Defects. *American Journal of Potato Research, 92*(1), 339–349.

Saiz-Rubio, V., & Rovira-Mas, F. (2020). From Smart Farming towards Agriculture 5.0: A Review on Crop Data Management. *Agronomy, 10*(207), 1–21.

Shanmugapriya, P., Rathika, S., Ramesh, T., & Janaki, P. (2019). Applications of Remote Sensing in Agriculture: A Review. *International Journal of Current Microbiology and Applied Sciences, 8*(01), 2270–2283.

Suarez, V. (2012). The Rise of Asia as the Centre of Global Potato Production and Some Implication for Industry. *Potato Journal, 39*(1), 1–22.

Tervonen, J. (2018). Experiment of the Quality Control of Vegetable Storage Based on the Internet-of-Things. *Procedia Computer Science, 130*, 440–447.

UN DESA. (2019). World Population Prospects 2019: Highlights. *Department of Economic and Social Affairs. World Population Prospects 2019, 424*(1), 1–39.

UNESCAP. (2017). Analysing Resource Efficiency Transitions in Asia and the Pacific. *Greening of Economic Growth Series, 10*(1), 1–46.

Wan, G., & Zhan, Y. (2011). *ADB Economics Working Paper Series Between-Country Disparities in MDGs: The Asia and Pacific Region* (Issue 278).

Wisskirchen, G., Thibault, B., Bormann, B. U., Muntz, A., Niehaus, G., Soler, G. J., & Von Brauchitsch, B. (2017). Artificial Intelligence and Robotics and their Impact on the Workplace. *IBA Global Employment Institute, 1*(4), 1–120.

Wu, Y. C. J., & Cheng, M. J. (2008). Logistics Outlook: An Asian Perspective. *International Journal of Integrated Supply Management, 4*(1), 4–15.

Yusianto, R., Marimin, M., Suprihatin, S., & Hardjomidjojo, H. (2019). Intelligent Spatial Logistics DSS for Tracking and Tracing in Horticultural Food Security. *International Seminar on Application for Technology of Information and Communication, ISemantic, 4*(1), 73–77.

Yusianto, R., Marimin, Suprihatin, & Hardjomidjojo, H. (2020a). Smart Logistics System in Food Horticulture Industrial Products: A Systematic Review and Future Research Agenda. *International Journal of Supply Chain Management, 9*(2), 943–956.

Yusianto, R., Marimin, Suprihatin, & Hardjomidjojo, H. (2020b). Spatial Analysis for Crop Land Suitability Evaluation: A Case Study of Potatoes Cultivation in Wonosobo, Indonesia. *International Seminar on Application for Technology of Information and Communication (ISemantic), 10*(2), 313–319.

Zai, Y. Y. M., Hadiguna, R. A., & Afrinaldi, F. (2018). A Review on Success Factors of Logistic Innovation in Agro-Industry. *International Journal of Engineering & Technology, 7*(9), 236–240.

13 Social media as collaborative and knowledge-sharing tools in Malaysian schools

Simin Ghavifekr

Introduction

Nowadays, the use of social media is not limited to any specific sector or any particular country, but it has penetrated to every ones' life in whole world. Global digital report shows continuous increase in the number of social media users in the world. It shows that social media is now taking part in almost all spheres of peoples' life. Similarly, the trend of using social media is rapidly growing in the education arena. Social media has many positive effects on education including better communication, timely information, socialising online, learning, enhancing skills, making a career among others. This is due to the potential of social media in increasing knowledge of the users through a facilitated knowledge-sharing environment (Muhammad Imran Rasheed et al., 2020; Mathrani & Edwards, 2020).

The proliferation of various social media platforms and applications enables efficient exchange of information benefiting the teaching and learning processes in academic institutions. Due to the influence and the rapid development of information and communication technology, students have gained wider and faster access to information through various digital means, such as social media (Body & Dominelli, 2017).

Among higher education institutions in Malaysia and in different parts of the world, more than 90% of students have access to social media through various devices, such as smartphones and computers, and an average of 60–80% of students recognise the usefulness of social media in their personal lives (Hashim & Zamani, 2015; Hwang et al., 2018; Kumar et al., 2020). Despite the popularity of using social media in terms of personal communication and entertainment, unlocking the potentials of social media as a collaborative and knowledge-sharing tool in schools and universities presents opportunities to improve teaching and learning. The utilisation of social media in education can provide useful platforms for students to get useful information as well as to connect with relevant learning networks. In addition, social network tools can offer students and educational institutions with several opportunities to improve learning methods (Ansari & Khan, 2020).

DOI: 10.4324/9781003163824-17

Through academic collaboration, social media creates opportunities for online learning through seemingly limitless interactions between students, their peers, instructors and other stakeholders. Given the speedy rate of information sharing at a click of a button on social media sites, students and teachers can maximise this connectivity in order to instantly share and acquire information. Also known as social networking sites, social media can be loosely defined as an Internet-based platform, a software or an application, designed to allow users to create and share their own content through text, video or audio forms (Kaplan & Haenlein, 2010). According to various studies, the most popular social media sites among the younger generation are the following: Twitter, Instagram, Facebook, YouTube, WhatsApp and WeChat (Wang et al., 2012; Rasiah, 2014; Tuzel & Hobbs, 2017). Similarly, studies have confirmed how the aforementioned social media applications are being used both as a complementary and primary teaching tool in secondary schools and universities (Lau & Sim, 2008; Stern & Willits, 2011).

Although the benefits of social media in terms of collaboration and knowledge sharing have been widely acknowledged, certain issues and challenges in terms of its usage in the academic setting need to be addressed and carefully examined. There remains some confusion with respect to the right mindset and behaviour in terms of using social media that many users fail to distinguish its personal and professional use (Carpenter & Harvey, 2019). Also, accessibility to social media sites can still be a problem in places where technological infrastructures are still underdeveloped (Bayuong et al., 2019). Other than that, security concerns over data sharing are perceived to be a threat especially when reports of hacking surface, which disrupts the teaching and learning process at an institutional level (Anderson, 2019). Thus, resolving these challenges begins with a conceptual understanding of how social media can be fully utilised as a tool for collaboration and knowledge sharing.

In understanding social media as collaborative and knowledge-sharing tool in the Malaysian setting, a contextual and conceptual lens needs to be employed. Contextually, the Ministry of Education has fully embraced the adoption of new technology in its aims to align Malaysia schools with international standards (Siew-Eng & Muuk, 2015). Likewise, Malaysian higher education institutions have also integrated different social media applications and functions in their learning management systems (Lim et al., 2014; Moghavvemi et al., 2018). According to a framework developed by Al-rahmi et al. (2015) to fully understand the adoption of social media in academic institutions in Malaysia, social media engagement can be measured according to its perceived intention, ease of use and usefulness in terms of knowledge sharing and collaborative learning. Thus, this conceptual chapter will discuss how Malaysian schools and universities use social media as a collaborative and knowledge-sharing tool in terms of its usefulness in teaching and learning, connecting stakeholders and improving learning management systems.

Challenges of using social media in education

Although technological advances, such as social media, have potentials in improving educational practices, educators from various academic settings from different parts of the world have expressed key challenges in terms of its use and regulation. The primary concerns in the social media usage in the education setting range from individual issues, technical deficiencies and security lapses.

From a socio-ecological perspective, Carpenter and Harvey (2019) identified the problems faced by Physical Education and Health teachers in using social media primarily in terms of setting the boundary between its personal and professional use, as well as other issues regarding credibility and privacy. The engagement provided by social media platforms also creates confusion in terms of ethical online practices due to dual responsibility and boundary issues (Boddy & Dominelli, 2017). In the American context, social media platforms are being used as a space to share political views, which could be misused and oftentimes lead to disputes between colleagues that could spill from the online to the real world (Carpenter & Harvey, 2019). Hence et al. (2017) recommend an understanding of the prevalent ethical concerns and attitudes, which can be used and propagated among users to promote ethical values leading to an increased awareness in the personal and professional usage of social media.

As programs integrating technology in secondary school curricula involve the use of social media, Greenhow and Lewin (2016) pointed out that the use of social media in secondary schools generally falls under the category of an informal learning tool in which the participation of students is perceived as merely for engaging in social connections or keeping up with the trend rather than a formal platform for meaningful discussion. In Israeli secondary schools, interactions between students and teachers on WhatsApp lead to an excessive use and overloading of messages through countless groups created by teachers and students themselves (Rosenberg & Asterhan, 2018). The richness and the depth of interaction tend to be in question as engagement in social media tools can be more of a distraction if expectations are not laid down for secondary school students to adapt to social media as a formal learning space, considering they are in their formative years (Greenhow & Lewin, 2016). Generally, improper and unguided usage of social media among secondary school students could lead to addiction problems, hyperactivity and sedentary attitudes and even socially unacceptable actions (Merelle et al., 2019). Thus, regulating social media usage among students could be taken into account in order to capitalise on the benefits of using this digital tool to improve learning.

In higher education, social media concerns range from data usage authorisation to adoption in instruction. Anderson (2019) raised growing concerns about unauthorised data usage generated by the users and collected by the institutions. Particularly in the case of students, personal data are either shared consciously or unconsciously due to the requirement posed by platforms to gain access to needed information or learning tools (Anderson, 2019). In addition, an interview with university lecturers rendered the following issues related to teaching and learning using social media: more complex communication; increase workload in monitoring students' progress and activities; adoption of new technology and lack of resource support from the university (Zhang et al., 2010). On the other hand, students voiced out a different set of issues, which are mostly related to attitude towards social media, such as addiction to sites, distraction from school-related tasks or content and improper communication using inappropriate expressions and comments (Zhang et al., 2010).

Generally, most of the concerns regarding the use of social media pertain to the confusion in the roles, attitudes and practices of the users. Among students and teachers, the challenge of balancing ideals and following norms are primarily due to the lack of clarity in social media usage, which should be communicated and consistently adhered to by the institutions and the society (Greenhow & Lewin, 2016; Boddy & Dominelli, 2017). Hence, it is imperative to define the primary purposes of social media in an academic setting as a tool for collaboration and knowledge sharing.

Social media for collaboration

As a starting point in addressing the challenges of using social media in an education setting, defining the intentions and objectives of social media in teaching and learning sets the parameters that clarify the roles and responsibilities of its users. Given that a significant number of studies attested students perceive social media as a personal communication tool (Henderson et al., 2013), a change in mindset is needed to realign social media with classroom learning objectives in order to develop 21st-century skills. Needless to say, a critical review of literature conducted by Henderson et al. (2013) identified several ways social media has been used in the classroom for collaborative teaching and learning by providing new opportunities for interaction and by creating venues to develop skills in collaboration.

For instance, primary school teachers relayed their experiences in using Moodle as an online forum and platform for group activities, and they also highlighted key concerns like monitoring and shaping students' behaviour while using the application (Clark et al., 2017). Likewise, middle school teachers from the United Kingdom maximised the Wiki platform so that students could have an online learning environment where they could assess each other's work and showcase it to an audience, who could provide valuable feedback for their work (Grant, 2009). In a Hong Kong secondary school, students use social media to collaborate with their peers in brainstorming and designing their writing projects with the guidance of progress markers developed by both teachers and students (Mak & Coniam, 2008). Furthermore, a review of literature on the use of Facebook in higher education institutions reveal how this social media site is primarily used to increase teacher-student or student-student interaction for improved learning performance and better engagement (Chugh & Ruhi, 2018).

Social media for knowledge sharing

Aside from collaboration, research in social media in education has examined the factors and explored the ways social media platforms are used as a knowledge-sharing tool. Yu et al. (2010) conducted a survey among primary and secondary school teachers from Taiwan to identify the causal factors behind knowledge-sharing behaviour in the use of blogs. The results revealed that the knowledge-sharing behaviour on social media is primarily driven by the intention of helping others, its usefulness or relevance and the sharing culture of the students defined by fairness and openness in usage (Yu et al., 2010). Similarly, Hwang, Lin, and Shin (2018) noted that the intention to share knowledge in a learning environment can be driven by a person's commitment to acquire and share information proactively in a formal situation. In a study among students from higher education institutions in Tanzania, the perceived relevance or usefulness of the social media platform, alongside ease of use and privacy, improves the adoption rate of social media as a knowledge-sharing tool (Lubua et al., 2017). Thus, for social media to be fully utilised in terms of sharing valuable knowledge in the classroom setting, there needs to be a synergy of personal, affective and structural factors to drive the process.

Aside from the aforementioned factors, social media as a knowledge-sharing tool has been reported to have been fully maximised in various classroom applications. Students from secondary schools in Israel reported how they use WhatsApp as a central mode of communication in terms of sending school-related updates and tasks, as well as for their teachers to monitor and relay disciplinary actions (Rosenberg & Asterhan, 2018). Similarly, WhatsApp is widely used in South African schools, together with other applications like Bluetooth and Share it, which teachers and students maximise to share information relevant to the discussion (Rwodzi et al., 2020). With regard to the use of Facebook, Chugh and Ruhi (2018) noted that this social networking site is deemed as an ideal knowledge platform due to its user-friendly and convenient interface although there are certain concerns on teachers' dominance and privacy., In addition to curriculum-related content, social media is also utilised in promoting cultural understanding through culture knowledge sharing as a part of an activity among secondary school students from the United States and Turkey, which leads to positive interaction and establishment of common ground between students from different cultures (Tuzel & Hobbs, 2017). Moreover, benefits of social media for knowledge sharing in educational institutions include making students feel more engaged in learning, creating deeper interactions between teachers and students and expanding learning communities beyond school walls (Muhammad Imran Rasheed et al., 2020). Results of previous research determined that the main positive aspect of social media is for a student's sense of belonging in an educational community. This is due to the fact that through social media, teachers can enhance interactions between students, between students and teachers and with people and resources outside the classroom (Ansari & Khan, 2020; Bigliardi et al., 2021).

Effective use of social media in Malaysian schools

As discussed in the previous sections, social media is widely used as a collaborative and knowledge-sharing tool in different academic settings in various parts of the world. With the dedication of the Malaysian government, through its Ministry of Education, to be at par with the educational transformation taking place across the globe, the Malaysian education system has embraced the digital revolution by ensuring that students are equipped with 21st-century skills and are adept in using technological tools, such as social media (Al-rahmi et al., 2020). The effective use of social media in Malaysian schools, in the primary, secondary and tertiary levels, can be further discussed according to its role in teaching and learning, connecting stakeholders and improving management systems.

Teaching and learning

Particularly in the advent of blended learning in secondary schools, social media tools are used by teachers to equip students with the skills they need in higher education and in the real world. In a qualitative study conducted by Siew-Eng and Muuk (2015), the English teachers from secondary schools in Sarawak, Malaysia reported how they create interesting lessons and motivate students with the use of social media tools so that students can gain access to information easily and apply them in a learning situation. Similarly in a literature class, teachers use social media as a form of integrating ICT with the teaching and learning of literary texts by accessing Facebook to share information, watching YouTube to gain access to multimedia content, and by writing on blogsites to practice their skills (Yunus & Suliman, 2014). The use of social media to improve writing skills of ESL students in secondary schools is reported to allow student to be fully and effectively engaged in the process and be exposed to various styles and perspectives through social media interaction, as long as teachers can regulate the learning process (Aziz & Yunus, 2019). Noticeably, the relevance of using social media in the teaching and learning of subjects related to language development skills can be attributed to the nature of social media platforms as venues for collaboration and communication (Yunus & Suliman, 2014; Siew-Eng & Muuk, 2015). Teachers from Malaysian secondary schools recognise the potentials of social media in developing reading and writing skills through guided processes and informed reading that could enable them to be open to various sources of information and manners of acquiring new knowledge.

Whereas social media in secondary schools in Malaysia is commonly used in language and literature classes, higher education instructors and students use social media platforms in a plethora of ways. In a team-based learning environment, Facebook was used as a teaching and learning tool in a higher education institution in order to allow students to collaborate effectively with their classmates and instructors by sharing their thoughts through posts and by uploading their portfolios for feedback from their audience (Rasiah, 2014). The reflection of the students who participated in this study revealed how Facebook was used as a medium of discussion and knowledge sharing, which allowed the students to have a sense of belongingness and a rich learning experience (Rasiah, 2014). As a complementary teaching and learning tool, YouTube was regarded as beneficial in terms of enhancing learning experience through entertainment and information as long as the video contents are integrated and linked clearly with the topic based on the perspectives of business and management students from one of Malaysia's top universities (Moghavvemi et al., 2018). Despite the perceived notion that Facebook and YouTube could be a source of distraction, students acknowledge the responsibility of managing their learning on social media platform by focusing on the task and spending less time on non-academic related content (Rasiah, 2014; Moghavvemi et al., 2018).

To increase student engagement in the teaching and learning process, instructors in higher education institutions in Malaysia used a variety of applications from social media sites. Alshuaibi et al. (2018) noted that cognitive engagement links social media usage and academic performance, which is characterised by the student's intention to commit to the learning process through the use of complex ideas and development of required skills. In a comparative analysis between social media usage of Malaysian and Australian university students, it was found that Malaysian students put more significance on gaining new knowledge and using social media for academic development because of cultural factors, such as the socio-cultural approach to education and the rigid education system with high expectations on students' performance (Balakrishnan et al., 2017). A mixed methods study conducted by Lim et al. (2014) among informatics students from Malaysia higher education institutions revealed the increased usage of social media tools such as Google+, LinkedIn and Facebook for academic purposes, which primarily serves the purpose of working on projects and assignments, sharing documents and information or updates. Because of the high ownership of devices among students and ease of access to technology through reliable internet connection in their campuses, higher education students can maximise their engagement in social media and explore its capabilities in enriching their learning experience (Lim et al., 2014; Alshuaibi et al., 2018).

Despite the prevalence of using social media in teaching and learning in secondary schools and higher education, a limited number of studies highlight the use of social media in Malaysian primary schools. Among fourth grade students, social media applications, such as Twitter, WeChat and Telegram, were reportedly to be widely used primarily because most of their friends use it and they find it easy to follow their favourite artists (Yunus et al., 2019). In that similar study, only a few students reported using social media applications to learn English or gain knowledge; however, they expressed their inclination towards using other platforms such as YouTube, Quizzis or Kahoot in making their lessons more fun (Yunus et al., 2019). In the case of rural primary schools, Bayuong et al. (2019) noted that Facebook, WhatsApp and YouTube tend to be widely used by students to practice their English writing skills by being comfortable in using the language in an online situation and also by being exposed to common English expressions used on social media sites. Although social media has increasing potentials in developing the linguistic capabilities of young learners, accessibility to the sites and the availability of the devices among primary school students impede the regular use of social media in primary schools in Malaysia (Bayuong et al., 2019; Yunus et al., 2019). Given the age restrictions of social media sites and the low ownership of devices among primary school students, partnership between parents and teachers needs to be forged so as to set the parameters in the usage of ICT devices for learning purposes.

Connecting stakeholders

In a framework designed by Kumar and Nanda (2019), continuous engagement in social media usage in higher education includes the central role of students, through various learning activities, as managed collectively by various stakeholders, such as instructors, management, marketing and ICT experts and the university administration. As such, social media use is not only confined to the four corners of the classroom, but this extends to how the stakeholders maximise its usage in ways like promoting the university in the society, conducting the admission process, maintaining student engagement, advancing career development opportunities and sustaining networks with alumni and other professional organisations (Kumar & Nanda, 2019). Through continuous engagement with students and other stakeholders as initiated by the university on social media platforms, higher education institutions create a positive image for themselves, not only among their current student but also among potential students and industry partners (Clark et al., 2017).

Among Malaysian higher education institutions, the practice of using social media to connect with stakeholders reflects the intentions of sustaining continuous engagement and promoting a positive image for the university as a 21st-century academic institution. The regular use of applications, such as Twitter or YouTube, motivates students to engage in the learning process with their peers and their teachers in a Malaysian public university (Alshuaibi et al., 2018). With regard to the performance of researchers from higher education institutions in Malaysia, the ease of using social media platforms to connect with people involved in the research process enabled the researchers to perform more efficiently and effectively (Al-rahmi et al., 2015). As such, the students and researchers in higher education institutions in Malaysia reported a high level of satisfaction in using social media in terms of connecting with their peers, instructors or supervisors as this allows them to easily interact to form decisions related to their tasks (Al-rahmi et al., 2015; Alshuaibi et al., 2018). Moreover, Irfan et al. (2017) acknowledged the potentials of using social media in promoting educational tourism, which could benefit Malaysian universities, in attracting potential local and international students through the global reach of social media platforms. For instance, private universities advertise on social media since a majority of their target students belong to the Generation Z, whose interest and inclination in using social media could be beneficial in introducing the programs and facilities offered by the university (Krishnan & Sajilan, 2014).

In Malaysian primary and secondary schools, the use of social media helps teachers connect primarily with the parents of their students and other stakeholders who can assist them in their professional or organisational tasks. Interviews conducted among music teachers revealed how they use different venues, whether face-to-face or online communication through social media platforms, to be able to coordinate with parents regarding the progress of their children although some teachers think that there should be clear boundaries set before opening communication lines with parents (Ang et al., 2019). Lau and Sim (2008) reported how secondary school mathematics and science teachers from Sarawak, Malaysia use social media tools in collaborating with other teachers and experts to make their job training more extensive. Although teachers noted that there should be further collaboration among teachers and the district administrators to address issues immediately (Lau & Sim, 2008). Needless to say, the ways by which social media tools are used to strengthen connection among stakeholders in primary and secondary schools in Malaysia need clearer parameters in order to maximise its potentials in forging relationships to improve teaching and learning.

Improving learning management systems

In different schools around the world, a thin line separates the conception and usage of social media sites and learning management systems. Although traditional learning management systems were designed to focus primarily on the delivery of instructional materials, assessments and feedback, social media influenced the way learning management systems are being developed to incorporate certain social media tools and applications that could be beneficial and interesting for all stakeholders, particularly the students

(Stern & Willits, 2011). Based on the assessment of students' needs, Stern and Willits (2011) highlighted that learning management systems integrated various social media features, such as having a dynamic course platform, which links prominent apps like Moodle, Twitter, YouTube and Google Docs with the main infrastructure of the university's learning management system in order to provide students and teachers with a seamless operation and navigation (Stern & Willits, 2011). Another example of social media integration in learning management system is the use of Facebook Group for the purpose of sharing announcements, course materials, scheduled tutorial sessions, online discussions and administrative concerns (Wang et al., 2012).

Certain studies conducted in Malaysian higher education institutions have reported how social media has been integrated to improve existing learning management systems to benefit teaching and learning, as well as administrative functions. Based on a case study from an open university in Malaysia, the integration of social media functions on learning management systems were reported to have increased the engagement of use among students in such a way that they can be involved in peer discussions and complete tasks online within a short period of time based on immediate feedback from their instructors (Rahman et al., 2010). Recently, the introduction of Google Classroom in Malaysian universities was noted by Kumar et al. (2020) to be perceived as useful by both students and instructors with its capabilities to allow seamless peer-to-peer interaction through a user-friendly interface design that resembles contemporary social media sites. However, certain issues arise such as privacy concerns, management of learning analytics and inadequacy of cloud storage. Despite the attempts to integrate various social media applications and functions on the interface of learning management systems in Malaysian higher education institutions, previous research noted that certain technological features could be added in order to provide a smooth navigation for students and instructors and to create a well-integrated framework that utilises the applications according to the curriculum and the needs of the students (Hashim & Zamani, 2015; Kumar et al., 2020).

Future directions of social media in Malaysian schools

The potentials of social media in Malaysian primary and secondary schools lie in further exploration as to how it could be used to improve critical thinking, linguistic and collaboration skills of students. Yunus et al. (2019) noted how social media could be useful in teaching ESL in primary schools, especially in creating an enjoyable environment in the development of writing skills of students; thus, certain factors could be determined to identify how social media functions and usage affect students' writing skills. As social media was reported to be used in allowing students to critically analyse literary texts and engage in collaborative tasks, ICT tools can be further developed in order to incorporate an interactive teaching and learning of literature to keep students exposed to a variety of literature from different parts of the world (Yunus & Suliman, 2014). Despite these potentials, accessibility to the social media sites remains a challenge in primary and secondary schools primarily because of the minimum age restrictions of social media sites (Balakrishnan et al., 2017). Likewise, most students in public primary and secondary schools do not have their own smart phones or laptops, which could enable them to use the sites without the supervision of their parents (Lau & Sim, 2008; Aziz et al., 2019). Thus, how to increase ownership of devices and accessibility of social media among primary and secondary school students in Malaysia could be a starting point for further exploration.

Whereas studies on social media usage in primary and secondary schools in Malaysia are limited due to issues on accessibility and availability, a wide array of research on how social media is utilised in Malaysian higher education institutions presents new avenues for investigation particularly in this era of digital revolution. In terms of improving academic performance, future research on social media could focus on how collaborative learning could be further enhanced using various tools and platforms (Al-rahmi et al., 2014). Especially during the time of a pandemic when online teaching and learning is fully implemented, social media sites can be used not only as a complementary tool but also a main platform where teachers and students can interact and exchange materials so as not to disrupt the learning process (Kumar et al., 2020; Rwodzi et al., 2020). Generally, the role of social media in higher education can be further established with measures that ensure its seamless integration with existing systems to allow students and instructors to access resources readily (Hashim & Zamani, 2015; Alshuaibi et al., 2018).

Although this paper has discussed how social media is used in the Malaysian education system through teaching and learning, connecting stakeholders and improving learning management systems, prospective research could be conducted to address the perceived issues and challenges in using social media in schools. As the learning environment has shifted to online due to the pandemic and government restriction, it could also be helpful to explore the prevalent conditions that could impede effective teaching and learning. For instance, the rise in cyberstalking and cyberbullying on social media sites such as Facebook, WhatsApp, LinkedIn and WeChat was noted by undergraduate students to have a negative effect on collaboration and information acquisition; hence, further examination of factors related to online interaction and behaviour could be conducted to shed light on these issues (Al-rahmi et al., 2020).

Conclusion and implication

The prominence of social media among young individuals has been defined by its perceived usefulness in terms of connecting people through instant communication and information acquisition. Although the personal uses of social media supersede its professional functions, the collaborative and knowledge-sharing platforms of social media enable learners to expand their learning opportunities and for educators to explore various ways to deliver content and instruction. As a collaborative tool, social media enables learners to interact with their peers and perform certain tasks together, such as brainstorming, designing and peer editing, which are not only limited between them, their classmates and instructors but also with experts from different parts of the world. As a knowledge-sharing tool, the functions of social media present a wide array of venues in which students can acquire and verify new information through various resources, which they can use to advance their understanding in their respective fields.

Given how social media is used in the Malaysian education setting, studies discussed in this conceptual chapter lead to an optimistic perspective on its role in cultivating 21st-century learners. The implications of these studies go beyond the personal use of social media since education institutions can further explore the seemingly limitless potentials of social media applications and functions in developing learners' cognitive and behavioural attributes. The schools and districts should take into consideration on exploiting the usefulness of various social media platforms to get the active involvement of all the stakeholders including parents. Moreover, the persistent and pertinent professional development needs to be provided for teachers by schools. This will facilitate teachers not only to cultivate and sustain a positive relationship with parents but also enhance their skills, knowledge and attitudes in using social media applications in delivering, exchanging and sharing information. Correspondingly, the implementation of social media applications as practical initiatives can nurture a better partnership between families and schools.

The result of this systematic review confirmed that use of social media for knowledge sharing and collaborative learning purposes plays an important role in schools. It also shows that utilising social media in schools can help in easier and faster communications and interaction between school's stakeholders. For example, social networks allow teachers to share ideas and lesson plans with each other faster and easier. Moreover, it will help teachers in transferring the resource materials with colleagues.

Although most of the studies conducted in Malaysia were in higher education, future research can focus on how social media is used by primary and secondary school students to develop their skills not only in reading and writing but also in other subjects like Maths and Science. Likewise, the government and academic institutions should further invest in reliable and sustainable technological infrastructure for students to access social media sites for uninterrupted teaching and learning. Nevertheless, with support from various stakeholders, students should be able to recognise the usefulness of social media sites in improving their learning capabilities to be better learners and citizens in this digitalised era.

References

Al-rahmi, W. M., Othman, M. S., & Musa, M. A. (2014). The improvement of students' academic performance by using social media through collaborative learning in Malaysian higher education. *Asian Social Science, 10*(8), 210–221.

Al-rahmi, W. M., Othman, M. S., & Yusuf, L. M. (2015a). Social media for collaborative learning and engagement: Adoption framework in higher education institutions in Malaysia. *Mediterranean Journal of Social Sciences, 6*(3 S1), 246.

Al-rahmi, W. M., Othman, M. S., & Yusuf, L. M. (2015b). The effect of social media on researchers' academic performance through collaborative learning in Malaysian higher education. *Mediterranean Journal of Social Sciences, 6*(4), 193–203.

Al-rahmi, W. M., Yahaya, N., Alturki, U., Alrobai, A., Aldraiweesh, A. A., Omar Alsayed, A., & Kamin, Y. B. (2020). Social media–based collaborative learning: the effect on learning success with the moderating role of cyberstalking and cyberbullying. *Interactive Learning Environments*, 1–14.

Alshuaibi, M. S. I., Alshuaibi, A. S. I., Shamsudin, F. M., & Arshad, D. A. (2018). Use of social media, student engagement, and academic performance of business students in Malaysia. *International Journal of Educational Management, 32*(4), 625–660.

Anderson, T. (2019). Challenges and opportunities for use of social media in higher education. *Journal of Learning for Development, 6*(1), 6–19.

Ang, K., Panebianco, C., & Odendaal, A. (2019). Exploring the role of the music teacher from the perspectives of parents and teachers in West Malaysia. *Malaysian Journal of Music, 8*, 52–67.

Ansari, J. A. N., & Khan, N. A. (2020). Exploring the role of social media in collaborative learning the new domain of learning. *Journal of Smart Learning Environment, 7*(9), 1–16. https://doi.org/10.1186/s40561-020-00118-7.

Aziz, N., Hashim, H., & Yunus, M. M. (2019). Using social media to enhance ESL writing skill among Gen-Z learners. *Creative Education, 10*(12), 3020–3027.

Balakrishnan, V., Teoh, K. K., Pourshafie, T., & Liew, T. K. (2017). Social media and their use in learning: A comparative analysis between Australia and Malaysia from the learners' perspectives. *Australasian Journal of Educational Technology, 33*(1), 81–97.

Bayuong, P. D., Yunus, M. M., & Suliman, A. (2019). The use of social media (SM) among pupils in a rural primary school in Sarawak, Malaysia. *Humanities & Social Sciences Reviews, 7*(5), 1272–1279.

Bigliardi, B., Ferraro, G., Filippelli, S., & Galati, F. (2021). The past, present and future of open innovation. *European Journal of Innovation Management.* Emerald Publishing Limited 1460-1060. doi:10.1108/EJIM-10-2019-0296.

Boddy, J., & Dominelli, L. (2017). Social media and social work: The challenges of a new ethical space. *Australian Social Work, 70*(2), 172–184.

Carpenter, J. P., & Harvey, S. (2019). There's no referee on social media: Challenges in educator professional social media use. *Teaching and Teacher Education, 86.* doi:10.1016/j.tate.2019.102904.

Chugh, R., & Ruhi, U. (2018). Social media in higher education: A literature review of Facebook. *Education and Information Technologies, 23*(2), 605–616.

Clark, M., Fine, M. B., & Scheuer, C. L. (2017). Relationship quality in higher education marketing: The role of social media engagement. *Journal of Marketing for Higher Education, 27*(1), 40–58.

Grant, L. (2009). I don't care do your own page: A case study of using wikis for collaborative work in a UK secondary school. *Learning, Media and Technology, 34*(2), 105–117.

Greenhow, C., & Lewin, C. (2016). Social media and education: Reconceptualizing the boundaries of formal and informal learning. *Learning, Media and Technology, 41*(1), 6–30.

Hashim, K. F., & Zamani, M. A. (2015). Social media adoption in higher education: A case study of Universiti Utara Malaysia. *Jurnal Teknologi, 77*(4), 33–39.

Henderson, M., Snyder, I., & Beale, D. (2013). Social media for collaborative learning: A review of school literature. *Australian Educational Computing, 28*(2), 1–15.

Hwang, Y., Lin, H., & Shin, D. (2018). Knowledge system commitment and knowledge sharing intention: The role of personal information management motivation. *International Journal of Information Management, 39*, 220–227.

Irfan, A., Rasli, A., Sami, A., & Liaquat, H. (2017). Role of social media in promoting education tourism. *Advanced Science Letters, 23*(9), 8728–8731.

Kaplan, A. M., & Haenlein, M. (2010). Users of the world, unite! The challenges and opportunities of social media. *Business Horizons, 53*(1), 59–68.

Krishnan, K. S. T., & Sajilan, S. (2014). The effects of social media on Gen Z's intention to select private universities in Malaysia. *Review of Integrative Business and Economics Research, 3*(2), 466–483.

Kumar, J. A., Bervell, B., & Osman, S. (2020). Google classroom: insights from Malaysian higher education students' and instructors' experiences. *Education and Information Technologies, 25*(5), 4175–4195.

Kumar, V., & Nanda, P. (2019). Social media in higher education: A framework for continuous engagement. *International Journal of Information and Communication Technology Education, 15*(1), 97–108.

Lau, B. T., & Sim, C. H. (2008). Exploring the extent of ICT adoption among secondary school teachers in Malaysia. *International Journal of Computing and ICT Research, 2*(2), 19–36.

Lim, J. S. Y., Agostinho, S., Harper, B., & Chicharo, J. (2014). The engagement of social media technologies by undergraduate informatics students for academic purpose in Malaysia. *Journal of Information, Communication and Ethics in Society, 12*(3), 177–194.

Lubua, E. W., Semlambo, A., & Pretorius, P. D. (2017). Factors affecting the use of social media in the learning process. *South African Journal of Information Management, 19*(1), 1–7.

Mak, B., & Coniam, D. (2008). Using wikis to enhance and develop writing skills among secondary school students in Hong Kong. *System*, 437–455.

Mathrani, S., & Edwards, B. (2020). Knowledge-sharing strategies in distributed collaborative product development. *Journal of Open Innovation: Technology, Market, and Complexity, 6*(194). doi:10.3390/joitmc6040194.

Mérelle, S., Kleiboer, A., Schotanus, M., Cluitmans, T. L., Waardenburg, C. M., Kramer, D.,... & van Rooij, A. (2017). Which health-related problems are associated with problematic video-gaming or social media use in adolescents? *Clinical Neuropsychiatry: Journal of Treatments Evaluation, 14*(1), 11–19.

Moghavvemi, S., Sulaiman, A., Jaafar, N. I., & Kasem, N. (2018). Social media as a complementary learning tool for teaching and learning: The case of YouTube. *The International Journal of Management Education, 16*(1), 37–42.

Muhammad Imran Rasheed, Muhammad Jawad Malik, Abdul Hameed Pitafi, Jawad Iqbal, Muhammad Khalid Anser &, Mazhar Abbas. (2020). Usage of social media, student engagement, and creativity: The role of knowledge sharing behavior and cyberbullying. *Computers & Education, 159*(December 2020), 104002.

Rahman, K. A., Ghazali, S. A. M., & Ismail, M. N. (2010). The effectiveness of learning management system (LMS) case study at Open University Malaysia (OUM), Kota Bharu Campus. *Journal of Emerging Trends in Computing and Information Sciences, 2*(2), 73–79.

Rasiah, R. R. V. (2014). Transformative higher education teaching and learning: Using social media in a team-based learning environment. *Procedia-Social and Behavioral Sciences, 123*, 369–379.

Rosenberg, H., & Asterhan, C. S. (2018). "WhatsApp, Teacher?"-student perspectives on teacher-student Whatsapp interactions in secondary schools. *Journal of Information Technology Education Research, 17*, 205–226.

Rwodzi, C., De Jager, L., & Mpofu, N. (2020). The innovative use of social media for teaching English as a second language. *The Journal for Transdisciplinary Research in Southern Africa, 16*(1), 1–7.

Siew-Eng, L., & Muuk, M. A. (2015). Blended learning in teaching secondary schools' English: A preparation for tertiary science education in Malaysia. *Procedia-Social and Behavioral Sciences, 167*, 293–300.

Stern, D. M., & Willits, M. D. (2011). Social media killed the LMS: Re-imagining the traditional learning management system in the age of blogs and online social networks. In Wankel, C. (Ed.) *Educating educators with social media (cutting-edge technologies in higher education* (Vol. 1). Bingley: Emerald Group Publishing Limited (pp. 347–373). https://doi.org/10.1108/S2044-9968(2011)0000001020.

Tuzel, S., & Hobbs, R. (2017). The use of social media and popular culture to advance cross-cultural understanding. *Comunicar: Media Education Research Journal, 25*(1), 63–72.

Wang, Q., Woo, H. L., Quek, C. L., Yang, Y., & Liu, M. (2012). Using the Facebook group as a learning management system: An exploratory study. *British Journal of Educational Technology, 43*(3), 428–438.

Yu, T. K., Lu, L. C., & Liu, T. F. (2010). Exploring factors that influence knowledge sharing behavior via weblogs. *Computers in Human Behavior, 26*(1), 32–41.

Yunus, M. M., & Suliman, A. (2014). Information & communication technology (ICT) tools in teaching and learning literature component in Malaysian secondary schools. *Asian Social Science, 10*(7), 136–152.

Yunus, M. M., Zakaria, S., & Suliman, A. (2019). The potential use of social media on Malaysian primary students to improve writing. *International Journal of Education and Practice, 7*(4), 450–458.

Zhang, S., Flammer, C., & Yang, X. (2010). Uses, challenges, and potential of social media in higher education. In C. Wankel (Ed.), *Cutting-edge social media approaches to business education: Teaching with LinkedIn, Facebook, Twitter, second life, and blogs* (pp. 217–224). Charlotte, NC: Information Age Publishing.

14 Emergence of social media as a collaborative and knowledge-sharing tool of health information during pandemic

Samrat Kumar Mukherjee, Vivek Pandey, Ankit Singh and Ajeya Jha

Introduction

Social media is a new means of communication that helps users to communicate with each other through email, images, pictures and music. More than 40% of the world's people use social media and over 1.5 billion are frequent users every day (Appel et al., 2020). One of the most remarkable uses for health reasons is social media (Hagg et al., 2018). Many people are aware of health problems and collaborate through social media with healthcare professionals (Antheunis et al., 2013). The strongest benefit of this mode of interaction is that it provides the opportunity to promote mass communication and disease surveillance (Huo et al., 2019).

The world came to an abrupt end and unforeseen halt in March 2020 when the World Health Organization (Lekhraj et al., 2020) announced a global coronavirus pandemic, and the public learned that COVID-19 was not a distant news threat, but a true, deadly virus. While the Internet has been the first source of knowledge for patients (Martino et al., 2017), 63% of social media users have been sharing news and information with each other for years (Schmidt et al, 2017). Despite many threats and hurdles, the expectation that social media could play a key role as a medium for dialogue between authorities and people is becoming increasingly widespread (Liu et al., 2020). Social media offers an opportunity for health providers, physicians, consultants and health agencies to promote more informed decision making between populations and individuals relevant to health or care. Dr. Li Wenliang, who has tried to alert his colleagues of a possible outbreak of a serious acute respiratory disorder on social media (Hegarty, 2020). Social media has now been an integral aspect of people's lives, and those investigations will easily produce large quantities of personal and general information. They often seem to be a valuable method to be used by health officials in a sudden and rapidly changing situation, such as the coronavirus pandemic (Obiała et al., 2020).

When the pandemic began, people quickly shifted to respond to new guidelines for protection and social distancing. Visits to the doctor were carried out on iPads. Some patient support groups have performed somewhat

DOI: 10.4324/9781003163824-18

well in seeking to provide social media support (Carragher p., 2020). During the early stages of the pandemic, both objectively demonstrated and unconfirmed information about COVID-19 circulated to social media, in particular Twitter, Instagram and Facebook. Scientifically validated facts included safety precautions formally supported by the government, such as keeping social distances, wearing masks and using hand sanitisers. However, social media also disseminates unconfirmed reports on the causes and effects of spread of infection (Cato et al., 2021).

Purpose of the study

The purpose of the research is to understand how social media is used for collaboration and knowledge sharing of health information. It is also to find challenges faced during usage of social media for collaboration and knowledge sharing of health information. The paper also attempts to underline effective usage of social media in this respect.

The research questions on which the review paper has been based are:

* Why are those people using social media for collaboration and knowledge sharing for their source of information?
* What is the effective usage of social media for collaboration and knowledge for their health information?
* What are the challenges faced during usage of social media for collaboration and knowledge tool for their health information?

Social media for collaboration

Social media is a communications medium used in healthcare for the sharing and acquisition of content, professional communication and support of patients (Barnes et al., 2019; Carroll et al., 2019). The social media allows the curation of content that is important for a particular region or field by using hashtags, the equivalent of one keyword. In 2016, the #PedsICU has been set up to match child vital treatment material on the popular social media network Twitter (Barnes et al., 2016; Kochanek et al., 2017). Social media could serve as a huge means of exchanging pandemic knowledge and perspectives in real time in the paediatric critical care environment. Social networking is the big equaliser in terms of knowledge sharing. Social media provides quick education updates from across the globe through community and academic hospitals and all levels of resources. As COVID-19 evolved on and expanded across the continents, the association of international and national stakeholders (for example, @WHO, @CDCgov) started to use social media to widely exchange knowledge. In the country's most severely affected by the epidemic, including Italy, Spain and the US Clinicians started sharing their prospects and expertise in COVID-19 (Kudchadkar and Carroll, 2020).

In particular, the COVID-19 epidemic emphasised the need to implement a complete plan for social media networking to facilitate and enhance crisis response (Mirbabaie et al., 2020). Crisis management measures (Bunker et al., 2015), intelligence search and broadcast (Boss et al., 2018), collection and donation of funds (Starbird and Palen, 2012) and hierarchy-free cooperation are provided on social media sites (Schlagwein and Hu, 2017). At the same time, contact between social media can also have a negative influence on sense generation and decision making due to their personalisation of content, facilitating convergence behaviour haphazard and enabling anti-social conduct (Bunker et al., 2019). Government and Media Organizations (MOs) also use social media in their communications plan in order to communicate with people at risk, distribute alert messages and offer information alerts after a crisis (Graaf and Meijer, 2019; Palen et al., 2010). There are thus two problems with the usage of social media by these entities: firstly, to use social media as an additional medium to send messages; and secondly, to reach for useful information from locals in the crisis region, where people are directly affected (Bruns and Burgess, 2014; Ehnis and Bunker, 2012). The ongoing pandemic of COVID-19 highlights that a lack of early reliable and truthful knowledge will lead to the spread of rumours, misleading information and information overload to 'fill the void' and dramatically escalate the consequences of the epidemic as it affects social behaviour. When there is a high level of information and knowledge confusion, people are searching for information online and, in particular, social media to fill their knowledge gap (Mirbabaie et al., 2020).

Social media for knowledge sharing

In the current pandemic of COVID-19, social media has the ability, if used safely and effectively, to provide fast and reliable means of dissemination of key information. Free and quick access to high-quality knowledge from verifiable sources is valuable in optimising global medical response to emergencies such as the latest pandemic of COVID-19 (Chan et al., 2020). Social media is one of the most powerful contact mechanisms in the world today. There were 4.54 billion active users of the Internet and 3.8 billion active users of social media by January 2020 (Kaya, 2020). Social media is a medium to facilitate communication and bring people together by exchanging contents, known as user-generated communication (Michaelidou et al., 2011). In the perspective of working organisations, social media also has become an essential knowledge source as a tool for looking for information and finding accessible, which develops through collaboration among employees (Leonardi et al., 2013; Nah and Saxton, 2013). The use of social media sites provides greater opportunities than traditional tools such as search engines or databases for fast information flows between individuals operating around geographical areas (Panahi et al., 2016).

People are constantly seeking facts or awareness for their own gain through social media. An individual is not born with experience, and both formal and informal communications will lead to the process of obtaining insight from others according to their expertise. The knowledge-seeking habits of people have all been strengthened by social media apps, such as Facebook, blogs and wiki. In this context, people may accomplish a variety of personal or corporate goals or access resources such as those accessible on the Internet, in which Knowledge seekers can communicate and provide access to internal and external sources of information outside their geographic boundaries (Ahmed et al., 2019).

Social networking networks can provide a cost-effective and fast way to spread ideas during a global pandemic. Social media in medical education is constantly being used as a platform. Health professionals consider it as a powerful educational instrument (Sakusic et al., 2021).

Many countries like America, Great Britain and Canada have taken action to improve social distance, which is why the role of the social media has increased in interacting and sharing people's knowledge. Social media offers many contact capabilities (such as audio, video, talk, photo, day, etc.); several politicians, celebrities, journalists, government officials and many more joined these channels to share knowledge about their common experiences (Cogley, 2020). Many people have posted photos and memories on Twitter and Facebook posts, which also raise panic among other consumers (Mao, 2020). At present, people are also using social media, so they can get useful input from local virtual networks on Facebook, WhatsApp and other social media networks. Traditional literature is insufficient to offer advice on these aspects because social networks and social experiences via social media have altered customer shopping habits and behaviours (Naeem, 2021).

Challenges of using social media

Social media also played an important part in raising public health consciousness and knowledge; however, false news, hostility and bigotry have also been misused amid epidemics and civil unrest (Depoux et al., 2020; Diwanji, 2020; Larson, 2018, 2020). Even before the first COVID-19 case was detected in India, India was affected by the social media hysteria and the stocking up of masks and sanitisers. Fake news such as mass killings of people in China and the threat of expanding the lockdown has escalated the panic, causing people to escape from quarantine or isolation and to flee before lockdown and even when lockdown is required. Logos and website ties to national and foreign health departments, television outlets and major journals are unfortunately misused in such false news (Kadam and Atre, 2020). Increased pandemic concerns, tendency of doctors to maintain the one-way relationships, confusion in terms of ethical online practices, another risk of the social media sites, operated by health departments or states, are the increased pandemic concerns attributable to false news and disinformation (Abdoli, 2020). The general public, who have less information about pandemic, have been confused with much misinformation related to diagnosis and treatment. The example of the risks involved with poor health communication can be taken from Nigeria, where health officials discovered multiple cases of overdose of chloroquine after news of its effectiveness for the treatment of pandemic was published in the media (Busari and Adebayo, 2020). World Health Organization (WHO) has partnered with several social networking sites and decided to counter this wrong information and endorse important updates from healthcare agencies (Statt, 2020).

The engagement provided by social media platforms also creates confusion in terms of ethical online practices due to dual responsibility and boundary issues (Boddy and Dominelli, 2017). In the American context, social media platforms are being used as a space to share political views, which could be misused and oftentimes lead to disputes between colleagues that could spill from the online to the real world (Carpenter and Harvey, 2019). Hence, Body and Dominelli (2017) recommend an understanding of the prevalent ethical concerns and attitudes, which can be used and propagated among users to promote ethical values leading to an increased awareness in the personal and professional usage of social media.

Due to the pandemic and subsequent 'infodemic' content, filtering has been introduced by social media businesses at an alarming pace. It may affect convictions and result in 'real world harm' to transmit false or misleading information purposely or not communicated. As a result, it is understandable that social media companies have been framed to reduce the damage of collective reaction in the fight against disinformation (Baker et al., 2020). A large amount of potentially hazardous misinformation about the pandemic has been generated and most of it has been circulated over social networks. This fake news is made up of multiple aspects of an epidemic that is capable of affecting public safety, exasperating crisis management once again. These rumours about pandemic spread faster than the virus, and proof should also be given to the public and shown. Experts have recommended numerous strategies regarding usage of social media to correct myths about health, including timely expert guidance, daily public health knowledge and a correction programme with periodic contact between general people. This rectification programme would be effective if it is implemented rapidly and clearly, though proof should also be presented and displayed to the public along with the relevant document (Sahni & Sharma, 2020).

Although social media can help with health contact and communications, many health departments and doctors only use it to inform their patients and to maintain the one-way relationships. Another problem for the management of health-related media in social media is the failure to control posts. Negative commentary, tweets and talks are often skewed and the views of others are misinterpreted. The widespread application of social media activity in all communities is health awareness management. It is important to remember that for various reasons, many patients cannot access social media (Rafiki, 2020).

Social media hysteria has travelled further than COVID-19 has spread (Wilson and Chen, 2020). In several cases, a metonymic principle may be identified here, where symbols closely relating to the physical epicentre crisis (archaic quarantine and containment imagery) were frequently linked to locations and individuals linked to this archaic imagery. Chinese restaurants, Chinese visitors, Asian products, etc., have led to general mistrust and outburst of racism. One of the first victims of viral racism was Chinese-looking residents who never set their foot in China (King, 2015).

Social media like Facebook, Twitter, YouTube, Instagram, Snapchat and WhatsApp have nowadays become a big source of news and knowledge in public, but unhappily it causes more panic and spreads false information or false news in developing countries like Pakistan. The majority of the population who see disinformation about COVID-19 believes that what they are reading is real, which causes fear. People in Pakistan are inclined to spread misinformation and fuel distrust of something that is not actually real. Misinformation, particularly about COVID-19, can trigger panic (Hussain, 2020).

Effective use of social media

The use of social media is difficult. It is a source of content, entertainment and interaction. This reflects what's on our heads as well. According to Forbes.com, 6.7 million users discussed coronavirus on social media in one day (28 February 2020) (Brandon, 2020). On 11 March, less than two weeks later, analytics firm Sprinklr announced a new high of nearly 20 million mentions of coronavirus-related words (Molla, 2020). The most certainly pandemic is what our thoughts are.

Social media provides the pharmaceutical industry with an excellent forum to hit every nook and corner of the globe. Social media is one of the media for sharing facts, principles and solutions with patients in the pharmaceutical industry (Chatterjee, 2012).

Social media provides a significant to modest effect on healthcare objectives. The general public believe that social media provides an important to moderate influence on the involvement of patients, while some consider social networks to have a significant effect on the quality of treatment and provider involvement (Volpp and Mohta, 2017).

But there are still several aspects of social media that may be of immense use to those who feel lonely or isolated besides taking care of our physical selves by eating healthy, staying productive and having enough sleep (Covid, C. D. C. et al., 2020). We should also track our mental health. During pandemic, social media has played a vital role in increasing stress about the COVID-19 outbreak in Iraqi Kurdistan (Ahmad and Murad; 2020). The American Psychological Association advises alleviating fear by developing a sense of normality and retaining social networks. This can be achieved by connecting to others through video chat services, e-mails or messaging apps. They often promote the exchange of valuable knowledge with friends and relatives during these meetings as a means to help them cope with their own fear (Widerhold, 2020).

Social media, for example, is now more than one part of our lives, how we use it to deal with social differences and, while it can have opportunities for stronger connectivity, it certainly has its deficiencies and risks (Cuello-Garcia, 2020).

Telehealth and social media seem to be on a right track that may potentially help doctors drive efforts to better control chronic conditions in population health. As telehealth continues to gain momentum and individuals are looking for new ways to connect with doctors and their own healthcare, social media seems to be an obvious way to boost these goals (Sanborn, 2018).

People who are not diagnosed with the pandemic should receive regular treatment without the risk of exposure to other patients in the hospital, especially those who are with higher risk of contracting the disease (e.g. the elderly and those with underlying diseases) (Smith et al., 2019). Using social media as a telemedicine tool during epidemic situations has the ability to enhance epidemiological science, disease prevention and clinical case management (Monaghesh and Hajizaadeh, 2020; Ohannessian, 2015; Zhou et al., 2020).

The authorities of China, Singapore and Australia have informed that the psychological side effects of pandemic were illustrated, and have shown concerns that the long-term effects of fear and panic could be more damaging than pandemic (AGDH, 2020; Lai, L., 2020; NHCPRC, 2020). Pandemic has reduced the chance to physically interact with family and friends, and it leads to loneliness. It might increase the anxiety and depressive symptoms (Smith, 1985). If these are left unattended, these psychological symptoms might affect people in a long run. Providing psychological treatment can ensure that the patient's mental well-being is monitored properly. The delivery of resources, like social media, will likely benefit patients maintaining and dealing with acute and acute psychological well-being (Zhou et al., 2020).

Generally speaking, the merits of social media include rapid and continuous access, as well as their interactive existence, which is important for the rapid initiation of care and in line with the concept of equal access. However, usage of social media relies on the quality and pace of the internet, which has sometimes been a challenge, but according to many experts social media, have a significant role in doctors' fast decisions and the timely initiation of therapy and preventive measures. The experience during pandemic can also be helpful in resolving potential problems in the screening and prevention of other diseases. It can lead to circumstances in which cautious and timely care is accomplished to decrease the stress on health units, especially in underdeveloped areas (Taheri et al., 2020).

In response to public health emergencies, social media consumers generate and exchange timely health updates globally. Meanwhile, Governments and Leaders of the health sector have strongly adopted social media, including the 2001 anthrax attack in several US cities to contain the damage created by health crises (Reynolds and Seeger, 2005), Beijing's 2009 H1N1 flu outbreak (Hu and Zhang, 2014) and California's 2015 measles epidemic (Meadows et al., 2019). The effective use of social media during pandemic can be further discussed according to its role in providing support and knowledge sharing.

Health information support

One of the main advantages for people who use social media is that content offers social support, particularly for people with health issues or medical conditions (Ouyang et al., 2016). Social support is described as "the individual feeling valued and cared for by their social network as well as how well the person is embedded into a network of communication and social obligation" (Stephens and Petrie, 2015). Following previous studies (Yang et al., 2018), this study explores Wuhan residents obtained while accessing COVID-19 health information on WeChat as a multidimensional definition of information-based, emotional and peer-related help.

Informational support

People are encouraged to access health information on social media because of the opportunities of social support in the form of health decision-making information (Uchino et al., 2018). Informational support for individuals using social media helps them with stronger self-esteem and improved perceptions of social capital (Selkie et al., 2020), including positive mental health results (McConnell et al., 2015). In the meanwhile, information support reduces potential risks and strengthens coping techniques that protect mental health (McConnell et al., 2015). In the face of stress factors in a health crisis, knowledge support can help to mitigate possible threats, resulting in increased mental health support (Villagonzalo et al., 2019).

Emotional support

Emotional support can be explained as "information that meets the mental or emotional needs of the person" (Mattson and Hall, 2011). Emotional support helps the patient to meet their emotional needs. Emotional support examples include "sharing personal challenges," "motivational support that feels like a warm blanket wrapped around you" (Van Uden-Kraan et al., 2008; Mukherjee et. al., 2019) and "motivate those who cope with similar issues" (Bartlett and Coulson, 2011).

Esteem support

This support can be explained as "a contact that enhances one's appreciation or confidence in the abilities of a person to manage a problem or perform a necessary task" (Mattson and Hall, 2011). This kind of encouragement helps a person to take the actions effectively, confidently and with happiness. Examples of esteem like "getting motivation from the motivation of others patient's" (Chiu and Hsieh, 2013), "share experiences about a new treatment to find encouragement before starting it" (Coulson, 2013; Mukherjee et al., 2020) and "rituals of confirming each other's endeavors to follow health instructions" (Wentzer and Bygholm, 2013).

Network support

Definition of network support is "communication that affirms an individual's belonging to a network or reminds him/her of support available from the network" (Mattson and Hall, 2011). It is that kind of support that repeats people, regardless of the state they face. Network support examples include "meeting other patients who had gone through similar experiences" (Bers et al., 2010), "a means to connect and motivate others in similar situations" (Colineau and Paris, 2010) as well as "fostering relationships based on shared attributes" (Frost & Massagli, 2008).

Conclusion

Ever since its emergence social media is widespread, preferred and a popular platform for communication. Such a potential invited the attention of healthcare providers also to initiate dialogue with patients ostensibly to promote better and informed decisions. During the ongoing pandemic, social media burst with communication, including those related to healthcare, and though it has had immense beneficial impact globally, it also exposed the challenges to such healthcare collaborations. That it is fraught with deeply harmful tendencies is an understatement. This study has been undertaken to identify the collaboration challenges in healthcare communication. Our findings are that these include significant potential to spread hazardous misinformation, greatly enhance pandemic based anxiety, tendency of healthcare providers to sustain one-way relationships and confusion in terms of ethical online practices. It also concludes that social media can be effective in this context by instilling health information support, informational support, emotional support, esteem support and network support.

Implications of the study for the regulators are to appreciate the potential harmful capacity of social media-based healthcare communications that come up with policies to control the same if not eliminate it together. We have to keep in mind that this is not the last pandemic that humanity faced, more pandemics in near future are imminent. Scientists will be working to developing vaccination and treatments the regulators should plan to promote an international shared data space for highly infectious diseases. This may help in overcoming challenges identified in this paper. This calls for huge investment in technology and manpower but is worth it for its promising value and far-reaching social good. If it appears impossible or too challenging, then it is advocated to develop a national shared data space or health information systems for community health data sharing. Implications for information systems and technology scholars are to invest their capabilities and efforts to building such shared platforms and to keep them updated and free from flaws using AI and IOT tools. Implications for information providers are to ensure correct, ethical, balanced information without creating any panic. They must avoid holding to one-way communication and encourage the general public also to have their say. Additionally, they must address issues related to security, privacy, biases, ethics and the digital divide. Since general public is in great need of supports related to informational, emotional, esteem and networking, information providers must be sensitive to this and ensure such features are a part of their communication systems.

The general public also has the responsibility to understand the challenges posed by communicating through social media and avoid sensationalising information. They must learn to identify and report unethical instances to regulatory bodies. They also need to play a role in monitoring harmful, exaggerated and unethical information.

References

Abdoli, A., & Heidarnejadi, S. M. (2020). Opportunities and challenges of social media in outbreaks: A concern for COVID-19. *Ethics, Medicine and Public Health*, *15*, 100557.

Ahmad, A. R., & Murad, H. R. (2020). The impact of social media on panic during the COVID-19 pandemic in Iraqi Kurdistan: Online questionnaire study. *Journal of Medical Internet Research*, *22*(5), e19556.

Ahmed, Y. A., Ahmad, M. N., Ahmad, N., & Zakaria, N. H. (2019). Social media for knowledge-sharing: A systematic literature review. *Telematics and Informatics*, *37*, 72–112.

Antheunis, M. L., Tates, K., & Nieboer, T. E. (2013). Patients' and health professionals' use of social media in health care: Motives, barriers and expectations. *Patient Education and Counseling*, *92*(3), 426–431.

Appel, G., Grewal, L., Hadi, R., & Stephen, A. T. (2020). The future of social media in marketing. *Journal of the Academy of Marketing Science*, *48*(1), 79–95.

Australian Government Department of Health. Coronavirus (2020). Available at: https://www.health.gov.au.

Baker, S. A., Wade, M., & Walsh, M. J. (2020). <? covid19?> The challenges of responding to misinformation during a pandemic: Content moderation and the limitations of the concept of harm. *Media International Australia*, *177*(1), 103–107.

Barnes, S., Riley, C., & Kudchadkar, S. (2016). 416: Social media for dissemination of pediatric critical care content: A hashtag analysis. *Critical Care Medicine*, *44*(12), 180.

Barnes, S. S., Kaul, V., & Kudchadkar, S. R. (2019). Social media engagement and the critical care medicine community. *Journal of Intensive Care Medicine, 34*(3), 175–182.

Bartlett, Y. K., & Coulson, N. S. (2011). An investigation into the empowerment effects of using online support groups and how this affects health professional/patient communication. *Patient Education and Counseling, 83*(1), 113–119.

Bers, M. U., Beals, L. M., Chau, C., Satoh, K., Blume, E. D., DeMaso, D. R., & Gonzalez-Heydrich, J. (2010). Use of a virtual community as a psychosocial support system in pediatric transplantation. *Pediatric Transplantation, 14*(2), 261–267.

Boddy, J., & Dominelli, L. (2017). Social media and social work: The challenges of a new ethical space. *Australian Social Work, 70*(2), 172–184.

Brandon, J. (2020). 6.7 Million people just mentioned the coronavirus on social media in one day. Here's Why. *4th March.*

Bruns, A., & Burgess, J. (2014). Crisis communication in natural disasters: The Queensland floods and Christchurch earthquakes. *Twitter and Society [Digital Formations], 89*, 373–384.

Bunker, D., Levine, L., & Woody, C. (2015). Repertoires of collaboration for common operating pictures of disasters and extreme events. *Information Systems Frontiers, 17*(1), 51–65.

Bunker, D., Stieglitz, S., Ehnis, C., & Sleigh, A. (2019, June). Bright ICT: Social media analytics for society and crisis management. In *International working conference on transfer and diffusion of IT* (pp. 536–552). Springer, Cham.

Busari, S., & Adebayo, B. (2020). Nigeria records chloroquine poisoning after Trump endorses it for coronavirus treatment. *CNN.* Available online at: https://www.cnn. com/2020/03/23/africa/chloroquine-trump-nigeria-intl/index. html.

Carpenter, J. P., & Harvey, S. (2019). "There's no referee on social media": Challenges in educator professional social media use. *Teaching and Teacher Education, 86.* doi:10.1016/j.tate.2019.102904

Carragher. P. (2020). Virtual Support Groups Find Success Amid Pandemic. Available at: https://moffitt.org.

Carroll, C. L., Dangayach, N. S., Khan, R., Carlos, W. G., Harwayne-Gidansky, I., Grewal, H. S.,... & Wu, A. (2019). Lessons learned from web-and social media-based educational initiatives by pulmonary, critical care, and sleep societies. *Chest, 155*(4), 671–679.

Cato, S., Iida, T., Ishida, K., Ito, A., Katsumata, H., McElwain, K. M., & Shoji, M. (2021). The bright and dark sides of social media usage during the COVID-19 pandemic: Survey evidence from Japan. *International Journal of Disaster Risk Reduction, 54*, 102034.

Covid, C. D. C., Team, R., COVID, C., Team, R., COVID, C., Team, R., ... Sauber-Schatz, E. (2020). Severe outcomes among patients with coronavirus disease 2019 (COVID-19)—United States, February 12–March 16, 2020. Morbidity and mortality weekly report, *69*(12), 343.

Chan, A. K., Nickson, C. P., Rudolph, J. W., Lee, A., & Joynt, G. M. (2020). Social media for rapid knowledge dissemination: early experience from the COVID-19 pandemic, *Anaesthesia, 75*(12), 1579–1582.

Chatterjee, S. (2012). Social CRM and its impact on pharmaceutical industry. *International Journal of Multidisciplinary Research, 2*(1), 344–351.

Chiu, Y. C., & Hsieh, Y. L. (2013). Communication online with fellow cancer patients: Writing to be remembered, gain strength, and find survivors. *Journal of Health Psychology, 18*(12), 1572–1581.

Cogley, M. (2020). Has social media turbocharged panic buying by UK shoppers? Available at: https://www.telegraph.co.uk/technology/2020/03/10/has-social-media-turbocharged-panic-buying-uk-shoppers/.

Colineau, N., & Paris, C. (2010). Talking about your health to strangers: Understanding the use of online social networks by patients. *New Review of Hypermedia and Multimedia*, *16*(1–2), 141–160.

Coulson, N. S. (2013). How do online patient support communities affect the experience of inflammatory bowel disease? An online survey. *JRSM Short Reports*, *4*(8), 2042533313478004.

Cuello-Garcia, C., Pérez-Gaxiola, G., & van Amelsvoort, L. (2020). Social media can have an impact on how we manage and investigate the COVID-19 pandemic. *Journal of Clinical Epidemiology*, *127*, 198–201.

de Graaf, G., & Meijer, A. (2019). Social media and value conflicts: An explorative study of the Dutch police. *Public Administration Review*, *79*(1), 82–92.

De Martino, I., D'Apolito, R., McLawhorn, A. S., Fehring, K. A., Sculco, P. K., & Gasparini, G. (2017). Social media for patients: Benefits and drawbacks. *Current Reviews in Musculoskeletal Medicine*, *10*(1), 141–145.

Depoux, A., Martin, S., Karafillakis, E., Preet, R., Wilder-Smith, A., & Larson, H. (2020). The pandemic of social media panic travels faster than the COVID-19 outbreak, *Journal of Travel Medicine*, *27*(3), taaa031.

Diwanji, S. (2020). Fake news in India-statistics and facts. *Statista, March*, *2*.

Ehnis, C., & Bunker, D. (2012). Social media in disaster response: Queensland police service-public engagement during the 2011 floods. ACIS 2012 Proceedings. 107.

Frost, J., & Massagli, M. (2008). Social uses of personal health information within PatientsLikeMe, an online patient community: What can happen when patients have access to one another's data. *Journal of Medical Internet Research*, *10*(3), e15.

Hagg, E., Dahinten, V. S., & Currie, L. M. (2018). The emerging use of social media for health-related purposes in low and middle-income countries: A scoping review. *International Journal of Medical Informatics*, *115*, 92–105.

Hegarty, S. (2020). The Chinese doctor who tried to warn others about coronavirus. *BBC News*, *6*. https://www.bbc.com/news/world-asia-china-51364382.

Hu, B., & Zhang, D. (2014). Channel selection and knowledge acquisition during the 2009 Beijing H1N1 flu crisis: A media system dependency theory perspective. *Chinese Journal of Communication*, *7*(3), 299–318.

Huo, J., Desai, R., Hong, Y. R., Turner, K., Mainous III, A. G., & Bian, J. (2019). Use of social media in health communication: Findings from the health information national trends survey 2013, 2014, and 2017. *Cancer Control*, *26*(1), 1073274819841442.

Hussain, W. (2020). Role of social media in covid-19 pandemic. *The International Journal of Frontier Sciences*, *4*(2), 59–60.

Kadam, A. B., & Atre, S. R. (2020). Negative impact of social media panic during the COVID-19 outbreak in India. *Journal of Travel Medicine*, *27*(3), taaa057.

Kaya, T. (2020). The changes in the effects of social media use of Cypriots due to COVID-19 pandemic. *Technology in Society*, *63*, 101380.

King, N. B. (2015). Mediating panic: The iconography of 'new' infectious threats, 1936–2009. *Empires of panic: Epidemics and Colonial Anxieties*, 181–202.

Kochanek, P. M., Kudchadkar, S. R., & Kissoon, N. (2017). Guiding pediatric critical care medicine toward a bigger "impression" in 2017 and beyond. *Pediatric Critical Care Medicine*, *18*(5), 403–404.

Kudchadkar, S. R., & Carroll, C. L. (2020). Using social media for rapid information dissemination in a pandemic:# PedsICU and coronavirus disease 2019. *Pediatric Critical Care Medicine, 21*(8), e538.

Lai, L. (2020). Fear and panic can do more harm than the coronavirus, says PM Lee Hsien Loong. Available at: https://www.straitstimes.com.

Larson, H. J. (2018). The biggest pandemic risk? Viral misinformation. *Nature, 562*(7726), 309–310.

Larson, H. J. (2020). Blocking information on COVID-19 can fuel the spread of misinformation. *Nature, 580*(7803), 306–307.

Lekhraj Rampal, M. B. B. S., & Seng, L. B. (2020). Coronavirus disease (COVID-19) pandemic. *Medical Journal of Malaysia, 75*(2), 95.

Leonardi, P. M., Huysman, M., & Steinfield, C. (2013). Enterprise social media: Definition, history, and prospects for the study of social technologies in organizations. *Journal of Computer-Mediated Communication, 19*(1), 1–19.

Liu, Q., Zheng, Z., Zheng, J., Chen, Q., Liu, G., Chen, S.,... & Ming, W. K. (2020). Health communication through news media during the early stage of the COVID-19 outbreak in China: Digital topic modeling approach. *Journal of Medical Internet Research, 22*(4), e19118.

Mao, F. (2020). Coronavirus panic: Why are people stockpiling toilet paper. *BBC News, 4.* https://www.bbc.com/news/world-australia-51731422.

Mattson, M., & Hall, J. G. (2011). *Health as communication nexus: A service-learning approach.* Iowa, US: Kendall Hunt Publishing Company.

McConnell, E. A., Birkett, M. A., & Mustanski, B. (2015). Typologies of social support and associations with mental health outcomes among LGBT youth. *LGBT Health, 2*(1), 55–61.

Meadows, C. W., Meadows, C. Z., Tang, L., & Liu, W. (2019). Unraveling public health crises across stages: Understanding Twitter emotions and message types during the California measles outbreak. *Communication Studies, 70*(4), 453–469.

Menon, I. S., Sharma, M. K., Chandra, P. S., & Thennarasu, K. (2014). Social networking sites: An adjunctive treatment modality for psychological problems. *Indian Journal of Psychological Medicine, 36*(3), 260–263.

Michaelidou, N., Siamagka, N. T., & Christodoulides, G. (2011). Usage, barriers and measurement of social media marketing: An exploratory investigation of small and medium B2B brands. *Industrial Marketing Management, 40*(7), 1153–1159.

Mirbabaie, M., Bunker, D., Stieglitz, S., Marx, J., & Ehnis, C. (2020). Social media in times of crisis: Learning from Hurricane Harvey for the coronavirus disease 2019 pandemic response. *Journal of Information Technology, 35*(3), 195–213.

Molla, R. (2020). How coronavirus took over social media. *Vox. Com.*

Monaghesh, E., & Hajizadeh, A. (2020). The role of telehealth during COVID-19 outbreak: A systematic review based on current evidence. *BMC Public Health, 20*(1), 1–9.

Mukherjee, S. K., Kumar, J., Jha, A. K., & Rani, J. R. (2019). Role of social media promotion of prescription drugs on patient belief-system and behaviour. *International Journal of e-Collaboration (IJeC), 15*(2), 23–43.

Mukherjee, S. K., Kumar, J. K., Jha, A. K., & Pandey, J. R. (2021). Dynamics of Social Media Promotion of Prescription Drugs and Resulting Patient Belief Systems. In Jingyuan Zhao (Ed.), *E-Collaboration Technologies and Strategies for Competitive Advantage Amid Challenging Times* (pp. 144–170). IGI Global. DOI: 10.4018/978-1-7998-7764-6.ch005.

Naeem, M. (2021). Do social media platforms develop consumer panic buying during the fear of Covid-19 pandemic. *Journal of Retailing and Consumer Services*, *58*, 102226.

Nah, S., & Saxton, G. D. (2013). Modeling the adoption and use of social media by nonprofit organizations. *New Media & Society*, *15*(2), 294–313.

National Health Commission of the People's Republic of China, Ministry of Cicil Affairs of the People's Republic of China (2020). Notice on Strengthening the Psychological Assistance and Social Work Services in the Response to the New Coronary Pneumonia Epidemic Disease. www.nhc.gov.cn/jkj.

Obiała, J., Obiała, K., Mańczak, M., Owoc, J., & Olszewski, R. (2021). COVID-19 misinformation: Accuracy of articles about coronavirus prevention mostly shared on social media. *Health Policy and Technology*, *10*(1), 182–186.

Ohannessian, R. (2015). Telemedicine: Potential applications in epidemic situations. *European Research in Telemedicine/La Recherche Européenne en Télémédecine*, *4*(3), 95–98.

Ouyang, A., Inverso, N. A., Chow, S. M., Kumar, A., & Zhong, B. (2016). Mo1639 "Listening" to IBS Patients in the 21st Century: Offerings From an on-line self help and support group. *Gastroenterology*, *150*(4), S739.

Palen, L., Anderson, K. M., Mark, G., Martin, J., Sicker, D., Palmer, M., & Grunwald, D. (2010). A vision for technology-mediated support for public participation & assistance in mass emergencies & disasters. *ACM-BCS Visions of Computer Science 2010,7*, 1–12.

Panahi, S., Watson, J., & Partridge, H. (2016). Information encountering on social media and tacit knowledge sharing. *Journal of Information Science*, *42*(4), 539–550.

Rafiki, A. (2020). Opportunities and challenges of social media to the Islamic banks in Indonesia. In *Economics, Business, and Islamic Finance in ASEAN Economics Community* (pp. 227–251). IGI Global.

Reynolds, B., & W. SEEGER, M. A. T. T. H. E. W. (2005). Crisis and emergency risk communication as an integrative model. *Journal of Health Communication*, *10*(1), 43–55.

Ross, B., Potthoff, T., Majchrzak, T. A., Chakraborty, N. R., Ben Lazreg, M., & Stieglitz, S. (2018, January). The diffusion of crisis-related communication on social media: An empirical analysis of Facebook reactions. In *Proceedings of the 51st Hawaii International conference on system sciences*. University of Hawai'i at Mānoa.

Sahni, H., & Sharma, H. (2020). Role of social media during the COVID-19 pandemic: Beneficial, destructive, or reconstructive? *International Journal of Academic Medicine*, *6*(2), 70.

Sakusic, A., Markotic, D., Dong, Y., Festic, E., Krajinovic, V., Todorovic, Z.,... & Gajic, O. (2021). Rapid, multimodal, critical care knowledge-sharing platform for COVID-19 pandemic. *Bosnian Journal of Basic Medical Sciences*, *21*(1), 93.

Sanborn, B. J. (2020). *Telemedicine and social media interest advance population health*. Available at: https://www.healthcarefinancenews.com.

Schlagwein, D., & Hu, M. (2017). How and why organisations use social media: Five use types and their relation to absorptive capacity. *Journal of Information Technology*, *32*(2), 194–209.

Schmidt, A. L., Zollo, F., Del Vicario, M., Bessi, A., Scala, A., Caldarelli, G.,... & Quattrociocchi, W. (2017). Anatomy of news consumption on Facebook. *Proceedings of the National Academy of Sciences*, *114*(12), 3035–3039.

Selkie, E., Adkins, V., Masters, E., Bajpai, A., & Shumer, D. (2020). Transgender adolescents' uses of social media for social support. *Journal of Adolescent Health, 66*(3), 275–280.

Smith, A. C., Thomas, E., Snoswell, C. L., Haydon, H., Mehrotra, A., Clemensen, J., & Caffery, L. J. (2020). Telehealth for global emergencies: Implications for coronavirus disease 2019 (COVID-19). *Journal of Telemedicine and Telecare, 26*(5), 309–313.

Smith, E. M. (1985). Ethnic minorities: Life stress, social support, and mental health issues. *The Counseling Psychologist, 13*(4), 537–579.

Starbird, K., & Palen, L. (2012, February). (How) will the revolution be retweeted? Information diffusion and the 2011 Egyptian uprising. In *Proceedings of the ACM 2012 conference on computer supported cooperative work*. Association for Computing Machinery, New York, NY, United States, 7–16. doi. org/10.1145/2145204.2145212.

Statt, N. (2020). Major tech platforms say they're 'jointly combating fraud and misinformation' about COVID-19. *The Verge*. https://www.theverge. com/2020/3/16/21182726/coronavirus-covid-19-facebook-google-twitter-youtube-joint-effort-misinformation-fraud.

Stephens, M. H., & Petrie, K. J. (2015). Social support and recovery from disease and medical procedures. 735–740.

Taheri, M. S., Falahati, F., Radpour, A., Karimi, V., Sedaghat, A., & Karimi, M. A. (2020). Role of social media and telemedicine in diagnosis & management of COVID-19; An experience of the Iranian Society of Radiology. *Archives of Iranian Medicine, 23*(4), 285.

Uchino, B. N., Bowen, K., de Grey, R. K., Mikel, J., & Fisher, E. B. (2018). Social support and physical health: Models, mechanisms, and opportunities. In *Principles and concepts of behavioral medicine* (pp. 341–372). Springer, New York, NY. https://doi.org/10.1007/978-0-387-93826-4_12.

van Uden-Kraan, C., Drossaert, C., Taal, E., Seydel, E., & van de Laar, M. (2008). Self-reported differences in empowerment between lurkers and posters in online patient support groups. *Journal of Medical Internet Research, 10*(2), e18.

Villagonzalo, K. A., Arnold, C., Farhall, J., Rossell, S. L., Foley, F., & Thomas, N. (2019). Predictors of overall and mental health-related internet use in adults with psychosis. *Psychiatry Research, 278*, 12–18.

Volpp, K. G., & Mohta, N. S. (2017). Social networks to improve patient health. https://catalyst.nejm.org/doi/pdf/10.1056/CAT.18.0285.

Wentzer, H. S., & Bygholm, A. (2013). Narratives of empowerment and compliance: Studies of communication in online patient support groups. *International Journal of Medical Informatics, 82*(12), e386–e394.

Wiederhold, B. K. (2020). Using social media to our advantage: Alleviating anxiety during a pandemic. *Cyberpsychology, Behavior, and Social Networking, 23*(4), 197–198.

Wilson, M. E., & Chen, L. H. (2020). Travellers give wings to novel coronavirus (2019-nCoV). *Journal of Travel Medicine, 27*(2), taaa015.

Yang, F., Zhong, B., Kumar, A., Chow, S. M., & Ouyang, A. (2018). Exchanging social support online: A longitudinal social network analysis of irritable bowel syndrome patients' interactions on a health forum. *Journalism & Mass Communication Quarterly, 95*(4), 1033–1057.

Zhou, X., Snoswell, C. L., Harding, L. E., Bambling, M., Edirippulige, S., Bai, X., & Smith, A. C. (2020). The role of telehealth in reducing the mental health burden from COVID-19. *Telemedicine and e-Health, 26*(4), 377–379.

Index

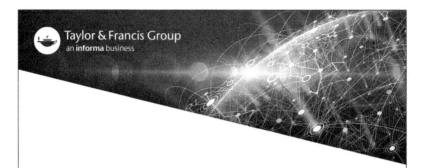

Printed in the United States
by Baker & Taylor Publisher Services